EYEWITNESS TRAVEL

MOSCOW

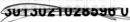

EYEWITNESS TRAVEL

MOSCOW

Main Contributors:
Christopher and Melanie Rice

DK

LONDON, NEW YORK,
MELBOURNE, MUNICH AND DELHI
www.dk.com

Project Editor Marcus Hardy
Art Editor Marisa Renzullo
Editors Catherine Day, Jane Oliver, Lynda Warrington
Designers Gillian Andrews, Carolyn Hewitson,
Paul Jackson, Elly King, Nicola Rodway
Visualizer Joy Fitzsimmons
Map Co-Ordinators Emily Green, David Pugh

Main Contributors
Christopher Rice, Melanie Rice

Maps
Maria Donnelly (Colourmap Scanning Ltd)

Photographer
Demetrio Carrasco

Illustrators
Stephen Conlin, Richard Draper, Stephen Gyapay,
Claire Littlejohn, Chris Orr & Associates

Printed and bound in China

First published in Great Britain in 1998
by Dorling Kindersley Limited
80 Strand, London WC2R 0RL

14 15 16 17 10 9 8 7 6 5 4 3 2 1

Reprinted with revisions 2000, 2001, 2004, 2007, 2010, 2013, 2015

Copyright 1998, 2015 © Dorling Kindersley Limited, London
A Penguin Random House Company

A CIP catalogue record is available from the British Library

ISBN 978-1-40937-005-5

Floors are referred to throughout in accordance with
European usage; ie the "first floor" is the floor above ground level.

MIX
Paper from
responsible sources
FSC www.fsc.org **FSC™ C018179**

**The information in this
DK Eyewitness Travel Guide is checked regularly.**
Every effort has been made to ensure that this book is as up-to-date as possible
at the time of going to press. Some details, however, such as telephone numbers,
opening hours, prices, gallery hanging arrangements and travel information are
liable to change. The publishers cannot accept responsibility for any consequences
arising from the use of this book, nor for any material on third party websites, and
cannot guarantee that any website address in this book will be a suitable source of
travel information. We value the views and suggestions of our readers very highly.
Please write to: Publisher, DK Eyewitness Travel Guides, Dorling Kindersley,
80 Strand, London, WC2R 0RL, UK, or email: travelguides@dk.com.

Front cover main image: The Cathedral of the Nativity in the Kremlin, Suzdal

◀ Detail of the gilded dancing statues on the Fountain of the Republics, All-Russian Exhibition Centre

Contents

How to Use
this Guide **6**

Socialist-Realist sculpture of Soviet
farm workers at the All-Russian
Exhibition Centre *(see p147)*

Introducing
Moscow

The Cathedral of the Annunciation in the
Kremlin *(see p62)*

The vaulted main hall of the Faceted Palace *(see p64)*

Ulitsa Arbat – popular for its shops and eateries *(see pp72)*

St Basil's Cathedral
(see pp110–11)

HOW TO USE THIS GUIDE

This guide will help you to get the most from your visit to Moscow. It provides expert recommendations together with detailed practical information. *Introducing Moscow* maps the city and sets it in its geographical, historical and cultural context, and the quick-reference timeline on the history pages gives the dates of Russia's rulers and significant events. *Moscow at a Glance* is an overview of the city's main attractions. *Moscow Area by Area* starts on page 52 and describes all the important sights, using maps, photographs and illustrations. The sights are arranged in three groups: those in Moscow's central districts, those a little further afield, and finally those beyond Moscow which require one- or two-day excursions. Hotel, restaurant and entertainment recommendations can be found in *Travellers' Needs*, while the *Survival Guide* includes tips on everything from transport and telephones to personal safety.

Finding your Way around the Sightseeing Section

Each of the seven sightseeing areas is colour-coded for easy reference. Every chapter opens with an introduction to the area it covers, describing its history and character. For central districts, this is followed by a Street-by-Street map illustrating a particularly interesting part of the area; for sights further away, by a regional map. A simple numbering system relates sights to the maps. Important sights are covered by several pages.

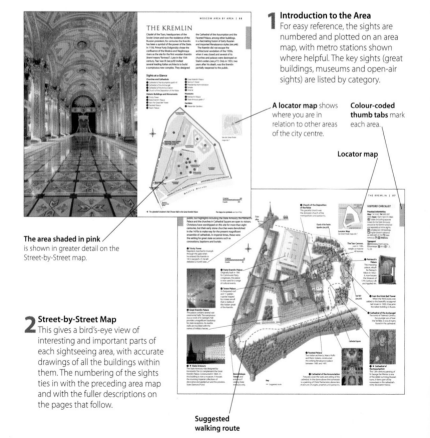

1 Introduction to the Area
For easy reference, the sights are numbered and plotted on an area map, with metro stations shown where helpful. The key sights (great buildings, museums and open-air sights) are listed by category.

A locator map shows where you are in relation to other areas of the city centre.

Colour-coded thumb tabs mark each area.

Locator map

The area shaded in pink is shown in greater detail on the Street-by-Street map.

2 Street-by-Street Map
This gives a bird's-eye view of interesting and important parts of each sightseeing area, with accurate drawings of all the buildings within them. The numbering of the sights ties in with the preceding area map and with the fuller descriptions on the pages that follow.

Suggested walking route

Moscow Area Map

The coloured areas shown on this map *(see pp16–17)* are the five main sightseeing areas into which central Moscow has been divided for this guide. Each is covered in a full chapter in the Moscow Area by Area section *(pp52–127)*. The areas are also highlighted on other maps throughout the book. In Moscow at a Glance *(pp38–51)*, for example, they help you locate the most important sights that no visitor should miss. The maps' coloured borders match the coloured thumb tabs at the top corner of each page.

Numbers refer to each sight's position on the area map and its place in the chapter.

Practical information lists all the information you need to visit every sight, including a map reference to the Street Finder maps *(pp228–45)*

3 Detailed information on each sight
All the important sights are described individually. They are listed to follow the numbering on the area map at the start of the section. The key to the symbols summarizing practical information is on the back flap.

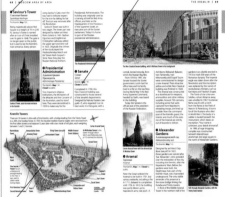

Illustrated maps show in detail the layout of extensive sights.

A **visitors' checklist** provides the practical information you will need to plan your visit.

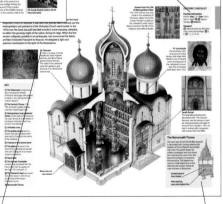

4 Moscow's Major Sights
These are given more extensive coverage, sometimes two or more full pages. Historic buildings are dissected to reveal their interiors; museums and galleries have colour-coded floorplans to help you find important exhibits.

Stars indicate the best features or works of art.

Story boxes provide details on famous people or historical events.

INTRODUCING
MOSCOW

GREAT DAYS IN MOSCOW

The Russian capital, having endured wars, revolutions and drastic social change, is today a place where the past and present combine to captivate and charm. From the multi-coloured onion domes of churches to the graves of Soviet heroes, reminders of the city's past are on almost every corner. Galleries like the Tretyakov are treasure troves of art, while the State Armoury contains treasure pure and simple, from Fabergé eggs to diamonds galore. These itineraries will help visitors find their way around; they are arranged first by themes and then by length of stay. Price guides on pages 10–11 include cost of food and admission fees.

Moscow's Past

Two adults allow at least $150

- **First stop Red Square**
- **Heroes and villains**
- **Colourful domes of St Basil's Cathedral**
- **Inside the Kremlin**

Morning

A whistle-stop tour through Russian history begins with a stroll across **Red Square** *(see p108)*, a vast expanse that accommodated huge military parades during the Soviet era. From here, head into **Lenin's Mausoleum** *(see p109)* to pay your respects to the leader of Russia's historic 1917 revolution. Afterwards, follow the path to the Kremlin Walls, to see the graves of other well-known Soviets including the ruthless dictator Joseph Stalin, and Yuriy Gagarin, the first man to orbit the planet. From the Kremlin Walls, make your way to **St Basil's Cathedral** *(see pp110–11)*, one of Russia's enduring symbols. According to legend, Ivan the Terrible had the cathedral's architect blinded to ensure that he would never again create anything to rival its beauty.

Afternoon

Feeling peckish? Make your way to Kamergerskiy pereulok, just off **Tverskaya ulitsa** *(see p91)*. This pleasant, traffic-free zone is in one of the city's main shopping districts and has a good choice of restaurants and cafés offering flavours from all over the world.

Afterwards, you can visit the **Kremlin** itself *(see pp54–69)*. Long the seat of power in Russia, the complex of cathedrals and palaces was not open to the public until the death of Stalin in 1955. Tickets are sold for separate sights, but be sure not to miss the collection of royal treasures at the **State Armoury** *(see pp66–7)* or icons and gilded frescoes at the **Cathedral of the Assumption** *(see pp60–61)*. Make time, too, for **Ivan the Great's Bell Tower** *(see p59)*. The 200-tonne behemoth of a bell outside the tower is the largest in the world.

Art works by local street artists for sale on Old Arbat (ulitsa Arbat)

Art & Architecture

Two adults allow at least $160

- **Treasures of Tretyakov**
- **Lunch in the park**
- **Exploring Old Arbat**

Morning

Start the day with a visit to the world-class **Tretyakov Gallery** *(see pp120–23)*. The priceless collection of Russian art includes

Historic Red Square, with the distinctive onion domes of St Basil's Cathedral in the distance

◄ Painting of Red Square by Appolinari Mikhailovich Vasnetsov (1856–1933)

Riverboat on the Moskva river, passing by the Kremlin

the 15th-century *Trinity* icon by Andrey Rublev and *The Appearance of Christ to the People*, a colossal work that took artist Aleksandr Ivanov 20 years to paint. The gift shop is a good place to stock up on souvenirs.

For a bite to eat, take a wander through leafy **Alexander Gardens** *(see p69)*, which has a good choice of cafés including pizzerias and an English-style pub.

Afternoon
Suitably refreshed, head for **Old Arbat** *(see pp72–73)*. Once the favoured haunt of writers, artists and poets, this lively pedestrianized area is a good place to seek out mementos of the Soviet era, such as flags, statuettes and old bits of Red Army kit, from the many stalls and shops that line the streets. There are also a few shops specializing in traditional icons.

The area has some fine examples of Russian architecture including the 19th-century **Pushkin House-Museum** *(see p75)*, which gives visitors a good idea of what life in Moscow was like when this literary giant lived here. Afterwards, take a detour down Krivoarbatskiy pereulok to peek at **Melnikov House** *(see p74)*, a cylindrical building designed in the 1920s by Konstantin Melnikov, one of Russia's greatest Constructivist architects. For dinner, try **Mari Vanna** *(see p187)*, by Patriarch's Pond, for pancakes, caviar and perhaps a glass or two of vodka.

A Family Day

Family of four allow at least $130

- A gentle river cruise
- Exploring Gorky Park
- The magical circus

Morning
In summer there is nothing more pleasant than taking a **Moscow River Cruise** *(see p221)*. Winding through the heart of the city, the double-decker river boats pass several major sights including the Kremlin and the Cathedral of Christ the Saviour. Jump ship at **Gorky Park** *(see p131)*, where the many activities include ice skating along the park's frozen paths in winter, and boating on the lakes or cycling in summer. The park is a good picnic spot. There are also a few good restaurants within the grounds; try **Bar Strelka** *(see p186)*.

Afternoon
Later, head off to the **Old Circus** *(see p199)* for a breathtaking display by world-renowned acrobats and trapeze artists. The antics of the circus's performing bears and tigers are not to everyone's taste, however. The colourful marionettes of the **Moscow Puppet Theatre** *(see p199)* are a worthwhile alternative.

History & Fresh Air

Two adults allow at least $80

- A fortified convent
- Famous graves
- A trip to the country

Morning
Hop on the metro for **Novodevichiy Convent** *(see pp132–3)*, where you can soak up some of the 16th-century atmosphere of this fortified religious complex. Novodevichiy's nearby cemetery reads like a *Who's Who* of Russian history and contains the graves of literary luminary Anton Chekhov and political heavyweight Nikita Khrushchev.

Afternoon
Afterwards, take the metro to **Kolomenskoe** *(see pp140–41)*, a country estate much loved by the tsars that is now a museum of architecture. Enjoy a lunch of traditional Russian food in one of the small wooden buildings. Highlights include the 16th-century Church of the Ascension and a log cabin built for Peter the Great. The park is also a wonderful place for a walk along the Moskva river, especially in winter when it often freezes over.

16th-century Cathedral of the Virgin of Smolensk, Novodevichiy Convent

2 Days in Moscow

- Admire the views of Red Square from within St Basil's Cathedral
- Marvel at the Kremlin's fine buildings
- Ponder the beauty of the Russian soul at the Tretyakov Gallery

Day 1
Morning Head for the vast expanse of **Red Square** (p108) and the iconic onion domes of **St Basil's Cathedral** (pp110–11). Explore the labyrinthine passages that connect the cathedral's eight chapels before joining the queue for the polished-granite **Lenin Mausoleum** (p109). The neighbouring **Historical Museum** (p108) holds an intriguing collection that's well worth a visit.

Afternoon Visit the **Kremlin** (pp54–69) for a fascinating tour of its historic buildings – don't miss the 14th-century **Cathedral of the Assumption** (pp60–61); afterwards, buy a separate ticket to visit the **State Armoury**'s (pp66–7) fabulous collection of aristocratic treasures.

Day 2
Morning Leave plenty of time for your visit to the **Tretyakov Gallery** (pp120–23) since the queues to get in are often lengthy and the collection itself is huge – the world's largest of Russian art. Look out for the exquisite 12th-century icons and the absorbing canvases by Ilya Repin, Russia's renowned Realist painter.

Afternoon Take the metro to Smolenskaya station, from where you'll emerge beneath the **Foreign Ministry** (p72), one of Stalin's monolithic gothic skyscrapers known as the Seven Sisters. Stroll along the pedestrianized **Ulitsa Arbat** (pp72–3), a delightful street lined with historic buildings once inhabited by artists and

The lavish interior of Yeliseyevsky Food Hall, on Tverskaya Ulitsa

artisans. A short distance away is the **Pushkin House-Museum** (p75) where newly wed Alexander Pushkin spent some of his happiest months. It provides an illuminating insight into the poet and author's private life. Continue along the street, past buskers and street artists, and browse the wares of the many colourful galleries, boutiques and souvenir shops.

3 Days in Moscow

- Be awed by the State Armoury's gleaming treasures
- Experience a 19th-century shopping mall at GUM
- Admire some of the world's greatest paintings in the Pushkin State Museum of Fine Arts

Day 1
Morning Prepare to be dazzled by the **State Armoury**'s (pp66–7) stunning collection of treasures, carriages and weaponry amassed by generations of Russian rulers. Highlights include the giant Orlov diamond and ten priceless Fabergé eggs. You'll need a separate ticket to visit the rest of the **Kremlin** (pp54–69). Don't miss the golden domed **Cathedral of the Assumption** (pp60–61), where Ivan the Terrible was crowned in 1547.

Afternoon No trip to Moscow would be complete without a visit to **Red Square** (p108). Queue up for your chance

to gaze upon the wax-like body of Lenin in his **Mausoleum** (p109), then explore the eight chapels within the stunning **St Basil's Cathedral** (pp110–11). Afterwards, take a look inside **GUM** (p109), a gleaming 19th-century shopping mall that is jammed with big-name boutiques.

Day 2
Morning Pay a visit to the immense **Cathedral of Christ the Saviour** (p76), built as a replica of the original 19th-century cathedral that was blown up by the Soviets in 1931. A short walk away you'll encounter the queue for the **Pushkin State Museum of Fine Arts** (pp80–83). Unless you intend to spend a whole day or more absorbing the overwhelming collection, plan your visit ahead by browsing the online catalogue.

Afternoon Move on to the historic **Ulitsa Arbat** (pp72–3) for a pleasant stroll. Artists and artisans once worked along this cobbled, pedestrianized street, and Alexander Pushkin lived here briefly with his wife – the house is now the **Pushkin House-Museum** (p75). A more recent addition (1953), is the **Foreign Ministry** (p72), one of Stalin's skyscrapers, which towers over one end of the street.

Day 3
Morning Head out for a walk along **Tverskaya Ulitsa** (p91), once Moscow's grandest street, where historic buildings vie for space with shiny modern structures. The splendid **Yeliseyevsky Food Hall** (p91) is a lovely example of old Moscow, while a visit to the **Museum of Contemporary History** (p99) gives a fascinating overview of the more recent past.

Afternoon Queue up for the chance to see a fantastic array of Russian art at the **Tretyakov Gallery** (pp120–23). What started out as one man's private collection back in 1856 has since become the world's largest collection of Russian art.

5 Days in Moscow

- Enjoy beautiful views of the city from Sparrow Hills
- Step back in time at the Chambers of the Romanov Boyars
- Encounter a Soviet-era exhibition at VVTs

The façade of the Tretyakov Gallery, home to the world's largest collection of Russian art

Day 1

Morning From Okhotny Ryad metro station, head to **Red Square** (p108), passing through **Resurrection Gate** (p107), a copy of the 17th-century gate destroyed by Stalin to allow troops easier access to the square. Take a tour of **St Basil's Cathedral** (pp110–11) before queuing for a glimpse of Lenin's embalmed body in the polished-granite **Mausoleum** (p109).

Afternoon The **Kitay Gorod** area (pp102–3) has some fascinating buildings – start with the **Church of St George** (p104), with its green domes, and the 17th-century **Church of the Trinity in Nikitniki** (p105). For an illuminating impression of Moscow's medieval life, visit the **Chambers of the Romanov Boyars** (pp104–5) and the **Old English Court** (p104).

Day 2

Morning Pop into the huge replica of the 19th-century **Cathedral of Christ the Saviour** (p76) before enjoying the world-class art collection at the **Pushkin State Museum of Fine Arts** (pp80–83).

Afternoon After a tour of the **Kremlin**'s imposing cathedrals and state buildings (pp54–69), head to the **State Armoury** (pp66–7) for the dazzling collection of diamonds, jewellery and weaponry.

Day 3

Morning Take a stroll along **Ulitsa Arbat** (pp72–3), one of Moscow's most famous streets. Buskers and street artists entertain passers-by here, and renowned writer and poet Alexander Pushkin once lived at what is now the **Pushkin House-Museum** (p75).

Afternoon Hop on the metro to Sportivnaya station, from where it is a short walk to the lovely UNESCO-listed **Novodevichiy Convent** (pp132–3). Nearby, at Universitet station, you'll find **Sparrow Hills** (p131), dominated by the Stalinist **Moscow State University** building. This is a great spot for sweeping views of the city.

Day 4

Morning Start the day with a morning of art appreciation at the **Tretyakov Gallery** (pp120–23). The world's largest collection of Russian art includes several rooms of ancient Orthodox icons.

Afternoon Explore the leafy streets of **Zamoskvoreche** (pp116–27) and its many pretty churches and mansions. The baroque **Church of St Clement** (pp124–5) and the onion-domed **Church of the Resurrection in Kadashi** (p124) are two of the best.

Day 5

Morning Enjoy an early stroll through **Gorky Park** (p131), a lovely expanse of riverside gardens that is iced over in winter for skating. Then take the metro to VDNKh station, where you'll encounter the futuristic **Monument to the Conquerors of Space** (p147) before passing through the towering gates of the **All-Russian Exhibition Centre (VVTs)** (p147). The star exhibit here is a Vostok rocket like the one used by Yuri Gagarin, the first man in space.

Afternoon A walk along **Tverskaya Ulitsa** (p91) will acquaint you with both Moscow's past and present – the **Museum of Contemporary History** (p99) is packed with fascinating displays on the city's recent history, while the **Yeliseyevsky Food Hall** (p91) is a splendid example of 19th-century architecture.

The Fountain of the Republics at the All-Russian Exhibition Centre

Putting Moscow on the Map

The Russian Federation (usually simply known as Russia) stretches from the Baltic to the Pacific. With an area of 17 million sq km (6.6 million sq miles), it was the largest of the USSR's 15 republics and is now the world's largest country, almost twice the size of the US. Moscow, the capital with 12 million inhabitants, lies at the heart of European Russia. St Petersburg is Russia's second largest city. Russia is a member of the CIS – a commonwealth of most of the former Soviet republics.

Murmansk

White Sea

Arkhangelsk

M18

FINLAND

Lake Ladoga

Vologda

NORWAY

3 4

Oslo

Dalälven

1

SWEDEN

Helsinki

St Petersburg

Kristia-
nsand

Stockholm

Tallinn

M11

Novgorod

M10

Frederiks-
havn

Gothenburg

ESTONIA

Pärnu

Lovat

MOSCOW

See inset
map above

Varberg

Oskarshamn

Tartu

Pskov

DENMARK

Liepāja

Riga

LATVIA

M12

M1

Smolensk

Tula

Baltic
Sea

LITHUANIA

Orsha

Copenhagen

Klaipėda

Vilnius

M:

Kaliningrad

Minsk

M20

Orël

Koszalin

Olsztyn

BELARUS

Hamburg

Szczecin

POLAND

Białystok

Gomel

Berlin

Odra

Warsaw

M1

M13

Pripyat

GERMANY

A2

A13

Wrocław

Radom

M17

Kiev

Dnepr

A4

Kraków

Prague

Lviv

UKRAINE

A3

CZECH
REPUBLIC

Danube

Košice

Dnestr

A8

SLOVAKIA

Vienna

Bratislava

MOLDOVA

M23

Munich

AUSTRIA

Budapest

Chisinau

Odessa

A10

HUNGARY

ROMANIA

SLOVENIA

Zagreb

Braşov

Venice

Timişoara

Sevastopol

Bologna

CROATIA

M12

BOSNIA-
HERZEGOVINA

Bucharest

A1

Constanţa

A12

Florence

Belgrade

Black
Sea

Ancona

Split

SERBIA

BULGARIA

Varna

ITALY

Adriatic
Sea

MONTENEGRO

Burgas

A14

KOSOVO

Sofia

Rome

Dubrovnik

Skopje

A1

Istanbul

03

A1

Tirana

MACEDONIA

A2

04

Naples

Bari

ALBANIA

Bursa

Ankara

GREECE

TURKEY

Mezen

Ukhta

Pechora

Vychegda

Syktyvkar

Kotlas

Kirov

Moscow and Environs

M8

Kirzhach

A108

M10

Lobnya

Sheremetevo

Istra

Noginsk

M7

M9

A108

A107

MOSCOW

Zhukovskiy

Ruza

Moskva

Vnukovo

M5

Domodedovo

A108

M1

M2

Podolsk

A107

Moskva

M3

M4

0 kilometres   40

0 miles   40

Chekhov

Kolomna

Kazan

R U S S I A N

Ufa

Sibay

Ural

Yaroslavl

F E D E R A T I O N

Orsk

M7

Vladimir

Ulyanovsk

Oka

Samara

Orenburg

M5

Aktobe

Yrgyz

Ryazan

Uralsk

Shubarkudyk

Shalkar

M5

Saratov

K A Z A K H S T A N

Balashov

Don

M5

Makat

Ustyurt Plateau

Aral
Sea

Volgograd

Volga

Atyrau

Kharkov

Donets

Astrakhan

Beyneu

Mariupol

Rostov-na-Don

Elista

Fort-
Shevchenko

Sea of
Azov

Caspian
Sea

Putting Russia on the Map

Arctic Ocean

RUSSIAN FEDERATION

○ Moscow

KAZAKHSTAN

MONGOLIA

CHINA

Pacific
Ocean

AFRICA

INDIA

Key

══════ Motorway

══════ Major road

══════ Minor road

─────── Railway

══════ International boundary

─────── Ferry route

0 kilometres   200

0 miles   200

For keys to symbols see back flap

Central Moscow

Most of Moscow's sights are situated in the city centre, within the area bounded by the Garden Ring and the Boulevard Ring. In this book the centre has been divided into five sightseeing areas, while two further sections cover the outskirts and day trips into the countryside. Each of the central areas has a distinctive character, with the sights in each one lying within easy walking distance of each other. All of these sights are also well served by public transport.

Hotel National
Located in the heart of Tverskaya, close to the Bolshoi Theatre (see pp92–3), the National (see p91) is an eclectic mixture of Style Moderne and Classical style.

Ulitsa Arbat
Running the length of what was a suburb in 15th-century Moscow, ulitsa Arbat (see pp72–3) is today a crowded, pedestrianized street, lined with shops and restaurants.

The Kremlin
The heart of the city, the Kremlin (see pp54–69) has dominated Russian life for over 800 years. Its buildings are from the 15th to 20th centuries.

Tretyakov Gallery
Across the river from Moscow's other main sights, the Tretyakov Gallery (see pp120–23) houses a vast collection of Russian art.

0 metres   400
0 yards   400

RED SQUARE & KITAY GOROD

PETROVSKIY BULVAR

STRASTNOY BULVAR

ROZHDESTVENSKIY BULVAR

SRETENSKIY BULVAR

BOL DMITROVKA UL

ULITSA PETROVKA

UL BOL LUBYANKA

CHRISTOPRUDNYY BULVAR

ULITSA POKROVKA

PEREULOK POKROVSKIY BULVAR

TVERSKAYA ULITSA

NEGLINNAYA ULITSA

NIKOLSKAYA ULITSA

NOVAYA PL

STARAYA PL

SOLYANKA

YAUZSKIY BULVAR

TEATRALNAYA PR

Upper Monastery of St Peter

Sandunovskiy Baths

Convent of the Nativity of the Virgin

Turgenevskaya

Chistye prudy

Menshikov's Tower

Moscow Arts Theatre

Kuznetskiy Most

Former KGB HQ

MAYAKOVSKY Museum

Bolshoi Theatre

Teatralnaya

Hotel Metropol

Lubyanka

History of Moscow Museum

Kitay Gorod

UL MAROSEYKA

Church of St Vladimir

Hotel National

Okhotnyy Ryad

Ploshchad Revolyutsii

Monastery of the Epiphany

Ivanovskaya Convent

Kazan Cathedral

Church of the Trinity in Nikitniki

Resurrection Gate

GUM

Moscow State University

Lenin Mausoleum

Manège

Senate

Arsenal

Biblioteka im Lenina

Aleksandrovskiy Sad

RED SQUARE KRASNAYA PL

KREMLIN

Borovitskaya

Cathedral of the Assumption

St Basil's Cathedral

Old English Court

Chambers of the Romanov Boyars

KITAYGORODSKIY PROEZD

Great Kremlin Palace

Cathedral of the Archangel

State Armoury

Cathedral of the Annunciation

NAB

BOL MOSKVORETSKIY MOST

MOSKVORETSKAYA NABEREZHNAYA

KREMLEVSKAYA NABEREZHNAYA

Moskva Москва

SOFIYSKAYA NABEREZHNAYA

BOLSHOY KAMENNYY MOST

BOLOTNAYA PLOSHCHAD

Malyy Moskvoretskiy Most

BOLOTNAYA ULITSA

Chugunyy Most

PYATNITSKAYA ULITSA

BOL ORDYNKA

Church of the Resurrection in Kadashi

Novokuznetskaya

Malyy Kamennyy most

Tretyakov Gallery

Tretyakovskaya

BOLSHAYA TATARSKAYA ULITSA

Church of St Nicholas in Pyzhy

Church of St Clement

UL BOL POLYANKA

Convent of SS Martha and Mary

NOVOKUZNETSKAYA UL

VISHNYAKOVSKIY PEREULOK

UL BAKRUSHINA

ZAMOSKVORECHE

Tropinin Museum

Bakhrushin Theatre Museum

Paveletskaya (circle)

ULITSA VALOVAYA

St Basil's Cathedral
Located in Red Square *(see p108)*, west of the historic district of Kitay Gorod, St Basil's *(see pp110–11)* is probably Russia's most enduring image.

Key

     Major sight

     Place of interest

For keys to symbols *see back flap*

THE HISTORY OF MOSCOW

From her 12th-century origins as an obscure defensive outpost, Moscow came to govern one sixth of the earth's surface and cast her shadow even further. The story of her rise is laced with glory and setbacks, including the two centuries when St Petersburg was the capital of Russia and Moscow lived the life of a dignified dowager.

The First Settlers

The forested area around Moscow was sparsely populated, but the fertile lands of southern Russia and Ukraine had long supported trade routes between the Orient and Europe. It was here that the Slavs, the ancestors of the Russian people, first settled. They came from Eastern Europe in the 6th century, and established isolated villages along the major rivers. In the 8th century they came into contact with the Varangians (Vikings), who navigated these waterways to trade amber, furs and fair-skinned slaves.

Bloodthirsty and fearless, this lacquer box shows Mongol warriors riding into battle

Kievan Rus

Endemic in-fighting between the Slavic tribes was quelled when Rurik, a Varangian chief, assumed power in the region. Rurik settled in Novgorod, but his successor Oleg took Kiev and made it his capital. In 988 Grand Prince Vladimir I, a descendant of Rurik, was baptised into Orthodox Christianity *(see p139)* and married the sister of the Byzantine emperor. Vladimir's conversion deeply affected the future of

Russia, which remained an Orthodox country right into the 20th century.

The Mongol Invasion

By the 12th century, Kiev's supremacy had already been challenged by the powerful Russian principalities to the north, including Rostov-Suzdal *(see p163)*, of which the wooden kremlin at Moscow formed part. As a result, when the fierce horse-borne Mongols invaded in 1237, the disunited Russians fell easy victims to the well-organized troops of Batu Khan. For the next 240 years the Russian principalities paid an exorbitant yearly tribute to the khans, though they were left to govern themselves.

Rurik, Varangian chief

800	900	1000	1100	1200

c. 800 Varangians arrive in the region to trade and find local tribes in conflict

988 Grand Prince Vladimir I converts to Christianity

1147 Moscow first documented, as the site of a small fortress

1156 Prince Yuriy Dolgorukiy builds Moscow's first wooden kremlin

1240 Mongols control most of Rus after the sack of Kiev

862 Rurik takes Novgorod and establishes a Varangian stronghold

882 Rurik's successor Oleg takes Kiev and makes it capital

863 Missionaries Cyril and Methodius invent the Cyrillic alphabet, based on the Greek one; literacy grows with the spread of Christianity

1108 The town of Vladimir *(see p163)* is founded

1223 First Mongol raid

1236–42 Prince Aleksandr Nevskiy of Novgorod defeats first the invading Swedes and then the Teutonic Knights

◀ The symbol of Moscow, St George and the Dragon, on a 15th-century icon housed in the Tretyakov Gallery

The Rise of Moscow

In the 14th century, the Mongols chose Moscow's power-hungry Grand Prince Ivan I, "Kalita" or "Moneybags" (1325–40), to collect tribute from all their conquered principalities, giving the city supremacy over its neighbours. Ivan had already shown his obsequiousness by crushing a revolt against the Mongols led by his neighbour, the Grand Prince of Tver. Yet the Mongols were sealing their own fate, for, as Moscow flourished under their benevolence, she ultimately became a real threat to their power. Within 50 years an army of soldiers from several Russian principalities, led by Moscow's Grand Prince Dmitriy Donskoy (1359–89), inflicted their first defeat on the Mongols, and the idea of a Russian nation was born.

It was not until the reign of Ivan III, "the Great" (1462–1505), when Moscow ruled a kingdom which stretched as far as the Arctic Ocean and the Urals, that the Mongols were finally vanquished. Ivan married the niece of the last emperor of Byzantium, who had fled Constantinople when it had fallen to the Ottomans in 1453. This increased Moscow's prestige further, and particularly her claim to being the last defender of true Orthodoxy. Ivan also sought to assert Moscow's status through a grand building programme. He started the tradition of importing foreign architects, including the Italians *(see p46)* who built the present Kremlin walls.

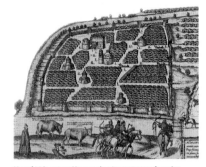

Map of 16th-century Moscow, showing neat rows of wooden houses and several churches behind the city's first stone walls

Ivan the Terrible

It was Ivan the Great's grandson, Ivan IV, "the Terrible" (1533–84), who transformed himself from Grand Prince of Moscow to "Tsar of All the Russias". During his reign Russia expanded beyond the Urals into Siberia and strong trading links were established with England. Moscow's walls were strengthened for, even as late as 1571, the Crimean Mongols continued to venture sporadic attacks on the Russian capital.

Yet, powerful though he was, Ivan suffered dreadful paranoia. After the death of his beloved wife Anastasia, he became convinced that she had been poisoned by the boyars *(see p22)* and set up Russia's first police state. A sinister force of black-hooded agents called the *oprichniki* murdered whole villages to stamp out the tsar's supposed enemies. Ivan also imposed restrictions on the aristocracy and peasantry alike, establishing those autocratic traditions that were to prove the country's downfall. Ivan's more

Ivan the Terrible (1533–84)

1328 Ivan I becomes Grand Prince of Vladimir	**c.1345** St Sergius founds the Trinity Monastery of St Sergius *(see pp164–7)*	**1380** Dmitriy Donskoy defeats the Mongols at the pivotal Battle of Kulikovo *(see p163)*	**1453** Constantinople, previously Moscow's Orthodox ally, falls to the Ottomans	**1470s** The Cathedral of the Assumption is built
1300		**1350**	**1400**	**1450**
1300 Metropolitan See is transferred from Kiev to Vladimir	**1328** Metropolitan See is transferred from Vladimir to Moscow **1325–40** Ivan I rules Moscow and strengthens its position	**1367** Dmitriy Donskoy rebuilds Kremlin walls in limestone *Rebuilding of the Kremlin walls*		**1462–1505** Reign of Ivan III **1476** Ivan III stops paying tribute to Mongols

immediate legacy was his contribution to the end of the Varangian dynasty, the murder of his only competent son, also named Ivan, in a paranoid rage.

The Time of Troubles

This ushered in a period known as the Time of Troubles. For 14 years, Ivan's retarded son Fyodor (1584–98) ruled under the guidance of Boris Godunov, a former and much-hated *oprichnik*. When Fyodor died childless, Godunov installed himself in the Kremlin, but he soon become target of a pretender to the throne. The pretender claimed to be Ivan the Terrible's dead youngest son Dimitry, sought support from Poland and marched on Moscow with an army of 4,000 in 1604. With the death of Boris Godunov in 1605 he was installed on the throne. The pretender was soon to enrage the Moscow boyars, who killed him, and replaced him with Vasiliy Shuiskiy, a boyar of some distinction. Faced with a second "False Dmitry" marching on Moscow in 1607, Shuiskiy appealed to Sweden for help only to provoke a new Polish intervention. The Poles reached Moscow in 1610 and Shuiskiy was then deposed by the boyars. In the north, the Swedes used the internal instability of Russia to capture Novgorod. Only in these desperate circumstances did the Russians finally unite to expel the occupying Poles, under the leadership of Minin and Prince Pozharskiy *(see p111)*. The siege of the Kremlin thus ended in 1612.

Boris Godunov (1598–1605)

The First Romanovs

Determined to put an end to this period of anarchy, Moscow's leading citizens came together to nominate the 16-year-old Mikhail Romanov, great-nephew of Ivan's first wife Anastasia, as hereditary tsar, thus initiating the 300 year rule of the Romanovs. Under Mikhail (1613–45), who ruled with his father Filaret, the patriarch of Moscow, Russia recovered from her exhausting upheavals. His greatest legacy, however, was his heir Alexis (1645–76). An intelligent and pious man, Alexis tried to modernize the state. He oversaw the first codification of Russian law and encouraged an influx of foreign technicians, against the will of the Church. During the reign of Alexis the Church saw difficult times due to the schism between the reformers, led by Patriarch Nikon *(see p59)*, and the conservative Old Believers. Nikon, however, grew too important for his own good which resulted in Alexis asserting the power of the State over the Church.

Ambassadors of the Council of the Realm entreating young Mikhail Romanov to accept the tsar's crown in 1613

1485 Ivan III commissions Italian architects to rebuild the Kremlin walls	1533–84 Reign of Ivan IV	1561 Building of St Basil's Cathedral is completed		1589 Moscow attains status of Patriarchate	1613 Mikhail is elected first tsar of the Romanov dynasty	1653–67 Religious schism between Patriarch Nikon and the Old Believers
1500		**1550**		**1600**		**1650**
1478 Ivan III revokes Novgorod's charter of independence	1547 Ivan IV takes title "Tsar"	1570 Ivan IV orders massacre of Novgorod	1571 Mongols raid Moscow	1610 Moscow falls to the Poles but they are driven out two years later	1654–67 Second war with Poland	
	1552 Victory over Mongols as Ivan IV takes town of Kazan		1598–1605 Reign of Boris Godunov		*Patriarch Nikon*	

Medieval Moscow

Moscow developed in 400 years from an isolated wooden fortress (kremlin), built in 1156, into a thriving capital city, described by a Dutch envoy as "shining like Jerusalem from without, but like Bethlehem inside". Its circle of outer walls enclosed a series of smaller districts centred on the Kremlin, whose wooden stockade was replaced with white limestone in 1367 to protect the city from Mongol raids, and by massive brick walls in 1495. It boasted a clutch of stone cathedrals, befitting its role as the "Third Rome" after the fall of Constantinople in 1453. Next to the Kremlin lay Red Square, where public spectacles ranged from executions to fairs. The rest of the city housed boyars, merchants, servants, hawkers and artisans.

Extent of the City
▨ 13th century ▢ 1590

The public sauna (banya) was always sited near water, isolated where possible from the dense crush of wooden housing.

Andrey Rublev (c.1370–1430)
Moscow's finest icon painter, Andrey Rublev is seen here painting a fresco at the Monastery of the Saviour and Andronicus (see p142). Icons (see p63) were used for the religious education of the people.

A Silver Kovsh
Originally made in wood, this ceremonial drinking vessel, known as a kovsh, began to be crafted in metal in the 14th century. Elaborately decorated kovshi were often given by the tsar to favoured subjects. These treasured artifacts would be displayed as a symbol of wealth when not in use.

The Walled City
Vasnetsov's (see p146) painting of the Kremlin in the 15th century shows the warren of wooden houses which surrounded the palaces and churches. Among them were the renowned Kremlin workshops.

Boyars and Merchants
Though richly dressed, boyars (noblemen) in medieval Russia were largely illiterate and often crude in their habits. Their material needs were looked after by merchants who traded in furs from the north and silk from Turkey.

THE HISTORY OF MOSCOW | **23**

Foreigners in Moscow

From the 16th century, foreign diplomats and traders began to visit the isolated and xenophobic Russia. The adventurer Richard Chancellor, who attempted to find the northwest passage to the Orient but ended up in Russia, managed to negotiate a trading treaty with Ivan the Terrible.

Where to see Medieval Moscow

The Kremlin's medieval buildings include its Cathedrals of the Assumption *(see pp60–61)*, the Archangel *(p62)* and the Annunciation *(p62)*. The State Armoury *(pp66–7)*, also in the Kremlin, displays medieval artifacts and armour while the daily life of the nobility is recreated in the Chambers of the Romanov Boyars *(pp104–5)*. St Basil's Cathedral *(pp110–11)* also dates from this time.

The dining room in the Chambers of the Romanov Boyars.

Wooden houses could be bought pre-fabricated from a market outside the city walls. They quickly replaced houses that were lost in Moscow's frequent fires.

Limestone walls, erected by Dmitriy Donskoy *(see p20)*

Cathedral of the Assumption

Building a Cathedral

During the reign of Ivan I (1325–40), when the first stone Cathedral of the Assumption was built, Metropolitan Peter moved to Moscow to be head of the Orthodox Church. This manuscript illustration shows him blessing the new cathedral.

Small trading vessels thronged the banks of the Moskva river, unloading goods for the growing city. Russia's rivers were her trading routes and were far more efficient than travel by land.

Ivan the Terrible

Though Ivan IV's reign (1533–84) did much to benefit Russia, he certainly deserved his epithet. Among the many souls on his conscience was his only worthy son and heir, Ivan, killed in a fit of rage which the tsar regretted for the rest of his life.

Peter the Great

The extraordinary reign of Alexis's son Peter I, "the Great", really put Russia back on her feet. Brought up in an atmosphere of reform, Peter was determined to make Russia a modern European state. In 1697, he became the first tsar ever to go abroad, with the particular aim of studying shipbuilding and other European technologies. On his return, he began immediately to build a Russian navy, reformed the army and insisted on Western-style clothing for his courtiers. At Poltava in 1709, Peter dramatically defeated the Swedes, who had been a threat to Russia for a century, and stunned Europe into taking note of an emerging power.

Vasiliy Surikov's portrayal of Peter the Great watching Streltsy Guards being led to their deaths in 1698, as punishment for their earlier rebellion

Peter's effect on Moscow was double-edged. At the age of 10 he had seen relatives murdered in the Kremlin during the Streltsy Rebellion. This revolt had sprung from rivalry between his mother's family, the Naryshkins, and that of his father's first wife, the Miloslavskiys, over the succession.

In the end Peter was made co-tsar with his half-brother Ivan, but developed a pathological distrust of Moscow. He took a long-awaited and grim revenge on the Streltsys 16 years

Tsar Peter the Great (1682–1725)

later, when he executed over a thousand of them. He also began to build a new city on the boggy banks of the Neva to the north and ordered the imperial family and government to move. In 1712 he declared the cold, damp St Petersburg capital of Russia. For the next 200 years Moscow was Russia's second city.

Tsarina Elizabeth (1741–62)

The Petticoat Period

After Peter the Great's death in 1725, Russia was ruled by women for most of the 18th century: Catherine I, Anna, Elizabeth and Catherine II. Though they were all crowned in the Cathedral of the Assumption (see pp60–61), most preferred to live in Europeanized St Petersburg. However, Elizabeth, Peter's boisterous, fun-loving daughter, insisted on living in Moscow periodically. During Peter's reign constructions in stone outside St Petersburg had been banned, but under Elizabeth a flurry of new buildings appeared in Moscow, especially since some of Russia's leading families preferred to live there.

1696 Ivan dies. Peter I is sole ruler	1698 The Streltsys are crushed	1721 Peter I replaces patriarchiate with less-powerful church synod		1741–62 Reign of Elizabeth	1773–4 Pugachev Rebellion
	1700–21 Great Northern War against Sweden	1730–40 Reign of Anna			1768–74 First Russo-Turkish War

1700		1725		1750

1682 The Streltsy Rebellion; Peter I is co-tsar with half-brother Ivan V and his half-sister Sophia as regent	1709 Great Russian victory at the Battle of Poltava	1712 Capital is transferred to St Petersburg	1725–7 Reign of Catherine I	Tsarina Anna	1762 Peter III is killed. His wife seizes the throne as Catherine II
			1727–30 Reign of Peter II. Moscow is capital for two years		1755 Mikhail Lomonosov founds Moscow University

Elizabeth founded Russia's first university in Moscow *(see p96)*, under the guidance of Russia's 18th-century Renaissance man, the poet, scientist and academic Mikhail Lomonosov. But Moscow was still protected from the Westernization affecting the capital and thus retained a more purely Russian soul and identity.

Catherine the Great

In 1762 Catherine II, "the Great", a German princess, usurped the throne of her feeble husband Peter III with the help of her lover Grigoriy Orlov, a guards officer. Under her energetic, intelligent leadership, the country saw another vast expansion in its prestige and made territorial gains at the expense of Turkey and its old adversary Poland. Catherine purchased great collections of European art and books (including Voltaire's library) and in 1767 published her *Nakaz* (Imperial Instruction) upon which a reform of Russia's legal system was to be based. Unsurprisingly, this modern European monarch regarded Moscow as inward-looking and backward and spent little time there.

Catherine the Great (1762–96)

19th-Century Moscow

Napoleon's invasion in 1812 and the heroic part played in his defeat by Moscow *(see pp26–7)* appeared to reinvigorate the city. Aleksandr Herzen *(see p73)* claimed that "Moscow was again made the 'capital' of the Russian people by Napoleon", and, indeed, the destruction of two thirds of the city by fire resulted in a bold new architectural plan. The Napoleonic Wars also marked a turning point in Russian political history, as soldiers returned from Europe bringing with them the seeds of liberal ideas. Far from the court of Nicholas I, the Iron Tsar, Moscow became a fertile environment for underground debate among early revolutionaries such as Herzen and the Decembrists. Yet most of Moscow society was trapped in a comfortable and conservative cocoon, financed by the system of serfdom. With the Emancipation of the Serfs in 1861, however, the economic strength of most nobles was radically curtailed. The freed serfs who were too poor to buy their own land, flocked to the factories of mercantile and industrial entrepreneurs. In Moscow, at the old heart of the empire, these entrepreneurs came to usurp the position of the aristocrats, making vast fortunes from trade, textiles, railways, banking and publishing, and financing a renaissance in the Russian arts on the proceeds.

The Bolshoi Theatre, favoured by Moscow's aristocracy, along with balls and lavish suppers, for an evening's entertainment

1787–92 Second Russo-Turkish War	**1805–7** War with France; Russia is defeated at battles of Austerlitz, Friedland	*Tsar Nicholas I*	**1835** First modern law code comes into effect	**1851** The Nicholas Railway between Moscow and St Petersburg is opened	**1853–6** Crimean War

1800   **1825**   **1850**

1796 Death of Catherine II. Paul I accedes

1801 Paul I is assassinated. Alexander I becomes tsar and begins a programme of reforms

1807 Treaty of Tilsit

1812 Napoleon invades Moscow but has to retreat

1816–19 Emancipation of serfs in Baltic provinces

1825 Nicholas I becomes tsar. The Decembrist Rebellion is crushed in St Petersburg

1855 Nicholas I dies. Alexander II succeeds

1861 Emancipation of all serfs

1863–9 Tolstoy publishes *War and Peace*

War and Peace

Russia's glorious rise to the ranks of a world power accelerated in the period between 1800 and 1830. Even though she suffered severe defeats against France, including the Battle of Austerlitz (1805), she rose in power after signing the Treaty of Tilsit in 1807 and becoming an ally of France. The uneasy peace ended in 1812, with the invasion of Napoleon's Grande Armée. But Russia turned disaster into victory and in 1814–15, Tsar Alexander I sat down to decide Europe's future at the Congress of Vienna. The war marked an important cultural shift in Russia as liberal Western European political ideas first filtered into the country, although their time had not yet come.

Extent of the City

1812, before the fire

Areas razed by the fire

The Kremlin was damaged more by the looting of the French than by the fire outside.

Alexander I (1801–25)
The handsome young tsar was initially infected by the ideals of enlightened government, but became increasingly influenced by his reactionary advisers.

Napoleon stayed in the tsar's apartments for a few days before retreating to safety outside the city.

The French soldiers soon fell to undisciplined drinking and looting.

Moscow Burning

After Field Marshal Mikhail Kutuzov's retreat at Borodino, the French army was able to enter Moscow, but Muscovites set light to their city and fled. In just four days, two thirds of the city burnt down, leaving the army without shelter or provisions. Combined with Alexander I's refusal to negotiate while Napoleon remained on Russian territory, this resulted in the French emperor's defeat.

Battle of Borodino, September 1812
The Battle of Borodino (*see p160*) lasted 15 hours, causing the death of 70,000 men, half of them French. Yet Napoleon declared the battle a victory and advanced on Moscow.

Retreat of Napoleon's Grande Armée
Facing the winter without supplies, the army began its retreat in October. Only 30,000 out of 600,000 men made it back.

Empire Style
Many things, from chairs to plates, were designed in the popular Empire style *(see p47)*. This cup and saucer with a Classical motif were made at the Popov factory near Moscow in 1810.

Where to see Neo-Classical Moscow

Pediment, Kuskovo Palace

Early examples of Neo-Classicism can be seen at the palaces of Ostankino *(see pp146–7)* and Kuskovo *(pp144–5)*, at Pashkov House *(p84)* and at Moscow Old University *(p96)*. The fire of 1812 allowed vast areas to be developed to an Empire-style city plan. Bolshaya Nikitskaya ulitsa *(p95)*, ulitsa Prechistenka *(p76)* and Theatre Square *(p90)* are lined with fine buildings from this time.

Moscow University
It was after the Napoleonic Wars that the University of Moscow, founded in 1755, gained a reputation as a hotbed of liberalism. However, political discussions still had to be conducted at secret salons.

Alexander Pushkin
The great Romantic poet Alexander Pushkin *(see p75)* captured the spirit of the time. Pushkin and his wife Natalya were often invited to court balls, such as the one shown here. This enabled Nicholas I to keep an eye on the liberal poet as well as on his enchanting wife.

New fires were started deliberately throughout the city, on the orders of the tsarist governor.

The river proved no barrier to the fire, whipped up by a fierce wind.

The Millstone of Serfdom
In the shadow of the nobility's easy life, and to a great extent enabling it, were millions of serfs toiling in slavery on large estates. This painting shows a serf owner settling his debts by selling a girl to a new master.

The End of an Empire

Though the 1890s saw rapid advances in industrialization, Russia experienced a disastrous slump at the turn of the 20th century. Nicholas II's diversionary war with Japan backfired, causing economic unrest, adding to the misery of the working classes and finally culminating in the 1905 Revolution. On 9th January 1905, a demonstration in St Petersburg carried a petition of grievances to the tsar and was met by bullets. News of this "Bloody Sunday" spread like wildfire and strikes broke out all over the country. To avert further disaster Nicholas had to promise basic civil rights, and an elected parliament, which he, however, simply dissolved whenever it displeased him. This high-handed behaviour, along with the imperial family's friendship with the "holy man" Rasputin, further damaged the Romanovs' reputation.

The outbreak of World War I brought a surge of patriotism which the inexperienced Nicholas sought to ride by taking personal command of the troops. By late 1916, however, Russia had

The Bolshevik by Boris Kustodiev, painted in 1920

lost 3,500,000 men, morale at the front was very low and supplies of food at home had become increasingly scarce.

Revolution and Civil War

In early 1917 strikes broke out in St Petersburg. People took to the streets, jails were stormed and the February Revolution began. The tsar was forced to abdicate and his family was placed under house arrest. Exiled revolutionaries flooded back into the country to set up workers' and soldiers' soviets. Elected by the workers as an alternative to an unelected provisional government they formed a powerful anti-war lobby. In October the leadership of the Bolsheviks, urged on by Lenin, decided on an armed uprising, under the rallying cries of "All power to the soviets!" and "Peace, bread and land". In the early hours of 26th October, they arrested the provisional government in St Petersburg's Winter Palace.

Within months the Bolsheviks had shown themselves as careless of democracy as the tsar, dismissing the constituent assembly and setting up their own secret police, the Cheka.

Tsar Nicholas II surrounded by his wife Alexandra, their four daughters and Tsarevich Alexis in 1913

Tatiana — Olga — Maria — Anastasia

In March 1918, however, the Bolsheviks stayed true to their promise and took Russia out of World War I, instead plunging the soldiers straight into a vicious civil war. The capital was moved back to Moscow, and from here Lenin and his government directed their "Red" army against the diverse coalition of anti-revolutionary groups known as the "Whites". When White soldiers got closer to the exiled Romanovs in Yekaterinburg in July 1918, the royal family was brutally butchered by its captors. But the Whites were a disparate force, and by November 1920 Soviet Russia was rid of them, only to face two years of appalling famine.

Cathedral of Christ the Saviour, torn down on the orders of Stalin as part of his new city plan *(see pp76–7)*

A 1937 propaganda poster showing Joseph Stalin

The Stalin Years

In the 5 years after Lenin's death in 1924, Joseph Stalin used his position as General Secretary of the Communist Party to remove rivals such as Leon Trotsky and establish his dictatorship.

The terror began in the countryside, with the collectivization of agriculture which forced the peasantry to give up their land, machinery and livestock to collective farms in return for a salary. During this time, and in the ensuing famine of 1931–2, up to 10 million people are thought to have died.

The first major purge of intellectuals took place in urban areas in 1928–9. Then, in December 1934, Sergey Kirov, the local party leader in Leningrad, was assassinated on the secret orders of Stalin, although the murder was blamed on an underground anti-Stalinist cell. This was the catalyst for 5 years of purges, by the end of which over a million people had been executed and some 15 million arrested and sent to labour camps, where they often died.

In his purge of the Red Army in 1937–8, Stalin dismissed or executed three quarters of his officers. When the Germans invaded in 1941 they were able to advance rapidly, subjecting Leningrad to a horrendous siege of nearly 900 days. But Moscow was never taken since Hitler, like Napoleon before him, underestimated both the harshness of the Russian winter and his enemies' willingness to fight.

After the German defeat, the Russian people, who had lost over 20 million souls in the war, were subjected to a renewed internal terror by Stalin, which lasted until his death in 1953.

1917 The Russian revolution *(see pp30–31)*

1918 Civil War starts. Capital moves to Moscow

1920

1921 Lenin bans all opposition. NEP (New Economic Policy) is introduced

1922 Stalin becomes General Secretary

1924 Lenin dies

1932 Socialist Realism becomes the officially approved style in art

1934 Leningrad Party Secretary Sergey Kirov is murdered; purges begin

1940

1939 Nazi-Soviet pact

1941 Hitler attacks Soviet Union, reaches outskirts of Moscow. Siege of Leningrad

1947 The term "Cold War" is coined

Sergey Kirov

The Russian Revolution

The Russian Revolution, which began in St Petersburg and made Moscow once more a capital city, was pivotal to the history of the 20th century. By late 1916, with Russia facing defeat in World War I and starvation at home, even ministers and generals were doubting the tsar's ability to rule. In 1917 there were two uprisings: the February Revolution, which began with massive strikes and led to the abdication of Nicholas II; and the October Revolution, which overturned the provisional government and swept the Communists to power. They emerged victoriously from the Civil War that followed, to attempt to build a new society.

Extent of The City

▦ 1917   ☐ Today

Many soldiers deserting from the front were happy to put on the new Red Army uniform instead.

The Ex-Tsar
Nicholas II, seen here clearing snow during his house arrest outside St Petersburg, was later taken with his family to Yekaterinburg in the Urals. There, in 1918, they were shot and their bodies thrown down a mine shaft.

Middle class people as well as the poor took part in the Revolution.

Reds Outside The Kremlin

In October, the fight for control of the Kremlin was intense in comparison to the one in St Petersburg. The Bolshevik seizure was reversed after 3 days, and it took the revolutionaries another 6 days to overcome loyalist troops in the fortress and elsewhere in the city.

Women took part in demonstrations and strikes.

Comrade Lenin
A charismatic speaker, depicted here by Viktor Ivanov, the exiled Lenin returned in April to lead the Revolution. By late 1917 his Bolshevik party had gained power.

Revolutionary Plate
Ceramics with revolutionary themes, mixed with touches of Russian folklore, were produced to commemorate special events. This plate marks the founding of the Third International Communist group in 1919.

Leon Trotsky
The intellectual Trotsky played
a leading military role in the
Revolution. In 1928, during the
power struggle after Lenin's death,
he was exiled by Stalin. He was
murdered in Mexico, in 1940,
by a Stalinist agent.

Propaganda
One hallmark of the Soviet
regime was its powerful
propaganda. Many
talented artists were
employed to design
posters, which spread the
Socialist message through
striking graphics. During
the Civil War (1918–20),
posters such as this one
extolled the "pacifist army
of workers" to support
War Communism.

Banner proclaiming
freedom to the world

Avant-Garde Art
Even before 1917, Russia's
artists had been in a state
of revolution, producing
the world's first truly
abstract paintings. A fine
example of avant-garde art
is *Supremus No. 56*, painted
in 1916 by Kazimir Malevich.

Old and young were swept away
by the revolutionary fervour.

New Values
Traditions were radically
altered by the Revolution;
instead of church weddings,
couples exchanged vows
under the red flag. Loudly
trumpeted sexual equality
meant that women had to
work twice as hard – at
home and in the factories.

| **February** Revolution in St Petersburg | **March** The tsar is persuaded to abdicate. Provisional government is led by Prince Lvov | **October** Bolsheviks storm Winter Palace in St Petersburg, after signal from *Aurora,* and oust provisional government | **March** Bolsheviks sign Brest Litovsk peace treaty with Germany, taking Russia out of World War I. Capital is moved to Moscow |

1917   **1918**

July Kerenskiy becomes prime minister of provisional government

Battleship Aurora

1918 January Trotsky becomes Commissar of War

December Lenin forms the Cheka (secret police)

July Start of Civil War. Tsar and family murdered in prison at Yekaterinburg

The Washington Dove of Peace (1953), a Russian caricature from the days of the Cold War

Behind the Iron Curtain

In 1956, 3 years after Stalin's death, his successor, Nikita Khrushchev, denounced his crimes at the 20th Party Congress and the period known as "The Thaw" began. Thousands of political prisoners were released and books critical of Stalin were published. In foreign affairs, things were not so liberal. Soviet tanks invaded Hungary in 1956 and in 1962 Khrushchev's decision to base nuclear missiles on Cuba brought the world to the brink of nuclear war. When Leonid Brezhnev took over in 1964, the

intellectual climate froze once more. The first 10 years of his office were a time of relative plenty, but beneath the surface there was a vast black market and growing corruption. The party *apparatchiks*, who benefitted from the corruption, had no interest in rocking the boat. When Brezhnev died in 1982, the Politburo was determined to prevent the accession of a younger generation. He was succeeded by the 68-year-old Andropov, followed by the 72-year-old Chernenko.

Glasnost and Perestroika

It was only in 1985, when the new leader, 53-year-old Mikhail Gorbachev, announced his policies of *perestroika* (restructuring) and *glasnost* (openness), that the true bankruptcy of the old system became apparent. Yet he had no idea of the immense changes that they would bring in their wake. For the first time since 1917 the elections to the Congress of People's Deputies in 1989 contained an element of true choice, with rebels such as human-rights campaigner Andrey Sakharov and Boris Yeltsin winning seats. In the autumn and winter

Mikhail Gorbachev with George Bush

of that year the Warsaw Pact disintegrated as country after country in Eastern Europe declared its independence from the Soviet Union. Local elections within the Union in 1990 brought nationalist candidates to power in the republics and democrats in the most important Russian local councils.

First in Space

Under Khrushchev the Soviet Union achieved her greatest coup against the West, when she sent *Sputnik 1* into space in 1957. That same year the dog Laika was the first living creature in space, on *Sputnik 2*. She never came back but, four years later, Yuriy Gagarin made history as the first man in space, returning as a hero. The Soviets lost the race to put a man on the moon, but the space programme was a powerful propaganda tool, backing the claims of politicians that Russia would soon catch up with and overtake the West.

Sputnik 2 and the space dog Laika, 1957

1950–53 Korean War	1961 Building of Berlin Wall. Yuriy Gagarin is first man in space	1964 Brezhnev takes over the role of General Secretary after Krushchev		1979 USSR invades Afghanistan	1980 Moscow Olympics are boycotted by the West	1984 Chernenko replaces Andropov
	1953 Stalin dies		1968 Soviet troops enter Czechoslovakia to suppress "Prague Spring"			
1950	**1960**		**1970**		**1980**	
1955 Warsaw Pact	1957 *Sputnik 1* is launched	1962 Cuban missile crisis	1969 Strategic Arms Limitation Talks (SALT) with USA	1982 Brezhnev dies and is replaced by Andropov		1986 Chernob nuclear disaster
1956 Stalin denounced at 20th Party Congress. Hungarian uprising crushed		1961 Stalin's body is removed from the Kremlin Mausoleum	*Leonid Brezhnev*	1985 Gorbachev is elected General Secretary of Communist Party		

Communist hero fallen from grace after the 1991 coup

In 1991 the Baltic Republics and Russia herself seceded from the Soviet Union. With his massive victory in the election for President of the Russian Republic, Yeltsin gained the mandate he needed to deal the death blow to the Soviet Union. It came after the military coup against Gorbachev in August 1991, when Yeltsin's stand against the tanks in Moscow made him a hero. After Gorbachev's return from house arrest in the Crimea, Yeltsin forced him to outlaw the Communist Party. By the end of the year the Soviet Union was no more as all the republics declared their independence.

Moscow
850-years poster

quadrupled between 1991 and 1997. No amount of nightclubs seemed able to soak up their desire to party. Much of the city was renovated in 1997 in honour of Moscow's 850th anniversary. The Cathedral of Christ the Saviour (see p76), demolished by Stalin in 1931, was rebuilt as part of the restoration programme. This was also a sign of the renewed importance of the Orthodox Church, which was forced underground during the Soviet era. Churches have filled once again for weddings, baptisms and religious holidays. The crime rate fell from its dizzying high in 1995, as the city's criminal groups, or *mafiya*, resolved their territorial battles. President Putin's second term in office from 2004 until 2008 saw Russia grow rich on oil dollars, and living standards rose dramatically, especially in the capital. However, the global financial crisis in 2009 hit the country hard.

Vladimir Putin was re-elected President in 2012 for a third term, with Dmitry Medvedev as Prime Minister.

Moscow Today

The 1990s had a profound effect on the drab old Moscow of Soviet times. With Russia's vast natural resources attracting a rush of inward investment, Moscow saw the lion's share of that money passing through its hands. A wealthy elite, the "New Russians", suddenly had a vastly improved standard of living and, for instance, car ownership in the city

A church wedding, popular once more since religion has gained new importance among the young

1989 USSR leaves Afghanistan

1994 Reconstruction programme in city initiated

2000 Vladimir Putin becomes President of Russia

2008 Putin becomes Prime Minister while Dmitry Medvedev takes office as President

Vladimir Putin

1990   2000   2010   2020

1991 Yeltsin is elected president of Russia. August coup fails; the USSR is dissolved in December

Boris Yeltsin with the Russian flag

2004 Chechen separatists seize school in Beslan; more than 300 left dead after special forces storm the building

2012 Putin becomes President for the third time

MOSCOW THROUGH THE YEAR

Muscovites are ready to celebrate at any time and take their public holidays seriously. Flowers play a particularly important role, from mimosa for International Women's Day to lilac as a symbol that summer is on its way. All the official holidays, as well as some local festivals such as City Day, are marked with concerts and night-time fireworks all over the city. Music, whether classical, folk or contemporary, is the central theme of a large number of festivals, bringing in talent from all over the world. For really big celebrations top Russian and international singers perform for crowds of thousands in Red Square. Even without an official holiday, people love to get out and about, whether skiing in winter, picnicking in spring or summer, or gathering mushrooms in autumn.

Folk performers celebrating Maslenitsa

Spring

When flocks of rooks appear in the city, usually in late March, and the violets and snowdrops bloom, spring is reckoned to have arrived.

To warm themselves up after the months of cold, locals celebrate *maslenitsa*, the feast of blini-making, before Lent. Willow branches with catkins are gathered as a symbol of the approaching Palm Sunday and on Forgiveness Sunday, just before Lent, people ask forgiveness of those they may have offended in the past year. Wealthy

Easter service, Trinity Monastery of St Sergius (see pp164–7)

Muscovites usually make a first visit to their *dacha* at this time to put the garden in order and to plant their own fruits and vegetables.

March

Maslenitsa, end Feb–early Mar. Pancake Week heralds the coming of spring with concerts and carnivals across the city.

International Women's Day (*Mezhdunarodnyy zhenskyy den*), 8 Mar. Men buy flowers for their womenfolk and congratulate them on the holiday with the words *"s prazdnikom"*.

Moscow International Film Festival, biannually in Mar and Oct. A glamorous event attended by celebrities and the general public.

Easter Sunday (*Paskha*), Mar–early May, following the Orthodox calendar. Churches are filled with chanting and candles. After the greeting *Khristos voskres* (Christ is risen) and the reply *Voistinu voskres* (He is truly risen), people kiss one another three times.

April

April Fools' Day (*Den durakov*), 1 Apr. Russians play tricks with particular glee.

Cosmonauts' Day (*Den kosmonavtiki*), 12 Apr. Space exploration was one of the glories of the Soviet Union and is celebrated with fireworks.

Moscow Easter Festival, mid-Apr–mid-May. Nation-wide classical music event with concerts at various city venues.

Alternative Festival, end Apr–May. Annual modern music festival in Gorky Park.

War veterans on parade in Red Square on Victory Day

May

Labour Day (*Den truda*), 1 May. A much more low-key event than it once was, with impromptu concerts.

Victory Day (*Den pobedy*), 9 May. War veterans fill Red Square in memory of the 1945 Nazi surrender.

Night at the Museum, mid-May. Moscow's museums stay open through the night.

Border Troopers' Day (*Den pogranichnika*), 28 May. Retired Border Troopers gather at the Bolshoi Theatre and in Gorky Park to get drunk, sing and watch fireworks.

Average Daily Hours of Sunshine

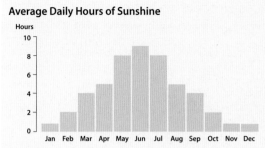

Hours

Sunshine Chart
Moscow is often thought of as a cold and snowy city. However, it has more hours of sunshine in the summer months than many cities in northern Europe. May, June and July are the sunniest months. The short, cold days of winter provide a stark contrast, with an average of only around one hour of sunshine a day.

Summer

Life in Moscow is much less hectic in July and August as most enterprises close down for their summer breaks and many Muscovites move out of the city, either to their *dacha* or to spend holidays abroad. Although most of the theatres also close or go on tour for these two months, there is still plenty going on in and around the city for the visitor to enjoy. Some of the large estates and stately homes outside Moscow, such as Kuskovo *(see pp144–5)* and Ostankino Palace *(see pp146–7)*, hold outdoor concerts at this time of year. Gorky Park offers a number of options on a fine summer day – from hiring a rowing boat or pedalo to enjoying a picnic. Outdoor cafés and bars are a favourite with Muscovites

Women dressed in national costume

remaining in the city; establishments compete to have the most sought-after summer terrace.

June
Trinity Sunday *(Troitsa)*, late May late Jun. Believers and atheists alike go to tidy the graves of their loved ones and drink a toast to their souls.
Tchaikovsky International Competition, Jun, held every four years (next in 2015 and 2019). One of the world's most prestigious musical awards *(see p200)*. Concerts are held throughout the city.
Manor Jazz Festival, first week of Jun. Large open-air festival with classic and contemporary jazz, funk, swing, blues and rock in the leafy grounds of Arkhangelskoe Manor on the outskirts of Moscow.
Day of Russia *(Den Rossii)*, 12 Jun. One of the country's newest holidays marks the day

Russia became independent of the Soviet Union in 1991.
International Music Festival, May–Jun. World music is performed at concert halls throughout the city.

July
St John the Baptist Day *(Ivan Kupala, or Ivanov den)*, 6 July. Popular pagan holiday. Bonfires are lit around the city and youths leap over the flames to test their bravery. Couples leap together as a sign of their commitment to each other.
Navy Day *(Den voenno-morskovo flota)*, first Sunday after 22 July. Spectacular fireworks are accompanied by costumed celebrations across the city. Since Moscow is not a port city, celebrations are not on as lavish a scale as those held in St Petersburg.
Afisha Picnic Festival, late Jul. This one-day music festival in Mosow's Kolomenskoe Park *(see pp140–41)* attracts 50,000 visitors to enjoy both renowned international artists and local independent musicians.

August
Summer Music Festival, throughout Aug. Evening recitals of classical music featuring distinguished graduates of the Moscow Conservatory.
Moscow Annual Airshow, end of Aug, in the town of Zhukovskiy, south-east of Moscow. A chance to see famous Russian aeroplanes.
Russian Cinema Day, 27 Aug. Showings of favourite, mostly Russian, films on television and in cinemas all over the city.

Relaxing on a summer's day at an outdoor café in Arbat

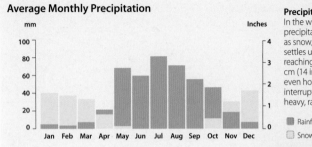

Average Monthly Precipitation

Precipitation Chart
In the winter months, precipitation falls mainly as snow, most of which settles until the spring, reaching a depth of 35 cm (14 in). In summer, even hot days are often interrupted by brief, but heavy, rain showers.

▓ Rainfall (from axis)
▢ Snowfall (from axis)

Autumn

City life begins to pick up as people return from the country and prepare their children for school. In the last weeks of August, Moscow is filled with posters noting the advent of the school year and shops are packed with parents buying new school clothes and books. Theatres open again in September, with premieres of plays and operas.

The crisp autumn weather is perfect for mushroom gathering. Muscovites often head out early in the morning to the forests around the city to hunt for white (the favourite) and brown mushrooms, orange-cap bolens, chanterelles and oyster mushrooms. However, dangerously poisonous as well as edible mushrooms abound and gathering them is best left

Chanterelle mushrooms

to the experts. Other popular autumnal pastimes include horse riding at the Hippodrome and taking a boat trip along the Moskva river.

September

New Academic Year (*Novyy uchebnyy god*), 1 Sep. The first day back at school. Those going for the first time often take flowers with them.

City Day (*Den goroda*), first Sunday in Sep. Celebrations are held all over the city to mark the founding of Moscow in 1147 (*see p19*). More low-key than it once was as this is also the anniversary of the Beslan massacre in 2004.

October

Talents of Russia (*Talanty Rossii*), 1–10 Oct. Festival of classical music, with musicians from all over the country.

Children with flowers for teachers at the start of the new school year

Kremlin Cup, mid–late Oct. Russia's biggest tennis tournament at the Olympic Stadium.

November

Students of the Moscow ballet schools give the first of their annual winter performances at various venues. This is the worst month to visit as Moscow is dirty and slushy.

Day of National Unity (*Den Narodnogo Edinstva*), 4 Nov. Holiday to replace the Day of Reconciliation (previously called the Day of the Great October Revolution).

Public Holidays

New Year's Holiday (1–5 Jan)

Russian Orthodox Christmas (7 Jan)

Defender of the Fatherland Day (23 Feb)

International Women's Day (8 Mar)

Easter Sunday (Mar/Apr/May)

Labour Day (1 May)

Victory Day (9 May)

Day of Russia (12 Jun)

Day of National Unity (4 Nov)

Open-air folk dancing at Moscow's City Day celebrations

Average Monthly Temperature

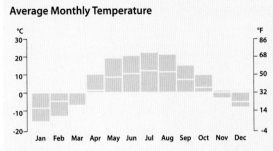

Temperature Chart
The chart shows the average minimum and maximum temperatures for each month. Winter temperatures well below freezing may seem daunting, and do limit the length of time it is possible to stay out, but the cold is dry and can be exhilarating and there is very little wind.

Winter

As the ice thickens and the snow deepens, people head outdoors. Gorky (see p131), Sokolniki and Luzhniki parks become the venues for ice-skating and skiing. The hardened locals, the so-called "walruses", break the ice at Serebryaniy Bor on the western outskirts of Moscow to take a dip early every morning.

In the midst of winter sports come New Year and Christmas. New Year is the big holiday, while Christmas is celebrated on 7 January, in accordance with the Orthodox calendar. Many people also still celebrate Old New Year which falls a week later on 14 January.

One great pleasure of this season is the Christmas ballet, *The Nutcracker*, performed at the Bolshoi Theatre (see pp92–3) largely by children.

December
New Year's Eve (*Novyy god*), 31 Dec. Still the biggest holiday of the year, New Year's Eve is celebrated with the local *shampanskoe* (sparkling wine). This is primarily a family celebration: at circuses and balls, actors dress up as the traditional bringers of presents, the Snow Maiden and Grandfather Frost. More recently, people have begun gathering in Red Square to see in the New Year.

Svyatoslav Richter December Nights (*Dekabrskie vechera imeni Svyatoslava Rikhtera*), throughout Dec. Classical music dedicated to the Russian pianist at the Pushkin State Museum of Fine Arts (see pp80–83).

Russian Winter (*Russkaya zima*), end Dec–mid-Jan. Classical music festival.

Fisherman fishing through a hole in the ice

January
Russian Orthodox Christmas (*Rozhdestvo*), 7 Jan. Christmas is celebrated in a quieter fashion than Easter, with a traditional visit to an evening service on Christmas Eve, when bells ring out through the frosty air from all over Moscow. Children's celebrations are held at various venues, including the Great Kremlin Palace (see p65). The parties are called *Yolka* (Christmas tree).

Christmas Festival of Sacred Music, mid-Jan. International and Russian choirs perform at the Moscow International House of Music.

Ice Sculpture Festival in Gorky Park. This festival lasts for several months, but it is never possible to tell exactly when it will start. It depends entirely on the weather and some years can start as early as December. During the festival Gorky Park is taken over by numerous ice sculptures, usually of fairy-tale characters, which remain in the park until the thaw.

Tatyana's Day (*Tatyanin den*), 25 Jan. St Tatyana's day is largely a holiday for students rather than a religious holiday, since the decree founding Moscow University (see p96) was signed on this day in 1755.

Street entertainer

February
International Festival of the Orthodox Church, throughout Feb. The music and cultural heritage of the Orthodox Church is celebrated in various city venues.

Valentine's Day (*Den svyatovo Valentina*), 14 Feb. Now a part of Moscow's calendar, although it is not as popular as it is in the West.

Defenders of the Fatherland Day (*Den zashchitnika Otechestva*), 23 Feb. Known to most as "Man's Day", this day originally commemorated men in the armed forces, but now celebrates men in general.

An ice sculpture of an octopus, part of the festival in Gorky Park

MOSCOW AT A GLANCE

More than 100 places of interest are described in the *Area by Area* section of this book. These range from the historic treasures of State and Church, enclosed within the Kremlin walls, to galleries housing incomparable religious icons among spectacular collections of Russian and Western art. The city's liveliest streets and most beautiful parks, which offer different attractions in winter and summer,

are also included. To help make the most of a visit, the next 12 pages offer a guide to the very best that Moscow has to offer. Museums and architecture each have their own section, and there is a special feature on Moscow's grandiose metro stations. The sights mentioned here are cross-referenced to their own full entries for ease of use. Below is a selection of the top sights that no visitor should miss.

Moscow's Top Ten Attractions

Bolshoi Theatre
See pp92–93.

St Basil's Cathedral
See pp110–11.

Tretyakov Gallery
See pp120–23.

Kolomenskoe
See pp140–41.

Kremlin Sights

State Armoury
See pp66–7.

Red Square
See p108.

Lenin Mausoleum
See p109.

Cathedral of the Assumption
See pp60–61.

Pushkin State Museum of Fine Arts
See pp80–83.

Kuskovo
See pp144–5.

◀ St Basil's Cathedral in Red Square, with its colourful onion domes

Moscow's Best: Metro Stations

Not many of the world's underground railways can claim to be
tourist attractions and artistic monuments in their own right. The
Moscow metro is an exception. Its station platforms and concourses
resemble miniature palaces with chandeliers, sculptures and lavish
mosaics. Moreover, this is one of the busiest and most efficient metro
networks in the world. Some of the finest stations are shown here and
further information can be found on *pp42–3*. Practical details about
using the metro are given on *pp222–3*.

Belorusskaya
Named after the nearby
Belorusskiy railway station,
Belorusskaya has a central
hall with mosaics of rural
scenes and a tiled floor based
on a traditional pattern
from a Belorussian rug.

TVERSKAYA
(See pp86–99)

Mayakovskaya
A bust of poet Vladimir
Mayakovsky stands in this
station, which is named in
his honour. Recesses in the
ceiling contain a series of
mosaics depicting planes
and sporting scenes.

ARBATSKAYA
(See pp70–85)

Kievskaya
Large, ostentatious
mosaics decorate the walls
of this station. They
include idealized
scenes representing
Russia's friendship
with the Ukraine
and pictures of
Soviet agriculture.

Kropotkinskaya
Clean lines and simple colours
distinguish this elegant station,
designed by Aleksey Dushkin in
the 1930s. It is named after the
anarchist, Prince Pyotr Kropotkin.

Park Kultury
Niches in the walls of this station's central hall hold white,
marble bas-relief medallions. These show people
involved in various recreational activities such as
ice-skating, reading, playing chess and dancing.

Teatralnaya
The differing cultures of the republics of the former Soviet Union provide the theme for this station. The ceiling panels depict some of their national costumes.

Komsomolskaya
This is the main entrance to Komsomolskaya station, named in honour of the Communist Youth League (Komsomol) which helped to construct the metro.

RED SQUARE AND KITAY GOROD
(See pp100–115)

REMLIN
e pp54–69)

ZAMOSKVORECHE
(See pp116–127)

| 0 metres | 750 |
| 0 yards | 750 |

Ploshchad Revolyutsii
The main hall of this station contains lifesize bronze statues of ordinary citizens, such as a farmer, who helped to build the Soviet State.

Novokuznetskaya
A bas-relief frieze runs along the central hall of this station, which was constructed in 1943. The frieze shows a variety of Russian military heroes, such as World War II soldiers.

Exploring the Moscow Metro

When the idea of an underground railway was first proposed for Moscow in 1902 the idea was rejected by one local newspaper as "a staggeringly impudent encroachment on everything Russian people hold dear in the city of Moscow". By the 1930s, however, the need for better transportation had become urgent as the population of the city more than doubled to meet the demands of rapid industrialization. Two prominent young Communists, Nikita Khrushchev and Lazar Kaganovich, were entrusted with building a metro that would serve as a showcase for socialism and the achievements of workers and peasants.

Members of the Communist Youth League helping to build the metro

Building the Metro

Construction work on the metro began in December 1931, during the period of Stalin's first Five Year Plan of 1928–33. The Communist Party decreed that "the whole country will build the metro", so workers – both men and women – were drafted in from all over the Soviet Union. They were assisted by soldiers of the Red Army and by over 13,000 members of the Communist Youth League (Komsomol).

The latter worked as volunteers in their free time and their massive contribution was commemorated by naming **Komsomolskaya** after them. The materials, too, came from different parts of the country: rails from the steelworks of Kuznetsk, marble from the Urals and Caucasus and granite from Karelia and the Ukraine.

Work was completed on the first 11.6-km (7.2-mile) section of track, linking Sokolniki with **Park Kultury**, in February 1935 and the first 13 stations were opened in May. Many of those who had worked on the project

were subsequently rewarded with medals, including the much-coveted Order of Lenin. Construction work continued rapidly and by 1939 there were 22 stations serving over one million passengers.

Metro Decoration

Some of the Soviet Union's finest artists were employed to decorate the metro. Working within the confines of Socialist Realism *(see p137)*, many dealt with themes such as the Revolution, national defence and the Soviet way of life.

The earliest metro stations are generally regarded as the most architecturally successful. **Mayakovskaya**, designed by Aleksey Dushkin in 1938, won the Grand Prix at the New York World's Fair. Its spacious halls are supported by columns of stainless steel and marble. **Kropotkinskaya** (1935) and **Ploshchad Revolyutsii** (1938) are also by Dushkin. The main hall of the latter has a series of marble-lined arches. On either

side of each stands a life-sized bronze figure cast by sculptor Matvey Manizer. Red Guards, workers, sailors, sportsmen and women, a Young Pioneer and a mother and child are among the "everyday heroes" who made the Revolution possible or helped to build the subsequent Soviet State.

Several stations, including **Komsomolskaya**, consist of two or more linked sections on different metro lines. One of Komsomolskaya's two sections, on the Sokolnicheskaya line, was built in 1935. Its decor is relatively restrained, with rose-coloured marble pillars and majolica panels by Yevgeniy Lanseray showing heroic metro workers. The other station, on the circle line, was completed 17 years later and is much more ostentatious, with florid stucco mouldings and glittering chandeliers. Designed by leading architect Aleksey Shchusev, it was also a prizewinner at the New York World's Fair. The glittering mosaics showing military

Metro Statistics

The Moscow metro is still expanding, but there are already 194 stations and about 325 km (202 miles) of track. Almost 10,000 trains operate every day, travelling at speeds of up to 90 km/h (56 mph). The Moscow metro carries 8–9 million passengers per day, more than the London and New York systems combined. During peak periods trains arrive at stations every 90 seconds.

The simple, yet stylish, Mayakovskaya, designed by Aleksey Dushkin

parades and figures from Russian history are the work of artist Pavel Korin.

Martial themes predominated during and after World War II. At **Novokuznetskaya** (1943), for example, architects Vladimir Gelfreikh and Igor Rozhin commissioned a bas-relief frieze from Nikolay Tomskiy showing Russian military heroes as diverse as Minin and Pozharskiy *(see p111)* and Field Marshal Kutuzov *(see p160)*.

Many of the stations built in the 1940s and 1950s extol the virtues of the Soviet regime. Ceramic panels at **Teatralnaya** (1940) celebrate the arts of the former Soviet Republics, while mosaics at **Belorusskaya** (1952) and **Kievskaya** (1937 and 1954) show healthy, happy peasants celebrating agricultural abundance. These ignore the terrible famine that resulted from Stalin's forced collectivization policy of the early 1930s.

In the Soviet mind, athletic prowess was the natural preparation for heroic achievement. Sport and recreation are the twin themes of the bas-reliefs by artist Isaak Rabinovich at **Park Kultury** (1935 and 1950).

Even the station exteriors above ground were designed to work as propaganda. Seen from above, the entrance to **Arbatskaya** (1935) is in the shape of the Soviet red star.

Although financial constraints impose limits, artistic leeway was still possible in the design of some of the newer stations such as **Chekhovskaya** (1987), and **Park Pobedy**, the world's deepest metro station, completed in 2003.

Part of Komsomolskaya, designed by architect Aleksey Shchusev

The Metro and War

The early metro lines were laid deep underground so that they could be used as bomb shelters in times of war. By November 1941 German troops had reached the outskirts of Moscow and the Soviet Union was fighting for survival. **Mayakovskaya**, completed just three years earlier, became the headquarters of the Anti-Aircraft Defence Forces. It was in the station's central hall that Stalin addressed generals and party activists on the anniversary of the October Revolution in 1941.

Kirovskaya (now known as **Chistye Prudy**) was the headquarters of the General Staff throughout World War II. Stalin and his advisors planned the first offensives against the Nazis here. Consequently, the metro system became an important symbol of resistance to the Nazi invasion. In fact, its propaganda value was deemed so great that the

Revolutionary figures at Belorusskaya

designs for the mosaics at **Novokuznetskaya** were made in Vladimir Frolov's workshop in Leningrad, now St Petersburg, during the siege of the city. Frolov died of exposure after he had completed the work.

Metro Museum

The history and workings of the Moscow metro are fully explained in this interesting museum, located above the main hall of Sportivnaya on Sparrow Hills *(see p131)*. Some rather dated photomontages show the construction of the track and stations. There are numerous displays including models of trains and escalators, a reconstruction of a driver's cabin and the first ticket, sold in 1935.

🏛 **Moscow Metro Museum**
Sportivnaya metro. **Tel** (495) 622 7309.
Open 9am–4:30pm Tue–Fri,
10am–4:30pm Sat.

Where to see the Metro

Arbatskaya **Map** 6 E1
Belorusskaya **Map** 1 C2
Chekhovskaya **Map** 2 F4
Chistye Prudy **Map** 3 C4
Kievskaya **Map** 5 B2
Komsomolskaya **Map** 4 D2
Kropotkinskaya **Map** 6 E2
Mayakovskaya **Map** 2 E3
Novokuznetskaya **Map** 7 B3
Park Kultury **Map** 6 D4 & 6 E3
Ploshchad Revolyutsii **Map** 3 A5
Teatralnaya **Map** 3 A5

The entrance to Arbatskaya, in the shape of the Soviet red star

Moscow's Best: Architecture

Visitors to Moscow are often pleasantly surprised by the wealth and variety of architecture the city has to offer. As well as magnificent palaces and cathedrals, such as those in the Kremlin, there are also smaller churches and chapels, homely boyars' residences, imposing Neo-Classical mansions and some beautiful municipal buildings. A stark contrast to this older architecture is provided by early 20th-century Constructivist buildings and Communist landmarks such as Stalinist-Gothic skyscrapers. For further information about architecture, see pp46–7.

Moscow Old University
The colonnade of pillars on the front of this building and its ochre and white colouring are typical Neo-Classical features.

Gorky House-Museum
Stunning stained-glass windows grace the Gorky House-Museum, a Style-Moderne masterpiece built by Fyodor Shekhtel in 1900.

TVERSKAYA
(See pp86–99)

ARBATSKAYA
(See pp70–85)

Cathedral of the Assumption
A miraculous fusion of Renaissance and Early-Russian styles, this superb cathedral was built in 1475–9 to a design by Italian architect Aristotele Fioravanti.

Foreign Ministry
This is one of seven skyscrapers designed in a hybrid style often referred to as Stalinist Gothic. The Foreign Ministry building was finished in 1952 shortly before Stalin's death.

Pashkov House
The Neo-Classical Pashkov House, which has been restored, has a colonnaded porch with relief sculptures.

Polytechnical Museum
The central part of the Polytechnical Museum, built in 1877, is the work of Ippolit Monighetti. It is an outstanding example of Russian Revival, a style that draws heavily on the architecture of Russia's past.

St Basil's Cathedral
Pointed roofs over the entrance steps and tiers of arched gables typify the stunning architectural diversity of this cathedral, built in 1555–61 for Ivan the Terrible.

RED SQUARE
AND KITAY
GOROD
(See pp100–115)

REMLIN
ee pp54–69)

Old English Court
Presented to an English trade delegation in 1556, this 16th-century, whitewashed, stone house has a wooden roof and few windows.

AMOSKVORECHE
(See pp116–127)

| 0 metres | 750 |
| 0 yards | 750 |

Church of the Resurrection in Kadashi
This Moscow-Baroque church has tiers of ornate limestone carvings in place of the kokoshniki gables normally seen on Early-Russian churches. The church's onion domes, previously an unusual jade green colour, are now gilded.

Exploring Moscow's Architecture

Russian architecture has always been innovative. The medieval Novgorod, Yaroslavl and Pskov schools of architecture developed several of the distinctive features found on Moscow's churches. These included the onion dome, rounded *zakomary* gables and *kokoshniki* gables, which are semi-circular or shaped like the cross-section of an onion. In later centuries Moscow's architects became increasingly influential, developing new styles, such as Constructivism, and giving a Russian flavour to others.

The Baroque Gate Church of the Intercession at Novodevichiy

Study in the Chambers of the Romanov Boyars

Early Russian

Moscow's earliest buildings were constructed entirely from wood. From around the 14th century, stone and brick began to be used for important buildings, but wood continued to be the main building material until the great fire of 1812 *(see p26)* when much of the city was burnt to the ground.

The majority of Moscow's oldest surviving buildings are churches. One of the earliest is the Cathedral of the Saviour in the **Monastery of the Saviour and Andronicus** *(see p142)*. In the 15th and 16th centuries the tsars employed a succession of Italian architects to construct prestigious buildings in the Kremlin. They combined the Early-Russian style with Italian Renaissance features to create magnificent buildings such as the **Cathedral of the Assumption** *(see pp60–61)*.

Another 16th-century innovation was the spire-like tent roof, used, for example, on **St Basil's Cathedral** *(see pp110–11)*. In the mid-17th century Patriarch Nikon banned its use, insisting that plans for new churches must be based on ancient Byzantine designs.

The majority of Moscow's early secular buildings have not survived. The few exceptions include the ornate 16th-century **Chambers of the Romanov Boyars** *(see pp104–5)* and the charming early 16th-century Old English Court *(see p104)*.

Baroque

The Bridge Tower (1670s) at **Izmaylovo Park** *(see p143)* is an early example of Moscow Baroque. Its filigree limestone trimmings and pilaster decoration, set against a background of red brick, are typical of the style. The gate churches in the **Novodevichiy Convent** *(see pp132–3)*, the buildings of the **Krutitskoe Mission** *(see p142)* and the spectacular **Church of the Resurrection in Kadashi** *(see p124)*, with its limestone ornamentation carved to resemble lace, are also fine examples of this style of architecture.

A number of Baroque buildings, including the **Church of the Intercession in Fili** *(see p130)*, were built with money from the wealthy and powerful Naryshkin family. This has led to Moscow Baroque also being known as Naryshkin Baroque.

Neo-Classical

The Accession of Catherine the Great in 1762 heralded a new direction for Russian architecture. She favoured the Neo-Classical style, which drew on the architecture of ancient Greece and Rome. This style has been used to great effect in the **Pashkov House** *(see p84)*, thought to have been designed by Vasiliy Bazhenov in 1784 (sadly, the building is now covered by hoarding).

Bazhenov's assistant, the prolific Matvey Kazakov, demonstrated the flexibility of Neo-Classicism in his designs

The New Patriotism

The reconstruction of the city's pre-Revolutionary buildings, including the **Kazan Cathedral** *(see p107)* and the **Cathedral of Christ the Saviour** *(see p76)*, is evidence of a growing nostalgia for Russia's past, and a renewed interest in the nation's architectural heritage. The revival of the Orthodox Church, in particular, has led to the restoration of hundreds of churches across Moscow.

The Cathedral of Christ the Saviour, rebuilt in 1994–7

for a wide range of buildings, including churches, hospitals, the **Moscow Old University** *(see p96)* and the **House of Unions** *(see pp90–91)*. He is best known for the **Senate** *(see pp68–9)* in the Kremlin.

The huge fire that followed Napoleon's brief occupation of the city in 1812 led to a whole-sale reconstruction. Moscow's nobility built new homes along **ulitsa Prechistenka** *(see p76)* in the newly fashionable Empire style. Leading architects of this more decorative style included Afanasiy Grigorev and Osip Bove, who designed **Theatre Square** *(see p90)*.

A Neo-Classical bas-relief in the House of Unions, built in the 1780s

Historicism and Style Moderne

Historicism replaced Neo-Classicism in the mid-19th century. It arose from a desire to create a national style by reviving architectural styles from the past. The **Great Kremlin Palace** *(see p65)* and **State Armoury** *(see pp66–7)*, both designed by Konstantin Ton around 1840, are typical. They combine various styles including Renaissance, Classical and Baroque. Ton also designed the extravagant

The Style-Moderne Gorky House-Museum

The House of Friendship, a wonderful example of Eclecticism

Byzantine-style **Cathedral of Christ the Saviour** *(see p76)*, finished in 1883 and rebuilt in 1994–7.

Eclecticism combined past and present architectural styles from all over the world to create fantastical buildings such as the **House of Friendship** *(see p97)*, which was designed by Vladimir Mazyrin in 1898.

Traditional wooden architecture and folk art were rich sources of inspiration for the architects that formulated the Russian-Revival style. The flamboyant **Historical Museum** *(see p108)* and **Polytechnical Museum** *(see p112)* are fine examples of the genre. However, the finest, and most functional, is **GUM** *(see p109)* designed by Aleksandr Pomerantsev.

Style Moderne was a radical new architectural style akin to Art Nouveau. One of the earliest examples is the **Hotel Metropol** *(see p90)*, designed in 1899 by Englishman William Walcot. The greatest advocate of Style Moderne was Fyodor Shekhtel. The mansion he built for Stepan Ryabushinskiy is now the **Gorky House-Museum** *(see p97)*. It is highly unconventional and uses mosaic friezes, glazed brick and stained glass to stunning effect.

Mosaic of irises from the frieze around the Gorky House-Museum

Architecture after the Revolution

Constructivism was a novel attempt to combine form and function, and was the most popular style to emerge in the decade after the Revolution. The offices of the newspaper **Izvestiya**, on Pushkin Square *(see p99)*, were designed by Grigoriy Barkhin in 1927. His use of glass and reinforced concrete to create geometrical designs is typical of the Constructivist style.

Another leading Constructivist was Konstantin Melnikov. The unique **Melnikov House** *(see p74)*, which consists of two interlocking cylinders, is the home that he built for himself in 1927. In the 1930s Stalin formulated a grand plan to rebuild large areas of the city. He favoured a new monumental style and Constructivism went out of vogue. The monumental style is exemplified by Aleksey Shchusev's grandiose "proletarian" apartments at the lower end of Tverskaya ulitsa and culminates in Stalinist Gothic. This term is used to describe the seven matching skyscrapers erected at key points in the city in the 1940s and 1950s. The **Foreign Ministry** building *(see p72)*, designed by architects Mikhail Minkus and Vladimir Gelfreikh, is typical of this style, which is often called "wedding-cake" architecture.

Moscow's Best: Museums

Moscow has more than 80 museums offering a fascinating insight into the history and culture of the people of Russia. Some, such as the Tretyakov Gallery and State Armoury, have collections including works by world-famous artists and craftsmen, while others house exhibits of local or specialist interest. Among the most evocative are those commemorating the lives of artists, writers and musicians. The rooms where they lived and worked have been lovingly preserved. For further information on museums *see pp50–51.*

State Armoury
This elaborate 17th-century enamel work is exhibited in the State Armoury, along with a dazzling array of gold and silverware, jewellery and royal regalia. The current Armoury building was constructed in 1844 on the orders of Tsar Nicholas I.

Shalyapin House-Museum
Portraits of the opera star Fyodor Shalyapin on display in his former home include formal paintings, images of him on stage and drawings by his children.

TVERSKAYA
(See pp86–99)

ARBATSKAYA
(See pp70–85)

Pushkin State Museum of Fine Arts
As well as a fine collection of Byzantine and Western European art from the 8th to the 18th centuries, this gallery houses artifacts from ancient Egypt, Greece and Rome, including this Egyptian funeral mask.

0 metres	750
0 yards	750

Tolstoy House-Museum
For over 20 years this traditional house was the winter home of Leo Tolstoy, author of the epic novel *War and Peace.* It is now an evocative museum which recaptures the daily lives of the writer and his family.

Lenin Mausoleum
The red and black pyramid of the Lenin Mausoleum was erected in 1930 to a design by architect Aleksey Shchusev. It contains the embalmed body of Vladimir Lenin, the first Soviet leader.

Mayakovsky Museum
This thought-provoking museum commemorates the revolutionary poet, playwright and artist Vladimir Mayakovsky. The abstract exhibits in this room symbolize his childhood in Georgia.

Chambers of the Romanov Boyars
The restored interiors and luxurious clothes and possessions in this house effectively evoke the daily lives of the Moscow aristocracy in the 16th and 17th centuries. The house was constructed for boyar Nikita Romanov.

RED SQUARE AND KITAY GOROD
(See pp100–115)

EMLIN
pp54–69)

ZAMOSKVORECHE
(See pp116–127)

Further Afield

0 kilometres 4
0 miles 2

Kuskovo was the rural estate of the aristocratic Sheremetev family in the 18th century.

Kolomenskoe
was a favourite country residence for Tsar Alexis Mikhailovich. An open-air museum of architecture now forms part of the estate.

Tretyakov Gallery
Valentin Serov's *Girl with Peaches* (1887) in the Tretyakov Gallery is part of the largest collection of Russian art in the world.

Exploring Moscow's Museums

Wherever visitors' interests lie, whether it be in painting and the fine arts, science, the Revolution, the history of the Russian theatre or the lives of the nobility, there will be something in Moscow's museums to appeal to them. A number of house-museums have preserved the former homes of important cultural figures, such as novelist Leo Tolstoy. As well as the many museums in the city, there are a number of country estates in the area around Moscow. Several of these, including Kuskovo and Kolomenskoe, are easily accessible by metro and make good half-day or day excursions (see p227). However, it is worth bearing in mind that a number of museums are currently undergoing much-needed renovation and, in some cases, ideological reassessment.

The elegant drawing room of the Lermontov House-Museum

Young Acrobat on a Ball, Picasso, in the Gallery of European and American Art

Painting and Decorative Arts

The world's most important collection of Russian art is on display in the **Tretyakov Gallery** (see pp120–23). The gallery owns over 160,000 works, but only a fraction of them are on show at any one time. They include, among others, paintings by most of the group of artists called the Wanderers (peredvizhniki). The gallery's extensive collection of Post-Revolution (20th-century) art is now housed in the **Tretyakov on Krymsky Val** (see p137). The **Tropinin Museum** (see pp126–7) has a fine collection of works by the 19th-century portrait artist Vasiliy Tropinin and his contemporaries.

The **Department of Private Collections** (see p77) is a new gallery, housed in a 19th-century building. It exhibits previously unseen drawings, watercolours, sketches and paintings, mainly by Russian artists of the 19th and 20th centuries.

On the same street, the **Pushkin State Museum of Fine Arts** (see pp80–83) and The **Gallery of 19th- and 20th-Century European and American Art** (see p77), are two of Moscow's finest art galleries. The former displays old masters such as Botticelli, Rubens and Rembrandt, while the latter boasts a superb collection of Impressionist and Post-Impressionist paintings.

A superb collection of decorative and applied art spanning the last seven centuries or so is housed in the **State Armoury** (see pp66–7) in the Kremlin. There are rooms devoted to arms and armour, jewellery, gold and silverware, religious vestments and imperial regalia.

A 16th-century Persian shield on display in the State Armoury

House-Museums

The houses and apartments where many important Russian cultural figures lived have been preserved as museums. The sturdy, timber-framed **Tolstoy House-Museum** (see p136) contains many personal possessions that belonged to Leo Tolstoy. The novelist and his family spent many winters in the house. Among their regular visitors was the playwright Anton Chekhov. The house where this writer began his career in the 1880s is also open to the public as the **Chekhov House-Museum** (see p98). Across the road from Chekhov's house is the **Shalyapin House-Museum** (see p85) where the great opera singer, Fyodor Shalyapin, lived. Visitors can enjoy the beautifully furnished rooms while listening to old recordings of his singing.

The **Stanislavskiy House-Museum** (see p95) is the former home of Konstantin Stanislavskiy, theatrical director and the co-founder of the Moscow Arts Theatre (see p94). It contains costumes, props and other memorabilia.

Along with a few items once owned by Alexander Pushkin, the **Pushkin House-Museum** (see p75) contains an interesting display of pictures that show what Moscow was like in 1831, when the poet lived here. The **Bely House-Museum** (see p75), in the building next door, was once the home of the Symbolist poet, Andrei Bely. Nearby is the **Skryabin House-Museum** (see p74), the last home of composer Aleksandr Skryabin. The tower blocks of Novyy Arbat dwarf the **Lermontov House-Museum** (see pp84–5), the simple timber house where Pushkin's contemporary, the poet Mikhail Lermontov, was brought up in the early 1830s.

The extraordinary life of Vladimir Mayakovsky is brilliantly realized in the displays in the **Mayakovsky Museum** (see p113). This apartment, near the former KGB building (see p114), is where the Futurist poet lived from 1919 to 1930.

The artist Viktor Vasnetsov designed his own home. In his studio, now the **Vasnetsov House-Museum** (see p146), visitors can see his enormous canvases based on folk tales.

The **Tchaikovsky House-Museum** (see p161) at Klin still contains furnishings used by composer Pyotr Tchaikovsky, including the desk where he finished his Sixth Symphony.

Country Estates

Several palaces and estates on the outskirts of Moscow are open to the public. **Ostankino Palace** (see pp146–7), built in the 18th century for the fabulously wealthy Sheremetev family, is famous for its exquisite theatre, where serf actors and musicians once took the stage. **Kuskovo** (see pp144–5) was also built for the Sheremetevs. In the palace's beautiful gardens is a ceramics museum.

A number of superb 16th- and 17th-century buildings still stand at the former royal estate of **Kolomenskoe** (see pp140–41). Also on the estate is a fascinating museum of wooden architecture.

Picturesque, Gothic-style ruins are all that remain of the palace at **Tsaritsyno** (see p139). This ambitious project was commissioned by Catherine the Great. The original building was not to her liking so she ordered that it should be rebuilt, but the palace was never finished.

Works of art by 19th- and 20th-century Russian artists are on show at the **Abramtsevo Estate-Museum** (see p162), which was formerly an artists' colony.

Sweet wrappers, boxes and scales in the Museum of Modern History

History Museums

A number of museums and other sites in and around the city provide fascinating glimpses into Moscow's past.

The **Historical Museum** (see p108) traces the history of Russia from the ice age to the present day. Permanent collections include the 13th-century Mongol Invasion of Eastern Europe and the Russian Orthodox Church in the 16th and 17th Centuries.

The life of the boyars (see p22) in Moscow in the early 17th century is re-created in the **Chambers of the Romanov Boyars** (see pp104–5).

Visitors interested in Napoleon's winter invasion of Russia in 1812 (see pp25–7) will want to make the day trip to **Borodino** (see p160). This was the scene of one of the bloodiest encounters of the campaign. There are more than 30 monuments around the battlefield and a museum nearby tells the story of the battle. They may also like to visit the **Borodino Panorama Museum** (see p131) on Kutuzovskiy prospekt. This circular pavilion contains an enormous painting of the famous battle.

The monumental scale of the **Lenin Mausoleum** (see p109), containing Lenin's embalmed body, gives an insight into the importance of the role played by Lenin (see pp29–30) in 20th-century Russian history.

Displays at the **Museum of Contemporary History** (see p99) cover Russian history from 1900 until the collapse of the Soviet Union in 1991. Sweet wrappers depicting Marx and Lenin and home-made grenades are among the exhibits.

The **Museum of the Great Patriotic War** (see p131) has maps, models and dioramas of major battles from World War II, shown largely from a Soviet viewpoint.

Specialist Museums

Among the city's handful of specialist museums is the **Polytechnical Museum** (see p112), which charts important developments in science and technology in Russia.

The **Bakhrushin Theatre Museum** (see p127) houses an exciting collection of theatre memorabilia, including ballet shoes worn by Taglioni, while the **Shchusev Museum of Architecture** (see p152) gives a history of Russian architecture.

A model of a reactor from a nuclear power station, one of the displays at the Polytechnical Museum

The imposing Cathedral of Christ the Saviour and Patriarshy Bridge ▶

MOSCOW AREA BY AREA

THE KREMLIN

Citadel of the Tsars, headquarters of the Soviet Union and now the residence of the Russian president, for centuries the Kremlin has been a symbol of the power of the State. In 1156, Prince Yuriy Dolgorukiy chose the confluence of the Moskva and Neglinnaya rivers as the site for the first wooden Kremlin (*kreml* means "fortress"). Late in the 15th century, Tsar Ivan III *(see p20)* invited several leading Italian architects to build a sumptuous new complex. They designed

the Cathedral of the Assumption and the Faceted Palace, among other buildings, in a fascinating fusion of Early-Russian and imported Renaissance styles *(see p46)*.

The Kremlin did not escape the architectural vandalism of the 1930s, when it was closed and several of its churches and palaces were destroyed on Stalin's orders *(see p77)*. Only in 1955, two years after his death, was the Kremlin partially reopened to the public.

Sights at a Glance

Churches and Cathedrals
5 *Cathedral of the Assumption pp60–61*
6 Cathedral of the Archangel
7 Cathedral of the Annunciation
9 Church of the Deposition of the Robe

Historic Buildings and Monuments
1 Trinity Tower
2 State Kremlin Palace
4 Ivan the Great Bell Tower
8 Faceted Palace
10 Terem Palace

11 Great Kremlin Palace
13 Saviour's Tower
14 Presidential Administration
15 Senate
16 Arsenal

Museums
3 Patriarch's Palace
12 *State Armoury pp66–7*

Gardens
17 Alexander Gardens

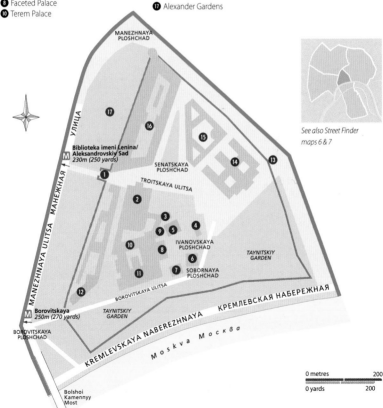

See also Street Finder maps 6 & 7

◀ The splendid St Andrew's Hall (Throne Hall) in the Great Kremlin Palace

For keys to symbols *see back flap*

Street by Street: The Kremlin

The Kremlin is home to the Russian president and the seat of his administration. As a result less than half of it is accessible to the public, but highlights including the State Armoury, the Patriarch's Palace and the churches in Cathedral Square are open to visitors. Christians have worshipped on this site for more than eight centuries, but their early stone churches were demolished in the 1470s to make way for the present magnificent ensemble of cathedrals. In imperial times, these were the setting for great state occasions such as coronations, baptisms and burials.

❶ Trinity Tower
Napoleon marched in triumph through this gate when he entered the Kremlin in 1812 *(see pp25–7)*. He left defeated a month later.

Ticket office

0 metres		50
0 yards		50

❷ State Kremlin Palace
Originally built in 1961 for Communist Party congresses, the palace is now used for a range of cultural events.

❿ Terem Palace
A chequered roof and 11 golden cupolas topped by crosses are all that is visible of this hidden jewel of the Kremlin.

⓫ Great Kremlin Palace
The palace contains several vast ceremonial halls. The sumptuous stucco work of St George's Hall provides a magnificent backdrop for state receptions. Its marble walls are inscribed with the names of military heroes.

⓬ ★ State Armoury
The State Armoury was designed by Konstantin Ton to complement the Great Kremlin Palace. Constructed in 1844–51, this building is now a museum. It houses the stunning imperial collections of decorative and applied art and the priceless State Diamond Fund

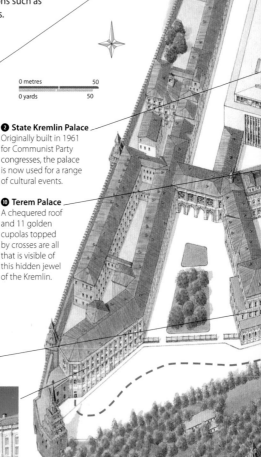

Borovitskaya Tower, and entrance if visiting State Armoury only.

Key

— Suggested route

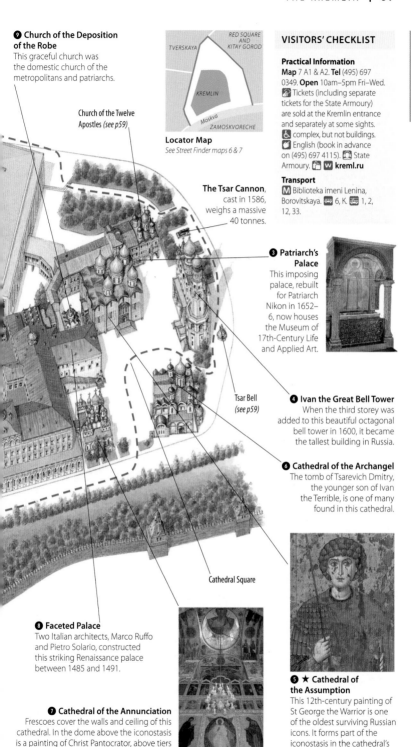

❾ Church of the Deposition of the Robe
This graceful church was the domestic church of the metropolitans and patriarchs.

Church of the Twelve Apostles *(see p59)*

Locator Map
See Street Finder maps 6 & 7

The Tsar Cannon, cast in 1586, weighs a massive 40 tonnes.

Tsar Bell *(see p59)*

Cathedral Square

VISITORS' CHECKLIST

Practical Information
Map 7 A1 & A2. **Tel** (495) 697 0349. **Open** 10am–5pm Fri–Wed. 🎫 Tickets (including separate tickets for the State Armoury) are sold at the Kremlin entrance and separately at some sights. ♿ complex, but not buildings. 📷 English (book in advance on (495) 697 4115). 🎧 State Armoury. 🌐 **kreml.ru**

Transport
Ⓜ Biblioteka imeni Lenina, Borovitskaya. 🚌 6, K. 🚎 1, 2, 12, 33.

❸ Patriarch's Palace
This imposing palace, rebuilt for Patriarch Nikon in 1652–6, now houses the Museum of 17th-Century Life and Applied Art.

❹ Ivan the Great Bell Tower
When the third storey was added to this beautiful octagonal bell tower in 1600, it became the tallest building in Russia.

❻ Cathedral of the Archangel
The tomb of Tsarevich Dmitry, the younger son of Ivan the Terrible, is one of many found in this cathedral.

❽ Faceted Palace
Two Italian architects, Marco Ruffo and Pietro Solario, constructed this striking Renaissance palace between 1485 and 1491.

❼ Cathedral of the Annunciation
Frescoes cover the walls and ceiling of this cathedral. In the dome above the iconostasis is a painting of Christ Pantocrator, above tiers of pictures of angels, prophets and patriarchs.

❺ ★ Cathedral of the Assumption
This 12th-century painting of St George the Warrior is one of the oldest surviving Russian icons. It forms part of the iconostasis in the cathedral's richly decorated interior.

Trinity Tower, with the modern Palace of Congresses on the right

❶ Trinity Tower
Троицкая башня
Troitskaya bashnya

The Kremlin. **Map** 7 A1.

This tower takes its name from the Trinity Monastery of St Sergius (see pp164–7), which once had a mission nearby. The tower's Trinity Gate used to be the entrance for patriarchs and the tsars' wives and daughters. Today it is one of only two that admit visitors. The other is in the Borovitskaya Tower (see p68) to the southwest.

At 76 m (249 ft) high, the seven-storey Trinity Tower is the Kremlin's tallest. It was built in 1495–9 and in 1516 was linked by a bridge over the Neglinnaya river to the Kutafya Tower. The river now runs underground

and the Kutafya Tower is the sole survivor of the circle of towers that were originally built to defend the Kremlin walls.

In September 1812 Napoleon triumphantly marched his army into the Kremlin through the Trinity Gate – they left only a month later when the Russians set fire to the city (see pp26–7).

❷ State Kremlin Palace
Государственный Кремлёвский дворец
Gosudarstvennyy Kremlevskiy dvorets

The Kremlin. **Map** 7 A1. **Open** for performances only.

Commissioned by Russian premier Nikita Khrushchev in 1959 to host Communist Party conferences, the Palace of Congresses is the Kremlin's only modern building. It was completed in 1961 by a team of architects led by Mikhail Posokhin. Roughly 120 m (395 ft) long, the palace was sunk 15 m (49 ft) into the ground so as not to dwarf the surrounding buildings.

Until 1991 the 6,000-seat auditorium was the venue for political meetings. Now it is used by the Kremlin Ballet Company (see p200) and for staging operas and rock concerts.

❾ Patriarch's Palace
Патриарший дворец
Patriarshiy dvorets

The Kremlin. **Map** 7 A1. **Open** 10am–5pm Fri–Wed.

The metropolitans of the Russian Orthodox Church lived on the site of the current Patriarch's Palace for many years. In the 16th century, the patriarchate was created, and the patriarch took over from the metropolitans as the most senior figure in the Russian Church. As a result the bishops of Krutitsy became metro-politans (see p142) while the patriarch lived in the Kremlin.

When Nikon became the patriarch in 1652, he felt that the existing residence and the small Church of the Deposition of the Robe (see pp64–5) were not grand enough for him. He had the residence extended and renovated to create the Patriarch's Palace, with its integral Church of the Twelve Apostles. Completed in 1656, the work was carried out by a team of master builders led by Ivan Semenov and Aleksey Korolkov.

The palace is now the Museum of 17th-Century Life and Applied Art. It

Tsarevich Alexis's school book

comprises an exhibition hall and more than 1,000 exhibits drawn from the State Armoury collection (see pp66–7) and from churches and monasteries that were destroyed by Stalin in the 1930s (see p77).

Entry to the museum is up a short flight of stairs. The first room houses an exhibition on the history of the palace. In the Cross Chamber is a dazzling array of 17th-century patriarchs' robes. Some of Nikon's own vestments are on display, including a chasuble (sakkos), a set of beautifully carved staffs and a cowl made from damask and satin, and embroidered with gold thread.

Two rooms in the museum have been refurbished in the style of a 17th-century boyar's apartment. In one of them is a display of old, handwritten

Refurbished residence of a boyar in the Patriarch's Palace

books, including Tsarevich Alexis' primer. Each page features one letter of the alphabet and a selection of objects beginning with that letter.

The impressive Chamber of the Cross, to the right of the stairs, has an area of 280 sq m (3,013 sq ft). When this ceremonial hall was built, it was the largest room in Russia without columns supporting its roof. Its ceiling is painted with a delicate tracery of flowers. The room was later used for producing consecrated oil called *miro*, and the silver vats and ornate stove used still stand in the room.

Nikon's rejection of new architectural forms, such as tent roofs, dictated a traditional design for the Church of the Twelve Apostles. Located to the left of the stairs, it houses some brilliant icons, including works by master iconographers such as Semen Ushakov. The iconostasis dates from around 1700. It was brought to the church from the Kremlin Convent of the Ascension prior to its demolition in 1929.

Patriarch Nikon

A zealous reformer of the Russian Orthodox Church, Patriarch Nikon was so intent on returning it to its Byzantine roots that he caused his adversaries, the Old Believers, to split from the rest of the Church. Nikon also advocated the supremacy of Church over State, angering Tsar Alexis *(see p21)*. His autocratic style made him unpopular and he retreated to a monastery outside the city. He was deposed in 1667.

Ivan the Great Bell Tower, with the Assumption Belfry and annexe

❹ Ivan the Great Bell Tower

Колокольня Ивана Великого

Kolokolnya Ivana Velikovo

The Kremlin. **Map** 7 A1.

This elegant bell tower was built in 1505–8 to a design by Marco Bon Friazin. It takes its name from the Church of St Ivan Climacus, which stood on the site in the 14th century. The bell tower is called "the Great" because of its height. In 1600 it became the tallest building in Moscow when Tsar Boris Godunov added a third story to extend it to 81 m (266 ft).

The four-storey Assumption Belfry, with its single gilded dome, was built beside the bell tower by Petrok Maliy in 1532–43. It holds 21 bells, the largest of which, the 64-tonne Assumption Bell, traditionally tolled three times when the tsar died. A small museum on the first floor houses changing displays about the Kremlin. The tent-roofed annexe next to the belfry was commissioned by Patriarch Filaret in 1642.

Outside the bell tower is the enormous Tsar Bell. The largest in the world, it weighs over 200 tonnes. When it fell from the bell tower and shattered in a fire in 1701, the fragments were used in a second bell ordered by Tsarina Anna. This still lay in its casting pit when the Kremlin caught fire again in 1737. Cold water was poured over the hot bell and a large piece (displayed beside the bell) broke off.

The Tsar Bell, the largest in the world, with the 11.5-tonne section that broke off

❺ Cathedral of the Assumption

Успенский собор
Uspenskiy sobor

From the early 14th century, the Cathedral of the Assumption was the most important church in Moscow. It was here that princes were crowned and the metropolitans and patriarchs of the Orthodox Church were buried. In the 1470s Ivan the Great *(see p20)* decided to build a more imposing cathedral, to reflect the growing might of the nation during his reign. When the first version collapsed, possibly in an earthquake, Ivan summoned the Italian architect Aristotele Fioravanti to Moscow. He designed a light and spacious masterpiece in the spirit of the Renaissance.

★ **Frescoes**
In 1642–4, a team of artists headed by Sidor Pospeev and Ivan and Boris Paisein painted these frescoes. The walls of the cathedral were first gilded to give the look of an illuminated manuscript.

KEY

① **The Tabernacle** contains holy relics including the remains of Patriarch Hermogen, who starved to death in 1612 during the Polish invasion *(see p21)*.

② **The Tsarina's Throne** (17th–19th centuries) is gilded and has a double-headed eagle crest.

③ **Metropolitans' and patriarchs' tombs** line the walls of the nave and the crypt. Almost all of the leaders of the Russian Orthodox Church are buried in the cathedral.

④ **Orthodox cross**

⑤ **The golden domes** stand on towers inset with windows which allow light to flood into the interior of the cathedral.

⑥ **Frescoes in the central dome**

⑦ **The pillars** that stand in the centre of the cathedral are painted with over 100 figures of canonized martyrs and warriors.

⑧ **Royal Gate**

⑨ **The Harvest Chandelier** contains silver recovered from the French after their occupation of the city in 1812 *(see pp25–7)*.

⑩ **The Patriarch's Seat** was carved from white stone in 1653 for use by the head of the Russian Orthodox Church.

⑪ **Monomakh Throne**

Western door and main entrance

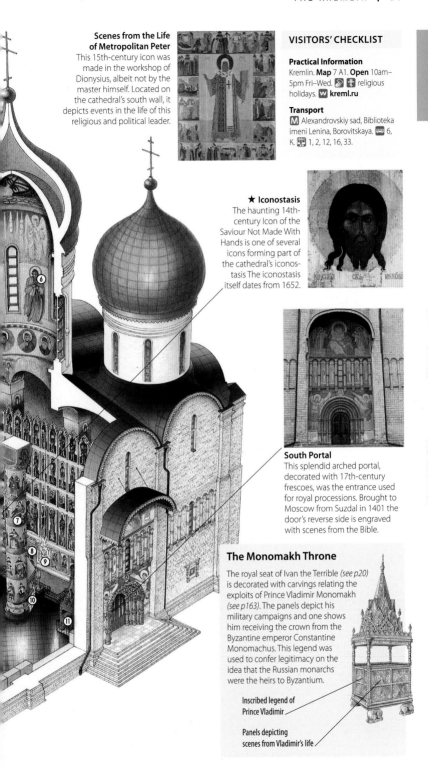

Scenes from the Life of Metropolitan Peter
This 15th-century icon was made in the workshop of Dionysius, albeit not by the master himself. Located on the cathedral's south wall, it depicts events in the life of this religious and political leader.

★ Iconostasis
The haunting 14th-century Icon of the Saviour Not Made With Hands is one of several icons forming part of the cathedral's iconostasis The iconostasis itself dates from 1652.

South Portal
This splendid arched portal, decorated with 17th-century frescoes, was the entrance used for royal processions. Brought to Moscow from Suzdal in 1401 the door's reverse side is engraved with scenes from the Bible.

The Monomakh Throne

The royal seat of Ivan the Terrible *(see p20)* is decorated with carvings relating the exploits of Prince Vladimir Monomakh *(see p163)*. The panels depict his military campaigns and one shows him receiving the crown from the Byzantine emperor Constantine Monomachus. This legend was used to confer legitimacy on the idea that the Russian monarchs were the heirs to Byzantium.

Inscribed legend of Prince Vladimir

Panels depicting scenes from Vladimir's life

❻ Cathedral of the Archangel

Архангельский собор
Arkhangelskiy sobor

The Kremlin. **Map** 7 A2.

This was the last of the great cathedrals in the Kremlin to be built. It was commissioned by Ivan III in 1505, shortly before his death. Designed by a Venetian architect, Aleviz Novyy, it combines Early-Russian and Italian Renaissance architecture. The most striking of the Italian features is the scallop shell motif underneath the *zakomary* gables *(see p46)*.

This site was the burial place for Moscow's princes and tsars from 1340, first in an earlier cathedral and then in the current building. The tombs of the tsars, white stone sarcophagi with bronze covers inscribed in Old Slavonic, are in the nave. The tomb of Tsarevich Dmitry, the youngest son of Ivan the Terrible *(see p20)*, has a carved, painted canopy above it. The tsars were no longer buried here after the capital city was moved to St Petersburg in 1712. Peter II, who died of smallpox in Moscow in 1730, was the only later ruler to be buried here.

The walls, pillars and domes of the cathedral are covered with frescoes painted in 1652–66 by a team of artists led by Semen Ushakov, the head of the icon workshop in the State Armoury *(see pp66–7)*. There are over 60 full-length idealized portraits of Russian rulers, as well as some striking images of the Archangel Michael, traditionally the protector of the rulers of early Moscow.

The fresco in the cathedral's central cupola depicts the threefold nature of God. The Father holds the Son on his lap and the Holy Spirit, in the form of a white dove, hovers between them.

The four-tiered iconostasis was constructed in 1680–81. However, the Icon of the Archangel Michael on the lowest tier dates from the 14th century.

❼ Cathedral of the Annunciation

Благовещенский собор
Blagoveshchenskiy sobor

The Kremlin. **Map** 7 A2. **Open** 10am–5pm Fri–Wed.

Unlike the other Kremlin cathedrals, which were created by Italians, this cathedral is a wholly Russian affair. Commissioned by Ivan III in 1484 as a royal chapel, it stands beside the Faceted Palace *(see p64)*, which is all that remains of a large palace built for Ivan III around the same time. The cathedral, built by architects from Pskov *(see p46)*, originally had three domes and open galleries on all sides but, after a fire in 1547, the corner chapels were added and the galleries

The glorious Cathedral of the Annunciation

were enclosed. On the south façade is the Groznenskiy Porch, added by Ivan the Terrible when he contravened church law by marrying for the fourth time in 1572. Barred from attending religious services, he could only watch through a grille in the porch.

The whole of the interior of the cathedral, including the galleries, is painted with frescoes. The painter of the artwork around the iconostasis is uncertain, but it may have been painted in 1508 by the monk Feodosius, the son of the icon painter Dionysius. The warm colours of the frescoes create an atmosphere of intimacy (this was the tsars' family church). At the same time the vertical thrust of the pillars draws the eye upwards to the cupola and its awe-inspiring painting of Christ Pantocrator (Christ as ruler of the universe).

Three of the greatest masters of icon painting in Russia contributed to the iconostasis, widely considered the finest in Russia. Theophanes the Greek painted the images of Christ, the Virgin and the Archangel Gabriel in the Deesis Tier, while the Icon of the Archangel Michael on this tier is attributed to Andrey Rublev. Several of the icons in the Festival Tier, including *The Annunciation* and *The Nativity* were also painted by Rublev. Most of the other icons in this tier, including the *The Last Supper* and *The Crucifixion* are the work of Prokhor Gorodetskiy.

The fresco in the central cupola of the Cathedral of the Archangel

The Art of Icon Painting in Russia

The Russian Orthodox church uses icons for both worship and teaching and there are strict rules for creating each image. Icons were thought to be imbued with power from the saint they depicted and were invoked for protection during wars. Because content was more important than style, old revered icons were often repainted. The first icons were brought to Russia from Byzantium. Kiev was Russia's main icon painting centre until the Mongols conquered it in 1240. Influential schools then sprang up in Novgorod and the Vladimir-Suzdal area. The Moscow school was founded in the late 14th century and its greatest period was during the 15th century, when renowned icon-painters such as Andrey Rublev and Dionysius were at work.

Theophanes the Greek (c.1340–1405) is thought to have painted this icon of the Assumption (ascent into heaven) of the Virgin Mary. Originally from Byzantium, Theophanes became famous first in Novgorod and then in Moscow. The figures in his icons are renowned for their delicate features and individual expressions.

The Virgin of Vladimir, from 12th-century Byzantium, is highly venerated and has had a profound influence on Russian iconography.

Iconostasis

Separating the sanctuary from the main part of the church, the iconostasis also symbolizes the boundary between the spiritual and temporal worlds. The icons are arranged in tiers (usually four, five or six), each with its own subject matter and significance.

Andrey Rublev became a monk at the Trinity Monastery of St Sergius *(see pp164–7)*. Later he moved to a monastery in Moscow. Rublev painted this icon of the Archangel Michael in about 1410. The benevolent appearance of the archangel is typical of Rublev's figures.

The Festival Tier depicts important feast days and holidays in the Russian Orthodox calendar.

The top tier of the iconostasis depicts patriarchs and prophets of the Old Testament.

Christ Enthroned is always shown at the centre of the Deesis Tier, and is normally flanked by the Virgin Mary and John the Baptist.

The Deesis Tier is the most important in the iconostasis and depicts saints, apostles and archangels.

An additional tier between the Local and Deesis Tiers often depicts the months of the year.

The Royal Gate, at the centre of the Local Tier, is usually decorated with panels showing the four apostles and the Annunciation – when Mary learns she is to bear the Son of God. The gate represents the entrance from the temporal to the spiritual world.

The Local Tier contains icons of saints with a strong link to the church, such as the church's namesake or saints after whom patrons of the church were named.

The enormous vaulted main hall of the Faceted Palace, which was lavishly repainted in the 1880s

⑧ Faceted Palace

Грановитая палата
Granovitaya palata

The Kremlin. **Map** 7 A2. **Closed** to public.

In the 19th century, the Faceted Palace, along with the Terem Palace, was incorporated into the Great Kremlin Palace. Named after its distinctive stonework façade, the Faceted Palace is all that is left of a larger 15th-century royal palace. It was commissioned by Ivan III *(see p20)* in 1485 and finished 6 years later. The Faceted Palace is the work of two Italian architects, Marco Ruffo and Pietro Solario.

The first floor of the Faceted Palace consists of the main hall and adjoining Sacred Vestibule. Both are decorated with rich frescoes and gilded carvings. The splendid vaulted main hall has an area of about 500 sq m (5,380 sq ft). It was the throne room and banqueting hall of the tsars and is now used for holding receptions.

On the palace's southern façade is the Red Staircase. The tsars passed down this staircase on their way to the Cathedral of the Assumption for their coronations. The last such procession was at the coronation of Nicholas II in 1896. In the Streltsy Rebellion of 1682 *(see p24)* several of Peter the

Great's relatives were hurled down the Red Staircase onto the pikes of the Streltsy guard.

Demolished by Stalin in the 1930s, the staircase was rebuilt in 1994 at great expense.

⑨ Church of the Deposition of the Robe

Церковь Ризположения
Tserkov Rizopolozheniya

The Kremlin. **Map** 7 A1.

Crowned by a single golden dome, this beautiful, but simply designed, church was built as the domestic church of the metropolitans in 1484–6. It was designed by architects from Pskov *(see p46)*.

The church is named after a Byzantine feast day, which celebrates the arrival, in the city of Constantinople, of a robe supposed to have belonged to the Virgin Mary. The robe is believed to have saved the city from invasion several times.

The exterior of the church has distinctive ogee arches, which are shaped like the cross-section of an onion and feature on many Russian churches from this period. They are a favourite device of the Pskov school of architecture. Inside the church,

The southern façade of the Faceted Palace, with the Red Staircase

the walls and slender columns are covered with 17th-century frescoes by artists including Ivan Borisov, Sidor Pospeev and Semen Abramov. Many depict scenes from the life of the Virgin. Others depict Christ, the prophets, royalty and the Moscow metropolitans.

The impressive iconostasis was created by Nazariy Istomin in 1627. To the left of the royal gate is a splendid image of the Trinity and to its right is the patronal Icon of the Deposition of the Virgin's Robe.

The small, single-domed Church of the Deposition of the Robe

❿ Terem Palace
Теремной дворец
Teremnoy dvorets

The Kremlin. **Map** 7 A2. **Closed** to public.

Commissioned by Tsar Mikhail Romanov *(see p21)*, the Terem Palace was built next to the Faceted Palace in 1635–7. It was constructed by a team of stonemasons led by Bazhen Ogurtsov. The palace takes its name from the *terem*, a pavilion-like structure with a red and white chequered roof on top of the main building. The interior has small, low-vaulted, simply furnished rooms.

The Tsar had five sumptuous rooms situated on the third floor of the palace. The ante-room, where boyars *(see p22)* and foreign dignitaries waited to be received, leads into the council chamber, where the tsar held meetings with boyars. Beyond this are the throne

The ornately decorated anteroom in the Terem Palace

room, the tsar's bedchamber and a small prayer room.

Most of the splendid Terem Palace is not visible from the areas of the Kremlin to which the public have access. The eleven richly decorated onion domes of the four palace churches, at one end of the palace, are all that can be seen.

⓫ Great Kremlin Palace
Большой Кремлёвский дворец
Bolshoy Kremlevskiy dvorets

The Kremlin. **Map** 7 A2. **Closed** to public.

The impressive 125-m (410-ft) façade of this yellow and white palace is best admired from the Kremlin embankment, outside the Kremlin walls. The Great Kremlin Palace was built to replace the 18th-century Kremlin Palace that previously

stood on the site but had become dilapidated. In 1837 Tsar Nicholas I commissioned the Great Kremlin Palace as the Moscow residence of the royal family, where they stayed when visiting from St Petersburg, then the capital. Designed by a team of architects led by Konstantin Ton *(see p47)*, it took 12 years to build. Ton's design integrated the Terem and Faceted Palaces with the new palace, creating a single complex. He also rebuilt the State Armoury *(see pp66–7)*.

On the palace's ground floor are the luxurious private rooms of the royal family. The state chambers, on the first floor, include several vast ceremonial halls. The imposing St George's Hall has white walls engraved in gold with the names of those awarded the Order of St George, one of Russia's highest military decorations.

Despite spending massive amounts on the interior, the tsar rarely used the palace. In the 1930s two of the halls were joined to form a huge meeting room for the Supreme Soviet. Now the palace's halls are used to receive foreign dignitaries.

The Great Kremlin Palace viewed from the Kremlin embankment

⑫ State Armoury

Оружейная палата

Oruzheynaya palata

The collection of the State Armoury represents the wealth accumulated by Russian princes and tsars over many centuries. The first written mention of a state armoury occurs in 1508, but there were forges in the Kremlin producing weapons and armour as early as the 13th century. Later, gold- and silversmiths, workshops producing icons and embroidery, and the Office of the Royal Stables all moved into the Kremlin. The original armoury was demolished in 1960 to make way for the State Kremlin Palace *(see p58)*. The current State Armoury was built as a museum on the orders of Nicholas I. It was designed by Konstantin Ton *(see p47)* in 1844 and was completed in 1851.

★ **Fabergé Eggs**
This egg, also a musical box, was made in 1904 in the St Petersburg workshops of the famous House of Fabergé. The egg forms part of a stylized model of the Kremlin.

Arms and armour made in the Kremlin workshops are on show here, along with items from Western Europe and Persia.

Carriages and Sledges
This magnificent collection includes the beautiful gilded summer carriage shown here. It was presented to Catherine the Great *(see p25)* by Count Orlov. The oldest carriage displayed was a gift from King James I of England to Boris Godunov.

First Floor

4

3

5

9

The State Diamond Fund

This dazzling exhibition of diamonds, crowns, jewellery and state regalia includes the famous Orlov Diamond. Taken from an Indian temple, it was one of many presents given to Catherine the Great by her lover Count Grigoriy Orlov. The tsarina had it mounted at the top of her sceptre. Also on show are Catherine's imperial crown, inset with almost 5,000 gems, and the Shah Diamond, which was given to Tsar Nicholas I by Shah Mirza.

The Orlov Diamond on the sceptre of Catherine the Great

Ground floor

Ambassadors' gifts, presented by visiting emissaries from the Netherlands, Poland, England and Scandinavia are displayed here.

Main entrance from the Kremlin grounds

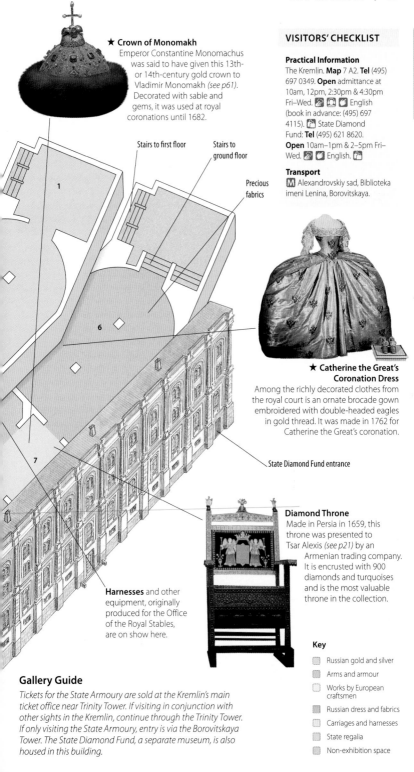

★ **Crown of Monomakh**
Emperor Constantine Monomachus was said to have given this 13th- or 14th-century gold crown to Vladimir Monomakh *(see p61)*. Decorated with sable and gems, it was used at royal coronations until 1682.

Stairs to first floor

Stairs to ground floor

Precious fabrics

★ **Catherine the Great's Coronation Dress**
Among the richly decorated clothes from the royal court is an ornate brocade gown embroidered with double-headed eagles in gold thread. It was made in 1762 for Catherine the Great's coronation.

State Diamond Fund entrance

Diamond Throne
Made in Persia in 1659, this throne was presented to Tsar Alexis *(see p21)* by an Armenian trading company. It is encrusted with 900 diamonds and turquoises and is the most valuable throne in the collection.

Harnesses and other equipment, originally produced for the Office of the Royal Stables, are on show here.

Key

- 🟦 Russian gold and silver
- 🟦 Arms and armour
- ⬜ Works by European craftsmen
- 🟦 Russian dress and fabrics
- 🟦 Carriages and harnesses
- 🟦 State regalia
- 🟦 Non-exhibition space

Gallery Guide

Tickets for the State Armoury are sold at the Kremlin's main ticket office near Trinity Tower. If visiting in conjunction with other sights in the Kremlin, continue through the Trinity Tower. If only visiting the State Armoury, entry is via the Borovitskaya Tower. The State Diamond Fund, a separate museum, is also housed in this building.

⓭ Saviour's Tower

Спасская башня
Spasskaya bashnya

The Kremlin. **Map** 7 B1.

Rising majestically above Red Square to a height of 70 m (230 ft), Saviour's Tower is named after an icon of Christ installed over its gate in 1648. The gate is no longer open to the public, but it used to be the Kremlin's main entrance. Every person

Saviour's Tower, once the main entrance to the Kremlin

using Saviour's Gate, even the tsar, had to indicate respect for the icon by taking his hat off. The icon was removed after the Revolution.

Saviour's Tower was built in two stages. The lower part was designed by Italian architect Pietro Solario in 1491. Bazhen Ogurtsov and Englishman Christopher Galloway added the upper part and tent roof in 1625. Originally the chimes of the clock played the *Preobrazhenskyy March* and *Kol' Slaven Nash Gospod' v Sione*. Now they play the Russian National Anthem.

⓮ Presidential Administration

Администрация Президента
Administraya Presidenta

The Kremlin. **Map** 7 A1.
Closed to public.

Two important religious institutions, the Monastery of the Miracles and the Convent of the Ascension, used to stand here. They were demolished in 1929 to make way for the

Presidential Administration. The building was originally used as a training school for Red Army officers, and later as the headquarters of the Presidium of the Supreme Soviet, an executive arm of the Soviet parliament. Today it is home to part of the Russian presidential administration.

The Presidential Administration

⓯ Senate

Сенат
Senat

Kremlin. **Map** 7 A1.
Closed to public.

Completed in 1790, this Neo-Classical building was constructed to house several of the Senate's departments. Designed by Matvey Kazakov *(see pp46–7)*, who regarded it as his best work, it is triangular, with a

Kremlin Towers

There are 19 towers in the walls of the Kremlin, with a bridge leading from the Trinity Tower to a 20th, the Kutafya Tower. In 1935 the double-headed imperial eagles were removed from the five tallest towers and replaced 2 years later with stars made of red glass, each weighing between 1 and 1.5 tonnes.

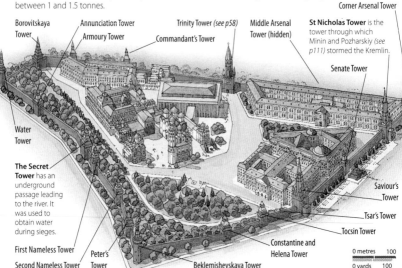

Borovitskaya Tower

Annunciation Tower

Armoury Tower

Trinity Tower *(see p58)*

Commandant's Tower

Middle Arsenal Tower (hidden)

Corner Arsenal Tower

St Nicholas Tower is the tower through which Minin and Pozharskiy *(see p111)* stormed the Kremlin.

Senate Tower

Water Tower

The Secret Tower has an underground passage leading to the river. It was used to obtain water during sieges.

First Nameless Tower

Second Nameless Tower

Peter's Tower

Beklemishevskaya Tower

Constantine and Helena Tower

Tocsin Tower

Tsar's Tower

Saviour's Tower

0 metres 100
0 yards 100

The Neo-Classical Senate building, with St Nicholas Tower in the background

central, domed rotunda, from which the Russian flag flies.

From 1918 to 1991, the Senate housed the Soviet government. Lenin had his office here and his family lived in a flat on the top floor. During World War II the Red Army Supreme Command, headed by Stalin, was based in the building.

Today the Senate is the official seat of the president of the Russian Federation.

Corner Arsenal Tower with the Arsenal and St Nicholas Tower

⑯ Arsenal

Арсенал
Arsenal

The Kremlin. **Map** 7 A1. **Closed** to public.

Peter the Great ordered the Arsenal to be built in 1701, but various setbacks, including a fire in 1711, delayed its completion until 1736. In 1812 the building was partly blown up by Napoleon's army *(see pp25–7)*.

Architects Aleksandr Bakarev, Ivan Tamanskiy, Ivan Mironovskiy and Evgraf Tyurin were commissioned to design a new Arsenal. Their attractive yellow and white Neo-Classical building was finished in 1828.

The Arsenal was constructed as a storehouse for weapons, ammunition and other military supplies. Around 750 cannons, including some that were captured from Napoleon's retreating troops, are lined up outside. Now the command post of the Kremlin guard, the interior and much of the exterior of the Arsenal are strictly out of bounds to visitors.

⑰ Alexander Gardens

Александровский сад
Aleksandrovskiy sad

The Kremlin. **Map** 7 A1.

Designed by architect Osip Bove *(see p47)* in 1821, these gardens are named after Tsar Alexander I, who presided over the restoration of the city, including the Kremlin, after the Napoleonic Wars. Before the gardens were built, the Neglinnaya river, part of the Kremlin moat, was channelled underground. The only visible reminder of its presence is the stone bridge linking Kutafya and Trinity towers.

In front of the Middle Arsenal Tower in the northern half of the

gardens is an obelisk erected in 1913 to mark 300 years of the Romanov dynasty. The imperial eagle was taken down after the Revolution and the inscription was replaced by the names of revolutionary thinkers, such as Karl Marx and Friedrich Engels.

The Tomb of the Unknown Soldier, a short distance away, was unveiled in 1967. Its eternal flame was lit with a torch from the flame at the Field of Mars in St Petersburg. It burns for all the Russians who died in World War II. The body of a soldier is buried beneath the monument, which bears an inscription, "Your name is unknown, your deeds immortal".

In 1996, a huge shopping complex was constructed beneath Manezhnaya ploshchad, the large square to the north of Alexander Gardens.

Path through Alexander Gardens, with the Trinity Tower behind

ARBATSKAYA

The name "Arbat" is thought to derive from a Mongol word meaning suburb, and was first applied in the 15th century to the entire area west of the Kremlin, then inhabited by the tsar's artisans and equerries. Though still commemorated in street names, the artisans moved elsewhere in the late 18th century. The aristocracy moved in and were followed by Moscow's professionals, intellectuals and

artists, attracted by the area's rambling backstreets, dilapidated cottages and overgrown courtyards. In the Old Arbat, with its pedestrianized main street, there are historic churches, timber houses and early 19th-century mansions around pereulok Sivtsev Vrazhek. Yet, not far away are the kiosks, cafés and huge Soviet-era apartment blocks and shops of the New Arbat.

Sights at a Glance

Museums and Galleries
1. Skryabin House-Museum
4. Pushkin House-Museum
5. Bely House-Museum
8. Gallery of 19th- and 20th-Century European and American Art
9. *Pushkin State Museum of Fine Arts pp80–83*
10. Department of Private Collections
13. Lermontov House-Museum
14. Shalyapin House-Museum

Cathedrals
7. Cathedral of Christ the Saviour

Historic Buildings
3. Melnikov House
11. Pashkov House

Streets and Squares
2. Spasopeskovskiy Pereulok
6. Ulitsa Prechistenka
12. Arbat Square

Restaurants *see p186*
1. Baba Marta
2. Barashka
3. Bar Strelka
4. Chocolate
5. Elardzhi
6. Korchma Taras Bulba
7. Obraz Zhizny
8. Shchisliva
9. Twenty-Two
10. Vostochnaya Komnata
11. White Rabbit
12. Zhurfak
13. Zu Café

See also Street Finder map 6

◀ The monumental Foreign Ministry building, one of the Seven Sisters skyscrapers built by Stalin   **For keys to symbols** *see back flap*

Street-by-Street: Old Arbat

At the heart of the Old Arbat is the pedestrianized ulitsa Arbat. It is lined with antique shops, boutiques, book stalls, pavement cafés and a variety of restaurants, from pizzerias and hamburger joints to lively examples of the traditional Russian pub (*traktir*). In the 19th century, the Old Arbat was the haunt of artists, musicians, poets, writers and intellectuals. Some of their homes have been preserved and opened as museums, and are among the district's many houses of that era that have been lovingly restored and painted in pastel shades of blue, green and ochre. Today, pavement artists, buskers and street poets give it a renewed bohemian atmosphere.

Spaso House is a grand Neo-Classical mansion. It has been the residence of the U ambassador since 193

This small garden contains a statue of the poet Alexander Pushkin.

Novyy Arbat ↑

PEREULOK KAMENNOY SLOBODY

SPASOPESKOVSKIY

KARMANITSKIY PEREULOK

SMOLENSKAYA PLOSHCHAD

❹ ★ Pushkin House-Museum
The poet Alexander Pushkin lived here just after his marriage in 1831. The interior of the house has been carefully renovated.

Ulitsa Arbat
By the time of the Soviet era, ulitsa Arbat had lost most of its 19th-century character. It was pedestrianized in 1985, however, and its lively shops, restaurants and cafés are now popular with Muscovites and visitors to the city alike.

Smolenskaya Ⓜ

DENEZHNYY PEREULOK

Georgian Centre

❺ Bely House-Museum
Andrei Bely, best known for two works, a novel, Petersburg, and his memoirs, lived in this flat for the first 26 years of his life. It is now a museum and the exhibits on display include this photo of Bely with his wife and the fascinating illustration, *Line of Life (see p75)*

The Foreign Ministry is one of Moscow's seven Stalinist-Gothic skyscrapers *(see p47)*.

❶ ★ Skryabin House-Museum
This comfortable apartment has been preserved as it was in 1912–15 when experimental composer Aleksandr Skryabin lived here. The furniture in the rooms is Style Moderne and the lighting is dim, since Skryabin disliked direct light.

Locator Map
See Street Finder map 6

The Vakhtangova Theatre was established here in 1921 by Yevgeniy Vakhtangov, one of Moscow's leading theatre directors. The current theatre building dates from 1947.

These pre-Revolution apartments, designed for wealthy Muscovites, are decorated with fanciful turrets and sculptures of knights.

BOLSHOY NIKOLOPESKOVSKIY PEREULOK

Arbat Square

ULITSA ARBAT

KALOSHIN PEREULOK

❷ Spasopeskovskiy Pereulok
On one side of this peaceful lane is the 18th-century Church of the Saviour on the Sands, with its white bell tower. It overlooks a secluded square and garden, a reminder that the Arbat was at that time a genteel suburb.

Pushkin Museum of Fine Arts

The Herzen House-Museum was the home of the radical writer Aleksandr Herzen for three years from 1843.

❸ Melnikov House
This unusual cylindrical house is now dwarfed by the apartments on ulitsa Arbat. It was built in the 1920s by Constructivist architect Konstantin Melnikov, who lived here until his death in 1974.

0 metres 100
0 yards 100

Key

— Suggested route

For keys to symbols see back flap

❶ Skryabin House-Museum

Дом-музей АН Скрябина

Dom-muzey AN Skryabina

Bolshoy Nikolopeskovskiy pereulok 11. **Map** 6 D1. **Tel** (499) 241 1901. Ⓜ Smolenskaya, Arbatskaya. **Open** 11am–6pm Wed & Fri–Sun, 1–9pm Thu. **Closed** last Fri of month. 🅿️

The apartment where the pianist and composer Aleksandr Skryabin (1872–1915) died, at the age of 43, has been preserved as it was when he lived there. Skryabin studied at the Moscow Conservatory *(see p96)*, where he established an international reputation as a concert pianist. He was also a highly original composer and musical theorist, best known for his orchestral works such as *Prometheus* and *A Poem of Ecstasy*. Skryabin's music had a great influence on the young Igor Stravinsky (1882–1971), and leading composer Sergei Rachmaninov (1873–1943) was a regular visitor.

Although Skryabin spent much of his time abroad giving concerts, he was an aesthete and paid considerable attention to furnishing and decorating his fashionable apartment. The lofty rooms house his pianos, autographed manuscripts and Style-Moderne furniture. However, the most original item

A room in Aleksandr Skryabin's apartment, with one of his pianos

The Classical-style Spaso House on Spasopeskovskaya ploshchad

on show is a device for projecting flickering light. Regular concerts are held in the rooms on the ground floor.

❷ Spasopeskovskiy Pereulok

Спасопесковский переулок

Spasopeskovskiy pereulok

Map 6 D1. Ⓜ Smolenskaya.

The charms of the Old Arbat have been preserved in this secluded lane and the peaceful adjoining square, Spasopeskovskaya ploshchad. In 1878, Vasiliy Polenov painted *A Moscow Courtyard*, depicting Spasopeskovskaya ploshchad as a bucolic haven in the midst of the city. Today the square still provides a respite from the hustle and bustle prevailing elsewhere.

Viktor Melnikov's studio in the Melnikov House

At the centre of Polenov's picture, now in the Tretyakov Gallery *(see pp120–23)*, is the white bell tower of the Church of the Saviour on the Sands (Tserkov Spas na Peskakh) from which the lane gets its name. This 18th-century church still dominates the square. In front of it is a small garden dedicated to the poet Alexander Pushkin.

The handsome Classical-style mansion standing on the far side of the square was built in 1913 as a private residence. Known as Spaso House, it has been the home of the US ambassador since 1933.

❸ Melnikov House

Дом Мельникова

Dom Melnikova

Krivoarbatskiy pereulok 10. **Map** 6 D1. Ⓜ Smolenskaya. **Closed** to public.

This unique house, almost hidden by office blocks, was designed by Konstantin Melnikov (1890–1974), one of Russia's greatest Constructivist architects *(see p47)*, in 1927.

Made from brick overlaid with white stucco, the house consists of two interlocking cylinders. These are studded with rows of hexagonal windows, creating a curious honeycomb effect. A spiral staircase rises through the space where the cylinders overlap, linking the light, airy living spaces. Melnikov's house was built for his family, but it was also to have been a prototype for future housing developments. However, his career was blighted when Stalin encouraged architects to adopt a new monumental style *(see p47)*. Although he had won the Gold Medal at the Paris World's Fair in 1925, Melnikov's work was ridiculed or ignored. However, he did remain in his house for the rest of his life, one of the very few residents of central Moscow allowed to live in a privately built dwelling.

Melnikov's son, Viktor Melnikov, had a studio in the house until his death in 2006.

Alexander Pushkin

Born in 1799 into Russia's aristocracy, Alexander Pushkin is Russia's most famous poet. He had established a reputation as both a poet and a rebel by the time he was 20. In 1820, he was sent into exile because the Tsarist government did not approve of his liberal verse, but eventually he was set free.

Pushkin's early work consisted of narrative poems such as *The Robber Brothers* (1821), and his most famous work is *Eugene Onegin* (1823–30), a novel in verse. From 1830 Pushkin wrote mostly prose. He developed a unique style in pieces such as *The Queen of Spades* (1834) and is credited with giving Russian literature its own identity.

Pushkin holds a special place in Russians' hearts and they treat his work and memory with reverence.

❺ Bely House-Museum

Музей-квартира
Андрея Белого
Muzey-kvartira Andreya Belovo

Ulitsa Arbat 55. **Map** 6 D2. **Tel** (499) 241 7702. Ⓜ Smolenskaya. **Open** 10am–6pm Wed & Fri–Sun, noon–9pm Thu. **Closed** last Fri of month. 🚫 📷 book in advance.

In the adjoining building to the Pushkin House-Museum is the childhood home of the symbolist writer Andrei Bely. Born Boris Bugaev in 1880, Bely later adopted the name by which he is known as a writer. He grew up here before becoming a student at Moscow University *(see p96)*, where he began to write verse. He is best known, however, for *Petersburg*, a novel completed in 1916.

Only two rooms have been preserved. A photographic exhibition on Bely's life and work is housed in one room. The most interesting item in the museum is the *Line of Life*, an illustration by Bely to show how his mood swings combined with cultural influences to direct his work.

❹ Pushkin House-Museum

Музей-квартира АС
Пушкина
Muzey-kvartira AS Pushkina

Ulitsa Arbat 53. **Map** 6 D2. **Tel** (499) 241 9293. Ⓜ Smolenskaya. **Open** 10am–6pm Wed & Fri–Sun, noon–9pm Thu. **Closed** last Fri of month. 🚫 📷 English (book in advance).

Alexander Pushkin rented this elegant, Empire-style apartment for the first 3 months of his marriage to society beauty Natalya Goncharova. They were married in the Church of the Great Ascension on Bolshaya Nikitskaya ulitsa *(see p95)* in February 1831, when she was 18 years old. Pushkin wrote to his friend Pyotr Pletnev: "I am married – and happy. My only wish is that nothing in my life should change; I couldn't possibly expect anything better."

However, by May 1831 Pushkin had tired of life in Moscow, and the couple moved to St Petersburg, where sadly a tragic fate awaited him. Gossip began to circulate there that Pushkin's brother-in-law, a French officer called d'Anthès, was making advances to Natalya. Upon receiving letters informing him that he was now the "Grand Master to the Order of Cuckolds", Pushkin challenged

d'Anthès to a duel. Mortally wounded in the contest, Pushkin died 2 days later.

The fascinating exhibition located in the museum's ground floor rooms gives an idea of what the city would have been like in the period when Pushkin was growing up, before the great fire of 1812. Among the prints, lithographs and watercolours are some unusual wax figures of a serf orchestra that belonged to the Goncharova family.

Pushkin and Natalya lived on the first floor. There are disappointingly few personal possessions here, although the poet's writing bureau and some family portraits are displayed. The atmosphere resembles a shrine more than a museum.

A portrait of Pushkin's wife, Natalya Goncharova

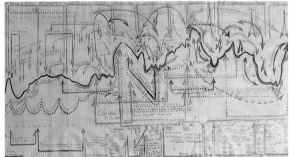

The *Line of Life* illustration drawn by the symbolist writer Andrei Bely

Stone eagles among the ornate decoration on No. 20 ulitsa Prechistenka

❻ Ulitsa Prechistenka

Улица Пречистенка

Ulitsa Prechistenka

Map 6 D3–E2. Ⓜ Kropotkinskaya.

Moscow's Aristocracy first settled in this street in the late 18th century and their elegant mansions still line it today. In Soviet times it was known as Kropotkinskaya ulitsa, after Prince Pyotr Kropotkin, a famous anarchist.

The Empire-style house at No.12 ulitsa Prechistenka is now the Pushkin Literary Museum (not to be confused with the Pushkin House-Museum, *see p75*). The house was originally designed for the Khrushchev family (no connection with Nikita Khrushchev) by Afanasiy Grigorev (*see p47*), one of the leading exponents of this style in Moscow. The building has a wooden frame, skilfully hidden by Classical columns and ornate stucco decoration.

Across the street is the Tolstoy Literary Museum which, unlike the Tolstoy House-Museum (*see p136*), concentrates on the man's work rather than his life. It was built in 1822, also to a design by Afanasiy Grigorev, for the noble Lopukhin family.

At No. 20 is an elegant two-storey mansion decorated with eagles, urns, heraldic symbols and scallop shells. Until 1861 it was home to General Aleksey

Lion at No. 16 ulitsa Prechistenka

Yermolov, a commander-in-chief in the Russian army. After the Revolution, the American dancer Isadora Duncan and the poet Sergey Yesenin lived here during their brief, tempestuous marriage. The two spoke no common language, and Yesenin stated his feelings by writing the Russian for "I love you" in lipstick on the bedroom mirror.

The most distinguished house is at No. 19. Rebuilt after the 1812 fire (*see p26*) for the Dolgorukov family, it has an ochre and white façade. The gallery within exhibits work by controversial artist Zurab Tsereteli, designer of the infamous Peter the Great statue on the banks of the Moscow river (*see p24*). Adjoining it, at No. 21, is another early 19th-century mansion, now the Academy of Arts, where exhibitions are sometimes put on.

❼ Cathedral of Christ the Saviour

Храм Христа Спасителя

Khram Khrista Spasitelya

Ulitsa Volkhonka 15. **Map** 6 F2. Ⓜ Kropotkinskaya.

Rebuilding this cathedral, blown up on Stalin's orders in 1931, was the most ambitious of the construction projects undertaken by the enterprising mayor of Moscow, Yuriy Luzhkov. The basic structure of the new cathedral was built

between 1994 and 1997. For much of the intervening time, the site was occupied by an outdoor swimming pool, but this was eventually filled in.

The project courted controversy from the start, both on grounds of taste and cost. In 1995 a presidential decree declared that not a kopek of public money should be spent on it – funds were to be raised through donations from the public, the Russian Church and foreign donors among the big multinational companies operating in Russia. However, in practice, the better part of the total bill of over US$200 million came from the state budget, which raised objections at a time when Muscovites were suffering extreme poverty.

The original cathedral was built to commemorate the miraculous deliverance of Moscow from Napoleon's Grande Armée (*see pp25–6*). Begun in 1839, but not completed until 1883, it was designed by Konstantin Ton (*see p47*). The cathedral was the tallest building in Moscow at that time, the gilded dome rising to a height of 103 m (338 ft) and dominating the skyline for miles around. It could accommodate more than 10,000 worshippers.

Boris Yeltsin lay in state here after his death in 2007, and in 1998, a small museum and a church on the ground floor opened to the public. There are spectacular views of the city from the dome.

Cathedral of Christ the Saviour, rebuilt in the 1990s at huge cost

Paul Cézanne's *Mont Ste Victoire*, painted in 1905

❽ Gallery of 19th- and 20th-Century European and American Art

Музей Галерея искусства стран Европы и Америки XIX–XX веков
Galeryeya Iskusstva Stran Evropi I Ameriki X1X–XX Vekov

Ulitsa Volkhonka 14. **Map** 6 F2.
Tel (495) 697 1546. **Open** 10am–7pm Tue–Sun (to 9pm Thu). Ⓜ Kropotkinskaya. 🖼 🏛 ♿ 🎧 🎞 📷

Before the revolution the Knyazhiy Dvor hotel, whose guests included Maxim Gorky and artist Ilya Repin, occupied this building. Now it is a museum displaying Impressionist and Post-Impressionist paintings that were previously shown in the Pushkin State Museum of Fine Arts next door. Some of the paintings are also from the St Petersburg's Hermitage.

Many were displayed in a Soviet-era museum of Western art that was opened in 1918 under orders from Lenin. The museum was closed in 1948 by Stalin, who considered the works "bourgeois propaganda".

The first of the gallery's three floors displays mainly European oil paintings from the first half of the 19th century, with works by artists such as Alexandre-Gabriel Decamps.

The real masterpieces are on the remaining two floors, however. Here, there are a number of paintings by Vincent Van Gogh, including *The Red Vineyard at Arles* (1888) and *Prisoners Exercising* (1890), as well as Pierre Auguste Renoir's *Nude* (1876) and *Bathing on the Seine* (1879). The same floor also holds Paul Cézanne's *Mont Ste Victoire* (1905) and a series of paintings by Paul Gauguin, including a fine selection from the artist's Polynesian period.

The third floor is just as impressive, and contains a number of works by Henri Matisse, including *Goldfish* (1911–12), and Pablo Picasso's *Girl Standing on a Ball* (1905). Russia is also represented, with paintings by Wassily Kandinsky, including *Improvisation No. 20a* (1911).

❾ Pushkin State Museum of Fine Arts

See pp80–83.

❿ Department of Private Collections

Отдел личных коллекций
Otdel lichnykh kollektsiy

Ulitsa Volkhonka 10. **Map** 6 F2.
Tel (495) 697 1610. **Open** 10am–7pm Wed–Sun (to 9pm Thu). Ⓜ Kropotkinskaya. 🖼 ♿ 🎞 📷 🏛 📶 W artprivatecollections.ru

This museum is based on private collections donated to the Pushkin State Museum. The largest is that of historian and public figure Ilya Zilberstein, which includes a vast range of work by prominent Russian artists such as Ivan Shishkin, Ilya Repin and Konstantin Somov. There are also works by Aleksandr Rodchenko, and rooms devoted to periodic specialist exhibitions.

Gallery of 19th- and 20th-Century European and American Art

Stalin's Plan for a Palace of Soviets

The original Cathedral of Christ the Redeemer was to have been replaced by a Palace of Soviets – a soaring tower, 315 m (1,034 ft) high, topped by a 100-m (328-ft) statue of Lenin. It was designed as the highlight of Stalin's reconstruction of Moscow, much of the rest of which was realized: broad boulevards, skyscrapers and the metro system *(see pp40–43)* are now familiar features of the city. The result was also, however, the destruction of many supposedly unnecessary buildings, especially churches and monasteries, even inside the Kremlin. The scheme for the Palace of Soviets was eventually abandoned and the cathedral was rebuilt in the 1990s.

Artist's impression of Stalin's proposed awe-inspiring Palace of Soviets

Detail of sculptures on the façade of the Cathedral of Christ the Saviour ▶

❾ Pushkin State Museum of Fine Arts

Музей изобразительных искусств имени АС Пушкина

Muzey izobrazitelnykb iskusstv imeni AS Pushkina

Founded in 1898, the Pushkin Museum houses a fine collections of works from antiquity to the early 19th century. Following the collapse of the Soviet Union *(see pp32–3)*, the curators admitted that they had countless works of art hidden away. Some of these are now on show, including Schliemann's "Treasures of Troy" excavations, which were taken from the Museum of Ancient History in Berlin by Soviet military authorities in 1945. The museum remains open while undergoing a major renovation programme. There are plans to open new galleries and an exhibition hall by 2018.

Room 23 houses mostly 18th–19th-century French paintings.

Museum Building
The design of the building borrows from Ancient Greece, Italy, France and Germany to create a suitably impressive façade and interior.

Stairs to ground floor

First floor

★ *Annunciation*
Painted around 1495–8 by Italian artist Sandro Botticelli, this work was originally part of a large altarpiece. It shows the angel Gabriel telling the Virgin Mary she is to bear the Son of God.

Room 3 houses Schliemann's "Treasures of Troy".

Gallery Guide

The ticket office is in the entrance hall. The displays are spread over two floors, but although the museum halls are numbered, the layout is not strictly chronological. The ground floor houses all of the works from ancient civilizations as well as Byzantine art and Italian, Dutch and Flemish art from the 13th to the 17th centuries. Spanish, Italian and French art from the 17th to the early 19th centuries is upstairs. The cloakroom and toilets are in the basement.

Key

- Collection of plaster casts
- Art of ancient civilizations
- Byzantine art and Italian art: 13th–16th centuries
- German, Dutch and Flemish art: 15th–17th centuries
- Spanish and Italian art: 17th–18th centuries
- French art: 17th–early 19th centuries
- Temporary exhibition space

Bucentaur's Return to the Pier by the Palazzo Ducale
Canaletto was known for his bold use of colour, exemplified in this scene of the Grand Canal (1727–9).

Room 10 is dedicated to Rembrandt and his School and includes drawings, etchings and six paintings by the great master.

Ahasuerus, Haman and Esther
In this biblical scene by Rembrandt (1660), the Persian king, Ahasuerus, is flanked by his Jewish wife and his minister, Haman. Esther, lit by a single ray of light, accuses Haman of plotting to destroy the Jews.

Stairs to first floor

★ ***Bacchanalia***
Based on the myth of the god of nature, vegetation and viniculture, Dionysus-Bacchus, this splendidly exuberant, sensual painting (c.1615) did not leave the possession of its artist, Peter Paul Rubens, his entire life.

Tickets and information

Entrance

Ground floor

★ ***Fayoum Portrait***
Painted in the 1st century AD, this is one of a collection of portraits discovered at a burial ground at the Fayoum oasis in Egypt in the 1870s. They were painted while the subjects were alive to be used as death masks.

Exploring the Pushkin State Museum of Fine Arts

In addition to the collection of plaster casts, the accumulated treasures of original work in the Pushkin State Museum of Fine Arts reflect the tastes of many private collectors, whose holdings were given to the museum. The largest of these belonged to the Egyptologist Vladimir Golenishchev who assembled some 6,000 items during his travels in Egypt. The museum also contains many important pieces of European art from the 13th to the early 19th centuries, including work by Rembrandt, Rubens, Van Dyck, Botticelli, Poussin and Canaletto, among many others.

Greek marble sarcophagus, dating from around AD 210

Collection of Plaster Casts

The huge collection of plaster casts fills ten rooms and offers a fine backdrop to the original works. Room 14, The Greek Courtyard, is devoted to Greek architecture and sculpture from the 4th and 5th centuries and includes a scale model of the Acropolis and Parthenon.

Room 15 reproduces the inner courtyard of the 14th-century palazzo de Podesta in Florence. On the first floor the collection continues with the art of ancient Greece and Rome, and Renaissance sculpture from Italy, the Netherlands and Germany. Room 29 is devoted entirely to the work of Michelangelo.

Art of Ancient Civilizations

The museum's archaeological exhibits come from as far afield as ancient Mesopotamia, Hindustan and the Mayan Empire. The display includes the renowned and remarkably vivid tomb portraits from Fayoum and two exquisite ebony

figurines of the high priest Amen-Hotep and his wife, the priestess Re-nai.

Another highlight is the fabulous Treasure of Troy display, with gold artifacts excavated from the legendary city in the 1870s. There is also an assortment of items from ancient Greece and Rome.

Byzantine Art and Italian Art: 13th–16th Centuries

Room 7 contains a small, but memorable collection of Byzantine icons, including miniature folding icons and ivory carvings from the 10th century. There is also some later work, such as the splendidly luminous *Twelve Apostles* painted by Constantinopolitan masters in the early 14th century.

Italian Medieval and Renaissance art is also represented here. There is a series of altar panels painted in the Byzantine tradition by Italian artists. Siena was a major artistic centre in

the 14th century and Simone Martini was a leading master of the Sienese school. His naturalistic images of St Augustine and Mary Magdalene, painted in the 1320s, are among the exhibits.

There are also a number of later religious pieces on show, including a triptych by Pietro di Giovanni Lianori. Two outstanding old masters painted in the 1490s are also displayed here: the superb *Annunciation*, painted by Sandro Botticelli, and the *Madonna and Child* by Pietro Perugino.

German, Dutch and Flemish Art: 15th–17th Centuries

The museum is particularly well endowed with German, Dutch and Flemish Renaissance art. Room 8 includes Pieter Breughel the Younger's *Winter Landscape with Bird Trap* (1620s) – a copy of a similar painting by his father, Breughel the Elder – and a strong collection by the Saxon court painter, Lucas Cranach the Elder. His *Virgin and Child* (c.1520), painted on wood, places the Virgin and Child in the context of a typical German landscape.

Rooms 9 and 11 are equally rich with masters. They include Anthony Van Dyck's accomplished portraits of the wealthy burgher, Adriaen

A section of the *Virgin and Child*, painted by Lucas Cranach the Elder in about 1525

Stevens, and his wife, Maria Boschaert, both painted in 1629, and some evocative landscapes by Jan Van Goyen and Jacob van Ruysdael. Also on show are still lifes by Frans Snyders, some delightful genre scenes by Jan Steen, Pieter de Hooch and Gabriel Metsu and several works by Peter Paul Rubens, including *Apotheosis of the Infanta Isabella* (1634) and, in place of honour, the characteristically flamboyant *Bacchanalia* (c.1615).

Six of Rembrandt's masterly canvases, along with some of his drawings and etchings, are displayed in Room 10 of the gallery. The paintings include the biblical *Ahasuerus, Haman and Esther* (1660), *Christ Driving the Money-Changers from the Temple* (1626) and the theatrical *The Incredulity of Thomas* (1634). However, it is perhaps the later *Portrait of an Old Woman* (1654), actually of the artist's mother, that demonstrates the great skill of the artist. Here, the shadowed, stooping figure seems almost weighed down by memories.

Spanish and Italian Art: 17th–18th Centuries

Room 18 of the gallery has a modest collection of Spanish paintings from the 17th century and only the most important are on display. Of note are the lifelike religious figures by Fransciso de Zurbarán, such as *The Infant Christ* (1635–1640) painted late in his life. However it is another Spanish master, Bartholomé Esteban Murillo, known for the warmth and emotion caught in his religious scenes and portraits, who is probably the best known. Works include *Girl Selling Fruit* and *Archangel Raphael and Bishop Domonte* (1680).

Of the Italian works on display here, the influence of Caravaggio is felt, particularly in *Christ is Crowned with Thorns* (c.1610) by the relatively unknown artist Tommaso Salini, and the great artist's pupil Domenico Fetti and his follower Bernardo Strozzi. The latter's *Old Coquette* (after 1630) shows a

grey-haired woman sitting in front of a mirror, while her maids giggle in the background. It is a grotesque yet poignant depiction of the cruelty of time. Another trend of the era was the academic style of the Bologna school. Guido Reni's work is exemplary. In *Adoration of the Shepherds* (c.1640) the careful composition and light colouring made his style very popular at the time.

Guido Reni's *Adoration of the Shepherds* (c.1640)

In the 18th century, it was the Venetian school that dominated Italian painting. In Room 17 the colourful *Betrothal of the Venetian Doge to the Adriatic Sea* (1729–30) by Canaletto is on display. The artist is widely considered the master of the style of urban landscape known as *veduta*.

Hercules and Omphale, painted in the 1730s by François Boucher

French Art: 17th–Early 19th Centuries

The Pushkin Museum is justly famous for its collection of French art, which includes paintings of classical and epic subjects by a variety of artists. 17th-century pieces are held in Room 21 and include a good collection by one of the greatest French painters of the period, Nicolas Poussin. He was an exponent of High Renaissance

styles, preferring balance and order in his work. The early piece *Victory of Joshua over the Amorites* (c.1625) shows an almost austere pictorial manner. Later work includes his poetic *Rinaldo and Armida* (early 1630s) and landscapes such as *Landscape with Hercules and Cacus* (1656). In the same room is the earliest known work by eminent Versailles painter and art theorist, Charles Lebrun. His *Crucifixion* (1637), painted when the artist was still a teenager, shows the influence of Rubens. Also on display is his portrait of the playwright Molière, painted much later.

Room 22 moves to the 18th century and the art of the French Rococo period. A leading exponent of the style, François Boucher, is well represented here. An early piece, and typical of the ornamental Rococo style, is *Hercules and Omphale* (1730s), which depicts the myth of Hercules, who was sold as a slave to Queen Omphale.

Finally, French art from the second half of the 18th century to the early 19th century is housed in Room 23. At this time, landscape became a popular genre and there are some fine examples by celebrated artists of the day Claude-Joseph Vernet and Hubert Robert. Sculpture is also on display here. Jean-Antoine Houdon's bronzes of Enlightenment thinker Voltaire brought him much fame.

Arbatskaya metro station and a cinema in Arbat Square

⓫ Pashkov House

Дом Пашкова

Dom Pashkova

Ulitsa Znamenka 6. **Map** 6 F1.
Closed to public. Ⓜ Borovitskaya,
Biblioteka imeni Lenina.

This magnificent mansion
was once the finest private
house in Moscow and enjoys
a wonderful hilltop location
overlooking the Kremlin. It was
built in the Neo-Classical style
in 1784–8 for the fabulously
wealthy Captain Pyotr Pashkov.
Pashkov encouraged his
architect, who is thought to
have been Vasiliy Bazhenov
(*see p46*), to surpass himself
with the grandeur of the design.
The mansion's height was
achieved by placing it on an
enormous stone base and the
building is surmounted by a
beautifully proportioned
rotunda. Surprisingly the most
impressive façade is to the
rear of the building, which
originally led to a garden.

In 1839, a relative of Captain
Pashkov sold the house to the
Moscow Institute for Nobles,
which occupied
the premises

until 1861. It was then taken over
by the Rumyantsev Museum,
which moved to the capital from
St Petersburg at that time. The
museum brought with it an art
collection and a library of more
than one million volumes.

The building has been
completely renovated, and can
be hired for private events – for
$160,000 for an evening!

⓬ Arbat Square

Арбатская площадь

Arbatskaya ploshchad

Map 6 E1. Ⓜ Arbatskaya.

A chaotic mass of kiosks,
traffic and underpasses,
Arbat Square is the link
between the vividly contrasting
areas of Old and New Arbat.
The area is popular with both
Muscovites and visitors.
Beneath the square, the
underpasses contain a society
of their own. Expect to come
across an impromptu rock
concert, kittens and puppies
for sale and, in late summer,
children selling bulbous,
hand-picked mushrooms
(though buying these may
not be advisable). The bright
neon lights along the
wide avenue of Novy
Arbat are a reminder
of the street's heyday
as Moscow's casino
district. In 2009, the
government banned
gambling, thus
putting an end to
the lucrative gaming
industry in Moscow.
The former casinos
have since been
converted into
late-night bars,

shops, entertainment centres
and restaurants.

The small white building at
the other end of the underpass
dates from 1909, but it was
redesigned three years later by
Fyodor Shekhtel (*see p47*) for the
pioneering Russian film studio
boss, Aleksandr Khanzhonkov.
Now known as the Arts Cinema
(*see p201*), it was one of the first
cinemas to open in Moscow.

A portrait of the poet and novelist
Lermontov (1814–41) as a child

⓭ Lermontov House-Museum

Дом-музей МЮ
Лермонтова

Dom-muzey MYu Lermontova

Ulitsa Malaya Molchanovka 2. **Map** 6
D1. **Tel** (495) 691 5298. Ⓜ Arbatskaya.
Open 10am–6pm Tue, Wed & Fri–Sun,
2–8pm Thu. 🖼

Tucked away behind the tower
blocks of the New Arbat is the
modest timber house that
was once home to Mikhail
Lermontov. The great Romantic
poet and novelist lived here
with his grandmother, Yelizaveta
Arseneva, from 1829–32 while
he was a student at Moscow
University. While here, he wrote
an early draft of his narrative
poem *The Demon* (1839).

Lermontov was more inter-
ested in writing poetry than in
his studies and left university
without graduating. He then
became a guardsman. However,
he was exiled to the Caucasus
for a year because of the bitter
criticisms of the authorities
expressed in his poem *Death of*

The imposing Pashkov House overlooking the Kremlin

Lermontov's tranquil study in the Lermontov House-Museum

a Poet (1837). This poem about the death of Pushkin *(see p75)* marked a turning point in Lermontov's writing and is generally agreed to be the first of his mature works. His most famous composition, the novel *A Hero of our Time*, was written in 1840. Lermontov died the next year, aged only 26. Like Pushkin, he was killed in a duel.

There are only five rooms in the museum, but each bears testament both to Lermontov's dazzling intellectual gifts and also to his zest for life. The study on the mezzanine was his favourite room. Here he would play the guitar, piano and violin, and even compose music.

The drawing room, which still contains many of its original furnishings, was often the site of lively dancing, singing and masquerades. Many of Lermontov's manuscripts are on display downstairs, together with drawings and watercolours, some by Lermontov himself.

⓮ Shalyapin House-Museum
Дом-музей Ф.И. Шаляпина
Dom-muzey FI Shalyapina

Novinskiy bulvar 25. **Map** 1 C5.
Tel (495) 605 6236. Ⓜ Smolenskaya,
Barrikadnaya. **Open** 11am–7pm Wed–
Sun. **Closed** last Thu of the month.
🈂 🎫 book in advance.

This is one of Moscow's newer house-museums and one of the best. The stone bust and inscription outside the yellow Empire-style mansion record that one of the greatest opera singers of the 20th century once lived here. The renowned Russian bass, Fyodor Shalyapin, occupied this large house from 1910 until he emigrated from Soviet Russia in 1922.

Born in Kazan in 1873, Shalyapin began his career in great poverty, working as a stevedore on the Volga before his unique vocal talent was discovered. He made his international debut at La Scala, Milan, in 1901, and went on to sing a variety of the great operatic bass roles, including *Don Quixote*, *Ivan the Terrible* and *Boris Godunov*.

Stone bust of opera singer Shalyapin

Shalyapin died in Paris in 1938, but his remains have since been returned to Russia and were reburied in the Novodevichiy Cemetery *(see p133)* alongside other famous Russians.

Shalyapin rehearsed with renowned musicians and composers in the concert room, where visitors can now listen to recordings of the master at work. There is also a wonderful Bechstein grand piano, which was presented to Shalyapin in 1913.

After performing for his guests, the celebrated singer would often take them next door for a game of billiards. He was not a very good loser and depending on his mood, his wife would only invite friends with grace enough to let him win. Items on display in the house include the singer's much treasured velvet armchair, complete with his favourite ashtray still balancing on the arm. A selection of his playing cards are laid out on a side table. The curious mementoes on the second floor include amusing portraits of the singer in his various operatic roles, as well as a splendid collection of theatrical costumes.

Pictures drawn by Shalyapin's children, on display in the sitting room

TVERSKAYA

At heart a commercial district, Tverskaya centres on the road of the same name, which originally led to St Petersburg and was the processional route used by the tsars. Now Moscow's premier shopping street, Tverskaya ulitsa underwent a major redevelopment in the 1930s during the huge reconstruction of Moscow ordered by Stalin (see p77). At that time many buildings were torn down so that the street could be widened and massive new apartment blocks were erected for workers. These looming grey buildings make the street a showcase of the monumental style of architecture (see p47) favoured by Stalin. The area's surprisingly tranquil backstreets have been home to many famous artists, writers and actors, and, despite Stalin's best efforts, still have some interesting pre-Revolutionary houses.

Sights at a Glance

Museums
9 Stanislavskiy House-Museum
15 Gorky House-Museum
16 Chekhov House-Museum
19 Bulgakov House-Museum
20 Museum of Contemporary History

Streets and Squares
2 Theatre Square
6 Tverskaya Ulitsa
8 Bryusov Pereulok
10 Bolshaya Nikitskaya Ulitsa
18 Patriarch's Ponds
21 Pushkin Square

Historic Buildings
1 Hotel Metropol
4 House of Unions
5 Hotel National
11 Moscow Conservatory
12 Moscow Old University
13 Manège
14 House of Friendship
17 Morozov Mansion

Monasteries
22 Upper Monastery of St Peter

Theatres
3 Bolshoi Theatre pp92–3
7 Moscow Arts Theatre

☐ Restaurants see pp186–7
1 As Eat Is
2 Bublik
3 Café Pushkin
4 Chicago Prime Steakhouse
5 Conversation
6 Dolkabar
7 El Gaucho
8 Hinkalnaya
9 Mari Vanna
10 Montalto
11 Pizza Peppe
12 Polo Club
13 Retseptor
14 Scandinavia
15 Ulliam's

See also Street Finder maps 2 & 3

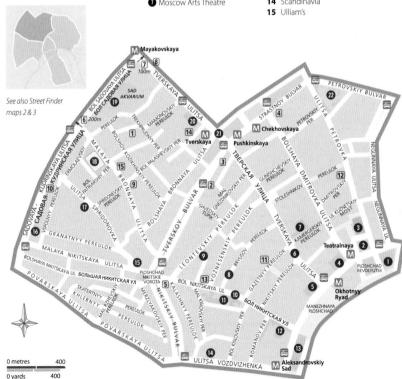

0 metres 400
0 yards 400

◀ The sumptuous interior of Yeliseyevsky Food Hall, on Tverskaya ulitsa

For keys to symbols see back flap

Street-by-Street: Around Theatre Square

Moscow's Theatreland is centred, quite appropriately, around Theatre Square. Dominating the square is one of the most famous opera and ballet stages in the world, the Bolshoi Theatre. The Malyy (Small) Theatre is on the east side of the square, while the Russian Academic Youth Theatre is on the west. Further to the west is the city's main shopping street, Tverskaya ulitsa, and two more theatres, the Yermolova Theatre and the Moscow Arts Theatre. There are also several excellent restaurants and bars in this lively neighbourhood.

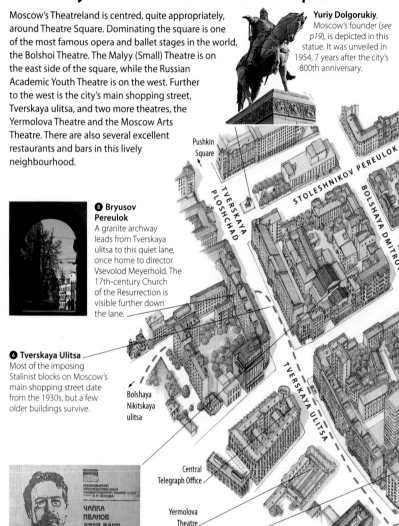

Yuriy Dolgorukiy, Moscow's founder (*see p19*), is depicted in this statue. It was unveiled in 1954, 7 years after the city's 800th anniversary.

Pushkin Square

❽ Bryusov Pereulok
A granite archway leads from Tverskaya ulitsa to this quiet lane, once home to director Vsevolod Meyerhold. The 17th-century Church of the Resurrection is visible further down the lane.

❻ Tverskaya Ulitsa
Most of the imposing Stalinist blocks on Moscow's main shopping street date from the 1930s, but a few older buildings survive.

Bolshaya Nikitskaya ulitsa

Central Telegraph Office

Yermolova Theatre

Okhotnyy Ryad

❼ Moscow Arts Theatre
This famous theatre will always be associated with the dramatist Anton Chekhov (*see p94*). Several of his plays, including *The Cherry Orchard*, were premiered here.

Lower Chamber of the Russian Parliament

❺ Hotel National
The National is a mix of Style Moderne and Classical style. Now restored, its decor is as impressive as it was before the Revolution, when it was Moscow's finest hotel.

Key

— Suggested route

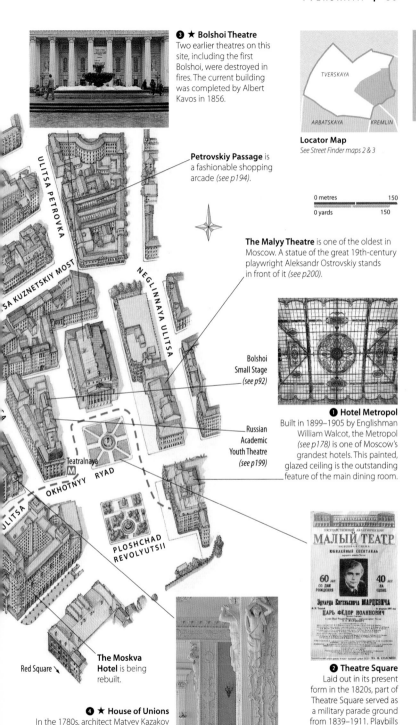

③ ★ Bolshoi Theatre
Two earlier theatres on this site, including the first Bolshoi, were destroyed in fires. The current building was completed by Albert Kavos in 1856.

Locator Map
See Street Finder maps 2 & 3

| 0 metres | 150 |
| 0 yards | 150 |

Petrovskiy Passage is a fashionable shopping arcade *(see p194)*.

The Malyy Theatre is one of the oldest in Moscow. A statue of the great 19th-century playwright Aleksandr Ostrovskiy stands in front of it *(see p200)*.

Bolshoi
Small Stage
(see p92)

① Hotel Metropol
Built in 1899–1905 by Englishman William Walcot, the Metropol *(see p178)* is one of Moscow's grandest hotels. This painted, glazed ceiling is the outstanding feature of the main dining room.

Russian
Academic
Youth Theatre
(see p199)

Teatralnaya Ⓜ

OKHOTNYY RYAD

ULITSA

PLOSHCHAD
REVOLYUTSII

The Moskva Hotel is being rebuilt.

Red Square ↘

④ ★ House of Unions
In the 1780s, architect Matvey Kazakov converted this Neo-Classical mansion into a noblemen's club. The trade unions took it over in the Soviet era.

② Theatre Square
Laid out in its present form in the 1820s, part of Theatre Square served as a military parade ground from 1839–1911. Playbills around the city advertise performances in the theatres on the square.

МАЛЫЙ ТЕАТР

ГОСУДАРСТВЕННЫЙ АКАДЕМИЧЕСКИЙ

ЮБИЛЕЙНЫЙ СПЕКТАКЛЬ

60 ЛЕТ
СО ДНЯ
РОЖДЕНИЯ

40 ЛЕТ
НА
СЦЕНЕ

Эдуарда Евгеньевича МАРЦЕВИЧА

ЦАРЬ ФЁДОР ИОАННОВИЧ

For keys to symbols *see back flap*

The statue of Aleksandr Ostrovskiy in front of the Malyy Theatre

❶ Hotel Metropol

Гостиница Метрополь

Gostinitsa Metropol

Teatralnyy proezd 2. **Map** 3 A5.
Tel (499) 501 7800. Ⓜ Teatralnaya.
See Where to Stay: p178.

The Hotel Metropol, built by William Walcot and Lev Kekushev in 1899–1905, is a fine example of Style-Moderne architecture *(see p47)*. The exterior walls sport a number of ceramic panels, including Mikhail Vrubel's large work at the top of the façade. Called *The Daydreaming Princess*, it is based on scenes from the play *La Princesse Lointaine*, written in 1895 by Edmond Rostand, author of *Cyrano de Bergerac*. The building also has ornate wrought-iron balconies and a superb painted glass roof in its Metropol Zal restaurant.

Over the years the Metropol has welcomed guests as varied and famous as Irish dramatist George Bernard Shaw and American pop star Michael Jackson.

❷ Theatre Square

Театральная площадь

Teatralnaya ploshchad

Map 3 A5. Ⓜ Teatralnaya, ploshchad Revolyutsii, Okhotnyy Ryad.

This elegant square is named after the theatres on three of its sides. Originally this area was marshy ground, regularly flooded by the Neglinnaya river. In the 1820s it was paved over and the square was laid out to a design by Osip Bove *(see p47)*. In 1839–1911 a military parade ground occupied part of the square. Today, Theatre Square is dominated by the Bolshoi Theatre.

On the square's east side is a converted private mansion that houses the Malyy (Small) Theatre *(see p200)*. The Malyy is particularly associated with playwright Aleksandr Ostrovskiy (1823–86), whose satirical plays were performed here. A sombre statue of him by Nikolay Andreev was erected in the forecourt in 1929.

The Russian Academic Youth Theatre *(see p199)*, with its elaborate Neo-Classical porch, stands on the square's west side. Originally designed by Osip Bove *(see p47)*, it was almost entirely rebuilt by Boris Freidenberg in 1882. The theatre has occupied this building since 1936.

To the northwest of Theatre Square is the Operetta Theatre *(see p200)*. In the 1890s the private opera company of the wealthy industrialist and arts patron Savva Mamontov (1842–1914) performed here. The careers of opera singer Fyodor Shalyapin *(see p85)*, composer Sergei Rachmaninov and artist Vasiliy Polenov, who designed sets and costumes, all began here with Mamontov's company.

In the centre of the square is a granite statue of Karl Marx. Sculpted in 1961 by Leonid Kerbel, it bears the words "Workers of the world unite!"

❸ Bolshoi Theatre

See pp92–3.

The well-proportioned Hall of Columns in the elegant, 18th-century House of Unions

❹ House of Unions

Дом Союзов

Dom Soyuzov

Bolshaya Dmitrovka ulitsa 1. **Map** 3 A5. **Tel** (495) 692 0736. **Open** for performances only. Ⓜ Teatralnaya, Okhotnyy Ryad.

This green and white Neo-Classical mansion was originally built in the first half of the 18th century. In the early 1780s, it was bought by a group of Moscow nobles who commissioned architect Matvey Kazakov *(see pp46–7)* to turn it into a noblemen's club. Kazakov added a number of rooms to the existing building including the magnificent ballroom, known as the Hall of Columns. It was here, in 1856, that Tsar Alexander II addressed an audience of the Russian nobility on the need to emancipate the serfs.

After the Revolution, trade unions took over the building, hence its current name.

The façade of the Hotel Metropol, designed by William Walcot

In 1924 the hall was opened to the public for more than a million people to file past Lenin's open coffin. Many of his closest colleagues were later tried here during the show trials of 1936–8 *(see p29)*. Stalin also lay in state here in 1953.

Nowadays the House of Unions is used for concerts and public meetings.

❺ Hotel National

Гостиница Националь

Gostinitsa Natsional

Mokhovaya ulitsa 15/1. **Map** 2 F5. **Tel** (495) 258 7000. Ⓜ Okhotnyy Ryad. ♿ 📷 See Where to Stay: p176.

Designed in 1903 by architect Aleksandr Ivanov, the Hotel National is an eclectic mixture of Style-Moderne and Classical-style architecture *(see pp46–7)*. The façade is decorated with sculpted nymphs and ornate stone tracery, but is topped by a mosaic from the Soviet era. This features factory chimneys belching smoke, oil derricks, electricity pylons, railway engines and tractors.

The National's most famous guest was Lenin, who stayed

Lobby of the Hotel National, with Style-Moderne windows and Classical statues

in room 107 at the hotel for a week, in March 1918, before he moved to the Kremlin.

The National was completely refurbished in the early 1990s and its Style-Moderne interiors have been faithfully restored to their original splendour.

❻ Tverskaya Ulitsa

Тверская улица

Tverskaya ulitsa

Map 2 F5, F4, E3. Ⓜ Okhotnyy Ryad, Tverskaya, Pushkinskaya.

Tverskaya ulitsa was the grandest thoroughfare in Moscow in the 19th century, when it was famous for its restaurants, theatres, hotels and purveyors of French fashions. Stalin's reconstruction of the city in the 1930s resulted in Tverskaya ulitsa being widened by 42 m (138 ft) and its name being changed to ulitsa Gorkovo to commemorate the writer Maxim Gorky. Many buildings were torn down to make way for huge apartment blocks to house party bureaucrats, such as those at Nos. 9–11. Other buildings were rebuilt further back to stand on the new, wider road. Now called Tverskaya ulitsa again, the street carries a huge volume of traffic. However, it is still one of the city's most popular places to eat out and shop.

At No. 7 is the Central Telegraph Office, a severe grey building with an illuminated globe outside. It was designed by Ilya Rerberg in 1927. Through the arch on the other side of the road is a green-tiled building with floral friezes and tent-roofed turrets. Built in 1905, this was the Moscow mission of the Savvinskiy Monastery. It is now luxury apartments and offices.

Tverskaya ulitsa, one of Moscow's most popular shopping streets

Further up the street is the soulless Tverskaya square, dominated by an equestrian statue of Moscow's founder, Prince Yuriy Dolgorukiy *(see p88)*. On the west side of the square is the red and white city hall. Designed in 1782 by Matvey Kazakov *(see pp46–7)*, it was the residence of the governor-general before the Revolution and later became the Moscow City Soviet or town hall. In 1944–6 extra storeys were added, more than doubling its height.

Beyond Tverskaya square, at No. 14, is Moscow's most famous delicatessen. Now known by its pre-Revolutionary name, Yeliseyevsky Food Hall *(see p194)*, in Soviet times it was called Gastronom No.1. In the 1820s this mansion was the home of Princess Zinaida Volkonskaya, whose soirées were attended by great figures of the day, including Alexander Pushkin *(see p75)*. In 1898 Grigoriy Yeliseev bought the building, and had it lavishly redecorated in Neo-Baroque style with stained-glass windows, crystal chandeliers, carved pillars, polished wood counters and large mirrors. The palatial food emporium now stocks a wide selection of imported and Russian delicacies.

❸ Bolshoi Theatre

Большой театр
Bolshoy teatr

Home to one of the oldest, and probably the most famous, ballet companies in the world, the Bolshoi Theatre is also one of Moscow's major landmarks. The first Bolshoi Theatre opened in 1780 and presented masquerades, comedies and comic operas. It burnt down in 1805, but its successor was completed in 1825 to a design by Osip Bove (*see p47*) and Andrey Mikhaylov. This building too was destroyed by fire, in 1853, but the essentials of its highly praised design were retained in Albert Kavos's reconstruction of 1856. A major refurbishment has reinstated a number of its original historic features and returned it to its former glory.

★ Royal Box
Situated at the centre of the gallery, the royal box, hung with crimson velvet, is one of over 120 boxes. The imperial crown on its pediment was removed in the Soviet era but has now been restored.

Neo-Classical Pediment
The relief on the Neo-Classical pediment was an addition by Albert Kavos during his reconstruction of the theatre. It depicts a pair of angels bearing aloft the lyre of Apollo, the Greek god of music and light.

★ Apollo in the Chariot of the Sun
This eye-catching sculpture by Pyotr Klodt, part of the original 1825 building, was retained by Albert Kavos. It depicts Apollo driving the chariot on which he carried the sun across the sky.

Entrance

Vestibule
Patrons entering the theatre find themselves in this grand tiled vestibule. Magnificent staircases, lined with white marble, lead up from either side of the vestibule to the spacious main foyer.

Grand Imperial Foyer
This ornately decorated room was known as the Beethoven Hall in the Soviet era. It is now used for occasional exhibitions. The stuccoed decoration on the ceiling includes about 3,000 rosettes and the walls are adorned with delicately embroidered panels of crimson silk.

Apollo and the Muses
The ten painted panels decorating the auditorium's ceiling are by Pyotr Titov. They depict Apollo dancing with the nine muses of Greek myth, each of which is connected with a different branch of the arts or sciences.

KEY

① **Eight-columned portico**

② **The auditorium** has six tiers and a seating capacity of 1,600. When Kavos rebuilt it he modified its shape to improve the acoustics.

③ **Main stage**

④ **The backstage area** provides jobs for over 700 workers, including craftsmen and women making ballet shoes, costumes and stage props.

⑤ **Artists' dressing room**

⑥ **The exhibition foyer** extends around the whole of the front of the building on the first floor. It hosts temporary exhibitions that are open during performances.

The Bolshoi Ballet in the Soviet Era

In the 1920s and 1930s new ballets conforming to Revolutionary ideals were created for the Bolshoi, but the company's heyday was in the 1950s and 1960s. Ballets such as *Spartacus* were produced and the dancers toured abroad for the first time to widespread acclaim. Yet a number of dancers also defected to the West in this period, in protest at the company's harsh management and a lack of artistic freedom.

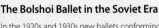

A production of *Spartacus* (1954), by Aram Khachaturian, at the Bolshoi

The single-domed Church of the Resurrection, built in 1629 on Bryusov Pereulok

❼ Moscow Arts Theatre

МХАТ имени АП Чехова

MKhAT imeni AP Chekhova

Kamergerskiy pereulok 3. **Map** 2 F5.
Tel (495) 629 8760/6748.
Ⓜ Teatralnaya, Okhotnyy Ryad.
Open performances only.
See Entertainment: p200.

The first ever performance at the Moscow Arts Theatre (MKhAT) took place in 1898. This venue was founded by a group of young theatre enthusiasts, led by the directors Konstantin Stanislavskiy and Vladimir Nemirovich-Danchenko.

The Moscow Arts Theatre entrance with *The Wave* bas-relief above

The MKhAT company had an early success with their production of Anton Chekhov's play *The Seagull* in the theatre's first year. When the play had been performed 3 years earlier in St Petersburg, it had been a disastrous flop; however, performed in Moscow using Stanislavskiy's new Method acting, it was extremely well received.

In 1902 architect Fyodor Shekhtel *(see p47)* completely reconstructed the interior of the theatre, adding innovations such as a central lighting box and a revolving stage. The auditorium had very little decoration, so that audiences were forced to focus on the stage and concentrate on the performance.

Stylized seagull on the exterior of the Moscow Arts Theatre

The theatre continued to flourish after the 1917 Revolution, despite its repertoire being restricted by state censorship. Most of the plays produced were written by Maxim Gorky, whose work was in favour with the government. The frustrations and compromises of the period were brilliantly satirized in the 1930s by Mikhail Bulgakov (who also worked as an assistant director in the theatre) in his novel *Teatralnyy Roman*. These problems continued and in the 1980s part of the company moved to the Gorky Arts Theatre on Tverskoy bulvar.

Today a variety of productions are staged at the Moscow Arts Theatre, including many of Anton Chekhov's plays.

❽ Bryusov Pereulok

Брюсов переулок

Bryusov pereulok

Map 2 F5. Ⓜ Okhotnyy Ryad, Arbatskaya.

A granite arch spanning Tverskaya ulitsa marks the entrance to this quiet side street. It is named after the Bruces, a Scottish family who were involved with the Russian court.

In the 1920s new apartments here were assigned to the staff of the Moscow state theatres. No. 17, for example, was the home of two actors from the Moscow Arts Theatre, Vasiliy Kachalov and Ivan Moskvin.

No. 12 was home to the avant-garde director Vsevolod Meyerhold, who directed premieres of Vladimir Mayakovsky's satires. Meyerhold lived here from 1928 until his arrest in 1939 at the height of Stalin's Great Purge *(see p29)*.

The Composers' Union was housed at Nos. 8–10. It was here that composers Sergey Prokofiev and Dmitriy Shostakovich were forced to read an apology for works that deviated from Socialist Realism *(see p137)*.

About halfway along Bryusov pereulok is the 17th-century single-domed Church of the Resurrection. This was one of the few churches to remain open during the Soviet era.

❾ Stanislavskiy House-Museum

Дом-музей КС

Станиславского
Dom-muzey KS Stanislavskovo

Leontevskiy pereulok 6. **Map** 2 E5.
Tel (495) 629 2442. Ⓜ Arbatskaya,
Tverskaya. **Open** noon–7pm Wed &
Fri, 11am–6pm Thu, Sat & Sun.
Closed last Thu of month. 🎨 📷 📱

This 18th-century mansion was the home of the great director and actor Konstantin Stanislavskiy.

Stanislavskiy found himself disillusioned with the conservative ethos of the old Moscow Theatre School, and created an outlet for his innovative ideas by founding the Moscow Arts Theatre (MKhAT) in 1898. After moving into this apartment, he converted his ballroom into a makeshift theatre where he rehearsed his experimental Opera Dramatic Group. The actors would step on stage from the adjacent Red Room, which served as a make-up studio and held furniture for rehearsals and classes. To this day, actors, directors and opera singers continue to perform here at weekends.

Stanislavskiy was indifferent to his surroundings and, for most of his life, slept in his study. Only when he fell ill in 1928 did he move into a purpose-built bedroom. He died here a decade later.

❿ Bolshaya Nikitskaya Ulitsa

Большая Никитская улица
Bolshaya Nikitskaya ulitsa

Map 2 F5, E5. Ⓜ Arbatskaya,
Okhotnyy Ryad, Biblioteka imeni
Lenina.

This historic street, once the main road to Novgorod, is named after the Nikitskiy Convent which was founded in the 16th century, but pulled down by Stalin in the 1930s.

Prominent aristocratic families such as the Menshikovs and Orlovs built their palaces here in the 18th century. The finest is the former residence of Prince

Stanislavskiy and Chekhov

Konstantin Stanislavskiy's successful production of Anton Chekhov's *The Seagull* took the theatre world by storm. Stanislavskiy's secret was his new school of Method acting, in which performers explored their characters' inner motives. Stanislavskiy and Chekhov collaborated on the premieres of other Chekhov plays and the success of the productions was such that their names have been linked ever since.

Konstantin Stanislavskiy in the play *Uncle Vanya* by Chekhov

Sergey Menshikov, which can be reached via Gazetniy pereulok. The pale blue façade was reconstructed following the great fire of 1812 (see pp26–7). The Neo-Classical rear façade, which survived the fire, dates from around 1775.

Just opposite the Moscow Conservatory (see p96), is the attractive white Church of the Little Ascension. Built around the end of the 16th century, it was restored in 1739 following a fire. Behind it is the Gothic tower of St Andrew's Anglican Church. It was built for Moscow's English community in 1882 by British architect Richard Freeman.

Stone relief on Church of the Great Ascension

The heavily ornamented red-brick building at Nos. 19–20 was once called the Paradise Theatre. It was renamed the Mayakovsky Theatre after the poet Vladimir Mayakovsky (see p113). His plays *Bath House* and *The Bed Bug* were premiered

here in 1928 and 1929, directed by avant-garde director Vsevolod Meyerhold. One of the greatest innovators of his era, Meyerhold was executed by the State in 1940, largely because his work did not agree with the canons of Socialist Realism (see p137).

About halfway along the road is Nikitskie Vorota ploshchad, named after the medieval gate that used to stand here. On the square is a modern white building with a sign in the shape of a large globe hanging beneath its porch. This is the ITAR-TASS news agency, the mouthpiece of the Communist Party in the Soviet era and now Russia's main news agency.

Opposite is the Church of the Great Ascension. Begun in 1798, it was rebuilt after the 1812 fire. Alexander Pushkin (see p75) married Natalya Goncharova here in 1831.

Sign in the shape of a globe hanging outside the ITAR-TASS news agency

The Bolshoy Zal (Great Hall) in the Moscow Conservatory

⓫ Moscow Conservatory

Московская консерватория

Moskovskaya Konservatoriya

Bolshaya Nikitskaya ulitsa 13/6. **Map** 2 F5. **Tel** (495) 629 9401. Ⓜ Arbatskaya, Pushkinskaya. **Open** performances only. Ⓦ mosconsv.ru

The largest music school in Russia was founded in 1866 by Nikolay Rubinstein, the brother of composer and pianist Anton Rubinstein.

One of the Conservatory's teachers was the young Pyotr Tchaikovsky, who taught here until 1878. On the forecourt is his statue, wielding a baton despite the fact that Tchaikovsky detested conducting. The work of Vera Mukhina, it dates from 1954. The pattern on the fore-court railings is made up of the opening notes from some of Tchaikovsky's works.

Portraits of famous com-posers adorn the walls of the light, airy Bolshoy Zal (Great Hall). Used for concerts since 1898, it is also the setting for the prestigious Tchaikovsky International Competition *(see p200)*. The Conservatory has a small museum that is open during perfomances.

The Conservatory has always been an important training ground for young Russian composers and performers. Among its best-known alumni are pianist-composers Sergei Rachmaninov and Aleksandr Skryabin *(see p74)*. Dmitriy Shostakovich, the great Soviet composer, lived nearby, at the Composers' Union on Bryusov

pereulok *(see p94)*. He taught at the Conservatory from 1942 until he fell from favour and was sacked 6 years later for "professional incompetence" during Stalin's Purges *(see p29)*.

⓬ Moscow Old University

Московский университет

Moskovskiy Universitet

Mokhovaya ulitsa 9. **Map** 2 F5. Ⓜ Okhotnyy Ryad, Biblioteka imeni Lenina.

Founded by the scholar Mikhail Lomonosov in 1755, this is the oldest university in Russia. It moved into this imposing building (now called the Old University) in 1793. Designed by Matvey Kazakov *(see pp46–7)*, it was extensively rebuilt by Domenico Gilardi after the 1812 fire *(see pp26–7)* and is a fine example of Neo-Classical architecture. Outside are statues of radical writers Nikolay Ogarev and

Statue of Mikhail Lomonosov

Aleksandr Herzen. In 1836 the university acquired a building on the far side of Bolshaya Nikitskaya ulitsa. In front of the New University is a statue of Mikhail Lomonosov. Nearby is the chapel of St Tatyana, whose feast day is celebrated by the students.

⓭ Manège

Манеж

Manezh

Manezhnaya ploshchad 1. **Map** 6 F1. **Tel** (495) 648 1717. Ⓜ Biblioteka imeni Lenina, Okhotnyy Ryad. **Open** exhibitions only. 🖼 ▯

The Manège was originally built in 1817 as a military parade ground to a design by General Augustin de Béthencourt. The 45-m- (148-ft-) wide roof had no supporting columns, leaving an uninterrupted floor space large enough for an infantry regiment to practise in.

In 1823–5 Osip Bove *(see p47)* added a colonnade and decorative frieze to the exterior.

The Manège became the Central Exhibition Hall in 1957 and it was at an exhibition here in 1962 that Nikita Khrushchev *(see p32)* famously condemned abstract art. The brunt of the attack was borne by the sculptor Ernst Neizvestniy but, curiously, in his will Khrushchev chose Neizvestniy to design his tombstone *(see p133)*. Fire partly destroyed the building in 2004 but it was swiftly rebuilt. Today the Manège is still mostly used to house exhibitions.

The Manège, designed by Augustin de Béthencourt in 1817

The extravagant interior of the 19th-century House of Friendship

⑭ House of Friendship

Дом дружбы
Dom Druzhby

Vozdvizhenka ulitsa 16. **Map** 6 E1. **Tel** (495) 690 2069. **M** Arbatskaya, Biblioteka imeni Lenina. **Open** performances only.

This incredible mansion has towers encrusted with stone shells and topped by lacelike stonework. Vladimir Mazyrin designed it at the end of the 19th century for the playboy Arseny Morozov, a member of the wealthy Morozov family *(see p98)*. The interior is just as showy; rooms include a hunting hall filled with carved animal heads. The only way to see inside is to attend a concert or lecture held here. In Soviet times the mansion was used by the Union of Friendship Societies, hence its name.

⑮ Gorky House-Museum

Дом-музей АМ Горького
Dom-muzey AM Gorkovo

Malaya Nikitskaya ulitsa 6/2. **Map** 2 E5. **Tel** (495) 690 0535. **M** Tverskaya, Arbat. **Open** 11am–5:30pm Wed–Sun. **Closed** last Thu of the month. 🎧 English.

A frieze of irises against a background of blue and purple clouds runs round the top of the yellow glazed-brick walls of this extraordinary mansion. Fyodor Shekhtel designed this masterpiece of Style-Moderne architecture *(see p47)* in 1900. The house belonged to arts patron and millionaire banker Stepan Ryabushinskiy until he left Russia with his family after the Revolution. In 1931 Stalin presented the mansion as a gift to the famous socialist writer Maxim Gorky.

The interior of the house is spectacular, featuring ceilings with elaborate mouldings, stained-glass windows and carved door frames. However, the *pièce de résistance* is the flowing staircase of polished Estonian limestone, which ends in a lamp resembling a jellyfish.

By the time Gorky moved to this house, his career as a novelist and playwright was in decline. While living here, he wrote only one play, *Yegor Bulychev and Others* (1932), and part of a novel, *The Life of Klim Samgin* (unfinished at his death). However his fame and his earlier support for the Bolshevik Party made him a useful propaganda tool for the Soviet government. He served this function by being president of the Union of Writers, which explains why the rooms are full of photos of the author in the company of aspiring dramatists, Young Pioneers and ambitious Communist officials.

On display are Gorky's hat, overcoat and walking stick, his remarkable collection of oriental carvings and many of his letters and books, including some first editions.

Shortly after Gorky died in 1936, Genrikh Yagoda, the former head of the NKVD (secret police), was accused of murdering him. Although the charge was probably fabricated, Yagoda was found guilty in one of the last of the notorious show trials *(see p29)*. Rumours persist that Gorky was killed on Stalin's orders.

The spectacular Style-Moderne staircase in the Gorky House-Museum

⑯ Chekhov House-Museum

Дом-музей АП Чехова
Dom-muzey AP Chekhova

Sadovaya-Kudrinskaya ulitsa 6.
Map 2 D5. **Tel** (495) 691 3837.
Ⓜ Barrikadnaya. **Open** 2–8pm Wed &
Fri, 11am–6pm Tue, Thu & Sat.
Closed last day of month. 🖼 ✉ 📷
book in advance.

Anton Chekhov (1860–1904)
lived in this two-storey house in
1886–90. It was later refurbished
in consultation with the
author's widow, actress
Olga Knipper-Chekhova, and
opened as a museum in 1954.
However, it is only partially
successful in re-creating a
period feeling and contains few
of Chekhov's possessions.

Chekhov was a qualified
doctor and was practising
medicine when he lived here,
as the brass plate by the front
door testifies. He shared the
house with his parents, his
brother, Mikhail, and his sister,
Mariya. As the family's main
breadwinner, Chekhov could
only write in his spare time, but
it was here that he created his
first major play, *Ivanov*. He also
wrote many short stories and
several one-act plays here.

Exhibits in the study, which
doubled as a consulting room,
include Chekhov's doctor's
bag, manuscripts and pictures,
including some of him with
Leo Tolstoy *(see p136)*.

Upstairs are a richly decorated living room and Mariya's
room, which, in some ways, is
the most attractive in the house.
Its furnishings include a sewing
machine, ornaments and
embroidered tablecloths.

An exhibition about
Chekhov's later career as a
playwright *(see p95)* includes
first editions of his works.

Picture of Chekhov (on the left) talking with
Leo Tolstoy, in the Chekhov House-Museum

The Gothic-style Morozov Mansion, designed by Fyodor Shekhtel

⑰ Morozov Mansion

Дом ЗГ Морозовой
Dom ZG Morozovoy

Spiridonovka ulitsa 17. **Map** 2 D4.
Ⓜ Mayakovskaya. **Closed** to public.

Fyodor Shekhtel *(see p47)*
built this house for his patron,
Savva Morozov, in 1893–8.
Savva Morozov was a wealthy
textiles manufacturer and
arts patron, a member of
one of the city's richest
merchant families.

The mansion was built in
the Gothic style to resemble
a baronial castle, with turrets,
gargoyles and arched windows.
Some of the stained-glass windows were designed by the
Symbolist artist Mikhail Vrubel.

⑱ Patriarch's Ponds

Патриаршие пруды
Patriarshie prudy

Map 2 D4. Ⓜ Mayakovskaya.

A few minutes' walk from the
busy Garden Ring is a secluded,
tree-lined square with a large
pond at its heart, named after
the patriarch who formerly
owned the land. For a long time
there has been only one pond,
though there used to be several.

Near the children's
playground is a bronze statue of
the 19th-century playwright
and writer of popular fables Ivan
Krylov. Sculptures of the
creatures from his stories are
dotted among the trees.

Patriarch's Ponds is probably
best known as the setting for
the opening scene in Mikhail
Bulgakov's novel *The Master and
Margarita*, in which the Devil

appears in Moscow and causes
havoc. Bulgakov lived nearby for
3 years during the 1920s.

Graffiti at Bulgakov's apartment by
enthusiasts of his work

⑲ Bulgakov House-Museum

Музей Булгаковский дом
Bulgakovskiy dom

Bolshaya Sadovaya ulitsa 10.
Map 2 D3. **Tel** (495) 970 0619.
Ⓜ Mayakovskaya. **Open** 1–11pm
Sun–Thu, 1pm–1am Fri–Sat. 📷

This cultural centre is
dedicated to Mikhail Bulgakov
(1891–1940), the Russian
author whose best-known
work, *The Master and Margarita*,
was not published until long
after his death. During his
lifetime, many of his satirical
plays were banned. Bulgakov
became so frustrated that
he wrote to Stalin asking
to be exiled. Instead, he was
given a job at the Moscow
Arts Theatre *(see p94)*. Many
of Bulgakov's possessions
are on display. Admirers can
also visit his former apartment
two doors along.

Maxim gun used in the Civil War, Museum of Contemporary History

⑳ Museum of Contemporary History

Музей современной истории
Muzey sovremennoy istorii

Tverskaya ulitsa 21. **Map** 2 E4. **Tel** (495) 699 6724. Ⓜ Pushkinskaya, Tverskaya. **Open** 10am–6pm Tue–Sun. ♿ 📷 English. 🖥 🌐 **sovr.ru**

A pair of stone lions guards this elegant red mansion, built in the late 18th century. The wings and Empire-style façade *(see p47)* were added some decades later. In 1831 the mansion became a gentlemen's club, known as the English Club, and until the Revolution, the Muscovite aristocracy drank and gambled here.

Ironically, this building, with all its aristocratic associations, became the Museum of the Revolution. However, since the Soviet Union broke up in 1991, the collections display a more objective view of 20th-century Russian history; the name of the museum has also been changed to reflect this shift.

Laid out chronologically, the exhibits cover 1900–91. They include home-made grenades, a Maxim gun on a converted carriage (used in the Civil War), sweet wrappers depicting Marx and Lenin and former premier Nikita Khrushchev's hat and camera from his 1959 trip to the United States. The so-called propaganda porcelain and gifts presented to Soviet rulers are also interesting.

㉑ Pushkin Square

Пушкинская площадь
Pushkinskaya ploshchad

Map 2 F4. Ⓜ Pushkinskaya, Tverskaya, Chekhovskaya.

The bronze statue of poet Alexander Pushkin was unveiled in the presence of two other Russian literary giants, Fyodor Dostoevsky and Ivan Turgenev, in 1880. The statue, located on the south side of Pushkin Square, was sculpted by Alexander Opekushin.

Pushkin has long epitomized the spirit of freedom in Russia and the statue occasionally became a rallying point for demonstrations in the 1960s and 1970s, which sometimes ended in clashes between the KGB and demonstrators.

Before the Revolution Pushkin Square was called Strastnaya ploshchad (Passion Square) after the 17th-century Convent of the Passion which

The statue of poet Alexander Pushkin, on Pushkin Square

used to stand here. The convent was demolished in 1935 to make way for the monstrous Rossiya cinema.

Just beyond the cinema, on Malaya Dmitrovka ulitsa, is the Church of the Nativity of the Virgin in Putinki. Built in 1649–52, this attractive church has clustered tent roofs, tiered *kokoshniki* gables *(see p46)*

and blue onion domes. On the northeast corner of the square stand the offices of the newspaper *Izvestiya*. Once an official mouthpiece of the Soviet government, *Izvestiya* is now one of Russia's independent daily newspapers.

㉒ Upper Monastery of St Peter

Высоко-Петровский монастырь
Vysoko-Petrovskiy monastyr

Petrovka ulitsa 28/2. **Map** 3 A3. **Tel** (495) 694 6437. Ⓜ Pushkinskaya, Chekhovskaya. **Open** 8am–7pm daily. 📷 book in advance.

This monastery was founded in the reign of Ivan I *(see p20)*. It was rebuilt in the late 17th century with sponsorship from the Naryshkin family, relatives of Peter the Great. Its six churches include the Church of the Metropolitan Peter after which the monastery is named. This single-domed church was built in 1514–17 to a design by Aleviz Novyy. The Church of the Icon of the Virgin of Bogolyubovo commemorates three of Peter the Great's uncles killed in the 1682 Streltsy Rebellion *(see p24)*. The Refectory Church of St Sergius has five cupolas and scallop shell decoration.

Iconostasis in the Baroque bell tower of the Upper Monastery of St Peter

Street-by-Street: Kitay Gorod

Commerce and religion go hand-in-hand in this ancient part of the city. The heart of Moscow's financial district is Birzhevaya ploshchad, and the surrounding area has been home to traders for centuries. Among the banks and offices are an increasing number of upmarket stores, especially lining Nikolskaya ulitsa, and the area now rivals Russia's best-known shopping arcade, GUM (see p109). At one time there were more than 40 churches and monasteries dotted about these narrow streets. Only around a dozen have survived and most of these are now undergoing painstaking restoration.

❻ Cathedral of the Epiphany
This cathedral was once part of the second oldest monastery in Moscow. Built between 1693–6, it is a fine example of florid Moscow Baroque.

Russian Supreme Court

NIKOLSKAYA ULITSA

BOGOYAVLENSKIY PEREULOK

Red Square

VETOSHNYY PEREULOK

BIRZHEVA PLOSHCH

ULITSA ILINKA

❼ Nikolskaya Ulitsa
Well-heeled shoppers now head to this street's boutiques and jewellery shops. Among its more colourful sights is the Gothic-style Synodal Printing House, which dates from the 19th century.

KHRUSTALNYY PEREULOK

The Old Merchants' Chambers (Staryy Gostinyy Dvor), dating from the 18th to 19th centuries, now houses a shopping arcade.

Church of St Barbara

Key
— Suggested route

❺ Ulitsa Ilinka
Halfway along ulitsa Ilinka is Birzhevaya ploshchad, where the former Stock Exchange is located. Constructed in 1873–5 by Aleksandr Kaminskiy, this attractive, pink, Classical-style building is now the home of the Russian Chamber of Industry and Commerce.

❶ Ulitsa Varvarka
Several historic churches line this ancient route out of Moscow. Among them is the Church of St Maxim the Blessed, which was paid for by Novgorod merchants trading in Kitay Gorod and consecrated in 1698.

Locator Map
See Street Finder maps 3 & 7

❹ ★ Church of the Trinity in Nikitniki
Commissioned by the wealthy merchant Grigoriy Nikitnikov and completed in 1635, the church is famous both for its exuberant architecture and for its vivid frescoes. It is currently closed for renovations.

This house belonged to Simon Ushakov, a leading 17th-century icon and fresco painter. He worked on the nearby Church of the Trinity in Nikitniki.

❸ ★ Chambers of the Romanov Boyars
Originally lived in by powerful boyar *(see p22)* Nikita Romanov, this palace is now a fascinating museum that evokes the life of noble families in the 16th and 17th centuries.

Kitay Gorod metro

Church of St George

ULITSA VARVARKA

Monastery of the Sign

❷ Old English Court
Restored to its 17th-century appearance, this merchants' residence was given to visiting English traders by Ivan the Terrible in the hope of securing arms and other goods from them.

TSA ILINKA

NIKOLSKIY PEREULOK

IPATEVSKIY PEREULOK

PEREULOK

0 metres 100
0 yards 100

For keys to symbols *see back flap*

❶ Ulitsa Varvarka

Улица Варварка
Ulitsa Varvarka

Map 7 B1–C1. Ⓜ Kitay Gorod.

The heart of the former merchants' quarter of Zaryade, ulitsa Varvarka is one of Moscow's oldest streets. It is named after the original Church of St Barbara (Varvara) the Martyr. This earlier building was demolished in 1796 to make way for a new pink and white Neo-Classical church of the same name, designed by Rodion Kazakov.

A little further along is the single-domed Church of St Maxim the Blessed. Built by traders from Novgorod to house the bones of St Maxim, it was consecrated in 1698. Between the two churches stands the Old English Court.

Across the road are the Old Merchants' Chambers (Staryy gostinyy dvor), which are fronted by a row of Corinthian columns. Italian architect Giacomo Quarenghi drew up plans for this market in 1790, and the work was supervised by Moscow architects Semen Karin and Ivan Selekhov. There are shops here and performances and exhibitions are held in the covered yard. Beyond the Church of St Maxim are the 17th-century Monastery of the Sign and the Palace of the Romanov Boyars.

At the end of ulitsa Varvarka is the Church of St George, built in 1657–8 by merchants from Pskov,

The five domes of the Church of St George on ulitsa Varvarka

a town known for its architects *(see p46)*. To the right, on Kitaygorodskiy proezd, is one of the few sections of the old city walls to survive. At the end of this street, beside the Moskva river, is the mid-16th-century Church of the Conception of St Anna.

❷ Old English Court

Старый английский двор
Staryy angliyskiy dvor

Ulitsa Varvarka 4a. **Map** 7 B1. **Tel** (495) 698 3952. **Open** 10am–6pm Tue, Wed & Fri–Sun, 1–9pm Thu. **Closed** last Fri of month. Ⓜ Ploshchad Revolyutsii, Kitay Gorod. 🅿 🖒 English (book in advance).

In 1553, while searching the northern coast of Russia for a passage to the east, the English merchant adventurer Richard Chancellor *(see p23)* was shipwrecked. He was taken to Moscow and received by Ivan the Terrible, whose desire to

trade with England later led him to propose marriage to Queen Elizabeth I. On returning to Russia in 1556, Chancellor and his trading mission were given this large property in Zaryade. It was to serve as a storage and trading house and as accommodation for English merchants.

In the mid-17th century, the estate passed into Russian hands and by the 1900s it had been extensively altered. After the Revolution *(see pp28–31)*, the house was restored. It later reopened as a museum during the official visit of Queen Elizabeth II to Russia in 1994.

Inside, an exhibition highlights the history of the Old English Court and its role in developing Anglo-Russian relations. Stone staircases lead down to the cellars and the official chamber used for negotiations and functions. English merchants fitted the Russian stove with an open hearth as a reminder of home.

❸ Chambers of the Romanov Boyars

Палаты бояр Романовых в Зарядье
Palaty Boyar Romanovikh

Ulitsa Varvarka 10. **Map** 7 B1. **Tel** (495) 698 1256. **Open** 11am–7pm Wed, 10am–6pm Thu–Mon. **Closed** first Mon of the month. Ⓜ Kitay Gorod. 🅿

Only the upper storeys of this palace can be seen from ulitsa Varvarka. This is largely because the palace is built on a steep slope leading away from the street down towards the Moskva river.

The palace was originally built by the boyar *(see p22)* Nikita Romanov in the 16th century. It was home to the Romanovs until 1613 when Mikhail Romanov *(see p21)* became tsar and the family moved to the Kremlin. The palace has been protected as a museum since 1859.

The main entrance is reached via a courtyard; a double-

A view along ulitsa Varkarva, with the Old English Court straight ahead

headed eagle, the Romanov family crest, adorns the archway leading to the courtyard.

The ground and first floors of the palace probably date from the 17th century. In the painted hall, personal effects of the early Romanovs are displayed, including gold dishes, ancient title deeds, ledgers inlaid with precious gems and the robes of Nikita's eldest son, Patriarch Fyodor Filaret. The rooms have been refurbished in the lavish style of the period, with walls covered in gilt-embossed leather or painted in rich reds, greens and golds.

In the 16th and 17th centuries even the richest families had to tolerate rather cramped and dim conditions. The portals in the palace are so low that a man of average height has to stoop, and little light is let in by the windows as they are made of mica, a translucent mineral, rather than glass.

In the mid-19th century the light and airy, wooden upper storey was added to the building. The main hall on this level has a beautifully carved wooden ceiling. An anteroom has a display of embroidery.

The vaulted cellars are the least interesting rooms and contain an odd mix of trunks, baskets and kitchen items.

Ornate dining room in the Chambers of the Romanov Boyars

Gilded iconostasis in the Church of the Trinity in Nikitniki

❹ Church of the Trinity in Nikitniki

Церковь Троицы в Никитниках
Tserkov Troitsy v Nikitnikakh

Nikitnikov pereulok 3. **Map** 7 C1.
Ⓜ Kitay Gorod. **Closed** to public.

Like the churches on ulitsa Varvarka, this marvellous church is dwarfed by monstrous post-war buildings that were formerly Communist Party offices. When it was founded in 1635 by the wealthy merchant, Grigoriy Nikitnikov, the church would have dominated the local skyline. It is at present closed while it is being restored.

The church has five green domes, a profusion of decoration and painted tiles, and tiers of *kokoshniki* gables *(see p46)*. The equally elaborate tent-roofed bell tower, which is linked to the main building by an enclosed gallery, was added shortly after the church was finished.

Carvings on the porch of the Church of the Trinity in Nikitniki

The Church of the Trinity is famous for its frescoes, which were finished in 1656, shortly after Nikitnikov died from the plague. They portray scenes from the Gospels, such as *The Parable of the Rich Man*, in direct, emotional terms.

Among the artists who made an important contribution to the church's decoration was the great fresco and icon painter Semen Ushakov. He painted a number of the frescoes and several of the panels in the splendid gilded iconostasis. Among his works is the *Annunciation of the Virgin*, which can be seen to the left of the Royal Gate *(see p63)* on the iconostasis. Members of the Nikitnikov family are commemorated in the frescoes in the corner Chapel of St Nikita the Martyr.

Semen Ushakov was a parishioner and his house is around the corner from the church on Ipatevskiy pereulok. It is an unremarkable 17th-century, red-brick building.

Striking 19th-century commercial buildings lining ulitsa Ilinka

❺ Ulitsa Ilinka

Улица Ильинка

Ulitsa Ilinka

Map 7 B1. Ⓜ Kitay Gorod.

In the 19th century this narrow but majestic street was the commercial heart of Kitay Gorod, and home to numerous banks and trading offices. Their richly decorated façades were intended to impress and are still the chief pleasure of a stroll along the street. Today, ulitsa Ilinka is once more the location of a number of commercial and financial institutions, including the Ministry of Finance.

The name Ilinka refers to the former Ilinskiy Monastery, of which no traces now remain. The monastery once stood where the 17th-century Church of St Elijah can now be seen, at No. 3. Further along, at No. 6, on the corner of Birzhevaya ploshchad, is a peach-coloured building with a Neo-Classical portico, which at present houses the Russian Chamber of Industry and Commerce. Originally these were the premises of Moscow's Stock Exchange, which was rebuilt by Aleksandr Kamenskiy in 1873–5, having first opened in 1836. At that time many of Moscow's merchants still wore long patriarchal beards and the traditional kaftan, and were used to dealing with one another in the street. They at first refused to enter the new Stock Exchange and, in the end, were coralled into the building by the police. Across the street

from this building is the former Trinity Sergius Hostel, which was the city mission of the Trinity Monastery of St Sergius (see pp164–7). Now part of the Russian Supreme Court, it was built by Pavel Skomoroshenko in 1876 and is a restrained example of the Russian-Revival style (see p47).

A building which formerly served as offices for the Soviet government stands at the corner of ulitsa Ilinka and Bolshoy Cherkasskiy pereulok. Uncompromisingly plain, with glazed tiles and rows of narrowly spaced windows, it was designed by Vladimir Mayat in the 1920s.

❻ Cathedral of the Epiphany

Собор Богоявления

Sobor Bogoyavleniya

Bogoyavlenskiy pereulok 2, stroenie 4. **Map** 3 A5. **Tel** (495) 698 3825. Ⓜ Ploshchad Revolyutsii. **Open** 8am–8pm daily. ✉

This splendid cathedral once formed part of the Monastery of the Epiphany, the second oldest monastery in Moscow. Founded in 1296 by Prince Daniil Aleksandrovich, father of Grand Prince Ivan (see p20), it was built on what at that time was the edge of the city.

The cathedral which stands today is an addition to the original medieval complex and dates from 1693–6. The wedding-cake pink building is distinguished by its massive but

refined tower, a masterpiece of Moscow Baroque (see p46). An abbot chamber and cells for monks were built at the end of the 17th century, and the bell tower was erected in 1739.

❼ Nikolskaya Ulitsa

Никольская улица

Nikolskaya ulitsa

Map 3 A5. Ⓜ Lubyanka, Ploshchad Revolyutsii.

By the end of the 12th century, this street, which is named after the Kremlin's St Nicholas Tower (see p68), had been settled by merchants and traders. Trading stalls and shops remained a feature of the street until the Revolution. Following a dowdy period under Communism, Nikolskaya ulitsa has since moved upmarket with the arrival of several expensive clothing stores and jewellers.

Through the courtyard at No. 7 is a gateway leading into the Zaikonospasskiy Monastery, which was founded in the 15th century or earlier. The name means Saviour Beyond the Icons and recalls the time when there was a brisk trade in icons here. The monastery church, with its dilapidated red brick tower and spire, dates from the 17th century. It is now open again for worship. From 1687 to 1814 the monastery also housed Moscow's first institute of higher education, referred to laboriously as the Slavic Greek Latin Academy.

Gothic-style façade of the Synodal Printing House, Nikolskaya ulitsa

Kazan Cathedral, a faithful 1990s reconstruction of the original cathedral

❽ Kazan Cathedral

Казанский собор
Kazanskiy sobor

Nikolskaya ulitsa 3. **Map** 3 A5.
Tel (495) 698 2726. M Okhotnyy
Ryad. **Open** 8am–8pm daily. ✉

This diminutive cathedral is a replica of an original demolished in 1936. Its predecessor was consecrated in 1637 and housed the Icon of the Kazan Virgin. The icon was revered because it had accompanied Prince Dmitriy Pozharskiy during his victorious campaign against the invading Poles 25 years earlier (see p111).

Detailed plans and photographs, kept by architect Pyotr Baranovskiy, assisted reconstruction of the cathedral in 1990–1993 (see p46). It was reconsecrated by Patriarch Aleksey II in the presence of President Boris Yeltsin and the mayor of Moscow, Yuriy Luzhkov. The Icon of the Kazan Virgin is a copy as the original was stolen in 1904.

❾ Resurrection Gate

Воскресенские ворота
Voskresenskie vorota

Krasnaya ploshchad. **Map** 3 A5.
M Okhotnyy Ryad, Ploshchad Revolyutsii.

Rebuilt in 1995 (see p46), this gateway, with its twin red towers topped by green tent spires, is an exact copy of the original completed on this site in 1680. The first gateway was demolished in 1931. Note the mosaic icons on the gate, one of which depicts Moscow's patron saint, St George, slaying the dragon.

Within the gateway is the equally colourful Chapel of the Iverian Virgin, which was originally built in the late 18th century to house an icon. Whenever the tsar came to Moscow, he would visit this shrine before entering the Kremlin (see pp54–69). Visitors should try to see the gate at night, when it is impressively lit up.

Among its pupils was the famous polymath and future founder of Moscow University, Mikhail Lomonosov (see p96).

At No. 15 are the fanciful Gothic-style spires of the Synodal Printing House. The pale blue building, with a lion and unicorn sculpted over its central window, contrasting with an incongruous hammer and sickle above, dates from 1810 to 1814. The courtyard is enhanced by a colourful chequered roof and walls of blue and white tiles. In the chambers previously on this site Ivan Fyodorov produced Russia's first printed book, *The Acts of the Apostles,* in 1564.

Next door, in the courtyard of No. 17, was the former Slavyanskiy Bazaar restaurant, which opened in 1870. Among its former patrons was Anton Chekhov (see p98). This restaurant was also where the theatre directors Konstantin Stanislavskiy and Vladimir Nemirovich-Danchenko began a meeting which concluded with the founding of the Moscow Arts Theatre (see p94).

Following a fire in 1993, the restaurant closed. It now houses the Moscow Chamber Musical Theatre.

On the opposite side of the road is a building that used to house the Chizhevskoe Inn, a combined inn and warehouse for traders passing through Kitay Gorod. In the courtyard behind it is the 17th-century Church of the Assumption.

Floodlit Resurrection Gate, inside which is the Chapel of the Iverian Virgin

Red Square

Resurrection Gate
Historical Museum
Kazan Cathedral
Kremlin Wall
GUM
Lenin Mausoleum
Kremlin
Lobnoe Mesto
Saviour's Tower
St Basil's Cathedral

The vast expanse of Red Square, with the Historical Museum at the far end

⑩ Red Square

Красная площадь

Krasnaya ploshchad

Map 7 B1. Ⓜ Ploshchad Revolyutsii, Okhotnyy Ryad. Historical Museum: **Tel** (495) 692 4019. **Open** 10am–6pm Mon, Wed & Fri–Sun, 11am–9pm Thu. **Closed** last Wed of the month.

Towards the end of the 15th century, Ivan III *(see p20)* gave orders for houses in front of the Kremlin to be cleared to make way for this square. It originally served as a market called the *torg*, but the wooden stalls burned down so often that the area later became popularly known as Fire Square. The current name dates from the 17th century and is derived from the Russian word *krasnyy*, which originally meant "beautiful" but later came to denote "red". The association between the colour red and Communism is purely coincidental.

Red Square, which is approximately 500 m (1,600 ft) in length, was also the setting for public announcements and executions. At its southern end, in front of St Basil's Cathedral *(see pp110–11)*, there is a small circular dais. Called Lobnoe Mesto, this is the platform from which the tsars and patriarchs would address the people. In 1606 the first "False Dmitry" *(see p21)*, a usurper of the throne, was killed by a hostile crowd. His body was finally left at Lobnoe Mesto.

Six years later, a second pretender to the throne, who

like the first "False Dmitry" was backed by Poland, took power. He was expelled from the Kremlin by an army led by the Russian heroes Dmitriy Pozharskiy and Kuzma Minin, who proclaimed Russia's deliverance from Lobnoe Mesto. In 1818, a statue was erected in their honour *(see p111)*. This now stands in front of St Basil's.

Red Square has also long been a stage for pageants and processions. Before the Revolution *(see pp28–31)*, the patriarch would ride an ass through Saviour's Gate *(see p68)* to St Basil's each Palm Sunday to commemorate Christ's entry into Jerusalem.

Religious processions were abolished in the Communist era. Military parades took their place and were staged each year on May Day and on the anniversary of the Revolution.

Lobnoe Mesto, the platform from which the tsar spoke

Rows of grim-faced Soviet leaders observed them from outside the Lenin Mausoleum. They, in turn, would be keenly studied by professional kremlinologists in the West trying to work out the pecking order.

Today the square is used for a variety of cultural events, concerts, firework displays and other public occasions. The red-brick building facing St Basil's Cathedral was constructed by Vladimir Sherwood in 1883 in the Russian-Revival style *(see p47)*. It houses the Historical Museum. The museum boasts over four million exhibits covering the rise and expansion of the Russian state.

In front of the museum's façade on Manezhnaya ploshchad is a statue by Vyacheslav Klykov of one of the heroes of World War II *(see p150)*, Marshal Georgiy Zhukov. This statue of him was unveiled in 1995 to mark the 50th anniversary of the end of World War II.

Aleksey Shchusev's Lenin Mausoleum, with the Kremlin Wall behind

⓫ Lenin Mausoleum

Мавзолей ВИ Ленина

Mavzoley VI Lenina

Krasnaya ploshchad. **Map** 7 A1.
Tel (495) 623 5527. Ⓜ Ploshchad
Revolyutsii, Okhotnyy Ryad.
Open 10am–1pm Tue–Thu, Sat & Sun.
🚫 Strictly no cameras, even if it is in
your bag.

Following Lenin's death in
1924, and against his wishes,
it was decided to preserve
the former Soviet leader's body
for posterity. The body was
embalmed and placed in a
temporary wooden mausoleum
in Red Square. Once it became
clear that the embalming
process had worked, Aleksey
Shchusev *(see p47)* designed
the current mausoleum of a
pyramid of cubes cut from red
granite and black labradorite.

Paying one's respects to Lenin's
remains was once akin to a
religious experience, and queues
used to trail all over Red Square.
In 1993, however, the goose-
stepping guard of honour was
replaced by a lone militiaman
and now the mausoleum attracts
mostly tourists. There are
rumours that Lenin will soon be
moved elsewhere or buried.

Behind the mausoleum at
the foot of the Kremlin Wall are
the graves of other famous
communists. They include
Lenin's successors, Joseph Stalin
(at one time laid alongside
Lenin in the Mausoleum),
Leonid Brezhnev and Yuriy
Andropov. Lenin's wife and
sister are also buried here, as
are the first man in space, Yuriy
Gagarin, writer Maxim Gorky
and American John Reed. The
last was honoured as the
author of *Ten Days that Shook
the World*, an account of the
October Revolution.

The glass-roofed interior of Russia's largest department store, GUM

⓬ GUM

ГУМ

GUM

Krasnaya ploshchad 3. **Map** 7 B1.
Tel (495) 788 4343. Ⓜ Ploshchad
Revolyutsii, Okhotnyy Ryad. **Open**
10am–10pm daily. ♿ Ⓦ **gum.ru**

Before the Revolution, this
building was known as
the Upper Trading Rows after
the covered market that used to
stand on the site. In fact, lines of
stalls used to run all the way
from here to the Moskva river.
GUM has three separate arcades
which are still called "lines". The
store's name, Gosudarstvennyy
universalnyy magazin, dates
from its nationalization in 1921.
The building was designed
by Aleksandr Pomerantsev
in 1889–93 in the then-
fashionable Russian-Revival
style. Its archways, wrought-
iron railings and stuccoed
galleries inside are especially
impressive when sunlight
streams through the glass roof.

There were once more than
1,000 shops here, selling goods
ranging from furs and silks to
humble candles. For a period,
however, during the rule of
Stalin *(see p29)*, GUM's shops
were requisitioned as offices.
Nowadays, Western firms like
Benetton, Estée Lauder and
Christian Dior dominate the
prestigious ground floor along
with a variety of Western-style
cafés and restaurants.

Embalming Lenin

"Do not raise monuments to him, or palaces to his name, do
not organize pompous ceremonies in his memory." Such were
the words of Lenin's widow, Krupskaya. Despite this, Lenin's body
was embalmed by two professors and, after a delay to see if the
process had worked, put on display. A laboratory is dedicated
to preserving the body, which needs regular applications of
special fluids. Rumours that parts or all of the body have been
replaced with wax substitutes are vigorously denied.

⓭ St Basil's Cathedral

Собор Василия Блаженного

Sobor Vasiliya Blazhennovo

Commissioned by Ivan the Terrible *(see p20)* to celebrate the capture of the Mongol stronghold of Kazan in 1552, St Basil's Cathedral was completed in 1561. It is reputed to have been designed by the architect Postnik Yakovlev. According to legend, Ivan was so amazed at the beauty of his work that he had him blinded so that he would never be able to design anything as exquisite again. The church was officially called the Cathedral of the Intercession because the final siege of Kazan began on the Feast of the Intercession of the Virgin. However, it is usually known as St Basil's after the "holy fool" Basil the Blessed whose remains are interred within. The cathedral's design, which was inspired by traditional Russian timber architecture, is a riot of gables, tent roofs and twisting onion domes.

★ **Domes**

Following a fire in 1583 the original helmet-shaped cupolas were replaced by ribbed or faceted onion domes. It is only since 1670 that the domes have been painted many colours; at one time St Basil's was white with golden domes.

KEY

① **The Chapel of St Basil**, the ninth chapel to be added to the cathedral, was built in 1588 to house the remains of the "holy fool", Basil the Blessed.

② **Chapel of the Three Patriarchs**

③ **Chapel of the Trinity**

④ **Bell tower**

⑤ **Tent roof on the Central Chapel**

⑥ **Central Chapel of the Intercession** – light floods in through the windows of the tent-roofed central church, which soars to a height of 61 m (200 ft).

⑦ **Chapel of St Nicholas**

⑧ **Chapel of St Varlaam of Khutynskiy**

⑨ **Tiered gables**

⑩ **The Chapel of the Entry of Christ into Jerusalem** was used as a ceremonial entrance during the annual Palm Sunday procession. On this day the patriarch rode from the Kremlin to St Basil's Cathedral on a horse dressed up to look like a donkey.

⑪ **Chapel of Bishop Gregory**

Entrance to the cathedral

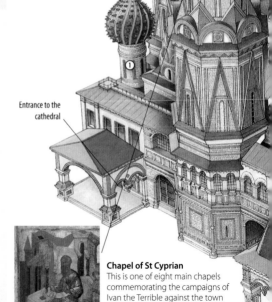

Chapel of St Cyprian

This is one of eight main chapels commemorating the campaigns of Ivan the Terrible against the town of Kazan, to the east of Moscow. It is dedicated to St Cyprian, whose feast is on 2 October, the day after the last attack.

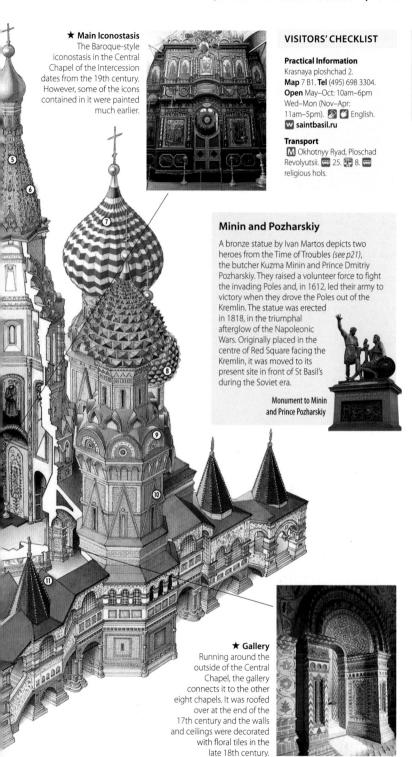

★ Main Iconostasis
The Baroque-style iconostasis in the Central Chapel of the Intercession dates from the 19th century. However, some of the icons contained in it were painted much earlier.

VISITORS' CHECKLIST

Practical Information
Krasnaya ploshchad 2.
Map 7 B1. **Tel** (495) 698 3304.
Open May–Oct: 10am–6pm
Wed–Mon (Nov–Apr:
11am–5pm). 🐾 🎧 English.
🔲 saintbasil.ru

Transport
Ⓜ Okhotnyy Ryad, Ploschad Revolyutsii. 🚌 25. 🚎 8. 🚌 religious hols.

Minin and Pozharskiy

A bronze statue by Ivan Martos depicts two heroes from the Time of Troubles *(see p21)*, the butcher Kuzma Minin and Prince Dmitriy Pozharskiy. They raised a volunteer force to fight the invading Poles and, in 1612, led their army to victory when they drove the Poles out of the Kremlin. The statue was erected in 1818, in the triumphal afterglow of the Napoleonic Wars. Originally placed in the centre of Red Square facing the Kremlin, it was moved to its present site in front of St Basil's during the Soviet era.

Monument to Minin and Prince Pozharskiy

★ Gallery
Running around the outside of the Central Chapel, the gallery connects it to the other eight chapels. It was roofed over at the end of the 17th century and the walls and ceilings were decorated with floral tiles in the late 18th century.

⑭ Ivanovskaya Hill

Ивановская горка
Ivanovskaya gorka

Map 3 C5. Ⓜ Kitay Gorod.

This hilly area takes its name from the Ivanovskiy Convent on the corner of ulitsa Zabelina and Malyy Ivanovskiy pereulok. The convent's rather neglected remains can be seen behind a twin-towered gateway and high encircling walls.

Yelena Glinska, mother of Ivan the Terrible *(see p20)*, founded the convent in 1533 as a gesture of thanks for the birth of her son. Later, however, it doubled as a prison for many years – its most famous inmate was Avgusta Tarakanova, the illegitimate daughter of Tsarina Elizabeth *(see p24)* and Count Aleksey Razumovskiy. She was educated abroad before being brought to Russia in 1785 and put into the convent under an assumed name. She spent the rest of her life here as a solitary nun, forbidden to receive any visitors except for the mother superior. She died in 1810.

Across the road is the Church of St Vladimir in the Old Gardens. It was built in 1514 by Italian architect Aleviz Novyy, but it was extensively altered at the end of the 17th century. Its name refers to the tsar's orchards, which used to occupy the slopes of the hill.

One of the pleasures of this area is exploring its unusually quiet backstreets. At the end of Malyy Ivanovskiy pereulok, which runs down from the Ivanovskiy Convent, is Podkolokolnyy pereulok (Lane Beneath the Bells). This street is dominated by the Church of St Nicholas the Wonderworker, which dates from the mid-17th century and is recognizable by its outsized red bell tower. Perhaps the most impressive church in the area is SS Peter and Paul on Petropavlovskiy pereulok. It was built in 1700 and contains an icon of the Bogolyubovskaya Virgin, which used to hang in a chapel near the gate to the city at the end of ulitsa Varvarka *(see p104)*.

To the north, at No. 10 Kolpachiy pereulok is the 17th-century mansion that reputedly belonged to the Ukrainian chief Ivan Mazepa. He fled to Turkish-controlled Moldova in 1709, after betraying Peter the Great *(see p24)* to the Swedes and then being defeated by him. Tchaikovsky set the story to music in his opera, *Mazepa*. The name of another street, Kokhlovskiy pereulok, may also have a Ukrainian link; Ukrainians used to be known as *khokhly* because of the tufts of hair they grew at the back of their shaved heads (*khokhly* means tufted in Russian). The most notable

Russian space programme exhibit at the Polytechnical Museum

building standing on ulitsa Maroseyka is the blue and white mansion at No. 17. This is now the Belorussian embassy.

⑮ Polytechnical Museum

Политехнический музей
Politekhnicheskiy muzey

Novaya ploshchad 3/4. **Map** 3 B5. **Tel** (495) 625 0614. **Open** 10am–6pm Tue–Sun. **Closed** last Fri of the month. Ⓜ Kitay Gorod, Lubyanka. 🅿 ⓦ **polymus.ru**

Designed by architect Ippolit Monighetti, the central section of this museum was built in 1877 and is a superb example of Russian-Revival architecture *(see p47)*. The north and south wings were added in 1896 and 1907 respectively.

The items on display were originally assembled for an exhibition staged in the Alexander Gardens *(see p69)* in 1872. This marked the 200th anniversary of the birth of Peter the Great, himself an enthusiastic amateur scientist.

The museum is a popular outing for schoolchildren. Its original collection has been expanded to trace the development of Russian science and technology during the 19th and 20th centuries. Exhibits range from early clocks and cameras to cars and space capsules. Every 2 hours there are demonstrations of devices such as robots, working models and sound equipment.

The Church of St Vladimir in the Old Gardens, on Ivanovskaya Hill

⓰ Choral Synagogue

ХоральнаяСинагога

Khoralnaya sinagoga

Bolshoy Spasoglinishchevskiy pereulok 10. **Map** 3 B5. **Tel** (495) 940 5557. **Open** 10am–6pm Mon–Fri. Ⓜ Kitay Gorod. 🚇 ✴ 8:30am Mon–Fri, 9am Sat & holidays. 🌐 synrus.ru

This magificent synagogue's Neo-Classical exterior features a large silver dome and yellow and white walls. Its construction began in 1887, largely funded by banker Lazar Polyakov, but was abandoned in 1891 after the governor ordered the expulsion of 20,000 of Moscow's Jews.

The synagogue eventually opened its doors in 1906 and continued to operate during the Soviet period. The interior is decorated in the Moorish style common to synagogues across Eastern Europe, with beautiful arabesques and wonderfully painted murals. The synagogue draws Jews from the city's growing community and from further afield.

Magnificent Neo-Classical exterior of the Choral Synagogue

⓱ Mayakovsky Museum

Музей-квартира ВВ Маяковского

Muzey-kvartira VV Mayakovskovo

Lubyanskiy proezd 3/6. **Map** 3 B5. **Tel** (495) 621 9387. **Open** 10am–6pm Fri–Tue, 1–9pm Thu. **Closed** last Fri of the month. Ⓜ Lubyanka. 🚇 ♿

Vladimir Mayakovsky, poet, iconoclast, exhibitionist and consummate self-publicist, was above all a revolutionary. In his short but eventful life his poetry, plays, film scripts and poster art gave a strident voice to the

The striking Constructivist entrance to the Mayakovsky Museum

Revolution and its vision of modernity. The terse and uncompromising agitprop posters he designed with Aleksandr Rodchenko are a prominent feature of the museum.

By nature, Mayakovsky was both provocative and extraordinary, and this is

Room designed to symbolize Mayakovsky's poetic origins

brilliantly reflected in this apparently anarchic museum. Huge frameworks of metal bars, designed in the Constructivist style influential in the 1920s, lean at fantastic angles and provide a backdrop for the other exhibits. Mayakovsky's artworks and belongings are intermingled: chairs, old boots, typewriters, painted cannon balls, large posters and photomontages, cracked mirrors, sewing machines and manuscripts.

Mayakovsky actually lived in this block from 1919 until his death in 1930: a single room on the fourth floor has been furnished to look as it would have done when he moved in. While living in this house, Mayakovsky continued his long-running love affair with Lilya Brik, the wife of his friend Osip Brik. This was also the period in which he wrote his best known plays, the caustic satires *The Bed Bug* and *Bath House*.

The last part of the exhibition deals with Mayakovsky's suicide at the age of 37. On display are two death masks, one black and one white. After his death, Stalin *(see p29)* praised Mayakovsky as the most talanted of Soviet poets and continued to use his work for propaganda purposes.

Vladimir Mayakovsky

Born in Georgia in 1893, Mayakovsky was brought up in Moscow, where he became involved in the revolutionary movement at the tender age of 14. Earning his revolutionary honours by being arrested three times in the space of two years, he was also drawn to the avant-garde and in 1912 became a founder of the Futurist movement by contributing to its manifesto, *A Slap in the Face for Public Taste*. Mayakovsky wholeheartedly endorsed the Revolution *(see pp28–31)*, becoming one of its most effective propagandists, but became increasingly disillusioned with the straitjacketed attitudes of Soviet society in the 1920s; this may have contributed to his suicide in 1930.

⑱ Lubyanka Square
Лубянская площадь
Lubyanskaya ploshchad

Map 3 B5. Ⓜ Lubyanka.

Synonymous with terror and the secret police, the name Lubyanka struck fear into the hearts of generations of Soviet citizens. In 1918, the Cheka (the forerunners of the KGB), led by the hated "Iron" Feliks Dzerzhinskiy, took over what had been the Rossiya Insurance Offices at the northern end of the square.

In the 1930s the building was extended and the enormous, underground Lubyanka Prison added, where the KGB interrogated, tortured, imprisoned and killed hundreds of thousands of people. By 1947 the incredible numbers of those accused in the course of Stalin's rule *(see p29)* led to the building of an additional wing, designed by Aleksey Shchusev *(see p47)*. Despite numerous changes of name

**Feliks Dzerzhinskiy
(1877–1926)**

(and protestations of changes in ethos), the Russian intelligence services still occupy the building.

A statue of Dzerzhinskiy used to stand in the centre of Lubyanka Square. It was unceremoniously toppled in front of a cheering crowd, following the unsuccessful coup against President Gorbachev in 1991 *(see p33)*. The statue can now be seen in the Graveyard of Fallen Monuments *(see p137)*. With a customary lack of irony, the Soviet authorities built Russia's largest toy store, Detskiy Mir, now closed, directly opposite the KGB headquarters in 1957.

⑲ Chistoprudnyy Bulvar
Чистопрудный бульвар
Chistoprudnyy bulvar

Map 3 C4. Ⓜ Chistye Prudy.

This road is part of the historic Boulevard Ring, which was laid out along the line of the old Belyy Gorod (White City) wall after the great fire of 1812 *(see p26)*. There are several fine houses located along Chistoprudnyy bulvar. At No. 19a is the elegant, Classical-style portico of the Sovremennik Theatre, which was built as a cinema by Roman Klein in 1914. Just beyond is the mansion where Sergey Eisenstein, director of *October* and *Battleship Potemkin*, lived from 1920 to 1934. Chistoprudnyy bulvar is part of the area which used to be known as Myasnitskaya after the butchers *(myasniki)* who worked here in the 17th century. The *myasniki* are still commemorated in the name of Myasnitskaya ulitsa, which runs from Lubyanka Square to Chistoprudnyy bulvar.

Detail of the fine stone carvings on the Church of the Archangel Gabriel

Between the carriageways of Chistoprudnyy bulvar is a large pond. It was created as a place for the butchers to dump offal and other waste products but, by 1703, the stench and risk of disease were so bad that the pond was cleared and renamed Chistye prudy (Clean Pond).

The beautiful, pale blue mansion just round the corner, at No. 22 ulitsa Pokrovka, was built between 1766 and 1772. Before the Communist coup in October 1917, the building used to be one of the best male secondary schools in Moscow, dating from 1861.

⑳ Church of the Archangel Gabriel
Церковь Архангела Гавриила
Tserkov Arkhangela Gavriila

Arkhangelskiy pereulok 15. **Map** 3 C4. Ⓜ Chistye Prudy. ♿ ⓟ

This church was constructed on the orders of Prince Aleksandr Menshikov, Peter the Great's advisor. With Peter the Great's backing, Menshikov rose from the position of lowly pie-seller to be one of most powerful men in Russia. It was typical of the flamboyant Menshikov that, when he commissioned the church from Ivan Zarudniy in 1701, he instructed the architect to make it just a little taller than the Ivan the Great Bell Tower *(see p59)*, until then the tallest structure in all of Russia.

Specialist stonemasons from Yaroslavl and Kostroma and Italian sculptors worked on the church, accounting for the beauty of the stone carvings and stuccoed festoons. The wooden spire was capped by a gilded angel and held an

The infamous former headquarters of the KGB on Lubyanka Square

expensive English clock, which chimed on the quarter-hour.

However, pious Muscovites remained unimpressed by the display of wealth and when the tower was destroyed by lightning in 1723 many saw in it the hand of God. The tower was rebuilt without the spire in 1773–80. The church was one of the few to remain open during the Soviet era and much of its interior decoration has survived.

Next to the tower is the small Church of St Fyodor Stratilit, which was heated in winter for the benefit of the parishioners. It was built in 1806, probably by Ivan Yegotov.

㉑ Perlov Tea House

Чай-кофе магазин
Chay-kofe magazin

Myasnitskaya ulitsa 19. **Map** 3 B4
Tel (495) 625 4656. **Open** 9am–9pm Mon–Fri, 10am–8pm Sat, 10am–7pm Sun. Ⓜ Chistye Prudy, Turgenevskaya. 🕿

This building was originally designed by Roman Klein in 1890 for the tea merchant Sergey Perlov. Five years later Perlov heard that the official representative of the Chinese emperor would be visiting Moscow. He commissioned Karl Gippius to redesign the shop in the hope of receiving him. The façade is a fanciful vision of the Orient, including serpents, dragons and pagoda-style details. The oriental theme is followed up inside with

Shelves of tea behind the counter of the elegant Perlov Tea House

lacquered columns and counters painted with dragons. The Chinese official mistakenly visited Perlov's nephew, who was also a tea merchant.

㉒ Convent of the Nativity of the Virgin

Рождественский монастырь
Rozhdestvenskiy monastyr

Ulitsa Rozhdestvenka 20. **Map** 3 A4.
Tel (495) 621 3986. **Open** 6am–8pm daily. Ⓜ Kuznetskiy Most, Trubnaya. 🕿

Converted to housing in Soviet times, this small cluster of buildings was neglected until 1991, when it was returned to the Russian Orthodox Church.

Founded in 1386 by Princess Maria Serpukhovskiy, daughter-in-law of Ivan I *(see p20)*, the convent was one of a ring of fortified monasteries constructed around Moscow.

The beautiful cathedral, commissioned between 1501 and 1505 by Tsar Ivan III *(see p20)*, has tiers of *kokoshniki* gables *(see p46)* and a cupola.

The small Church of St John of Zlatoust, with five domes, has also survived, along with a short section of the original brick ramparts. The yellow, tiered bell tower was designed by Nikolay Kozlovskiy in 1835.

The waiting area inside the luxurious Sandunovskiy Baths

㉓ Sandunovskiy Baths

Сандуновские бани
Sandunovskie bani

Neglinnaya ulitsa 14, building 3–7.
Map 3 A4. **Tel** (495) 625 4631.
Open 8am–10pm daily (last adm 8pm). Ⓜ Kuznetskiy Most, Trubnaya. 🕿 🕿
🆆 **sanduny.ru**

The original Sandunovskiy Baths were built for actor Sila Sandunov in 1808. In 1895 they were replaced by this building designed by Boris Freidenberg and with a decorative Beaux Arts façade.

The main entrance is through an ornate archway, decorated with sculptures of nymphs on horse-back, emerging from the sea and using triton shells as trumpets.

However, it is the sumptuous interiors, decorated in a flamboyant mix of Baroque, Gothic and Moorish styles, that make the baths famous. The Alhambra Palace in Spain was one of the sources of inspiration for the ornate decoration. The baths can accommodate up to 2,000 customers a day. The best, most expensive, rooms are located on the first floor. Here patrons can still buy birch twigs to beat themselves with, an essential part of a Russian steam bath.

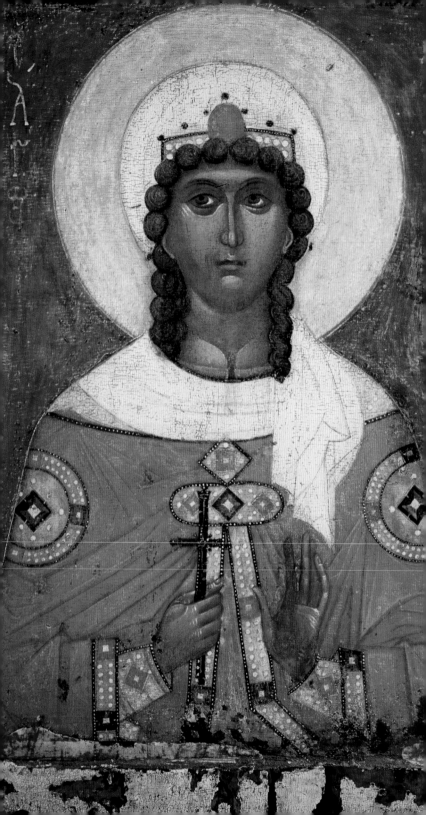

ZAMOSKVORECHE

First settled in the 13th century, Zamoskvoreche (literally "beyond the Moscow river") acted as an outpost against the Mongols. Its main road, Bolshaya Ordynka, was the route to the *Orda*, or Golden Horde, the Mongol headquarters on the Volga river. Later, under Ivan the Terrible, the Streltsy (royal guard) was stationed here. Artisans serving the court also moved in, living in areas according to their trades, each of which sponsored a church. These historic churches, now in varying states of repair, and the fact that the area was almost untouched by the replanning of the 1930s, give it a more old-fashioned atmosphere than the centre, which is dominated by massive Soviet architecture. In the 19th century wealthy merchants settled here, many of whom, such as Aleksey Bakhrushin and Pavel Tretyakov, were patrons of the arts. Based on its founder's acquisitions, the Tretyakov Gallery is the nation's most important collection of Russian art.

Sights at a Glance

Churches and Convents
❷ Church of the Resurrection in Kadashi
❸ Church of the Consolation
   of All Sorrows
❹ Church of St Clement
❺ Church of St Nicholas in Pyzhy
❻ Church of St Catherine
❼ Convent of SS Martha and Mary

Museums and Galleries
❶ *Tretyakov Gallery pp120–23*
❽ Tropinin Museum
❾ Bakhrushin Theatre Museum

Streets
❿ Sophia Embankment

Restaurants *see p188*
1 Aldebaran
2 Bottlebar
3 Brix
4 Correa's
5 Dorian Gray
6 Funky Lab
7 Karavaevi
8 Marukame
9 Oblomov
10 Punch and Judy

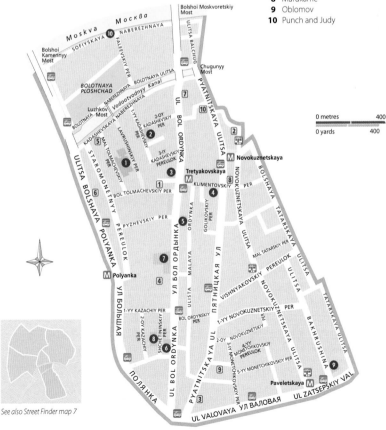

See also Street Finder map 7

◀ A 14th-century Russian icon on display at the Tretyakov Gallery

For keys to symbols *see back flap*

Street-by-Street: Around Pyatnitskaya Ulitsa

An old-fashioned atmosphere still prevails in the area around Pyatnitskaya ulitsa. The well-established streets are lined with attractive 19th-century churches and imposing Neo-Classical mansions. The busiest part of the district is the area around Tretyakovskaya metro. The market stalls on the station forecourt spill over onto Klimentovskiy pereulok, and nearby Pyatnitskaya ulitsa is the main shopping street. A short walk to the west is the stunning Tretyakov Gallery. To the north, the area is bordered by the Vodootvodnyy canal, which was built in 1783–6 to prevent the regular spring flooding of the Moskva river.

Vodootvodnyy Canal

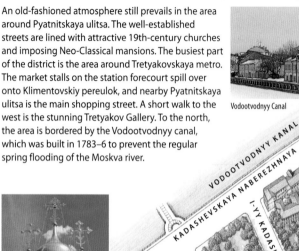

❷ ★ Church of the Resurrection in Kadashi
With its five onion domes and lavish limestone ornamentation this magnificent church is a fine example of the style known as Moscow Baroque *(see p46)*.

| 0 metres | 100 |
| 0 yards | 100 |

❶ ★ Tretyakov Gallery
The world's largest collection of Russian art is housed here. Taken down in the Soviet era, the statue of Pavel Tretyakov *(see p122)* has now been restored to its rightful place in front of the gallery.

The Demidov House was built in 1789–91 by a family of well-known industrialists.

❹ Church of the Consolation of all Sorrows
Two of Moscow's best-known architects contributed to this much-loved church. Vasiliy Bazhenov designed the bell tower and Osip Bove *(see p47)* the rotunda.

Church of St John the Baptist
has a distinctive green bell tower
and was built in the 18th century.

Kremlin

**The Church of SS
Michael and Fyodor,**
dating from the late 17th
century, is named after
two martyrs killed by
Mongols when they
refused to renounce
Christianity.

Cultural Centre of
Pan Slavism

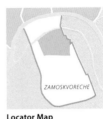

Locator Map
See Street Finder map 7

PYATNITSKAYA ULITSA

**Novokuznetskaya Metro
Station**, designed by Ivan
Taranov and Natalia Bykova,
was opened in 1943 at the
height of World War II, and
the design of the interior is
based on military subjects.

Key

— Suggested route

KLIMENTOVSKIY PEREULOK

Tretyakovskaya

Small shops on
Klimentovskiy pereulok
sell groceries, magazines,
perfumes and other goods.

The Dolgov House has
an elaborately decorated
Neo-Classical exterior.
This fine town house
was built in the 1770s
for a wealthy merchant
named Dolgov, possibly
by his son-in-law, Vasiliy
Bazhenov *(see p46)*.

❺ Church of St Clement
Building began on this splendid
Baroque church in 1720 and
continued in phases over the
next few decades: in 1756–8
a rectory and belfry were added.
The church has four black, star-
spangled domes and a central
golden dome.

For keys to symbols *see back flap*

❶ Tretyakov Gallery

Третьяковская галерея
Tretyakovskaya galereya

The Tretyakov Gallery was founded in 1856 by the wealthy merchant Pavel Tretyakov. He presented his private museum of Russian art to the city in 1892. His brother Sergey also donated a number of works and the gallery's collection has been expanding ever since. Today the Tretyakov has the largest collection of Russian art in the world. The building has a striking façade, designed by artist Viktor Vasnetsov, with a bas-relief of St George and the dragon at its centre. Many of the early 20th-century works from the collection are now housed in the Tretyakov on Krymsky Val, also known as the New Tretyakov (*see p137*).

Stairs down to ground floor

Portraits by Ivan Kramskoy (*see p122*)

First floor

The Rooks Have Come (1871)
This bleak winter scene by Aleksey Savrasov contains a message of hope: rooks are taken by Russians as a sign of the coming spring.

The Appearance of Christ to the People
is by the 19th-century Romantic artist, Aleksandr Ivanov (*see p123*).

Portrait of Arseny Tropinin, the Artist's Son (c.1818)
This portrait was painted by the renowned artist Vasiliy Tropinin. He was a serf for 47 years before gaining his freedom and finding commercial success.

Stairs from basement

Portraits by Ilya Repin (*see p122*)

Gallery Guide

The gallery has 62 rooms on two main floors. On entering the museum, visitors first descend to the basement ticket office, then head straight up to the first floor. Paintings are hung in chronological order in rooms 1–48, while rooms 49–54 display drawings and engravings. Russian jewellery is housed in the ground floor in room 55, while rooms 56–62 contain icons and jewellery.

★ **Demon Seated (1890)** This is one of several paintings by Mikhail Vrubel, who adopted a new, strikingly modern style. They are inspired by Mikhail Lermontov's Symbolist poem, *The Demon (see p84)*, with which Vrubel became obsessed.

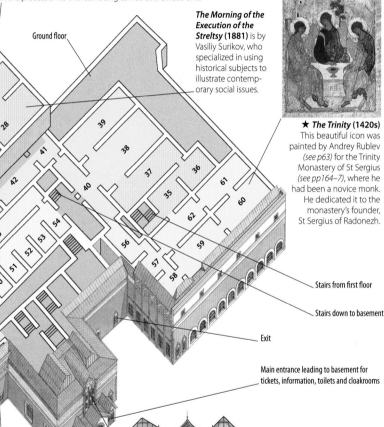

Religious Procession in Kursk Province (1881–3)
Ilya Repin painted this to show the different attitudes of those in the procession to the icon being carried at the head of it.

The Morning of the Execution of the Streltsy (1881) is by Vasiliy Surikov, who specialized in using historical subjects to illustrate contemporary social issues.

Ground floor

28
39
38
41
37 36
42
40 35 61
54 60
55 53 56 62
52 57 59
51 58
50

Russian jewellery

Main Façade
The gallery's façade was designed in 1902–04 by Viktor Vasnetsov. An example of the Russian-Revival style *(see p47)*, it has a frieze inspired by medieval manuscripts.

★ **The Trinity (1420s)**
This beautiful icon was painted by Andrey Rublev *(see p63)* for the Trinity Monastery of St Sergius *(see pp164–7)*, where he had been a novice monk. He dedicated it to the monastery's founder, St Sergius of Radonezh.

Stairs from first floor

Stairs down to basement

Exit

Main entrance leading to basement for tickets, information, toilets and cloakrooms

VISITORS' CHECKLIST

Practical Information
Lavrushinskiy pereulok 10.
Map 7 A3. **Tel** (495) 951 1362.
Open 10am–6pm Tue, Wed, Sat & Sun, 10am–9pm Thu & Fri.
tretyakov.ru

Transport
Tretyakovskaya. 6, K, 25.
1, 4, 8, 33, 62.

Key

18th and early 19th centuries

Second half of the 19th century

Late 19th and early 20th centuries

Drawings and watercolours of the 18th to 20th centuries

Icons and jewellery

Non-exhibition space

Exploring the Tretyakov Gallery

Although the gallery's collection began with the paintings donated by Pavel Tretyakov, it continued to expand after the Revolution as numerous private collections were nationalized by the Soviet regime. There are currently more than 160,000 Russian works in the collection. Paintings from after the Revolution – mainly Socialist-Realist works – are now exhibited in the New Tretyakov Gallery (*see p137*), while the main gallery displays Russian art ranging from the icons of the medieval period to early 20th-century paintings.

Pavel Tretyakov

Pavel Tretyakov began collecting Russian art in 1856 and was particularly interested in works by the Wanderers (*peredvizhniki*). His collection grew and in 1892 he donated it to the city of Moscow. His home was opened as a gallery and, much extended, still houses the collection today. Pavel Tretyakov was director of the gallery for the last 6 years of his life.

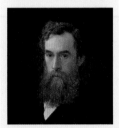

Portrait of Pavel Tretyakov (1876), by Ivan Kramskoy

Portrait of Countess Ursula Mniszek (1782) by Dmitriy Levitskiy

18th and Early 19th Centuries

Painting in Russia was exclusively religious in character for over 600 years. However, a profound transformation occurred in the 18th century as secular art from Europe began to influence Russian artists. Portrait painting came into its own with technically accomplished canvases by artists such as Vladimir Borovikovskiy (1757–1825), Fyodor Rokotov (c.1735–1808) and Dmitriy Levitskiy (1735–1822), whose *Portrait of Countess Ursula Mniszek* (1782) is among those in the gallery. The Romantic movement is represented in the collection by such pictures as Vasiliy Tropinin's (1780–1857) refined but sentimental portrait of his son and Orest Kiprenskiy's (1782–1836) famous *Portrait of the Poet Alexander Pushkin* (1827). Several of Aleksandr Ivanov's (1806–58) canvases are also displayed, including his outstanding *The Appearance of Christ to the People*. Begun in 1837, it took 20 years to finish.

Second Half of the 19th Century

The art of this period was dominated by Realism. In 1870 a group of artists founded the Association of Travelling Art Exhibitions. Its members, who became known as the Wanderers (*peredvizhniki*), began to produce "socially useful art" highlighting injustices and inequalities. One of the leaders of the movement was Vasiliy Perov (1834–82) whose satirical *Tea-drinking in Mytishchi* (1862) exposes hypocrisy among the clergy. Another Wanderer was Vasiliy Surikov (1848–1916), whose picture of *The Morning of the Execution of the Streltsy* (1881) instils new realism into a dramatic episode of Russian history. Ivan Kramskoy, the head of the group, aimed to portray the moral character of his subjects in paintings such as *Portrait of Pavel Tretyakov*.

Landscapes were popular subjects for the Wanderers and the gallery's many examples include Vasiliy Polenov's (1844–1927) *A Moscow Courtyard* (1878).

A number of works by Ilya Repin (1844–1930), the most versatile of the Wanderers, are on display. They include the enormous canvases *Religious Procession in Kursk Province* (1881–3); *They Did Not Expect Him* (1884–8) and *Ivan the Terrible and his Son Ivan on 16 November, 1581,*

Ivan the Terrible and his Son Ivan on 16 November, 1581 (1885), by Ilya Repin

Above the Eternal Peace (1894), painted by Isaak Levitan

and striking portraits of Repin's friends and contemporaries. Vasiliy Vereschagin (1842–1904), whose paintings are on display in room 27, was close to the Wanderers in the character of his work, which reflected his desire to achieve an objective creation of reality. One of Vereschagin's most famous works is *Apotheosis of War* (1871), depicting a pyramid of skulls with a plundered city in the distance. It was ironically dedicated to "all the great conquerors of the past, present and future". He was revolutionary in his approach to exhibitions, being the first artist in Russia to present his work in specially prepared environments, with darkened halls and black walls enhancing the mood of his paintings.

Late 19th and Early 20th Centuries

During the 1890s, the social ideals that inspired the Wanderers no longer appealed to a new generation of artists. Instead they rallied behind a call for "art for art's sake".

The innovative artist Mikhail Vrubel (1856–1910) was influenced by the poetry of the Russian Symbolists. Many of his dark works, such as *Demon Seated* (1890), also reflect his troubled mental state.

French painting had a huge impact on this and subsequent generations of artists. This influence can be seen in the Impressionist work *Paris,*

Boulevard des Capucines, painted in 1911 by Konstantin Korovin. The style of Valentin Serov's (1865–1911) early paintings was also close to Impressionism. His *Girl with Peaches* (1887) *(see p49)* is a portrait of the daughter of art patron Savva Mamontov.

In the decade leading up to World War I, Moscow was the centre of Russia's avant-garde movement, receptive to developments from abroad, such as Cubism and Futurism, as well as taking ideas from indigenous folk art, which inspired Primitivism. Primitivist works feature bold shapes and bright colours. *Staro Basmannaya – Board No. 1* (1916) by Vladimir Tatlin (1885–1953) and *Bathing Horses* (1911) by Natalya Goncharova (1881–1962) are among the works in this style.

The Transfiguration (c.1403), painted by a follower of Theophanes the Greek

Drawings and Watercolours

The gallery owns a substantial collection of sketches, lithographs and watercolours by artists from the 18th to 20th centuries but, to avoid exhibits being damaged by exposure to light, only a small proportion are on show at any time.

Among the watercolours are a delightful equestrian portrait by Karl Bryullov (1799–1852) and some preparatory biblical sketches by Aleksandr Ivanov. Landscapes by Isaak Levitan (1860–1900) and Ivan Shishkin (1832–98) contrast with delicate pencil portraits by artists as diverse as Ilya Repin, Valentin Serov and Konstantin Somov.

Icons and Jewellery

A fine collection of icons dating from the 12th to the 19th centuries is housed in the Tretyakov. One of the most revered icons is the 12th-century Virgin of Vladimir *(see p63)*, which originated in Byzantium.

The palette and style of Russian icon painting was derived from the Byzantine masters. However, masters such as Andrei Rublev and Daniil Chyomy raised iconography to new heights by modifying the style and lightening their palettes. A typical example is *The Transfiguration* (early 1400s) by a follower of Theophanes the Greek *(see p63)*. It depicts Christ emitting a divine light with the apostles prostrate at his feet.

Andrey Rublev's stunning icon *The Trinity* dates from around 1425–7.

Alongside it are icons by other masters of the Moscow school *(see p63)*.

Also on the ground floor is a room devoted to Russian jewellery from the 13th to the 20th centuries.

❷ Church of the Resurrection in Kadashi

Храм Воскресения в Кадашах

Khram Voskreseniya v Kadashakh

2-oy Kadashevskiy pereulok 7.
Map 7 B3. **Ⓜ** Tretyakovskaya.
Open 8am–7pm daily. **🔲** English
(book in advance on (495) 953 2291).

This five-domed church is among the most striking examples of Moscow Baroque *(see p46)* and is thought to have been designed by Sergey Turchaninov, favourite architect of Patriarch Nikon *(see pp59)*. The small group of buildings around it also includes a refectory and tiered bell tower. It was paid for by a wealthy guild of weavers who had moved into the street by the 17th century. Before that an earlier church stood here, in what was at that time the district of Kadeshevo, hence the name that survives today.

The church was built around 1687, and the slender, tapering bell tower added in the 1690s. Apart from the five gilded onion domes, the most notable features are the tiers of lace-like limestone balustrades just below the drums supporting the domes. The church also houses an art restoration workshop and two small museums.

❸ Church of the Consolation of All Sorrows

Церковь Богоматери Всех Скорбящих Радость

Tserkov Bogomateri Vsekh Skorbyashchikh Radost

Ulitsa Bolshaya Ordynka 20. **Map** 7 B3.
Ⓜ Tretyakovskaya. **Open** 7am–8pm daily.

Both the church of the Consolation of All Sorrows and the Neo-Classical yellow mansion opposite belonged to the Dolgovs, a wealthy merchant family. After completion of their

The Empire-style Church of the Consolation of All Sorrows

house in the 1770s, they commissioned the church from Vasiliy Bazhenov *(see p46)*, a relation by marriage. He first built a new belfry and refectory, which are among the few surviving buildings in Moscow by this talented architect, and then replaced the existing medieval church in 1783–91. It was finished by the Kumanins, another merchant family.

That church, however, was destroyed in the great fire of 1812 *(see p26)*. Another new one was designed by Osip Bove *(see p47)*, who was the architect in charge of Moscow's reconstruction after the fire. His Empire-style rotunda and dome were finished in 1833.

The interior is unusual in an Orthodox church due to its lavish Empire-style colonnade, theatrical iconostasis and exuberant sculpted angels. On display in the church's left aisle, originally dedicated to the Transfiguration, is the Icon of Our Lady of Consolation of All Sorrows. It is said to have miraculously cured the ailing sister of Patriarch Joachim in the 17th century.

❹ Church of St Clement

Церковь Святого Климента

Tserkov Svyatovo Klimenta

Klimentovskiy pereulok 7. **Map** 7 B3.
Ⓜ Tretyakovskaya. **Open** 10am–6pm daily.

This imposing, red-painted 18th-century church, named after the Roman Catholic

The bell tower and domes of the Church of the Resurrection in Kadashi

The remarkably decorated, 17th-century Church of St Nicholas in Pyzhy

constructed between 1670 and 72 in the area of the city once inhabited by the Streltsy, the royal guard, who provided the funds for it. Some of these men were later executed by Peter the Great for their role in the 1682 Streltsy Rebellion *(see p24)*. Funds were, in particular, generously lavished on the exterior decoration, which includes remarkable fretted cornices. The church's slender, tiered bell tower is one of the finest in the city, whilst the iconostasis contains some original icons as well as copies of more famous ones.

Pope St Clement, is now in a sadly decayed state. In 1756–8 the present refectory and belfry were built onto a church dating from the 1720s. This was pulled down in the 1760s when a new church was commissioned. The result is an outstanding example of late Moscow

Baroque. The design is thought to have been conceived by the Italian architect Pietro Antonio Trezzini. The building of the church was completed by 1774.

The red and white façade is crowned by four black domes with golden stars surrounding a fifth, golden, cupola. In the Soviet era, the Lenin State Library stored its books here, but services resumed in 2005.

❺ Church of St Nicholas in Pyzhy

Церковь Николая в Пыжах
Tserkov Nikolaya v Pyzhakh

Ulitsa Bolshaya Ordynka 27a/8.
Map 7 B3. **M** Tretyakovskaya.
Open 7:30am–8pm daily.

Small crowns, as well as the traditional crosses, decorate the silver domes of this splendid church. It was

Baroque domes of the Church of St Clement, completed in 1774

❻ Church of St Catherine

Церковь Екатерины
Tserkov Yekateriny

Ulitsa Bolshaya Ordynka 60/2.
Map 7 B3. **M** Tretyakovskaya.
Open 10am–6pm daily.

Originally a wooden church built by the cosmetic merchants' guild in the 16th century, Catherine the Great commissioned the architect Karl Blank to redesign and rebuild the church in the 1760s. It is dedicated to St Catherine of Alexandria who was beheaded in the 4th century on the orders of the Roman emperor Maximian for refusing to renounce her Christian faith.

The distinct architecture of the Church of St Catherine combines certain elements of Moscow Baroque and Rococo. Of interest are the ornate metal railings outside, which are superb and unique examples of 18th-century metalwork. Originally, they were located in the Kremlin between the Cathedral of the Archangel Michael and the Patriarchal Palace.

In 1931 the church was closed, its bell tower dismantled and almost all the icons (painted by Levitsky and Vasilevsky) were removed. It underwent further restoration in the 1990s and 2000s to return it to its former glory.

The Convent of SS Martha and Mary, founded in 1908 and designed by Aleksey Shchusev

❼ Convent of SS Martha and Mary

Марфо-Мариинская обитель

Marfo-Mariinskaya obitel

Ulitsa Bolshaya Ordynka 34.
Map 7 B4. **Tel** (495) 951 1139.
Ⓜ Tretyakovskaya, Polyanka.
Open 8am–8pm daily.

A low archway leads from the street to this secluded compound, containing what appear at first glance to be medieval buildings. In fact they date from 1908–12 and were designed by Aleksey Shchusev *(see p47)*.

The convent was conceived to house a dispensary, a clinic, a small women's hospital and a school. It was run by the Order of the Sisters of Charity which was founded by the Grand Duchess Yelizaveta Fyodorovna, sister-in-law of Tsar Nicholas II. She had turned to charitable work after her husband, Grand Prince Sergei (Tsar Nicholas II's uncle), was assassinated by a terrorist bomb in the troubled year of 1905 *(see p28)*. Yelizaveta also met a violent death: the day after the shooting of Tsar Nicholas II and his family in 1918, the Bolsheviks pushed her down a mine shaft with further members of the royal family. When designing the Church of the Intercession, the convent's main building, Shchusev carried out considerable research into Russian religious architecture, particularly that of the Pskov and Novgorod schools *(see p46)*. Shchusev's ingenious design juxtaposed a highly traditional style with Style-Moderne features such as boldly pointed gables, limestone carvings of mythical creatures and Slavonic script on the outer walls.

The artist Mikhail Nesterov, a protégé of industrialist and art patron Savva Mamontov *(see p162)*, was commissioned to design and paint the frescoes in the interior of the church. He also designed the pale grey and white habits of the nuns.

After the Revolution the Order of the Sisters of Charity was suppressed and the church was used as a workshop for restoring icons for a number of years. The nuns have now returned to staff the clinic.

❽ Tropinin Museum

Музей ВА Тропинина

Muzey VA Tropinina

Shchetininskiy pereulok 10. **Map** 7 B4.
Tel (495) 959 1103. Ⓜ Dobryninskaya,
Polyanka. **Open** 1–8pm Thu,
10am–6pm Fri–Mon. **Closed** last Mon
of the month. 🎫 📷 ♿

A highly talented portrait artist, Vasiliy Tropinin executed a staggering 3,000 paintings in his life. As well as painting figures in high society, he is noted as one of the first Russian artists to depict working people. Works spanning his career are displayed in this attractive museum set in a blue and white Neo-Classical house. The furnishings and ornaments are from Tropinin's time and are mostly in Empire style.

The museum's collection is based on works gathered by Feliks Vishnevskiy (1902–78). Having been a supporter of the Revolution, he was able to collect during the Soviet period when paintings were relatively cheap. In addition to Tropinin's oil portraits, there are works by

Girl in Ukrainian Dress painted by Vasiliy Tropinin

Vasiliy Tropinin (1776–1857)

Though born a serf in Karpovo near Novgorod, Vasiliy Tropinin's prodigious talent was recognized at an early age. He was sent to the St Petersburg Academy of Arts in 1798, but was withdrawn by his master and brought back to work as an interior decorator, pastry-cook and footman on his estates. Tropinin and his wife gained their freedom in 1823 and moved to Moscow, where Tropinin became a professional portrait artist. Unlike many other painters of the time, he did not limit himself to painting members of the aristocracy. Instead, his portraits depicted a cross-section of society, from peasants to nobles.

Some of the Empire-style furnishings in the Tropinin Museum

some of his contemporaries, including Orest Kiprenskiy and Dmitriy Levitskiy. Like Tropinin, they were students at the St Petersburg Academy of Arts.

❾ Bakhrushin Theatre Museum

Театральный музей имени А.А. Бахрушина
Teatralnyy muzey imeni AA Bakhrushina

Ulitsa Bakhrushina 31/12. **Map** 7 C5. **Tel** (495) 953 4470. Ⓜ Paveletskaya. **Open** noon–7pm Wed–Mon (last ticket 6pm). **Closed** last Mon of the month. 🅿 ♿ 📷 English (book in advance).

Founded in 1894 by Aleksey Bakhrushin, a merchant and patron of the arts, this museum contains probably the most important collection of theatre memorabilia in Russia. Spread over two floors, the exhibits range from sets and costumes to theatre tickets, programmes, advertisements and signed photographs.

The permanent exhibition begins in the study, where visitors can peruse a selection of Bakhrushin's personal belongings, as well as photographs and paintings depicting family life. From here, stairs lead down into the basement, which hosts temporary exhibitions on a variety of themes related to acting and the theatre.

Exhibits on 19th-century theatre include costumes and sets from the Ballets Russes. This famous company, formed by Sergey Diaghilev in 1909, revolutionized ballet. The sets include some designed by Michel Fokine, the company's inspired choreographer. A pair of ballet shoes belonging to Marie Taglioni, the renowned Italian-Swedish dancer who rose to fame following her father's creation of *La Sylphide* is also on show.

The room on 20th-century avant-garde theatre includes stage models created for outstanding directors Konstantin Stanislavskiy *(see p95)* and Vsevolod Meyerhold *(see p94)*.

View of the Kremlin from the Sophia Embankment

❿ Sophia Embankment

Софийская набережная
Sofiyskaya naberezhnaya

Map 7 A2. Ⓜ Kropotkinskaya, Borovitskaya, Novokuznetskaya.

Situated opposite the Kremlin, on the southern bank of the Moskva river, the Sophia Embankment stretches from the Bolshoi Kamennyy most (Great Stone bridge) to the Bolshoi Moskvoretskiy most (Great Moscow river bridge).

The embankment was built up to its current height at the end of the 18th century and was greatly improved in 1836. It offers spectacular views over the Kremlin and the city.

Novgorodians settled on the river bank in the 14th century and built the original Church of St Sophia. The present church dates from the mid-17th century. Aleksandr Kaminskiy added the bell tower in 1862.

The mansion at No. 14 was designed by Vasiliy Zalesskiy in 1893 for a sugar baron and is now the British ambassador's residence. The interiors are by Fyodor Shekhtel *(see p47)*.

Set design by Michel Fokine, on show in the Bakhrushin Theatre Museum

FURTHER AFIELD

Moscow's suburbs are generally rather bleak, but they conceal a surprising number of attractions, all accessible by metro. To the south of the centre lies a number of fortified monasteries, built to defend the city against the Mongols and the Poles. The most spectacular of them is Novodevichiy Convent, a serene 16th-century sanctuary with a glorious cathedral, but the Donskoy Monastery is also well worth a visit. The Danilovskiy Monastery, with its handsome cathedral, is the oldest in the city. Visitors to Moscow are often surprised at the beauty and variety of its green spaces. Gorky, Izmaylovo and Victory parks are the perfect places in which to relax, while Sparrow Hills offers fantastic views. The city's best-kept secrets, however, are the grand estates away from the centre in what was formerly countryside. There the Sheremetev family built two elegant Neo-Classical summer residences: Kuskovo and Ostankino. Both have beautifully preserved gardens and palaces full of fine paintings and period furnishings.

Sights at a Glance

Churches, Convents and Monasteries
❶ Church of the Intercession in Fili
❻ *Novodevichiy Convent pp132–3*
❽ Church of St Nicholas of the Weavers
❿ Church of St John the Warrior
⓫ Donskoy Monastery
⓬ Danilovskiy Monastery
⓯ Krutitskoe Mission
⓱ Monastery of the Saviour and Andronicus

Palaces
⓰ *Kuskovo pp144–5*
㉑ Ostankino Palace

Museums and Galleries
❼ Tolstoy House-Museum
❾ Tretyakov on Krymsky Val
⓭ *Kolomenskoe pp140–41*
⓴ Vasnetsov House-Museum

Historic Buildings
❷ White House
⓮ Tsaritsyno

Parks and Open Spaces
❸ Victory Park
❹ Sparrow Hills
❺ Gorky Park
⓲ Izmaylovo Park
⓳ Komsomolskaya Ploshchad
㉒ All-Russian Exhibition Centre (VVTs)

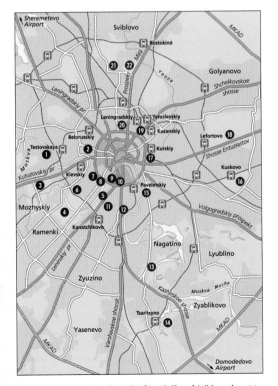

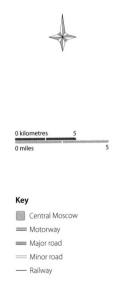

0 kilometres 5
0 miles 5

Key
▨ Central Moscow
━━ Motorway
▬▬ Major road
═══ Minor road
─── Railway

◀ The reconstructed wooden palace with its fairy-tale-like roofs in Kolomenskoe estate

For keys to symbols *see back flap*

❶ Church of the Intercession in Fili

Церковь Покрова в Филях
Tserkov Pokrova v Filyakh

Ulitsa Novozavodskaya 6. **Tel** (499) 148 4552. Ⓜ Fili. **Open** 8am–5pm Thu–Mon (May–Oct: upper church only).
🖼 🚻

This stunning church was commissioned by an uncle of Peter the Great, Prince Lev Naryshkin, and is in the style known as Moscow, or Naryshkin, Baroque *(see p46)*. Built by an unknown architect between 1690 and 1693, it is an extraordinary tiered structure of red brick, with lace-like ornamentation and pilasters of white stone.

Russian churches often comprise two buildings: a grand, unheated one for summer, and a smaller, simpler one that can be heated easily in winter.

Here, the winter church at ground level has changing displays of religious art. In front of it a double staircase rises to a terrace surrounding the upper summer church. This staircase would once have provided the setting for processions. Inside, there is an iconostasis, mainly the work of the 17th-century painter Karp Zolotarev, and a carved gilt pew used by Peter the Great.

The elegant Church of the Intercession in Fili, the city's best example of Moscow Baroque

Gilded crest on the clock tower of the White House

❷ White House

Белый дом
Belyy dom

Krasnopresnenskaya naberezhnaya 2. **Map** 1 B5. Ⓜ Krasnopresnenskaya. **Closed** to public.

A marble-clad building with a gilded clock tower, the White House is still a "must-see" for tourists interested in recent political history.

Once the seat of the Russian Federation's parliament, it first claimed the world's attention in August 1991 when it was the focus of resistance to the Communist hardliners' coup against Mikhail Gorbachev, the president of the Soviet Union. The rebels detained Gorbachev at his Black Sea villa, where he was holidaying at the time, so it was Boris Yeltsin, the president of the smaller Russian Federation, who led the opposition to the coup. The world watched as he passed through the lines of tanks surrounding the White House without anyone daring to arrest him. Then he climbed onto a tank to proclaim: "You can build a throne of bayonets, but you cannot sit on it for long".

The coup failed, and the victory of Yeltsin and his supporters was soon followed by the break-up of the Soviet Union and the end of Communist rule.

However, in September 1993, a reversal of roles occurred at the White House when Yeltsin became the besieger.

Hundreds of deputies locked themselves into it in protest when Yeltsin summarily suspended parliament over its increasing opposition to his new draft constitution. The siege ended after 2 weeks when army tanks bombarded the deputies into submission.

The charred building was quickly repaired, but never regained its former significance; today the Russian parliament occupies a building on ulitsa Okhotnyy ryad *(see p88)*, and the presidential offices are in the Kremlin *(see pp54–69)*.

The Triumphal Arch, celebrating Napoleon's defeat in the 1812 war

❸ Victory Park

Парк победы
Park pobedy

Kutuzovskiy prospekt. Ⓜ Kutuzovskaya. Museum of the Great Patriotic War: **Tel** (499) 148 5550. **Open** 10am–6pm Tue–Sun. **Closed** Last Thu of the month. ♿ Borodino Panorama Museum: **Tel** (499) 148 1927. **Open** 10am–6pm Sat–Thu. 🖼 🚻

Commemorating victory in the Great Patriotic War, the Russian name for World War II), Victory Park was originally intended to have a vast monument to Mother Russia at its centre. After the end of Communist rule, plans were scaled down and the park was finally completed in 1995, in time for the 50th anniversary of the end of the war.

The park is formally laid out, with straight alleys dividing the

The Stalinist-Gothic skyscraper of the Moscow State University

sparsely treed grass. The main, fountain-lined avenue leads from Kutuzovskiy prospekt to the central Nike Monument, a towering, 142-m (466-ft) obelisk designed by Zurab Tsereteli to honour the Greek goddess of victory.

Behind the monument is the domed, semicircular Museum of the Great Patriotic War. The dioramas, models, maps and weapons on show give an informative picture of the war as experienced by the Russians.

Just to the side of the central avenue is the simple Church of St George the Victorious, built in 1995, probably the first to be built in Russia after the Revolution. Next to it is a monument to war victims.

East along Kutuzovskiy prospekt are two large-scale memorials to the war of 1812 (see pp25–7). Moscow's final deliverance from the French is celebrated by the grand Triumphal Arch. It was designed by Osip Bove (see p47), with sculptures of Russian and Classical warriors by Ivan Vitali and Ivan Timofeev. Originally built on Tverskaya ulitsa in 1834, the arch was dismantled in the 1930s during street-widening. The sculptures were preserved and in 1968 the arch was rebuilt at its present site.

Further along the street, at No. 38, is the circular Borodino Panorama Museum, which contains a vast painting, 115-m (377-ft) long and 14-m (46-ft)

high. It was created by Franz Roubaud in 1912 to mark the centenary of the battle between Russian forces and Napoleon's army at Borodino (see pp160–61).

4 Sparrow Hills
Воробьёвы горы
Vorobevy gory

Ⓜ Universitet.

The summit of this wooded ridge offers unsurpassed views across the city. There is an observation point on ulitsa Kosygina and newly-wed couples traditionally come here to have their photograph taken against the panorama. It is also a favourite pitch for a large number of souvenir sellers.

The hills are dominated by the Moscow State University (MGU) building commissioned by Stalin, designed by Lev Rudnev and completed in 1953. At 36 floors high it is the tallest of the seven Stalinist-Gothic "wedding-cakes" (see p47).

The small, green-domed Church of the Trinity (1811) can also be seen close by, to the left of the observation platform. There are also a couple of long, but somewhat rickety, ski jumps on the hills.

On prospekt Vernadskovo, on the southeast edge of the hills, is the Palace of Youth and Creative

Plaque at the entrance to Gorky Park

Work, a studio complex built for the Communist youth organization. Also on this street are the silver-roofed New Moscow Circus (see p198) built in 1971, and the Nataliya Sats Children's Musical Theatre (see p199).

5 Gorky Park
Парк культуры и отдыха имени М. Горького
Park Kultury i otdykha imeni M. Gorkovo

Krymskiy val 9. **Map** 6 E4. Ⓜ Park Kultury, Oktyabrskaya. **Tel** (495) 237 0707. **Open** 24 hours daily. 🏖 ♿ ▯

Moscow's most famous park is named in honour of the writer Maxim Gorky and extends for more than 120 ha (297 acres) along the banks of the Moskva river. Opened in 1928 as the Park of Culture and Rest, it incorporates the Golitsyn Gardens, laid out by Matvey Kazakov (see p46) in the late 18th century, and a 19th-century pleasure park. During the Soviet era, loud-speakers were used to deliver speeches by Communist leaders across the park. Today the highlights include fairground rides, woodland walks, boating lakes, a 10,000-seat outdoor theatre and, in the winter months, an ice rink.

The park was immortalized in the opening scenes of Michael Apted's film *Gorky Park*. However, because of the tense political climate of 1983, the film was actually shot in Finland.

Outdoor ice-skating in Gorky Park, a popular activity in the winter months

❻ Novodevichiy Convent

Новодевичий монастырь
Novodevichiy monastyr

Probably the most beautiful of the semicircle of fortified religious institutions to the south of Moscow is Novodevichiy Convent, founded by Basil III in 1524 to commemorate the capture of Smolensk from the Lithuanians. Only the Cathedral of the Virgin of Smolensk was built at this time. Most of the other buildings were added in the late 17th century by Peter the Great's half-sister, the Regent Sophia. After Peter deposed her and reclaimed his throne in 1689 *(see p24)*, he confined her here for the rest of her life. In 1812 Napoleon's troops tried to blow up the convent but, according to a popular story, it was saved by the nuns, who snuffed out the fuses.

Gate Church of the Intercession
It is not known who designed this church, but it is believed to have been built in the second half of the 17th century.

KEY

① **Shoemaker's Tower**

② **Vorobeva Tower**

③ **Maria's Chambers** were used by the daughter of Tsar Alexis Mikhailovich, Maria.

④ **Church of St Ambrose**

⑤ **The Palace of Irina Gudunova** was home to the widow of Tsar Fyodor I.

⑥ **The Church of the Assumption** and adjoining refectory were built in the 1680s on the orders of the Regent Sophia.

⑦ **Refectory**

⑧ **Setunskaya Tower**

⑨ **Faceted Tower**

⑩ **Saviour's Tower**

⑪ **Nuns' cells**

⑫ **This guard house** is where the Regent Sophia was imprisoned.

⑬ **Naprudnaya Tower**

⑭ **Tsaritsa's Tower**

⑮ **St Nicholas' Tower**

⑯ **Tailor's Tower**

⑰ **Hospital**

Novodevichiy
Cemetery

| 0 metres | 25 |
| 0 yards | 25 |

★ **Cathedral of the Virgin of Smolensk**
The oldest building in the convent is the cathedral, built in 1524. The five-tier iconostasis, the rich frescoes and the onion domes all date from the 17th century.

Novodevichiy Cemetery

Many famous Russians are buried in this cemetery. Among the leading cultural figures are playwright Anton Chekhov, writers Nikolai Gogol and Mikhail Bulgakov, composers Sergey Prokofiev, Aleksandr Skryabin *(see p74)* and Dmitriy Shostakovich and opera singer Fyodor Shalyapin *(see p85)*. The cemetery is also the final resting place for many military and political dignitaries, including Nikita Khrushchev *(see p32)* and Boris Yeltsin.

The tombstone of Nikita Khrushchev

VISITORS' CHECKLIST

Practical Information
Novodevichiy proezd 1. **Tel** (499) 246 8526. **Open** 10am–5pm Wed–Mon. **Closed** some public hols. 🎫 ♿ grounds only. 📷 Cemetery: **Tel** (499) 246 6614. **Open** 10am–5pm daily.

Transport
Ⓜ Sportivnaya. 🚌 64, 132 *(see p227)*. 🚋 5, 15.

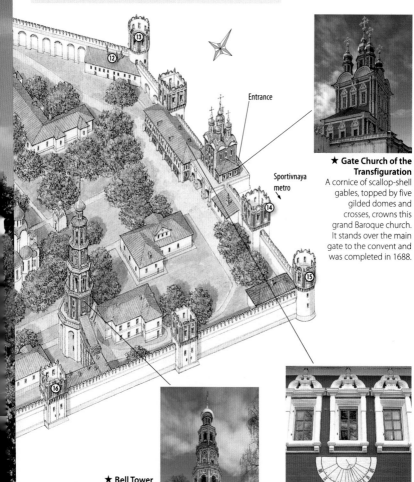

Entrance

Sportivnaya metro →

★ **Gate Church of the Transfiguration**
A cornice of scallop-shell gables, topped by five gilded domes and crosses, crowns this grand Baroque church. It stands over the main gate to the convent and was completed in 1688.

★ **Bell Tower**
Completed in 1690, this tower is one of the most exuberant examples of Baroque architecture in Moscow. The Church of St John the Divine occupies the second storey of the six-tiered, octagonal tower, which stands 72 m (236 ft) high.

Lopukhin Palace
This palace was built in 1687–9. After Peter the Great's death in 1725 his first wife, Yevdokiya Lopukhina, moved here from the Suzdal convent where she had been sent after Peter tired of her.

Magnificent towers and domed churches of Novodevichiy Convent, a UNESCO World Heritage Site ▶

❼ Tolstoy House-Museum

Музей-усадьба ЛН Толстого

Muzey-usadba LN Tolstovo

Ulitsa Lva Tolstovo 21. **Map** 6 D4.
Tel (499) 246 9444. Ⓜ Park Kultury.
Open 11am–6pm Tue, Wed & Fri–Sun,
noon–8pm Thu. 🅿 📷 English (book
in advance). Ⓦ **tolstoymuseum.ru**

The presence of one of Russia's greatest novelists can be felt in every corner of this evocative, wooden house. It was here that Leo Tolstoy (1828–1910) spent the winters between 1882 and 1901 with his long-suffering wife, Sofya Andreevna, and the nine surviving of their 13 children. The summers were spent on the Tolstoy ancestral estate at Yasnaya Polyana *(see p169)*, 200 km (124 miles) away.

The Moscow house was turned into a museum in 1921 on Lenin's orders and has been preserved much as it would have been when Tolstoy and his family resided here.

On the ground floor, the table in the dining room is laid with crockery. The evening meal in the Tolstoy household always began promptly at 6pm to the summons of the cuckoo clock on the wall. Next door is the "corner room" where, at one time, the elder sons, Sergey, Ilya and Lev, would retire to play Chinese billiards. The house

Leo Tolstoy

By the time Tolstoy was in his 50s, he was an author of international renown and had written his two great masterpieces *War and Peace* (1865–9) and *Anna Karenina* (1873–7). He continued to write fiction, but later renounced his earlier books and the world they depicted. Instead Tolstoy concentrated on his highly individual brand of Christian Humanism, a doctrine that included non-violence, vegetarianism and sexual abstinence. It was in this period that he wrote the stories *The Death of Ivan Ilych* and the *Kreutzer Sonata* and his last great novel, *Resurrection*, which strayed so far from Orthodoxy that the Holy Synod excommunicated him in 1901. Tolstoy left Moscow the same year for Yasnaya Polyana, where he devoted himself to the education of the peasants on the estate.

The dining room, with a painting of Tolstoy's favourite daughter, Mariya

exudes a sense of ordered, comfortable family life, but Tolstoy and his wife frequently quarrelled violently, largely on account of his wish to renounce society and live as simply as possible. The couple were reconciled for a short time when Vanya, their much-loved youngest child died from scarlet fever before reaching his seventh birthday. His memory is preserved in his small bedroom, where his high chair, rocking horse and books can be seen.

The bedroom of Tolstoy's second daughter, Tatyana, is crammed with ornaments and keepsakes. She was a talented artist and her own paintings and sketches are hung on the walls.

The stairs to the first floor open into the salon, a large hall where frequent

guests were treated to supper. They included the young Sergei Rachmaninov who accompanied the bass, Fyodor Shalyapin *(see p85)*, on the piano here, the artist Ilya Repin, whose portrait of Tatyana now hangs in the "corner room", the music critic Vladimir Stasov, and the writer Maxim Gorky *(see p97)* with whom Tolstoy would play chess. The drawing room next door was decorated by Sofya Andreevna herself.

The bedroom of Tolstoy's favourite child, Mariya, is rather spartan, testifying to her sympathy for her father's ideals and way of life.

At the far end of the upstairs passage is Tolstoy's study, a spacious room overlooking the garden. Reflecting his passion for austerity, the room is simply furnished in black leather. The plain, solid desk where he wrote his novel *Resurrection* is lit by candles. Rather than admit to being shortsighted, Tolstoy sawed off the ends of his chair legs to bring himself closer to his papers. In the adjoining washroom are dumbbells and a bicycle – evidence of his interest in keeping fit. Also on show are the tools he used for his hobby of shoe-making, with some of the pairs he made. The back stairs close by lead to the garden, which is only accessible to those taking a guided tour.

The simple desk in Tolstoy's study where he wrote his final novel, *Resurrection*

The luxurious interior of the Church of St Nicholas of the Weavers

❽ Church of St Nicholas of the Weavers

Церковь Святителя Николая в Хамовниках

Tserkov Svyatitelya Nikolaya v Khamovnikakh

Ulitsa Lva Tolstovo 2. **Map** 6 D4. **Tel** (499) 255 3071. Ⓜ Park Kultury. **Open** 7:30am–8pm daily. ♿

Dedicated to the patron saint of weavers, sailors and farmers, this spectacular church was founded in 1679 by local weavers (*khamovniki*). Their aim was to surpass the Church of the Resurrection in Kadashi (*see p124*), which was built a few years before by rival weavers across the river.

While staying at their winter home nearby, Tolstoy and his family used to attend services

here until his rift with the Church authorities. The church continued to function throughout the Communist era.

The exterior is decorated with vivid orange and green gables and topped with five golden domes, while the walls are decorated with patterned tiles imitating woven motifs.

Inside the church there is an iconostasis featuring a 17th-century Icon of St Nicholas. A separate Icon of the Virgin, Helper of Sinners, is reputed to perform miracles.

❾ Tretyakov on Krymsky Val

Третьяковская галерея на крымском валу

Tretyakovskaya galereya na Krymskom Valu

Krymskiy val 10. **Map** 6 F3. **Tel** (499) 230 7788. Ⓜ Park Kultury, Oktyabrskaya. **Open** 10am–7:30pm Tue–Sun. ♿ 🅰 🅲 English. 🆆 tretyakov.ru

This huge white box of a building is an annexe of the Tretyakov Gallery (*see pp120–23*) in the centre of town. It is devoted to Russian art from the early 1900s to the present. Most of the canvases here belong to the official movement known as Socialist Realism and reflect the cultural straitjacket imposed by Stalin (*see p29*). It had its roots in

the Wanderers movement of the 1860s, which was based on the principle that art has, first and foremost, a social role to play, though lyricism and beauty in paintings were also important (*see p122*). In contrast, the hard-hitting art of the Communist era served the state's interests, reflecting socialist goals and achievements. A few examples of the titles given to the paintings say it all: *Life is Getting Better; Building New Factories; Unforgettable Meeting* (between Stalin and a spellbound young woman). Technological achievements were also immortalized in pictures such as *The First Russian Airship*.

Many people will find the Modernist paintings at the beginning of the exhibition more aesthetically pleasing. These include pictures by previously outlawed artists, such as the *Black Square* by Kazimir Malevich and works by Constructivists such as Aleksandr Rodchenko and the brothers Georgiy and Vladimir Stenberg.

Outside, on the Moskva river embankment, is the Graveyard of Fallen Monuments, a collection of some of the sculptures removed from around Moscow at the end of the Soviet era. Pride of place belongs to the statue of the secret police chief, Feliks Dzerzhinskiy, which was taken down from outside the KGB headquarters (*see p114*) in 1991. A striking addition to the view from the gardens is a statue of Peter the Great by Zurab Tsereteli.

The vast statue of Peter the Great, erected in 1997, viewed from the Graveyard of Fallen Monuments

The Church of St Nicholas of the Weavers, topped by golden domes

The distinctive, colourful Church of St John the Warrior

⑩ Church of St John the Warrior
Церковь Иоанна Воина
Tserkov Ioanna Voina

Ulitsa Bolshaya Yakimanka 46.
Map 6 F4. **Tel** (499) 238 2056.
Ⓜ Oktyabrskaya. ✉

The plans for this famous church, attributed to the architect Ivan Zarudniy, are said to have been personally approved by Peter the Great *(see p24)*. Building work took place from 1709 to 1713 and the result is a notable example of Petrine Baroque, a style which had begun to flourish in St Petersburg, the tsar's new capital. The church's most eye-catching feature is a tiered octagonal tower, with an elegant balustrade and splendid coloured roof tiles forming bold, geometric designs.

St John the Warrior is one of the few churches to have stayed open after the Revolution and a number of historic works of religious art were transferred here for safekeeping. These can still be seen in the church and include the 17th-century Icon of the Saviour, which hung in a chapel near the Saviour's Tower in the Kremlin. Across the road is the extremely striking Igumnov House, which was built in 1893 for a rich

merchant by Nikolay Pozdeev. It is a typically flamboyant example of Russian-Revival architecture *(see p47)*, and now houses the French Embassy.

⑪ Donskoy Monastery
Донской монастырь
Donskoy monastyr

Donskaya ploshchad 1. **Tel** (495) 952 3570. Ⓜ Shabolovskaya. **Open** 7am–7pm daily. ♿ grounds only. ✉ 📷

The Donskoy Monastery was founded in 1593 by Boris Godunov to honour the Icon of Our Lady of the Don, credited with having twice saved Russia from the Mongols. The first time was in 1380 when Prince Dmitriy Donskoy carried the icon into battle at Kulikovo *(see p163)*. Boris Godunov also used it to rally his troops in 1591 against the army of Khan Kazy Girei. The crescent moons, or half boats, below many of the golden crosses on top of the monastery buildings, symbolize the church as a ship of salvation.

The modest scale of the original monastery is reflected in the beautifully understated Small Cathedral. The orthodox prelate, Archbishop Amvrosiy, killed by a mob during a riot

in 1771, is buried within. The remains of Patriarch Tikhon, who was imprisoned by the Bolsheviks after the Revolution, were secretly buried here until 1992 when they were moved to the Grand Cathedral.

The fortified outer walls and Grand Cathedral were added in the late 17th-century when the monastery acquired greater prestige under the patronage of the Regent Sophia.

Built in 1684–98 in the Moscow-Baroque style *(see p46)*, the New Cathedral is a towering brick building with five domes. Inside are a stunning seven-tiered iconostasis and frescoes painted in 1782–5 by Italian artist Antonio Claudio. The Icon of Our Lady of the Don is now in the Tretyakov Gallery *(see pp120–23)*, but a copy is on show in the Old Cathedral.

The Donskoy Monastery's imposing 17th-century Grand Cathedral

⑫ Danilovskiy Monastery
Даниловский монастырь
Danilovskiy monastyr

Danilovskiy val 22. **Tel** (495) 958 0502.
Ⓜ Tulskaya. **Open** 7am–8pm daily.
♿ 🌐 saintdaniel.ru

Founded by Prince Daniil in 1298–1300, the Danilovskiy Monastery is the city's oldest. It was used as a factory and youth detention centre after the Revolution, but since 1988 it has been the headquarters

The Russian Orthodox Church

Christianity was adopted as Russia's official religion in AD 988 when Vladimir I *(see p19)* married the sister of the Byzantine Emperor and had himself baptized in the Orthodox faith. In the 13th century monasteries became a focus for resistance against the invading Mongols. Thereafter the Church played a vital role in Russian life until the Revolution, when it was forced underground. As the Soviet Union broke up, the church revived and, in 1992, Boris Yeltsin became the first Russian leader to attend church services since 1917.

Delicate stone tracery on the Figured Gate at Tsaritsyno

of the Russian Orthodox Church, which has offices in its more modern, plainer buildings.

The green-domed Church of the Holy Fathers of the Seven Ecumenical Councils is the oldest of the three churches within the fortified walls. It was founded by Ivan the Terrible *(see p20)* in the 16th century. The main church, on the first floor, has a 17th-century iconostasis with contemporary icons.

At the heart of the monastery is the elegant yellow Cathedral of the Trinity, designed by Osip Bove *(see p47)* in 1833 and completed 5 years later.

The pretty pink bell tower in the northern wall contains the Gate Church of St Simeon the Stylite. It was built in 1730–32, but knocked down in the 1920s. The bells were sold to Harvard University, but have now been restored to the rebuilt gate and bell tower.

⑬ Kolomenskoe

See pp140–41.

⑭ Tsaritsyno
Царицыно
Tsaritsyno

Ulitsa Dolskaya 1. **Tel** (495) 321 6366. Ⓜ Orekhovo, Tsaritsyno. **Open** Apr–Oct: 11am–6pm Tue–Sun (to 8pm Sat, to 9pm Sun); Nov–Mar: 11am–6pm Wed–Sun (to 8pm Sat, to 7pm Sun). 🐾 ♿ 🅿 English (book in advance). 🖥 Grounds: **Open** 6am–midnight daily.

Catherine the Great *(see p25)* bought this tract of land in 1775 and changed its name from Chyornaya Gryaz (Black Mud) to Tsaritsyno (the Tsarina's Village). In doing so, she commissioned one of her most imaginative architects, Vasiliy Bazhenov *(see p46)*, to design and construct a lavish imperial palace which would rival any in St Petersburg.

Bazhenov conceived an innovative palace complex combining Gothic, Baroque and even Moorish styles and Catherine approved the plans. She visited the site in 1785 and, although construction was well under way, proclaimed herself dissatisfied. Bazhenov's young colleague Matvey Kazakov *(see pp46–7)* was told to rebuild the palace but, after a further decade of construction, lack of funds left it still incomplete.

Today the grounds boast charming lakes and woodland walks. Some of the ruins have been restored, but the forlorn remainder have a beauty which the completed palace might never have matched. Although the shell of Kazakov's Grand Palace is the most imposing building on the estate, some of Bazhenov's smaller structures are equally impressive. Visitors can see the Figured Gate with its elegant Gothic-style towers and lancet windows, the Figured Bridge and the ornate two-storey Opera House, one of the few buildings Catherine approved. The extraordinary Bread Gate, with its arch of sharply pointed stone "teeth", leads to the kitchens, while the Octahedron was built as the servants' quarters. The attractive Church of Our Lady of the Life-Giving Spirit was added in the 19th century.

A small museum on the estate displays icons, china, glass and some Fabergé eggs, as well as landscapes and architectural exhibits.

The iconostasis in the Church of the Holy Fathers, Danilovskiy Monastery

⑬ Kolomenskoe

Коломенское
Kolomenskoe

The earliest known reference to Kolomenskoe village is in the will of Ivan I
(see p20), dated 1339. By the 16th century Kolomenskoe was a favourite country
estate of the tsars. The oldest surviving building is the Church of the Ascension,
constructed in 1532. A superb wooden palace was built
for Tsar Alexis Mikhailovich *(see p21)* in 1667–71, but it was
demolished in the 18th century and rebuilt according to
its original plans in 2010. After the Revolution the park
was designated a museum of architecture, and
wooden buildings, such as Peter the Great's cabin
from Archangel, were moved here from all over
Russia. Also located on the estate is the Front Gate
Museum. Its exhibits include Russian craft objects,
such as tile paintings and woodcarvings.

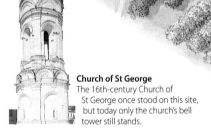

**★ Church of
the Ascension**
This magnificent
church was erected
by Basil III in 1532
to celebrate the
birth of his son Ivan
(later the Terrible).
It was the first tent-
roofed church to
be built in stone.

KEY

① **The Front Gate** was the
ceremonial entrance to Tsar Alexis'
palace. The chambers on either side
of it are now the Front Gate Museum.

② **Mead Brewery**

③ **Front Gate Museum**

④ **The Pavilion** is all that remains
of Alexander I's palace, built in 1825.

⑤ **Refectory**

⑥ **The Falcon Tower** was built in
1627. It was used as a water tower.

⑦ **This wooden gate tower** was
brought to Kolomenskoe from the St
Nicholas Monastery at Karelia in 1932.
It was built in 1692 from interlocking
sections without using a single nail.

⑧ **Front Gate Museum annexe**

⑨ **These ancient oaks** are said to
have been planted by Peter the Great.

⑩ **Bratsk Stockade Tower**

⑪ **The Boris Stone** (12th century)
bears the inscription, "Strong, brave,
holy Boris".

Church of St George
The 16th-century Church of
St George once stood on this site,
but today only the church's bell
tower still stands.

Model of Wooden Palace

Kolomenskoe underwent a major expansion during the reign
of Tsar Alexis Mikhailovich, father of Peter the Great. He added
a new centrepiece, an astonishing wooden palace with
fanciful barrel-shaped roofs, onion domes and carved
ornamentation, which visiting diplomats
described as the "eighth wonder of the
world". It was demolished in 1768 on
the orders of Catherine the Great.
Fortunately she had a model made,
according to which the palace was
reconstructed in 2010.

Church of St John the Baptist
Located to the south of the main estate, this church was commissioned by Ivan the Terrible to celebrate his accession to the throne in 1547.

Church of St John the Baptist

VISITORS' CHECKLIST

Practical Information
Prospekt Andropova 39.
Tel (499) 615 2768. Front Gate Museum & Churches:
Open 10am–5:30pm Tue–Sun. English (book in advance). Grounds:
Open 8am–9pm daily.

Transport
Kolomenskaya.

Peter the Great's Cabin
This simple log cabin was built for Tsar Peter the Great in 1702 when he visited Archangel (on the north coast of Russia). It was brought to Kolomenskoe in 1934 and its four low-ceilinged rooms restored.

0 metres 25
0 yards 25

St Saviour's Gate is the main entrance to the complex.

Kolomenskaya metro

★ Church of Our Lady of Kazan
Completed in 1650 for Tsar Alexis, this stunning church is an early example of Moscow Baroque (see p46). It is now open again for worship. A replica of the Icon of Our Lady of Kazan, which is believed to have helped Russia drive out Polish invaders in 1612, can be found inside the church.

⓯ Krutitskoe Mission

Крутицкое подворье

Krutitskoe podvorye

Krutitskaya ulitsa 11. **Map** 8 E5.
Tel (495) 676 3093. Ⓜ Proletarskaya.
Grounds: **Open** 8am–8pm daily.

The Metropolitan originally resided in the Kremlin, but after the creation of the patriarchate in the 16th century the bishops of Krutitsy became metropolitans *(see p58)*. The Mission's name derives from the Russian *krutoy*, meaning steep, and refers to the nearby bank of the Moskva river.

There is ongoing restoration work within a number of the buildings. They are dominated by the bulky Cathedral of the Assumption, which was built in 1685. The entire edifice, including the onion domes, is built of bricks.

A covered gallery links the cathedral to the Metropolitan's Palace via a double-arched gateway topped by a small pavilion or *teremok*. The gallery and pavilion are by Osip Startsev, who was famous in Russia in the late 17th century as a designer of religious buildings. The northern façade of the *teremok* is decorated with intricately carved window frames and turquoise tiles with yellow floral motifs.

The Metropolitan's Palace is a handsome, though plainer, red-brick building with pyramidal chimneys and an impressive staircase at the rear.

Since falling into disrepair early in the 19th century, the Mission has served as a barracks, a prison and, after the Revolution, a workers' hostel: their wooden living quarters did survive. Now, the youth movement of the Orthodox Church is based here.

⓰ Kuskovo

See pp144–5.

⓱ Monastery of the Saviour and Andronicus

Спасо-Андроников монастырь

Spaso-Andronikov monastyr

Andronevskaya ploshchad 10.
Map 8 F2. Ⓜ Ploshchad Ilyicha.
Open 11am–6pm Thu–Tue. Museum:
Tel (495) 678 1467. 🎫 ✉ 📷 (book in advance).

Travelling back from the city of Constantinople in 1360, Metropolitan Aleksey survived a storm at sea. To give thanks he founded the Monastery of the Saviour on the banks of the Yauza river. He then appointed the monk Andronicus to be the first abbot and to oversee the building works.

The best-known monk to have lived here was Andrey Rublev, Russia's most brilliant icon painter *(see p63)*. He is thought to have died and been buried here in about 1430, but the location of his grave is unknown. Rublev is commemorated by the monastery's Andrey Rublev

Icon of St John the Baptist, 15th century

The Cathedral of the Saviour, with characteristic *kokoshniki* gables

Museum of Old Russian Art. There are no icons by Rublev himself here, but some excellent copies of his works are on show, along with genuine pieces by his contemporaries. Original Rublev icons can be seen in the Tretyakov Gallery *(see pp120–23)*. The museum's collections, consisting of more than 150,000 paintings, sculptures and drawings, are on show in two of the monastery buildings. The 16th-century Abbot's House, decorated with tiles and just to the right of the main entrance, displays decorative arts of the 11th to 20th centuries. The Baroque Church of the Archangel Michael, built in 1691–94, displays Russian art of the 13th to 17th centuries. Highlights include the 17th-century Icon of the Tikhvin Virgin, originally from the Donskoy Monastery *(see p138)*, and paintings depicting the life of St Nicholas of Zaraysk, one of Russia's favourite saints.

The beautiful, single-domed Cathedral of the Saviour was built in either 1390 or 1425–7. If the former date is correct, this would make it the oldest church in Moscow. The original interior was destroyed by fire in 1812, but fragments of the frescoes have been restored. Traces of work by Rublev have survived around the altar windows.

Gateway at Krutitskoe, linking the cathedral to the Metropolitan's Palace

⑱ Izmaylovo Park

Парк Измайлово
Park Izmaylovo

Narodniy prospekt 17. **Tel** (499) 166
6119. Ⓜ Izmaylovskiy Park.
Open 24 hours. ♿ 🖥

One of the largest parks in
Europe, Izmaylovo covers
nearly 12 sq km (4.7 sq miles).
It features attractions such
as sports facilities, children's
amusements, cafés and woods,
as well as an outdoor theatre, a
famous flea market *(see p193)*, a
cathedral and the picturesque
remains of one of the tsars'
country estates.

Izmaylovo passed to the
Romanov family in the 16th
century and became one of
their favourite hunting lodges.
In 1663, Tsar Alexis *(see p21)* built
an enormous wooden palace
here and dedicated the land
to experiments in animal and
vegetable husbandry and
various cottage industries.

Peter the Great later spent an
idyllic childhood at Izmaylovo,
secluded from palace intrigues.
It was here that his lifelong
fascination with the sea began,
when he learned to sail an old
boat on a lake. The boat was
later nicknamed the "grandfather of the Russian navy".

The wooden palace has long
since disappeared, demolished
by Catherine the Great in 1767.
However, about 500 m (550 yds)
east of Izmaylovskiy Park metro,
the remains of other buildings
can be seen on an island near
the sports stadium. The lake
surrounding them was once
part of a network of 37 ponds

17th-century Cathedral of the Intercession, Izmaylovo Park

previously created by Tsar
Alexis for breeding fish and
irrigating experimental crops.
He planted exotic species such
as mulberry trees and cotton
and ordered seeds from his
ambassadors in England.

The island is reached over a
small bridge. The iron archway
at its far end was built in 1859
and led to three buildings
commissioned by Nicholas I
and designed by Konstantin
Ton *(see p47)* in the 1840s for
retired soldiers. Rising above
the trees ahead, behind the
remains of the
estate's walls,
are the five,
formidable black
domes of the
Cathedral of the
Intercession, built
in 1671–9. The
domes are tiled with
metallic "scales". The
zakomary gables
(see p46) beneath
them are beautifully
decorated with
"peacock's eye" tiles,
by Stepan Polubes,
a late 17th-century

Belorussian ceramicist
working in Moscow.

On the cathedral's right is
a tiered red-brick arch with a
tent roof. Built in 1671, this is
the Bridge Tower, all that remains
of a 14-span bridge that once
crossed the estate's extensive
waterways. Its tower was used
for meetings of the boyars'
council under Tsar Alexis. The
top tier of the bridge gives fine
views over the whole estate.

On the opposite side of
the cathedral from the Bridge
Tower stands the white, triple-
arched Ceremonial Gate. It was
designed by Terentiy Makarov
In 1682 and is one of two gates
that originally led to the palace.

The flea market, just to the
northwest of the lake, trails
down the hill from the concrete
tower blocks of the Izmaylovo
Hotel, offering an amazingly
eclectic variety of goods.
Muscovites come here in large
numbers to buy items such as
second-hand household goods
and vehicle parts. Tourists are
likely to be greeted by a storm
of shouts in English from people
selling their wares.

Triple-arched Ceremonial Gate, the surviving entrance to
the tsars' former estate, Izmaylovo Park

⓰ Kuskovo

Кусково
Kuskovo

For over 200 years before the Revolution, Kuskovo was the country seat of one of Russia's wealthiest aristocratic families, the Sheremetevs. The present buildings were commissioned by Count Pyotr Sheremetev after his marriage to the heiress Varvara Cherkasskaya in 1743. Among their 200,000 serfs were the architects Fyodor Argunov and Aleksey Mironov who played a major role in Kuskovo's construction, probably under the supervision of professional architect Karl Blank. Apart from the elaborate gardens, the main attraction is the two-storey wooden palace, completed in 1777. A ceramics museum, with a renowned collection of porcelain, occupies the Orangery.

Church of the Archangel Michael
Constructed in 1737–8, the church is the oldest building on the estate. The statue on its dome is of the Archangel Michael. The wooden bell tower and golden spire were added in 1792.

KEY

① **The Swiss Cottage** resembles a traditional Alpine chalet. It was designed by Nikolay Benoit in 1870.

② **Lake**

③ **The Dutch Cottage** was built in 1749 in the homely style of 17th-century Dutch architecture, in red brick and with stepped gables. The tiled interiors house Russian ceramics and glassware.

④ **Obelisk**

⑤ **The Hermitage** has distinctive rounded walls and is topped by a dome.

⑥ **Allegorical statue of the Greek river god Scamander**

⑦ **Statue of Minerva, Roman goddess of wisdom**

⑧ **Aviary**

⑨ **American Orangery**

⑩ **The Green Theatre** was used to stage open-air plays and concerts for an audience of 50 guests

⑪ **The Menagerie**, a semicircle of terracotta and white fenced pavilions, housed songbirds.

⑫ **Coach House**

⑬ **The kitchens** were housed in this large, imposing building, constructed in 1756–7.

0 metres 50
0 yards 50

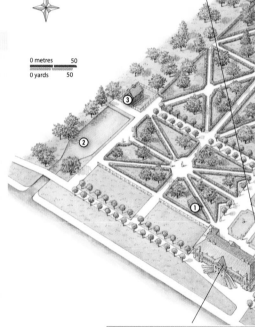

★ **Wooden Palace**
Surprisingly, this Neo-Classical palace is made entirely of wood, plastered and painted to resemble stone. Carriage ramps sweep up to the main portico, which is emblazoned with the crest of the Sheremetev family.

★ Orangery
With a central hall for dining and dancing, the Orangery was built in 1761–2. It is now a ceramics museum, based on the 18th–19th-century porcelain collection of Aleksey Morozov *(see p98)*. Pieces on show include Wedgwood, Meissen and items from various Russian factories.

VISITORS' CHECKLIST

Practical Information
Ulitsa Yunosti 2. **Tel** (495) 370 0160. **Open** mid-Apr–mid-Oct: 10am–6pm Wed–Sun; mid-Oct–mid-Apr: 10am–4pm Wed–Sun. **Closed** last Wed of the month. 🎫 tickets sold at main entrance for individual sights. 📷 book in advance. 📱 📖

Transport
Ⓜ Ryazanskiy prospekt, Vykhino. 🚌 133, 208 *(see p227)*.

★ Formal Gardens
The gardens were laid out in the French, geometrical style, which led to Kuskovo gaining a reputation as the Russian Versailles.

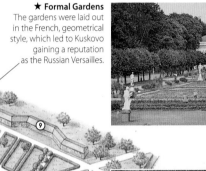

Italian Cottage
Russian architect Yuriy Kologrivov studied in Italy prior to designing this pavilion. It was built in 1754–5 in the style of a late-Renaissance villa and now contains displays of 18th-century paintings.

★ Grotto
Designed by Fyodor Argunov in the mid-18th century, the Grotto is the most remarkable of Kuskovo's pavilions. The cool, spacious interior is decorated with shells and porcelain embedded in sand and stucco.

Entrance

The majestic entrance to Leningradskiy station, on Komsomolskaya ploshchad

⑲ Komsomolskaya Ploshchad

Комсомольская площадь
Komsomolskaya ploshchad

Map 4 D2. Ⓜ Komsomolskaya.

The three railway stations on this large square are long-standing rivals for the affection of Muscovites. The oldest, Leningradskiy station (formerly Nikolaevskiy station), opened in 1851, serving as the terminus of the line from St Petersburg to Moscow. The building was designed according to the tenets of historicism by Konstantin Ton *(see p47)*, architect of the Great Kremlin Palace *(see p65)*.

In complete contrast is the turreted Yaroslavskiy station, rebuilt in 1902 by architect Fyodor Shekhtel *(see p47)*. The station is a colourful Style-Moderne building with a tiled frieze and an unusual, steeply pitched roof. The Trans-Siberian Railway starts here.

Shekhtel's radical design for his station goaded his rival, Aleksey Shchusev *(see p47)*, into adopting an equally bold approach when designing the third station, Kazanskiy, on the opposite side of the square. Begun in 1912, the station has a tiered central tower modelled on the citadel in the Mongol capital Kazan. The terminal was completed in 1926 and serves the Urals.

The porticoed pavilion of Komsomolskaya metro station *(see pp41–3)* is also a striking feature of the square. It is named after the Komsomol (Communist Youth volunteers) who helped to build it. It has a luxurious interior, lit by glittering chandeliers.

Komsomolskaya ploshchad itself is a seething mass of beggars, families with apparently everything they own in tow, street hawkers, drunks, drug dealers and, in the evenings, prostitutes. It has assumed an unnerving atmosphere to say the least, so it is advisable not to linger here long, especially at night.

⑳ Vasnetsov House-Museum

Дом-музей ВМ Васнецова
Dom-muzey VM Vasnetsova

Pereulok Vasnetsova 13. **Map** 3 A2. **Tel** (495) 681 1329. Ⓜ Sukharevskaya, Prospekt Mira. **Open** 10am–5pm Wed–Sun. **Closed** last Thu of the month. 🖼 ✉
Ⓦ tretyakovgallery.ru

A graphic artist, sculptor, painter, theatre designer and architect, Viktor Vasnetsov (1848–1926) was a member of the artists' colony set up by arts patron Savva Mamontov at Abramtsevo *(see p162)*. He is

Ornate roof of the wooden house designed by Viktor Vasnetsov

probably best known for the highly original façade of the Tretyakov Gallery *(see pp120–23)*, where many of his paintings are also housed. Vasnetsov designed this unusual house for himself and his family in 1893–4 and lived here until he died in 1926, at the age of 78. As an enthusiastic advocate of traditional Russian folk art and architecture, he employed peasant carpenters from Vladimir *(see pp168–9)* to build his remarkable, log-cabin-like, timber house with green roofs.

The ground-floor rooms display highly individual pieces of furniture, many designed by Vasnetsov and his similarly talented younger brother, Arkady (1856–1933). The stoves are decorated with tiles made by fellow artist Mikhail Vrubel (1856–1910).

A spiral staircase hung with 17th-century chain mail and weaponry leads up to the artist's studio, which resembles a vaulted medieval hall. This is the perfect backdrop for Vasnetsov's arresting canvases, many of which take figures from Russian legends as their subjects. For example, *Baba Yaga* portrays Russia's forest witch indulging in her favourite occupation, stealing children. *The Sleeping Princess*, painted in the last year of Vasnetsov's life, shows a scene from the fairy story, "Sleeping Beauty".

㉑ Ostankino Palace

Московский музей-усадьба Останкино
Moskovskiy muzey-usadba Ostankino

1-ya Ostankinskaya ulitsa 5. **Tel** (495) 683 4645. Ⓜ VDNKh. **Open** mid-May–Sep: 11am–7pm Wed–Sun; grounds to 9pm. 🖼 ♿ gardens only. 🎧 English.

Like the estate at Kuskovo *(see pp144–5)*, Ostankino was built by the serf architects Pavel Argunov and Aleksey Mironov for the Sheremetevs, one of Russia's richest families. Count Nikolay Sheremetev was a prominent patron of the arts and built his palace around a theatre, where a

Main façade of the imposing, Neo-Classical Ostankino Palace

company of 200 serf actors and actresses performed plays of his choosing. In 1800 the Count married Praskovia Zhemchugova-Kovaleva, one of the actresses. Secluded at their palace, they were able to shelter themselves from the disapproval of polite society, but sadly Praskovia died 3 years later. The count never recovered from the loss and left the palace, which fell into disuse.

Ostankino is a handsome palace, with a shallow green dome and impressive Classical 18th century interiors. The main building has an admirably restrained Neo-Classical façade. It was built in wood in 1792–8 and skilfully plastered over to look like brick and stone. It demonstrates the remarkable workmanship of Sheremetev's serf craftsmen. The halls are a wonder of *trompe l'oeil* decor. Carved wooden mouldings are painted to resemble bronze, gold and marble, parquet floors are patterned in birchwood and mahogany, while a huge crystal chandelier hangs from the frescoed ceiling of the main hall. The pavilion also serves as a sculpture gallery and among the sculptures is a Roman marble head of Aphrodite from the 1st century AD.

The *pièce de résistance* of the palace is the theatre, a breathtaking, elliptical hall with a superb painted ceiling supported by rows of Corinthian columns. In 1796 the building was partly reconstructed to allow the installation of an ingenious mechanical device which raised the auditorium floor so that the theatre

could also be used as a ballroom. In the summer, concerts of classical music are still held here.

On the road leading from the estate is the ornate Church of the Trinity with a cluster of green domes. It was built in 1678–83 for the Cherkasskiy family, who owned Ostankino estate before the Sheremetevs.

Theatre auditorium, Ostankino Palace, once home to Count Sheremetev's serf actors

㉒ All-Russian Exhibition Centre (VVTs)

Всероссийский Выставочный Центр (ВВЦ)

Vserossiyskiy Vystavochniy Tsentr (VVTs)

Prospekt Mira. **Tel** (495) 544 3400. Ⓜ VDNKh. Grounds: **Open** May–Sep: 9am–9pm (to 10pm Sat & Sun); Oct–Apr: 9am–8pm (to 9pm Sat & Sun). ♿ Pavilions: **Open** May–Sep: 10am–7pm (to 8pm Sat & Sun); Oct–Apr: 9am–8pm (to 9pm Sat & Sun). ♿ Botanical Gardens: **Open** May–Oct: 10am–8pm daily. Space Museum: **Open** 11am–7pm Tue–Sun (to 9pm Thu). 🎦 ♿ ✉

One of the city's main tourist attractions in Soviet times, the former Exhibition of Economic

Achievements of the USSR (VDNKh) has now become the All-Russian Exhibition Centre (VVTs), a vast park, shopping centre and exhibition site. VVTs remains a fascinating place for a visit, especially for enthusiasts of Soviet architecture. There are scores of massive pavilions, including a Pavilion of the Peoples of the USSR, guarded by a statue of Lenin. Its interior houses booths selling electrical goods and cosmetics.

The main entrance to the park is a huge triumphal arch, topped by the figures of a tractor driver and female collective farmer, holding up a sheaf of corn.

In the centre of the complex is the Fountain of the Republics, consisting of 15 gilded statues of maidens in national dress (representing the former Soviet republics) circling a golden wheat sheaf. Jets of water from the basin are sprayed 24 m (79 ft) into the air, and at night it is lit up.

Nearby is the entrance to the **Botanical Gardens**, which contain a small but pleasant Japanese Garden where tea is served. There are also numerous ponds and picnic spots.

Heading back towards VDNKh metro, it is hard to miss the Obelisk, a monument to the "Conquerors of Space". Over 100 m (328 ft) high, it represents a rocket lifting off. It was erected in 1964, 3 years after Yuriy Gagarin's historic flight. Underneath it is the **Space Museum**, one of the city's hidden treasures, containing Belka and Strelka (stuffed), the dogs who were the first creatures to return alive from space (Laika, more famous in the West, died), and *Vostok 1*, the tiny capsule in which Gagarin famously orbited the Earth.

Statue of tractor driver and farmer atop the main entrance of the VVTs

TWO GUIDED WALKS

Modern Moscow is, in many respects, the brainchild of Stalin. A sprawling city of around 12 million people, it is not a place that lends itself easily to a casual stroll. Stalin intended the city to awe, tearing down churches and any other buildings that got in the way of his plan for a Socialist megalopolis, and the capital's wide streets and imposing structures are a testament to his vision. Walking through Moscow, one can feel dwarfed by buildings that seem to have been designed for a larger race of being. One of the joys of life in the city, however, is finding

a quiet, forgotten corner, an unexpected moment of calm amid the bustle of city life. The two walks that follow present two very different aspects of the Russian capital. The first explores Moscow's busy centre, passing some often neglected, yet fascinating sights from both Russia's recent and distant past including the former headquarters of the KGB. The second walk provides a journey through Russian literature, from the giant statue of Dostoevsky outside the Russian State Library, to Patriarch's Ponds, straight from the pages of a modern Soviet classic.

CHOOSING A WALK

The Two Walks
This map shows the general area covered by the two guided walks in relation to the main sightseeing areas of Moscow.

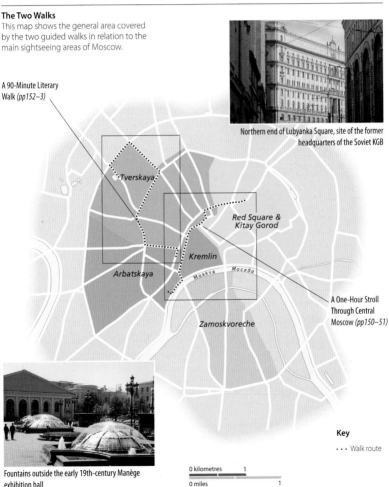

A 90-Minute Literary Walk (pp152–3)

Northern end of Lubyanka Square, site of the former headquarters of the Soviet KGB

Tverskaya

Red Square & Kitay Gorod

Kremlin

Arbatskaya

Moskva Москва

A One-Hour Stroll Through Central Moscow (pp150–51)

Zamoskvoreche

Fountains outside the early 19th-century Manège exhibition hall

Key

• • • Walk route

0 kilometres 1

0 miles 1

◄ Detail of the iron gate leading into Alexander Gardens, Kremlin, designed to commemorate the Russian victories over Napoleon

A One-Hour Stroll Through Central Moscow

Like any major capital, Moscow is a busy place and full of life. This walk, along the the quieter embankments and older streets, is a chance to explore the city's ancient heart, while avoiding many of the busier sections. Taking in such varied sights as the re-created Cathedral of Christ the Saviour, Red Square and the former KGB HQ, the route provides an excellent opportunity to appreciate Moscow's rich and eventful history of the distant, as well as more recent, past.

① Cathedral of Christ the Saviour, one of Moscow's main landmarks

Tips for Walkers
Along the Moscow River

The gilded dome of the Cathedral of Christ the Saviour ① (see p76) is immediately visible on exiting from Kropotkinskaya station. The original 19th-century cathedral was blown up on the orders of Stalin in 1931. This modern replica was completed in 2000. Explore the grounds to find a statue of Tsar Alexander II ②. After leaving the cathedral grounds turn left and walk along the embankment of the Moskva river, passing under Bolshoy Kamennyy Bridge. After the bridge turn left again in the

④ Water jets of an equestrian fountain, Alexander Gardens

direction of the Kremlin, and then cross the road at the traffic lights, under the watchful eyes of Moscow's traffic police. The guarded gate is Borovitskaya Tower ③, the presidential entrance to the Kremlin. When the President, or any other important figure, arrives traffic is held up throughout Moscow to allow the entourage, with its flashing blue lights, a clear road.

Around Alexander Gardens

Next, follow the pathway through Alexander Gardens ④ (see p69) past the Kremlin walls and turrets, including Trinity Tower ⑤ (see p58), the tallest of the Kremlin's fortifications. The gardens contain a number of cafés and the paths are a favourite place for Muscovites to take a stroll when the weather is fine. Look out for the fountains with characters from Russian fairy tales set against the wall of the shopping complex at the northern end of the gardens. Close to the park's exit are the monuments to the Hero Cities of the Soviet Union ⑥ (Moscow,

Leningrad, Kursk, etc.). They commemorate the bravery of the citizens of those cities that bore the brunt of the fighting during World War II. Next to these monuments is the Tomb of the Unknown Soldier, dedicated to the millions of Soviet soldiers who died in the battle against Fascism. Newly married couples often come here to pay homage to the fallen. Leaving Alexander Gardens, look to the right for an unusual view of Red Square ⑦ (see p108). Walking on, the statue of the earnest looking military man astride a horse is Marshal Georgiy Zhukov ⑧, the stout defender of Stalingrad and leader of the Soviet forces during the Battle of Kursk in 1943, the largest tank battle of World War II.

Continue past the statue of Zhukov for Resurrection Gate ⑨ (see p107) and another stunning view of Red Square. Walk through the gate: to the left is Kazan Cathedral ⑩ (see p107), a 1990s replica of the original, which, like the Cathedral of Christ the Saviour, was destroyed on Stalin's orders in 1936.

Key

••• Walk route

⑩ Kazan Cathedral, rebuilt after its destruction by the Communists

Head back through Resurrection Gate and turn right.

From Ploshchcad Revolyutsii to Lubyanka

Walk across to ploshchad Revolyutsii (Revolution Square) to find the chunky statue of Karl Marx ⑪. The inscription at the statue's base, urging the workers of the world to unite, grows more incongruous year by year as capitalism becomes the main economic model in Russia. Opposite the Karl Marx statue is the world famous

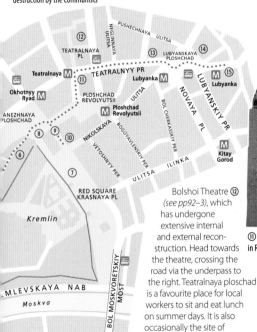

Bolshoi Theatre ⑫ (see pp92–3), which has undergone extensive internal and external reconstruction. Head towards the theatre, crossing the road via the underpass to the right. Teatralnaya ploschad is a favourite place for local workers to sit and eat lunch on summer days. It is also occasionally the site of demonstrations.

Next head up Teatralnyy proezd to No. 5, Detskiy Mir ⑬, which was the largest and most famous toy shop in Russia but which has been closed for renovation since 2008. A short distance away is Lubyanka Square (see p114), and, on it, the HQ of the former KGB ⑭. Here, during Communist Russia's darkest days, the state security agency carried out many of its interrogations. A plaque to Yuriy Andropov, the former Soviet General Secretary and KGB chief, is near the entrance. A statue of Feliks Dzerzhinskiy, founder of the Cheka (forerunners to the KGB), once stood in the square until it was toppled in 1991 by cheering crowds in one of the most symbolic events to take place during the death throes of the USSR. In a move that many have seen as equally symbolic, a plaque to Dzerzhinskiy has been placed within the grounds of what is now the HQ of the modern state security service, the FSB. To the right, on Lubyanskiy proezd, is the Mayakovsky Museum ⑮ (see p113), dedicated to the life of Vladimir Mayakovsky. One of Stalin's favourite poets, Mayakovsky eventually became disillusioned with Communism and committed suicide in this very building. It is a short walk from here to Lubyanka metro station.

⑪ Imposing statue of Marx in Revolution Square

Tips for Walkers

Starting point: Cathedral of Christ the Saviour.
Length: 3 km (2 miles).
Getting there: Kropotkinskaya metro station.
Stopping-off points: There are plenty of cafés and places to sit in Alexander Gardens.

⑧ Statue of war hero Marshal Zhukov, next to the Historical Museum

For keys to symbols *see back flap*

A 90-Minute Literary Walk

Russia has long been revered for its writers and Moscow is dotted with statues, monuments and other reminders of them. This walk highlights not only the well-known giants of Russian literature, such as Dostoevsky, but also lesser known yet important literary figures such as Pushkin, the father of Russian literature, Yesenin, a young idealist poet who took his own life, and Bulgakov, author of *The Master and Margarita*, a novel that conjures up a strange reality in which Moscow is visited by the devil himself. As well as sights directly relating to Russian literature, this walk also passes by other places of interest including theatres and newspaper offices.

⑤ Ornate façade of the 19th-century House of Friendship

③ Giant statue of Dostoevsky outside the Russian State Library

The Republics' Tree to the House of Friendship

Arriving at Borovitskaya metro station, take the city exit. Next to the stairs leading to the escalators is *The Republics' Tree* ①, a mural depicting the peoples of the 15 former Soviet republics. Take the escalators to street level. Turn left and follow the road to the corner for a view of the Manège ② *(see p96)*, an exhibition hall that was partially destroyed by a fire in 2005. To the left is the Russian State Library ③, and, outside it, the figure of Fyodor Dostoevsky (1821–81), the writer who helped to shape the 20th-century novel in works such as *Crime and Punishment* (1866). Further on, at No. 5, is the Shchusev Museum of Architecture ④, a former Bolshevik HQ. Take the underpass to the glitzy House of Friendship ⑤ *(see p97)*.

From Nikitskiy bulvar to Pushkin Square

Turning into Nikitskiy bulvar, cross the road to No. 7b ⑥,

where Nikolai Gogol (1809–52), author of the classic novel *Dead Souls* (1842), lived out his final years. It was here that he wrote the second volume of *Dead Souls*, but, having fallen under the influence of a religious fanatic, he destroyed the manuscript. Cross back over the road at the pedestrian crossing, pass the Museum of Oriental Art ⑦ at No. 12a, and then walk to the end of the road. The building opposite is ITAR-TASS ⑧, the Russian state news agency and the mouthpiece of the Communist Party in Soviet times. To the left is the Church of the Great Ascension ⑨, where Pushkin married Natalya Goncharova in 1831. West of the church, at No. 6, are the Alexei Tolstoy and Gorky House-Museums ⑩. Carry on up Tverskoy bulvar to the statue of the poet Sergey Yesenin ⑪. Born in 1895, he is best known for *Pugachev* (1922), a verse tragedy dealing with the peasant rebellion of 1773–5. Yesenin had a troubled life,

including an unhappy marriage to the American dancer Isadora Duncan, and killed himself in 1925.

Facing each other, slightly further up the road at Nos. 22 and 23 respectively, are the MKhAT Gorky Art Theatre ⑫, named for Maxim Gorky, the dramatist founder of Socialist Realism, and the Pushkin Theatre ⑬. At the end of the road, take the underpass and follow the tunnel to the left to enter Pushkin Square ⑭ where there is a monument to Alexander Pushkin (1799–1837), a hero of Russian literature. *Eugene Onegin* (1830), his novel in verse, is held by many to be the greatest masterpiece of Russian literature *(see p75)*.

⑧ Ground-floor window of ITAR-TASS, Russia's official news agency

Tverskaya ulitsa to Mayakovskaya Metro

Continue up Tverskaya ulitsa. On the right hand side of the street, at No. 18a, look out for a plaque (in Russian) noting that this was where Lenin's wife worked on the *Pravda*

⑳ Patriarch's Ponds, one of the city's most popular picnic spots

newspaper ⑮. Across the street, at No. 21, stands the red-bricked Museum of the Revolution, now renamed the Museum of Contemporary History ⑯ *(see p99)*. At the end of Tverskaya ulitsa, use the underpass to cross over to the statue of Vladimir Mayakovsky ⑰ (1893–1930). A poet of the revolution, Mayakovsky was one of the few writers permitted to travel abroad during the Soviet crackdown. He was a favourite of Stalin, who proclaimed that indifference to his works was a crime

(see p113). South of the statue is the Tchaikovsky Concert Hall ⑱ *(see p200)*, named after the composer of *The Nutcracker*. Heading down Bolshaya Sadovaya ulitsa, walk into the courtyard at No. 10 to pay a visit to two museums commemorating Bulgakov's life ⑲ *(see p98)*. Never a supporter of the Soviet regime, most of Mikhail Bulgakov's work was supressed during his lifetime. Continue on, taking the first left to reach Patriach's Ponds ⑳. This is the setting for the opening of Bulgakov's *The Master and Margarita*. From here, head back to Mayakovskaya metro station.

⑪ Statue of the troubled poet Sergey Yesenin on Tverskoy bulvar

Tips for Walkers

Starting point: The Republics' Tree, Borovitskaya metro station.
Length: 4 km (2 miles).
Getting there: Borovitskaya.
Stopping-off points: Pushkin Square has stalls selling food. Patriarch's Ponds is a good place for a picnic, with shops nearby. There are cafés along Nikitskiy bulvar and Tverskaya ulitsa.

(Map labels:)

ORUZHEYNYY PER

SADOVAYA-TRIUMFALNAYA UL

vskaya

LNAYA 'HAD

VORONTNOVSKIY PEREULOK

TVERSKAYA UL

UL MAL DMITROVKA

STAROPIMENOVSKIY PER

DEGTYARNYY PER

NASTASINSKIY PER

Pushkinskaya Ⓜ

⑯ ⑮

Tverskaya Ⓜ ⑭

PUSHKINSKAYA PLOSHCHAD

BOGOSLOVSKIY PER

BOLSHAYA BRONNAYA ULITSA

TVERSKOY BULVAR

⑬

⑪ ⑫

TVERSKAYA ULITSA

MAL GNEZDNIKOVSKIY PER

LEONTEVSKIY PEREULOK

VOZNESENSKIY PEREULOK

BRYUSOV PEREULOK

GAZETNYY PEREULOK

NIKITSKIY PEREULOK

⑧

BOL NIKITSKAYA UL БОЛ НИКИТСКАЯ УЛ

NIKITSKIY BULVAR

⑦

KALASHNYY PEREULOK

MAL KISLOVSKIY PEREULOK

BOL KISLOVSKIY PER

ROMANOV PER

Okhotnyy Ⓜ Ryad

MANEZHNAYA PLOSHCHAD

⑥

⑤ UL VOZDVIZHENKA

ARBATSKAYA PLOSHCHAD

Arbatskaya Ⓜ

④ ③

Aleksandrovskiy Sad

Biblioteka imeni Lenina Ⓜ

Borovitskaya ① Ⓜ

②

MOKHOVAYA ULITSA

MANEZHNAYA ULITSA

UL ZNAMENKA

BOROVITSKAYA PLOSHCHAD

Key

• • • Walk route

0 metres   300
0 yards   300

BEYOND MOSCOW

The magnificence of some of the palaces and churches outside Moscow and the historic interest of some of the towns make excursions there justly rewarding. Although parts of the landscape are unappealingly industrial, the large areas of true countryside are green, forested and dotted with villages of small wooden dachas.

Visitors may find it a good idea to take an organized tour *(see p220)* to out-of-town sights as public transport can be erratic, though perfectly feasible for those who prefer mixing with local daily life *(see p227)*. There are several places of historic and cultural importance within easy reach of the city. To the west is Borodino *(see p160)*, site of the great battle between Napoleon's army and Russian forces under the command of Field Marshal Mikhail Kutuzov. To the north is the magnificent Trinity Monastery of St Sergius *(see pp164–7)* and to the northeast the towns of the Golden Ring *(see p163)*. The political heyday of these towns was in the 12th and 13th centuries, before the rise of Moscow, and their churches and wooden buildings make them well worth exploring.

Also outside Moscow are houses lived in by two of Russia's most famous sons, Pyotr Tchaikovsky *(see p161)* and Leo Tolstoy *(see p136)*.

On Friday nights the trains and roads into the countryside are packed with families travelling to their dacha, a migration that leaves the capital rather deserted. Each dacha has a small plot of land that is used for growing fruit and vegetables. For some Muscovites this was, and often still is today, an essential source of food. In recent years, brick houses started to spring up where farmers used to grow crops, built for New Russians who have adopted Western commuter habits. However, many have been abandoned half-built as construction firms have gone out of business in the fast-changing economic climate.

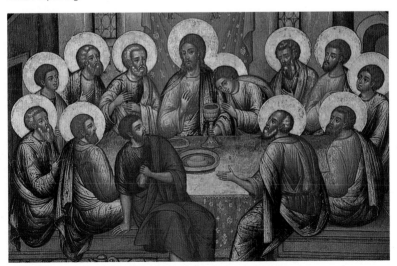

The Sacred Supper, painted in 1685, displayed in the Treasury at the Trinity Monastery of St Sergius

◀ A Neo-Classical colonnade in the formal gardens of Arkhangelskoe

Exploring the Moscow Region

Despite the numerous attractions of Moscow, it is well worth spending time in the surrounding region. Several country estates lie within easy reach of the city and make for delightful one- or two-day trips. Among them are Yasnaya Polyana, where Leo Tolstoy *(see p136)* lived for many years, the house in Klin rented by Pyotr Tchaikovsky and Abramtsevo Estate-Museum, a former artists' colony. However, the star attraction of the region is the Trinity Monastery of St Sergius. Once a place of pilgrimage for the tsars, this huge complex has several superb cathedrals.

Moscow is also an ideal base for visiting the Golden Ring towns, which include Pereslavl-Zalesskiy, Suzdal and Vladimir. Founded by Russians seeking shelter from invading tribes, these attractive settlements still have many historic buildings.

Tiles by artist Mikhail Vrubel on a bench at Abramtsevo

Key

- ═══ Motorway
- ─── Main road
- ⋯⋯ Minor road
- ─── Scenic route
- ─╍─ Main railway
- ─── Minor railway

Sights at a Glance

- ❶ Arkhangelskoe
- ❷ Borodino
- ❸ Tchaikovsky House-Museum
- ❹ Abramtsevo Estate-Museum
- ❺ *Trinity Monastery of St Sergius pp164–7*
- ❻ Pereslavl-Zalesskiy
- ❼ Suzdal
- ❽ Vladimir
- ❾ Yasnaya Polyana

The blue-domed Church of the Holy Spirit and the Chapel Over the Well, Trinity Monastery of St Sergius

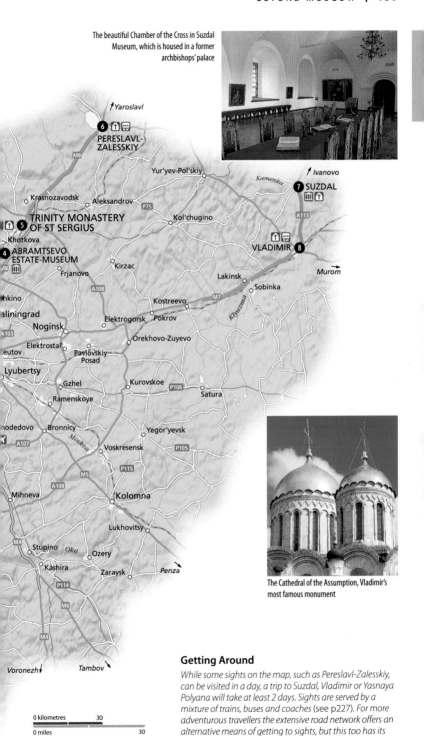

The beautiful Chamber of the Cross in Suzdal Museum, which is housed in a former archbishops' palace

The Cathedral of the Assumption, Vladimir's most famous monument

Getting Around

While some sights on the map, such as Pereslavl-Zalesskiy, can be visited in a day, a trip to Suzdal, Vladimir or Yasnaya Polyana will take at least 2 days. Sights are served by a mixture of trains, buses and coaches (see p227). For more adventurous travellers the extensive road network offers an alternative means of getting to sights, but this too has its problems (see p226). One of the best ways to visit sights outside Moscow is on an organized tour (see p220).

For keys to symbols *see back flap*

The southern, garden façade of the Neo-Classical, stucco-covered, wooden palace at Arkhangelskoe

❶ Arkhangelskoe

Архангельское
Arkhangelskoe

20 km (12 miles) W of Moscow. **Tel** (495) 363 1375. **Open** May–Oct: 10:30am–5pm Wed–Fri, 10:30am–6pm Sat & Sun; Nov–Apr: 10:30am–4pm Wed–Fri, 10:30am–5pm Sat & Sun. **Closed** last Wed of the month. Ⓜ Tushinskaya, then bus *(see p227)*. 🚹 🇬🇧 English (book in advance). ♿ pavilions and grounds only.

Most of the buildings on this country estate date from the 18th and 19th centuries. The charming Church of the Archangel Michael was completed in 1667, however, and gives the estate its name.

The Golitsyn family acquired the estate in 1703. In the 1780s Prince Nikolay Golitsyn began a wholesale rebuilding, including a new palace which was built to a design by the French architect Charles de Guerne. Constructed from wood, it was covered with stucco to give the effect of stone. When Golitsyn died in 1809, the estate was purchased by Prince Nikolay Yusupov. The palace's rooms are filled with fine furniture, fabrics and antiques. There is also an excellent art collection.

The formal gardens were laid out in the 18th century. Within them stand pavilions such as the Caprice Palace, built in 1819 for soirees. In 1910–16 a lavish mausoleum was erected for the Yusupov family, but it was never used because of the Revolution.

The painted dome of Yusupov mausoleum, built in 1910–16, at Arkhangelskoe

❷ Borodino

Бородино
Borodino

120 km (75 miles) W of Moscow. **Tel** (496) 385 1546. **Open** 9am–4:30pm Tue–Sun. **Closed** last Fri of the month. 🚆 Mozhaisk or Borodino, then bus *(see p227)*. 🚹 🅿 🇼 **borodino.ru**

One of the fiercest military confrontations of the 19th century took place at Borodino on 7 September 1812. For more than 15 hours Napoleon Bonaparte's Grande Armée and the Russian army, led by Field Marshal Mikhail Kutuzov, fought each other to a bloody impasse. It is estimated that 40,000 Russian

Monument to the fallen of Borodino

and 30,000 French soldiers were killed. Napoleon called it the "most terrible" of all his battles, but claimed victory on the grounds that the Russians were forced to continue their retreat to Moscow. Posterity, however, awarded the laurels to the Russians. The French followed the Russians, but arrived to find the city and the Kremlin deserted. The Muscovites then started a great fire *(see pp26–7)* in the city, and faced with a Russian winter in the open, the French were finally forced to retreat.

The battlefield covers over 100 sq km (40 sq miles), but the main places of interest are reasonably accessible. A museum, 1 km (0.5 mile) south of Borodino village, recounts the story of the battle with the aid of models and an illuminated map. More than 30 monuments are strewn around the area. Russia's most distinguished general to fall in battle, Prince Pyotr Bagration, was buried at the base of a column dedicated to the fallen just east of the museum. Nearby is the inn, now a museum, where Leo Tolstoy stayed to research the background for his epic novel *War and Peace*.

The small Empire-style Spasskiy Church

of 1822 was the first monument to be constructed on the battlefield. A re-enactment of the battle takes place every 7 September.

❸ Tchaikovsky House-Museum

Дом-музей ПИ Чайковского

Dom-muzey PI Chaykovskovo

90 km (55 miles) NW of Moscow. Ulitsa Tchaikovskogo 48, Klin. **Tel** (496) 245 8196. **Open** 10am–5pm Fri–Tue. **Closed** last Mon of the month. 🚇 Klin *(see p227).* 🅿 🔲 English. 🌐 tchaikovsky-museum.ru

In a letter to his brother Anatoly in May 1892, Pyotr Tchaikovsky wrote "I have rented a house in Klin. What a blessing it is to know that no-one will come, either to interrupt my work, or my reading or walking". Previous stays in the village of Frolovskoe near Klin had inspired some of his best music, including the ballets *The Sleeping Beauty* and *The Nutcracker*, and the opera *The Queen of Spades* based on Pushkin's novel

The reception area in the house at Klin, containing Tchaikovsky's piano

Tchaikovsky's wooden house in Klin, in the Russian countryside he loved so much

(see p75). Tchaikovsky enjoyed Klin for only a few months, as he died in 1893. In 1894 his younger brother, Modest, opened the estate to visitors. The ground floor of the clapboard house is closed to the public, but on entering the composer's rooms on the first floor visitors find themselves in a bright, spacious reception area. The walls are covered with photos of his family, his classmates at law school and fellow musicians. The grand piano in the centre of the room was a gift from the Russian firm Becker. Though an excellent pianist, Tchaikovsky never performed in public. The winner of the Tchaikovsky International Competition *(see p200)* gives a recital here on the composer's birthday, 7 May.

Tchaikovsky was a great collector of souvenirs. On a shelf behind the piano is a Statue of Liberty inkpot, which he brought back from his triumphant conducting tour of the United States in 1891.

The bedroom is separated from the reception area by a curtain. Warm and intimate, it contains Tchaikovsky's diminutive slippers and a beautiful coverlet made by his niece. Tchaikovsky finished his *Sixth Symphony*, the *Pathétique,* at the table by the window.

Also open to visitors are the handsome wood-panelled library and the study where Modest Tchaikovsky worked as the Klin archivist until his death in 1916. A memorial room to the composer holds some of his personal possessions, including his top hat, gloves and evening clothes.

Tchaikovsky habitually took a stroll in the garden before breakfast and after lunch. His favourite flowers, lilies of the valley, are still planted here.

Pyotr Tchaikovsky

Probably Russia's most famous composer, Tchaikovsky was born in 1840. After graduating initially in law, he studied music at the St Petersburg Conservatory. One of his teachers helped the young composer to get a job teaching music at the Moscow Conservatory *(see p96)* in 1866 where he then taught for the next 12 years. It was during this period that Tchaikovsky composed his first four symphonies and the ballet *Swan Lake* (1876). In 1877 he married a student from the Conservatory in an effort to suppress his homosexuality.

However, the marriage was unhappy and short-lived. Tchaikovsky composed prolifically in the 1880s, completing such works as the ballet *The Sleeping Beauty* (1889) and the overture *The Year 1812* (1880). In 1892 he moved to Klin, outside Moscow. He died of cholera in November 1893, while overseeing the premiere of his final work, the *Sixth Symphony*, in St Petersburg. It is rumoured that he drank infected water as a dignified form of suicide after the exposure of his homosexual affair with a young aristocrat.

Statue of Pyotr Tchaikovsky at the Moscow Conservatory

Iconostasis in the Church of the Saviour, Abramtsevo Estate-Museum

❹ Abramtsevo Estate-Museum
Музей-усадьба Абрамцево
Muzey-usadba Abramtsevo

60 km (35 miles) NE of Moscow.
🚉 Khotkova or Sergiev Posad, then bus *(see p227)*. **Tel** (496) 543 2470.
Open 10am–4pm Wed–Sun (to 6pm in summer). **Closed** last Thu of the month. 🅿️ ✉️ 🌐 **abramtsevo.net**

In the second half of the 19th century this delightful rural retreat became a hive of cultural activity. Until his death in 1859, the house was owned by the writer Sergey Aksakov, whose sons were leading Slavophile thinkers. The estate's creative legacy was continued in 1870 when it was acquired by Savva Mamontov, an industrialist and art patron. Mamontov's generosity and zeal led to the establishment of an artists' colony here, and to a re-evaluation of traditional Russian folk art and craftwork. The work of local peasant craftsmen, whose children were educated in the estate's school, was a source of inspiration for many of the artists.

Dotted around the estate are a number of remarkable buildings. The artists' studio, with a spectacular carved roof, was designed in 1872 by Viktor Gartman. Displayed here are ceramics by the two distinguished artists Valentin

Serov and Mikhail Vrubel. The *teremok*, meanwhile, is a free improvization on the typical peasant hut *(izba)*, and was originally built as a bathhouse by Ivan Ropet in 1873. It was later used as a guesthouse. Inside are the original wooden furnishings and ornaments, such as statuettes, kitchen utensils and a tiled stove.

The House on Chicken Legs stands on stilts. Designed by Viktor Vasnetsov, it is now a popular children's attraction, recalling the witch of Russian folklore, Baba Yaga, whose house in the forest is built on giant chicken legs.

A woodland path leads to the most remarkable building on the estate. The Church of the Saviour Not Made by Human Hand is modelled on the medieval churches of Novgorod, but was brought up to date by the addition of bands of painted majolica tiles to its walls of whitewashed brick. The church was built in 1881–2, to a design by Viktor Vasnetsov; the mosaic floor is also his work, while the icons were painted by Vasnetsov, Ilya Repin and his wife Vera, Vasiliy Polenov and Nikolay Nevrev. A small oratory holds Savva Mamontov's remains and those of his son Andrey, who died, aged 19, in 1891.

The manor house still contains Aksakov's original

Empire-style furnishings, left by Mamontov out of respect for his predecessor. Aksakov knew the novelists Nikolai Gogol and Ivan Turgenev, and, here, in the red sitting-room, Gogol would read aloud from his masterpiece, *Dead Souls*. The dining room features a beautiful, tiled corner fireplace and a profusion of paintings. The gaze, however, is drawn to a copy of Valentin Serov's arresting portrait of Vera, Savva Mamontov's daughter, seated at the dining table. Entitled *Girl with Peaches* (1887), the original can be found in the Tretyakov Gallery *(see p123)*.

❺ Trinity Monastery of St Sergius
See pp164–7.

❻ Pereslavl-Zalesskiy
Переславль-Залесский
Pereslavl-Zalesskiy

135 km (85 miles) NE of Moscow.
🚍 43,400. 🚉 Sergiev Posad, then bus *(see p227)*.

Founded as a fortress in 1152 by Yuriy Dolgorukiy, and overlooking Lake Pleshcheevo, Pereslavl-Zalesskiy was an independent princedom until 1302, when it came under the control of Moscow. Peter the Great *(see p24)* developed plans for the Russian navy here. Sights of interest include the 12th-century **Cathedral of the Transfiguration** and the **Goritskiy Monastery of the Assumption**, founded in the 14th century but dating mainly from the 17th–18th centuries.

Cathedral of the Goritskiy Monastery of the Assumption, Pereslavl-Zalesskiy

The History of the Golden Ring

The first important cities in Russia were Novgorod in the north and Kiev in the south, which were situated on trade routes connecting the Baltic and the Black Sea. From the 11th century, as hostile tribes invaded Kievan Rus *(see p19)* and many Russians were forced northward, new settlements were founded such as Rostov, Yaroslavl, Vladimir and Suzdal. Like Novgorod and Kiev, these towns flourished on trade from Western Europe, Byzantium and Central Asia, while Sergiev Posad, location of the Trinity Monastery of St Sergius *(see pp164–7)*, became an important centre for the Orthodox Church. Moscow was also founded during this era *(see p19)* and, by the 16th century, had become Russia's capital. By this time the cluster of towns northeast of Moscow had paled into insignificance, although in the 1960s their historic importance brought them the title the Golden Ring.

The Golden Ring

Prince Vladimir Monomakh *(see p61)* founded a small trading settlement in the late 11th century. It was named Vladimir in 1108. Monomakh's son, Yuriy Dolgorukiy *(see p19)*, expanded the town and it was later the capital of Northern Rus.

Andrey Bogolyubskiy, the son of Yuriy Dolgorukiy, moved his court to Vladimir in 1157, where his craftsmen were to re-create the splendour of Kiev. His boyars later murdered him for being a dictator.

A campaign by Suzdal against Novgorod in 1169 is the subject of this icon. Created by the 15th-century Novgorod School *(see p63)*, it recalls Sudzal's strength before Moscow became pre-eminent.

Angels denote that the campaign against the Mongols was blessed.

Dmitriy Donskoy

The Battle of Kulikovo *(see p20)*, in 1380, was a turning point in the history of the Golden Ring. The Mongols made many inroads into the area, sacking Suzdal in 1238 and demanding tribute from the Russians. Dmitriy Donskoy *(see p20)* won a decisive victory against them at Kulikovo, with a blessing, it is said, from monk Sergius of Radonezh *(see p167)*.

Many churches were built in the towns of the Golden Ring, a sign of their comparative wealth. Some wooden churches are preserved in a museum at Suzdal *(see p168)*.

❺ Trinity Monastery of St Sergius

Троице-Сергиева Лавра
Troitse-Sergieva Lavra

Founded around 1345 by Sergius of Radonezh *(see p167)*, the Trinity Monastery of St Sergius in the town of Sergiev-Possad is one of Russia's most important religious centres and places of pilgrimage. In 1608–10, during the Time of Troubles *(see p21)*, the monks survived a siege by the Polish army and in the 1680s the young Peter the Great found refuge here during the Streltsy Rebellion *(see p24)*. The monastery was closed down by the Communists in 1919, but was allowed to open again in 1946, when it became headquarters of the Russian Orthodox Church. The headquarters transferred to new premises at the Danilovskiy Monastery *(see pp138–9)* in 1988.

| 0 metres | 25 |
| 0 yards | 25 |

Chapel Over the Well
This delightful, Moscow-Baroque *(see p46)* chapel was built in the late 17th century to mark the site of a holy spring.

★ Trinity Cathedral
Built in 1422–3 over the grave of St Sergius, this splendid church contains an iconostasis painted by a team of artists led by Andrey Rublev *(see p63)*.

Palace of the Metropolitans
This grand palace was completed in 1778. It was the residence of the metropolitans and patriarchs in 1946–88.

★ Church of St Sergius and Refectory
The monks' refectory was built in 1686–92 with the Church of St Sergius at its eastern end. The colourful façade features pillars with vine leaf decoration and chequered walls. The interior is lavish.

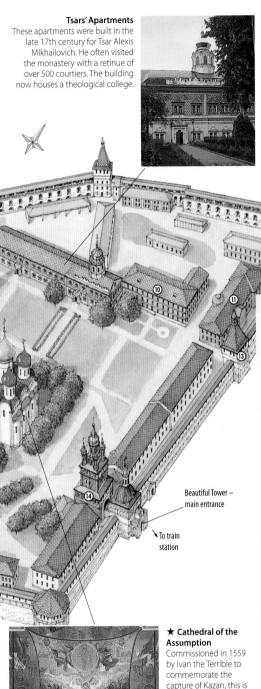

Tsars' Apartments
These apartments were built in the late 17th century for Tsar Alexis Mikhailovich. He often visited the monastery with a retinue of over 500 courtiers. The building now houses a theological college.

VISITORS' CHECKLIST

Practical Information
75 km (47 miles) NE of Moscow.
Tel (496) 540 5721. Cathedral:
Open 5am–8pm daily. Museum:
Open 10am–4pm Wed–Mon. 🖼
🎫 📷 💻 Grounds: **Open** 5am–8pm daily. ♿ grounds. 📷 book ahead. 🌐 stsl.ru

Transport
🚂 from Yaroslavskiy station
(see p227).

KEY

① **Church of the Holy Spirit**

② **Water Tower**

③ **Sacristy**

④ **Obelisk**

⑤ **Treasury**

⑥ **Hospital with Church of SS Zosima and Savvatiy**

⑦ **Carpenters' Tower**

⑧ **The Bell Tower** was begun in 1741 and completed 28 years later. Spectacular views can be obtained from its gallery.

⑨ **The Church of the Virgin of Smolensk** was built in 1745 to house the Icon of the Smolensk Virgin.

⑩ **School buildings**

⑪ **Library**

⑫ **The Duck Tower** was given its unusual name because of the legend that Peter the Great used to shoot ducks from its windows.

⑬ **Drying Tower**

⑭ **The Gate Church of St John the Baptist** stands over the main entrance. It was built in 1692–9 by the wealthy Stroganov family.

⑮ **Godunov's Tomb** is where Tsar Boris Godunov is buried with members of his family in a simple tomb. It was originally inside the cathedral, but later alterations put it outside. In Soviet times the tomb was opened and it was discovered that Boris Godunov's skull was missing.

Beautiful Tower – main entrance

To train station

★ **Cathedral of the Assumption**
Commissioned in 1559 by Ivan the Terrible to commemorate the capture of Kazan, this is the monastery's main cathedral. Its sumptuous interior was decorated by artists from Yaroslavl over a century later.

Exploring the Trinity Monastery of St Sergius

In the 14th century, Sergius of Radonezh built a small wooden church in the forests to the north of Moscow and consecrated it to the Holy Trinity. Many pilgrims were attracted to the site by reports of Sergius' piety. He organized them into a community and the Trinity Monastery was born. The monastery expanded as it gained wealth and influence and today the huge complex is enclosed by white walls around 1.6 km (1 mile) long. Its stunning churches, grouped around the spectacular Cathedral of the Assumption, are among the most beautiful in Russia.

The fortified Trinity Monastery of St Sergius seen from the southeast

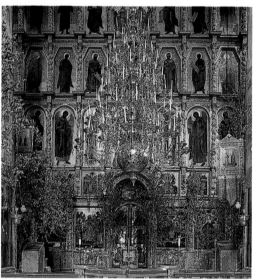

The superb 17th-century iconostasis in the Cathedral of the Assumption

Church of St Sergius and Refectory

The monks' refectory was built in 1686–92 using money donated by Peter the Great and his half-brother, Ivan V, in gratitude for the refuge given them by the monastery during the Streltsy Rebellion (see p24).

Baroque pillars on the Church of St Sergius and the Refectory

The exterior walls are divided into a series of panels, topped by carved scallop shells and separated by pillars decorated with sculpted vines. Each panel is painted so that it looks as though it has three-dimensional facets similar to those of the Faceted Palace (see p64) in the Kremlin. The refectory's main façade features a covered terrace with a wealth of ornamentation. At the eastern end of the refectory is the Church of St Sergius. Its iconostasis was brought here from Moscow's Church of St Nicholas on Ilinka in 1688. Delicate fretwork on the iconostasis seems to be metal, but is actually made of wood.

Cathedral of the Assumption

This magnificent cathedral, with its central golden cupola surrounded by four blue, star-spangled domes, is located at the heart of the monastery.

Ivan the Terrible commissioned the cathedral in 1559 to celebrate his defeat of the Mongols at Kazan (see p21). It was completed 26 years later to a design inspired by Aristotele Fioravanti's Cathedral of the Assumption (see pp60–61) in the Kremlin. Painters from the acclaimed Yaroslavl school of artists, led by Dmitriy Grigorev, took just 100 days to decorate the lofty interior in 1684. Their names are inscribed beneath a fresco of the Last Judgement on the west wall. The sumptuous five-tiered iconostasis dates from the same period but incorporates a number of icons from the 16th century.

Trinity Cathedral

This exquisite white cathedral is decorated with *kokoshniki* gables (see p46) above a triple-banded frieze and is the oldest stone building in the monastery. It was built over the tomb of St Sergius in 1422, the year of his canonization.

Christ in Majesty (1425–7) in the Trinity Cathedral's iconostasis

St Sergius' remains are now encased in a silver shrine inside the cathedral and are still a focus for visiting pilgrims.

The original decoration of the interior was the work of master artists Andrey Rublev and Daniil Chernyy. Most of their frescoes have since been painted over. Their iconostasis has survived, but Rublev's icon *The Trinity* (1420s) is a copy. The original is in the Tretyakov Gallery *(see pp120–23)*. Also in the iconostasis are two icons by renowned painter Simon Ushakov: *The Holy Face* (1674) and *Christ Enthroned* (1684).

Open rotunda over the holy spring, next to the Chapel Over the Well

Other Churches

There are five smaller churches within the monastery walls. The oldest is the Church of the Holy Spirit, built in 1476 by craftsmen from Pskov *(see p46)*, a town to the northwest of Moscow. The infirmary and its adjoining tent-roofed Church of SS Zosima and Savvatiy were constructed in 1635–8.

The Chapel Over the Well was built at the end of the 17th century over a holy spring. The open rotunda next to it was added in the 19th century. Pilgrims still come to fill bottles with holy water from the spring beneath the rotunda.

Just in front of the Church of St Sergius stands the small Church of St Micah. This single-domed church is named after one of St Sergius' pupils, who is buried beneath it.

The Baroque Church of the Virgin of Smolensk, a small,

The Holiest Monk

Sergius of Radonezh (c.1319–92) was born into a noble family but, with his brother, withdrew from the world and founded the Trinity Monastery. Sergius was instrumental in encouraging Russia's princes to unite against the Mongol invaders and, in 1380, Prince Dmitriy Donskoy, commander of the Russian army, asked for his blessing before attacking the Mongols at Kulikovo *(see p163)*. The Russian victory, along with the discovery that Sergius' body was miraculously unharmed in a Mongol attack on the monastery in 1408, led to Sergius' canonization in 1422.

A 16th-century icon of the appearance of the Virgin and Saints Peter and Paul to Sergius of Radonezh

blue and white rotunda, was built in 1745. The last of the monastery's churches to be constructed, it houses the Icon of the Smolensk Virgin.

Palaces and Museums

Gifts from the tsars are among the monastic treasures in the former Sacristy and Treasury. Visitors can see jewelled icon covers, exquisite crosses, icons, gospels in gilded covers, vestments and some wonderful tapestries, including the pall from the coffin of St Sergius.

Built in the late 17th century for Tsar Alexis Mikhailovich, the Tsar's Apartments are now used as a theological college. Parts of the slightly shabby exterior are

painted to appear faceted. In the southwest corner of the monastery is the 18th-century Palace of the Metropolitans. It was the first of the buildings to come back into religious use when the Soviets allowed the patriarchs and metropolitans to return in 1946.

Towers and Gate Churches

The Trinity Monastery was originally fortified in the reign of Ivan the Terrible *(see p20)*. Its formidable walls are 12 m (39 ft) high and date, in their present form, from the early 17th century. The monastery's main gate is in the Beautiful Tower. The frescoes on its archway depict the life of St Sergius. Behind the Beautiful Tower is the red-brick Gate Church of St John the Baptist.

At the north end of the walls is the Duck Tower, so called because Peter the Great shot ducks from its windows. The spire, with its carved duck, and the upper tiers were added in 1672–86.

The soaring, five-tiered, blue and white bell tower was built between 1741 and 1769.

One of the frescoes depicting scenes from St Sergius' life, on the archway of the Beautiful Tower

❼ Suzdal

Суздаль
Suzdal

---

200 km (124 miles) NE of Moscow.
🏙 12,100. 🚂 Vladimir, then bus.
🚌 *(see p227).* 🚍 Sun.

Nestling on the banks of the Kamenka river, Suzdal is the best preserved of the Golden Ring *(see p163)* towns. Its clusters of 17th- and 18th-century whitewashed churches, built by local merchants, and its streets of low, wooden houses with traditional carved eaves and windows mean that it is also one of the most attractive towns in the area.

The first records of Suzdal date from 1024. Shortly afterwards the founder of Moscow, Prince Yuriy Dolgorukiy *(see p19),* built the town's kremlin on a grassy rampart above the river. Its dominant building is the **Cathedral of the Nativity** with its blue, star-spangled domes. Although it was built in the 13th century, most of the current building dates from the 16th century. The south and west doors are of gilded copper, etched with biblical scenes. Frescoes dating from the 13th to the 17th centuries cover the interior walls. Next to it stands the former archbishop's palace,

The Cathedral of the Nativity, in the grounds of Suzdal's kremlin

now the **Suzdal Museum**. Its collection of icons and ancient art is housed in the main room, the magnificent Chamber of the Cross, one of the largest un-supported vaults in Russia. To the northeast, on Suzdal's main street, a long, arcaded building dating from 1806–11 was the former merchants' quarters.

Suzdal also contains five important religious foundations, including the **Monastery of St Euthymius**. Once the richest in the area, with more than 10,000 serfs at its disposal, the monastery has a com-manding position in the north of Suzdal, overlooking the town. Its fortified walls are almost 6 m (20 ft) thick. The monks' cells now house the **Museum of Arts and Crafts**, which has an impressive collection, including religious paintings and jewellery.

To the south of the monastery is the **Aleksandrovskiy Convent**. It was originally founded in 1240, but it burned down and was rebuilt in the 17th century. Its Cathedral of the Ascension was built at this time by Nataliya Naryshkina, mother of Peter the Great.

Rising from the meadows directly across the river here is the **Convent of the Intercession**. Founded in the 14th

Icon of St Nicholas, dating from the 15th century, in the Suzdal Museum

century, it was completed in the reign of Basil III in 1510–14. Its retreat houses offer overnight lodgings.

On the southwest edge of town is the **Suzdal Museum of Wooden Architecture** an open-air exhibition of wooden buildings brought from all over Russia. Particularly im-pressive is the Church of the Transfiguration, built in 1756. With domes made with over-lapping shingles, it was built without using any metal nails.

🏛 **Suzdal Museum**
Ulitsa Kremlyovskaya. **Tel** (492) 312 0444. **Open** Wed–Mon. 🎫
📷 English (book in advance).

🏛 **Museum of Arts and Crafts**
Ulitsa Lenina. **Tel** (492) 312 0444.
Open Tue–Sun. 🎫 📷 English (book in advance).

🏛 **Suzdal Museum of Wooden Architecture**
Ulitsa Kremlyovskaya. **Tel** (492) 312 0444. **Open** Wed–Mon. 🎫
📷 English (book in advance).

The Golden Gate, the entrance to Vladimir from the Moscow road

❽ Vladimir

Владимир
Vladimir

---

170 km (106 miles) NE of Moscow. 🏙 360,000. 🚂 🚌 *(see p227).* 🚍 daily.

Founded on the Klyazma river by Prince Vladimir Monomakh *(see p163)* in the late 11th century, Vladimir really began to flourish during the rule of his son, Prince Yuriy Dolgorukiy *(see p19).* In 1157 Dolgorukiy's heir, Prince Andrey Bogolyubskiy, brought his court here and made it the capital of the new principality of Vladimir-Suzdal. The town's heyday was in the

The 12th-century Cathedral of the Assumption in Vladimir

12th and early 13th centuries and most of the architectural monuments worth seeing date from this period. Like Suzdal, Vladimir was later eclipsed by Moscow in political importance, but it remained a significant trading centre. Today, Vladimir looks like any industrial city of the Soviet era, although, fortunately, the chemical plants and tyre factories are situated at some distance from the picturesque old part of the town, with its fine views.

When approaching Vladimir by the Moscow road, the visitor will still enter the city through the splendid **Golden Gate**. This was constructed in 1164, and combines the functions of both triumphal arch and defensive bastion. The icons above the archway were whitewashed by the Communists and have been restored. The gate now contains a small exhibition on military history.

A detail of the carved bas-reliefs on the Cathedral of St Dmitriy

A short stroll down the main street takes the visitor past the 19th-century trading arcades and shops to the **Cathedral of the Assumption**, Vladimir's most famous monument. Built in 1158–60, high above the banks of the Klyazma, it was originally decorated with prodigious quantities of gold and silver, precious gems, majolica tiles and white stone carvings. Craftsmen came from all over Russia, Poland and the Holy Roman Empire to contribute to what was then the tallest building in Russia. The coronation of many of Russia's princes, including Dmitriy Donskoy (see p20) and Aleksandr Nevskiy (see p19), took place here.

The cathedral was damaged by fire in 1185, and when it was repaired, four domes were added. When, in the 15th century, Ivan III wanted to build the Cathedral of the Assumption in Moscow (see pp60–61), he instructed his Italian architect, Aristotele Fioravanti, to use the cathedral of the same name in Vladimir as his model.

The famous Icon of the Virgin of Vladimir (see p63) used to hang in the cathedral, but it is now in the Tretyakov Gallery (see p123). However, some superb frescoes by medieval masters Andrey Rublev and Daniil Chernyy are still visible under the choir's gallery on the west wall. A short distance away is the **Cathedral of St Dmitriy**, built in 1194–7 by Prince Vsevolod III. A single-domed church of white limestone, its exterior is covered with more than a thousand bas-reliefs featuring griffons, centaurs, prancing lions and fantastic birds and plants, as well as a portrait of Vsevolod and his family. Over the window on the south wall is a carving of Alexander the Great ascending to heaven, a symbol of princely authority.

❾ Yasnaya Polyana

Ясная Поляна

Yasnaya Polyana

200 km (125 miles) S of Moscow. **Tel** (48751) 761 1 8. **Open** 9am–5pm Tue–Sun. **Closed** last Tue of the month. (see p227). English (book in advance).

The beloved country estate of Leo Tolstoy (see p136), Yasnaya Polyana is located in a peaceful valley surrounded by forests. Tolstoy was born on the estate in 1828. From the mid-1880s he spent the summers here with his wife and children, and moved here permanently without his family in 1901. The house and its contents are much as they were in Tolstoy's day. The rooms on show include the studies, where Tolstoy wrote *War and Peace* and *Anna Karenina*. Other buildings include the Dom Volkonskovo, where the serfs lived, and a pavilion for guests. Temporary exhibitions are housed in the former peasants' school.

Leo Tolstoy's house on his beloved family estate, Yasnaya Polyana

TRAVELLERS' NEEDS

WHERE TO STAY

The hotel situation in Moscow has improved dramatically since Russia became an independent state in 1992. At the top end of the market, countless new hotels have been built and grand old residences renovated, raising the standard of accommodation considerably. The mid-range sector has seen old Soviet hotels refurbished to Western standards and small family hotels established; while at the lower end, hostels have sprung up in converted apartments throughout the city. The hotels on pages 176–9 are arranged under five themes (historical, boutique, modern, luxury and chain), and listed by area and then by price. Prices are subject to rapid change, so always check in advance. There are travel and accommodation agencies, and it is possible to make a reservation at most hotels directly by phone or email. The best method, however, is to book in advance through a reliable online booking site.

The stunning marble reception area at the Radisson Royal (see p178)

Types of Hotel

Moscow's accommodation options fall into several broad categories: luxury hotels; mid-price and chain hotels; and budget options such as hostels, apartments and small hotels.

Luxury hotels are often foreign-owned or run as joint Russian–Western ventures. Many occupy historical buildings (some pre- and some post-Revolution) and have rooms combining period furniture with modern facilities. Service is similar to that in the best hotels in the West, but a double room will set you back at least 10,000 roubles a night. Hotels of this type are often referred to as Western-style.

The past decade has seen a surge in the availability of central hostels and mid-range hotels, so it is no longer necessary to venture further afield for budget options. It is also possible to rent out an apartment short-term, which can be a cheaper way to stay in a central location (see p175).

Fans of Soviet-era service and design may be disappointed to learn that in recent years most ex-Soviet hotels, including the iconic Hotel Ukraina, now the Radisson Royal (see p178), located in one of Moscow's Seven Sisters buildings, have been redeveloped as mid-range or top-of-the-range luxury hotels. The old Intourist Hotel on Tverskaya ulitsa has been turned into a luxury Ritz-Carlton (see p178).

Location of Hotels

Many of the hotels and hostels listed are within a 15-minute drive or metro ride of Moscow's city centre; others are a fair distance away, and this will be reflected in the price. When choosing a hotel, visitors should think about how they want to get around the city and take into consideration whether or not they will have a car, whether they want to get to the main sights on foot, or if their ability to read Cyrillic script is adequate to allow them to use buses and the metro with confidence.

Making a Reservation

To obtain a tourist visa, you must book a room in advance (see p206). However, this is little more than a formality that can be dealt with by a visa or travel agency; once in Moscow, it is possible to walk into any hotel and book a room on the spot. In practice, though, it is always best to make arrangements before arriving because many of the more expensive hotels may be booked up well in advance, particularly in the

The sleek bar area at the Ibis Moscow Paveletskaya (see p179)

◄ Radisson Royal, also known as Ukraina Hotel, housed in one of Stalin's magnificent Seven Sisters skyscrapers

The stylish entrance to the historic Hotel Golden Apple *(see p176)*

event of a major exhibition, while smaller hotels and hostels may have limited availability. All the hotels listed in this guide can be booked through online reservation sites such as www.booking.com and will accept reservations by phone or email. All the luxury hotels, well-known chain hotels and hostels have staff who speak reasonable English. Luxury hotels will usually ask for a credit card number as a deposit.

Facilities

All luxury hotels provide the facilities you would expect to find in an expensive hotel in the West. These include Wi-Fi, satellite television, business facilities such as meeting rooms and office services, mini-bars, a laundry service and 24-hour room service. All rooms have a bathroom with a bath or shower, or both. Fitness facilities and swimming pools are increasingly widespread, although they are not necessarily up to Western standards in the cheaper establishments. Most hotels have air-conditioned rooms.

All the larger hotels have bars and restaurants, and the luxury hotels feature some of the city's finest restaurants, but do not expect to find a bargain here. Continental breakfasts are the norm in luxury hotels and are usually served between 7:30am and 9:30am.

Apartments generally have free Wi-Fi access and flatscreen televisions, and they are comfortably furnished, often with a sofa bed for additional guests. Cooking facilities can range from just a kettle and microwave to a fully equipped kitchen replete with dishwasher and washing machine, so it's well worth enquiring in advance about what's available. Unlike hotel accommodation, apartments are usually serviced and cleaned twice a week or not at all for shorter stays.

Hostels vary enormously in terms of size and standards, but all offer free Wi-Fi as standard, and most have communal kitchens and living areas. Single-sex dormitories are available at a few places, but mixed dorms

are more commonplace. The better hostels are likely to provide individual lockers, access to a washing machine and, sometimes, hotel-style key cards for dormitories. Beware that smaller hostels may have limited shared bathroom facilities, which can cause lengthy queues in the mornings.

Registration

Foreign visitors to Russia receive a migration card upon arrival and are required by Russian law to register with the authorities within 7 days. The purpose of the registration is to notify the immigration authorities where visitors are staying during their visit to Russia. Failure to do so can cause delays and the possibility of a fine when leaving the country. Hotels are legally obliged to register guests upon arrival and sometimes charge a fee of between 500 and 1,500 roubles for this service; the same applies for apartment rentals. You will be asked to show your passport, Russian visa and migration card. Those staying with friends or Couchsurfing can either be registered by their hosts or register themselves at the nearest police station, usually for a nominal fee. Alternatively, visitors can arrange registration with a travel and visa agency in Moscow, such as **Real Russia**.

Spacious room with a view at the Ararat Park Hyatt *(see p178)*

Room with neutral colours and clean lines at Kadashevskaya *(see p178)*

Travelling with Children

Although the Russians idolize their children, this rarely seems to translate into hotel facilities for families. In most hotels it is possible to have an extra bed or cot put in a room for an additional fee, and most luxury hotels will also provide babysitters. Generally, however, hotels are more interested in business guests or tour groups, so do not expect to find extensive facilities for children or favourable room rates for families.

Payment

The rates given in this book are the standard rates quoted by each individual hotel. However, it is worth noting that business guests usually have cheaper rates negotiated at the expensive hotels by their companies, and that leisure weekend discounts are available at many luxury hotels, since most of their clients are business people who stay only during the week. The most efficient way for individual travellers to book a room is via online reservation sites such as www.booking.com, which guarantee that your payment is secure and offer the best possible range of prices.

Luxury hotels often quote prices in a foreign currency (usually US dollars). However,

it is illegal to pay in any currency other than roubles. The easiest way to pay in these hotels is undoubtedly with a debit or credit card, which eliminates the need to carry around large amounts of money. Beware that luxury hotels sometimes quote prices exclusive of VAT and city tax; this can add more than 30 per cent to the bill. Visitors should also note that tax rates in Russia are liable to change at short notice.

Breakfast is rarely included in room prices and can be another significant addition to the bill. The cost of making phone calls (international or local) from a hotel room can also be high. The local phone network *(see p214)* is cheaper, so buy a phone card and call from a public payphone.

Disabled Travellers

Most well-known chain and luxury hotels in Moscow have wheelchair access, as well as rooms equipped for disabled guests. However, it would be wise for disabled travellers to check in advance with their travel agents or the hotels to enquire about any specific needs.

Security

While many of the dangers of life in Moscow are exaggerated, hotels take security very seriously. Do not be surprised to see armed security staff with walkie-talkies patrolling the entrances of even the most refined establishments. Luxury and chain hotels all have safe-deposit boxes, and most hostels provide individual lockers, so

The Hilton Leningradskaya, housed in an imposing Stalinist skyscraper *(see p178)*

Bunk beds with privacy curtains at the Seasons Hostel *(see p177)*

guests generally have few problems with personal safety.

However, as in other cities, tourists are often targets for petty criminals. Take particular care when leaving the hotel, since pickpockets are known to hang around outside high-end tourist hotels.

Apartments

A good alternative to a hotel is a serviced apartment, which can be an attractive option for anyone who prefers to self-cater, particularly for families because you are not required to stick to set mealtimes as you would in a hotel. The length of time you can stay is usually flexible, and some companies offer good long-term deals. **Kvarthouse Apartments** and **Adrimi Apartments** rent out flats from 4,000 roubles per night, while **Moscow Suites Apartments** and **Weekend Inn Apartments** cater for high-end travellers, with Western-style apartments in the centre of town.

Budget Accommodation

Options for travellers on a tight budget have improved enormously with the advent of Couchsurfing (www.couch surfing.org) and the rise of conveniently located hostels at bargain prices.

Places such as **Godzillas**, **iVAN Hostel**, **Seasons Hostel** and **Z Hostel** are of a good standard and specifically cater to budget travellers, charging around 700 roubles per person per night for dormitory accommodation. Private doubles with shared bathrooms in hostels are usually around 2,500 roubles, while decent low-end hotels charge 3,500–5,000 roubles for an en-suite double. Hostels are generally clean and great for socializing; most include amenities such as breakfast, linen, Wi-Fi, entertainment and the use of a kitchen in the price.

Recommended Hotels

Moscow has its fair share of new buildings housing luxury or modern mid-range establishments, as well as old hotels in historical buildings full of character. The venues that have been listed on pages 176–9 are the best from the following categories: historical; boutique; modern; luxury; and chain. They are listed by price within each area. These lodgings have been featured for their excellent service, wide-ranging facilities or unique character.

Throughout the listings certain establishments have been highlighted as DK Choice. These offer a particularly special and memorable experience such as great views, period features, historical significance, special setting, unique ambience or a combination of these factors.

DIRECTORY

Registration

Real Russia
9 Bolshaya Mariyinaskaya.
Tel (499) 653 8574.
W realrussia.co.uk

Apartments

Adrimi Apartments
Tel (495) 795 6176.
W adrimi.ru

Kvarthouse Apartments
Tel (929) 616 0134.

Moscow Suites Apartments
Tel (495) 233 6429.
W moscowsuites.ru

Weekend Inn Apartments
Tel (495) 648 4047.
W weekend-inn.ru

Budget Accommodation

Godzillas
Bolshoy Karetnyy 6. **Tel** (495) 699 4223. W godzillashostel.com

iVAN Hostel
Petrovskiy pereulok 1/30, Apt. 23, Tverskoy. **Tel** (916) 407 1178.
W ivanhostel.com

Seasons Hostel
Bolshaya Ordynka 13/9, Zamoskvoreche.
Tel (495) 959 4742.
W seasonshostel.com

Z Hostel
Ulitsa Znamenka 15, Apt. 16, Khamovniki. **Tel** (495) 691 9844.
W z-hostel.ru

A modern and centrally located property rented by Moscow Suites Apartments *(see p177)*

Where to Stay

Historical

Tverskaya

iVAN Hostel ₽
*Petrovskiy pereulok 1/30, Apt. 23,
Tverskoy, 107031*
Tel (916) 407 1178 **Map** 2 F4
[W] ivanhostel.com
Mixed and single-sex dorms have
modern furnishings in this hostel
in a characterful old building.

Marco Polo Presnja ₽₽
*Spiridonyevsky pereulok 9,
Presnensky, 123104*
Tel (800) 9733 4226 **Map** 2 D4
[W] presnja.ru/thehotel-en.html
Built in 1904, this elegant hotel
has comfortable, individually
styled rooms.

Akvarel ₽₽₽
*Stoleshnikov pereulok 12, Bld. 3,
Tverskoy, 107031*
Tel (495) 502 9430 **Map** 2 F4
[W] hotelakvarel.ru
On a quiet cobbled street full of
historical buildings, this hotel has
modern, understated rooms.

DK Choice

National ₽₽₽
*Ulitsa Mokhovaya 15/1,
Tverskoy, 125009*
Tel (495) 258 7000 **Map** 6 F1
[W] national.ru
A fabulous hotel oozing period
charm, the National was briefly
home to the first Soviet
government in 1918; Lenin
stayed in room 107 for a week.
Today it boasts fantastic Kremlin
views, antique furniture and
high-ceilinged rooms, a lovely
spa centre and superb service.

Peking ₽₽₽
*Ulitsa Bolshaya Sadovaya 5,
Presnensky, 123001*
Tel (880) 0250 0550 **Map** 2 D3
[W] hotelpeking.ru
Occupying a striking Stalinist
building, the Peking will transport
you back to Soviet times.

Red Square and
Kitay Gorod

Sverchkov 8 Hotel ₽
*Sverchkov pereulok 8, Bld.1 ,
Basmanny, 101000*
Tel (495) 625 4978 **Map** 3 C4
[W] sverchkov-8.ru
This cosy hotel in a lovely
renovated mansion is comfortable,
despite showing signs of age.

Hotel Peter I ₽₽₽
Ulitsa Neglinnaya 17, Tverskoy, 127051
Tel (495) 925 3050 **Map** 3 A4
[W] hotel-peter1.ru/eng
Housed in a splendid 19th-
century building, this high-end
hotel has a spa and free Wi-Fi.

Savoy ₽₽₽
*Rozhdestvenka ulitsa, 3/6, Bld. 1,
Meshchansky, 109012*
Tel (495) 620 8500 **Map** 3 A3
[W] savoy.ru
First opened in 1913, this hotel – a
favourite of the Communist elite –
now attracts Hollywood A-listers.

Further Afield

Godzilla's Hostel ₽
Ulitsa Bolshoi Karetny 6
Tel (495) 699 4223 **Map** 3 A3
[W] godzillashostel.com
This legendary, fun hostel with
friendly staff offers rooms and
mixed dorms.

Golden Apple ₽₽₽
*Ulitsa Malaya Dmitrovka 11,
Tverskoy, 127006*
Tel (495) 980 7000 **Map** 2 E3
[W] goldenapple.ru/en
Each floor corresponds to a colour
of the rainbow at this stylish hotel
in a 19th-century building.

Boutique

Arbatskaya

Mercure Arbat ₽₽
*Smolenskaya ploschad 6,
Arbat, 121099*
Tel (495) 225 0025 **Map** 5 C1
[W] mercure.com
Rooms are spacious and elegantly
furnished here. The restaurant
serves French and Russian cuisine.

Adrimi Apartments, offering spacious,
well-equipped accommodation

Price Guide
Prices are based on one night's stay in
high season for a standard double room,
inclusive of service charges and taxes.
₽ up to ₽5,000
₽₽ ₽5,000 to ₽10,000
₽₽₽ over ₽10,000

Red Square and
Kitay Gorod

Kitai-Gorod Hotel ₽₽
*Lubyansky proezd 25, Bld. 2,
Basmanny, 101000*
Tel (495) 991 9971 **Map** 3 B5
[W] otel-kg.ru
This Soviet-era establishment
offers tastefully styled rooms and
good service.

Zamoskvoreche

Weekend Inn Apartments ₽
*Ulitsa Pyatnitskaya 10 Str.1 ,
Zamoskvorechye, 115035*
Tel (495) 648 4047 **Map** 7 B2
[W] weekend-inn.ru
Stylishly furnished rooms and
whole apartments are available
at this hotel. Outstanding service.

Medea Hotel ₽₽
*Pyatnitsky pereulok 4/1,
Zamoskvorechye, 115184*
Tel (495) 232 4898 **Map** 7 B3
[W] medea-hotel.ru/en
This small, comfortable hotel in
an 1860 building has Art
Nouveau features.

Further Afield

Blues Hotel ₽
*Ulitsa Dovatora 8, Khamovniki,
119048*
Tel (495) 961 1161
[W] eng.blues-hotel.ru
A cosy family-run hotel, Blues has
modern decor and a good
restaurant, The Crazy Hunter.

Congress-Park Volynskoe ₽₽
Ulitsa Starovolynskaya 9, 119501
Tel (499) 271 2802
[W] volynskoye.ru/en
Surrounded by lovely gardens,
this elegant hotel is just the
place for those seeking some
peace and quiet.

Danilovskaya ₽₽
*Bolshoy Starodanilovskiy
pereulok 5, 115191*
Tel (495) 954 0503
[W] danilovsky.ru/eng.htm
In a park next to Danilovskiy
monastery, this hotel fuses
modern style with a 12th-
century setting .

Gallery Avenue ₽₽
Ulitsa Shchepkina 32 Str. 1,
Meshchansky, 129090
Tel (495) 510 6737 **Map** 3 B2
W hotelgalery.ru/avenue_en/61
With murals and bright furniture,
this hotel has a quirky feel.

Gallery Park ₽₽
Ulitsa Derbenevskaya 11A, Bld.17,
115114
Tel (495) 788 3676 **Map** 8 E5
W hotelgalery.ru
This hotel has lovely design
features, with plenty of natural
light and reclaimed bricks.

Vorontsovsky ₽₽
Vorontsovsky pereulok 5/7, Bld. 2,
Tagansky, 109044
Tel (495) 663 9929 **Map** 8 E4
W vorontsovsky.ru/about-hotel
A hotel with stylish, comfortable
rooms and very large bathrooms.

Golden Ring ₽₽₽
Ulitsa Smolenskaya 5,
Khamovniki, 119121
Tel (495) 725 0100 **Map** 5 C2
W hotel-goldenring.ru/eng
Fully refurbished to five-star
standards, this Soviet-era hotel
has fantastic city views.

Hotel Garden Ring ₽₽₽
Prospekt Mira 14, Bld. 2,
Meshchansky, 129090
Tel (495) 988 3460 **Map** 3 B2
W gardenringhotel.ru
A great-value hotel in a typical
Moscow mansion, with a spa.

Modern
Arbatskaya
Landmark Hostel Arbat ₽
Starovagankovsky pereulok 15
Tel (499) 653 7044 **Map** 6 F1
W landmarkhostel.ru/en/
An immaculate hostel with
mixed and women-only dorms.

Moscow Suites Apartments ₽₽
22 ultisa Noviy Arbat, 119019
Tel (495) 233 6429 **Map** 6 F1
W moscowsuites.ru
These spotless, central apartments
have kitchens and all mod cons.
Free airport pick-up is included.

Tverskaya
Element ₽
Ulitsa Bolshaya Nikitskaya 24/1,
Bld. 5, Presnensky, 125009
Tel (495) 988 0064 **Map** 2 D5
W hotel-element.ru
A great-value hotel in an
excellent location, Element offers
smart and clean – if rather small –
rooms and cheerful service.

Elegantly furnished room in the Golden Apple

Home Hotel – Kamergersky ₽
Kamergerskiy pereulok 5, Apt. 11,
Tverskoy, 125009
Tel (495) 646 1665 **Map** 2 F5
W at-kamergersky.ru
This small, centrally located hotel
has simply furnished rooms and
shared bathroom facilities.

Pushkin ₽₽
Nastasyinskiy pereulok 5, Bld. 1,
Tverskoy, 127006
Tel (495) 201 0222 **Map** 2 E3
W otel-pushkin.ru
A comfortable hotel with high
standards and helpful staff. The
restaurant serves Russian and
European fare.

Red Square and Kitay Gorod
Day and Night Hostel ₽
Luchnikov pereulok 7/4, Bld. 6,
Basmanny, 101000
Tel (499) 504 8897 **Map** 3 B5
W daynighthostel.com
This central hostel with smart,
though slightly cramped
interiors offers both mixed
dorms and twin rooms.

Capital House ₽₽
Bolshoy Cherkasskiy pereulok 4/1,
Tverskoy, 109012
Tel (495) 739 0449 **Map** 3 B5
W us.capitalhouse.su/
Rooms are small and basic, but
spotless, at this hotel. In the
morning, pleasant staff serve
your choice of breakfast in bed.

Zamoskvoreche
Adrimi Apartments ₽
Ulitsa Bolshaya
Serpukhovskaya, 101000
Tel (495) 795 6176 **Map** 7 B5
W adrimi.ru
These large, furnished apartments
have full kitchen facilities. Staff are
on hand to answer queries.

DK Choice
Seasons Hostel ₽
Bolshaya Ordynka, 13/9, 115035
Tel (495) 959 4742 **Map** 7 B2
W seasonshostel.com
A spacious hostel boasting
bunks with individual curtains,
reading lights and lockers. There
are three bathrooms and a large
kitchen and dining area. Enjoy
home-made bread for breakfast.

Wals Hotel ₽
Ulitsa Dubininskaya 35, 115054
Tel (495) 959 6707 **Map** 7 C5
A decent-value option, Wals
Hotel is in a convenient location
with excellent transport
connections. It has an on-site café.

Aquamarine ₽₽
Ozerkovskaya naberezhnaya 26,
115184
Tel (495) 580 2828 **Map** 7 B2
W aquamarinehotel.ru
A tranquil hotel with smart
facilities and a restaurant.

Further Afield
Ananas Mini Hotel ₽
Ulitsa Barklaya 13/1, Filevsky Park,
121309
Tel (903) 112 4499
W hotelananas.ru
Basic, good-value rooms are set
over five floors, but with no lift.

Hostel University ₽
Prospect Vernadskogo 9 ap. 8, 119911
Tel (926) 353 0363
Popular with students, this basic
but well-maintained hostel has
large single-sex dorms.

Kvarthouse Apartments Leninsky ₽
Ulitsa Ordzhonikidze 6/9, 115419
Tel (929) 616 0134
An immaculate, roomy apartment
with excellent facilities.

For more information on types of hotel *see pages 172–5*

Lomonosov ₽
Michurinskiy prospekt 34,
Ramenki, 119192
Tel (495) 589 0809
W hotel-lomonosov.ru/en
This simple, clean hotel has
classical decor and large rooms.

RealTimeSchool Hostel ₽
Ulitsa Nezhinskaya 5, 119501
Tel (495) 442 5966
Within a wooded park, this hostel
in a Soviet-era building offers
great value.

Versal na Kutuzovskom ₽
Ploshchad Pobedy 1 E, 121293
Tel (903) 716 9100
W hotel-versali.com
A lovely small hotel with neatly
furnished rooms, a shared guest
kitchen and attentive staff.

Victory Hostel ₽
2 Pavlovskiy pereulok 26, entrance 1,
3rd Floor, Apt. 3, 115093
Tel (916) 747 4664
W victoryhostel.com
Three dorm rooms, each with a
shared bathroom, make up this
colourful, well-run hostel.

AST Hof ₽₽
Ulitsa Bolshaya Filevskaya 25,
Filevsky Park, 125309
Tel (495) 744 0700
W asthof.ru/en
It may have seen better days, but
this functional hotel is reasonable
value and close to a metro station.

Radisson Slavyanskaya ₽₽
Ploshchad Evropi 2, 121059
Tel (495) 941 8020
W radisson.ru
High standards in keeping with
the Radisson chain can be
enjoyed at this comfortable hotel.

Luxury
Arbatskaya

DK Choice

Lotte ₽₽₽
Novinskiy bulvar 8, Bld. 2,
Arbat, 121099
Tel (495) 745 1000　　**Map** 2 D5
W lottehotel.com
This hugely opulent central
hotel boasts vast, sumptuously
furnished rooms, an excellent
spa centre with underground
pool and two splendid
restaurants featuring menus
prepared by a Michelin-starred
chef. Part of a South Korean
hotel chain; the service
standards are second to none.

Tverskaya

Ararat Park Hyatt ₽₽₽
Ulitsa Neglinnaya 4,
Meshchansky, 109012
Tel (495) 783 1234　　**Map** 3 A4
W moscow.park.hyatt.com
Close to Red Square, this hotel has
a rooftop lounge with city views.

Intercontinental Tverskaya ₽₽₽
Ulitsa Tverskaya 22, Tverskoy, 125009
Tel (495) 787 8887　　**Map** 2 E3
W ihg.com
This stylish hotel has a spa and a
lovely restaurant.

Metropol ₽₽₽
Teatralny proezd 2, Tverskoy, 109012
Tel (499) 501 7800　　**Map** 3 A5
W metropol-moscow.ru
Lavish furnishings bordering on
the kitsch, and excellent service
can be enjoyed here. Free parking.

Ritz-Carlton ₽₽₽
Tverskaya 3, Tverskoy, 125009
Tel (495) 225 8888　　**Map** 2 E3
W ritzcarlton.com
An elegant hotel with impeccable
service and views of Red Square.

Red Square and Kitay Gorod

Nikolskaya Moscow ₽₽₽
Nikolskaya 12, Tverskoy, 109012
Tel (495) 967 7776　　**Map** 3 A5
W hotelnikolskaya.com
The lavish, elegant interior of this
hotel features lots of gold leaf.

Zamoskvoreche

Baltschug Kempinski ₽₽₽
Ulitsa Baltschug 1, 115035
Tel (495) 287 2000　　**Map** 7 B2
W kempinski.com
Enjoy elegant decor and river
views from the north-facing rooms.

Kadashevskaya ₽₽₽
Kadashevskaya naberezhnaya 26,
Yakimanka, 115035
Tel (495) 287 8710　　**Map** 7 A3
W kadashevskaya.com
Many of the ultra-modern stylish
rooms have delightful river views.

DK Choice

Swissôtel Krasnye Holmy ₽₽₽
Kosmodamianskaya
naberezhnaya 52, Bld. 6, 115054
Tel (495) 787 9898　　**Map** 7 C2
W swissotel.com/moscow
This landmark hotel with top-
rate facilities towers over
Moscow. Rooms with floor-to-
ceiling windows have
spectacular city views, as does
the 34th-floor City Space bar.

Hand-carved wooden ceiling and marble
staircase at the Hilton Leningradskaya

Further Afield

Crowne Plaza ₽₽
Krasnopresnenskaya naberezhnaya
12, Presnensky, 123610
Tel (495) 258 2222　　**Map** 1 B5
W cpmow.ru
High standards prevail at this
vast, good-value hotel in the
World Trade Centre.

Hilton Leningradskaya ₽₽₽
Ulitsa Kalanchevskaya 21/40,
Krasnoselsky, 107078
Tel (495) 627 5550　　**Map** 4 D2
W hilton.com
This colossal Stalinist skyscraper
still boasts the original hand-
carved wooden ceiling in its
lobby and Russian Empire-style
furniture throughout.

DK Choice

Radisson Royal ₽₽₽
Kutuzovsky prospekt 2/1,
Bld. 1, 121248
Tel (495) 221 5555　　**Map** 5 A2
W radisson.ru
This magnificent hotel occupies
the second highest of Stalin's
Seven Sisters skyscrapers (after
Moscow State University).
Highlights include the 30th-
floor bar with stunning city
views, a superb restaurant, pool
and the gleaming wall-to-
wall marble reception area.

Renaissance Moscow
Monarch Centre ₽₽₽
Leningradsky prospekt 31, Bld. 1,
Begovoy, 125284
Tel (749) 5995 0009
W marriott.com
This tasteful hotel offers a lovely
pool and spa area, and splendid
views from the rooftop terrace.

Chain

Arbatskaya

Arbat ₽₽
*Plotnikov pereulok 12,
Khamovniki, 119002*
Tel (499) 271 2801   **Map** 6 D2
W arbat.president-hotel.ru
Despite its tired interior, Arbat
offers good service and large
rooms, and is close to the metro.

Tverskaya

Assambleya Nikitskaya ₽₽₽
*Ulitsa Bolshaya Nikitskaya 12/2,
Presnensky, 125009*
Tel (495) 933 5001   **Map** 2 D5
W assambleya-hotels.ru
A spotless hotel, if rather on the
plain side, with attentive staff.

Courtyard Moscow
City Centre ₽₽₽
*Voznesenskiy pereulok 7,
Presnensky, 125009*
Tel (495) 981 3300   **Map** 2 E5
W marriott.com
A pleasant hotel with spacious
rooms and modern amenities.

Marriott Grand ₽₽₽
Ulitsa Tverskaya 26/1, Tverskoy, 125009
Tel (495) 937 0000   **Map** 2 E3
W marriott.com
This classy hotel has slightly
dated five-star facilities.

Zamoskvoreche

Ibis Moscow Centre
Bakhrushina ₽₽
Ulitsa Bakhrushina 11, 115184
Tel (495) 720 5301   **Map** 7 C4
W ibis.com
A modern hotel with attractive
wood decor in the public areas.

Ozerkovskaya ₽₽
*Ozerkovskaya naberezhnaya 50,
115054*
Tel (495) 951 9582   **Map** 7 C3
W ozerkovskaya.com
In a lovely setting facing the river,
this hotel offers large rooms.

Park Inn by Radisson Sadu ₽₽₽
*17 ulitsa Bolshaya Polyanka, Bld. 1,
Yakimanka, 119180*
Tel (495) 644 4844   **Map** 7 A3
W parkinn.com
A well-run hotel popular with
business travellers.

Further Afield

Maxima Irbis ₽
Ulitsa Gostinichnaya 1, 127106
Tel (495) 788 7272
W maximahotels.com
A good standard of comfort and
service are offered at this hotel.

Maxima Panorama ₽
Ulitsa Masterkova 4, 115280
Tel (495) 788 7272
W maximahotels.ru
A hotel with small, well-kept
rooms near Avtozavodskaya metro.

Maxima Zarya ₽
Ulitsa Gostinichnaya 4/9, 127106
Tel (495) 788 7272
W maximahotels.com
This comfortable venue is a larger
version of its nearby sister hotel.

Novotel Moscow Sheremetyevo
Airport ₽
*Airport Sheremetyevo Vladenie 3,
141400 Khimki*
Tel (495) 626 5900
W novotel.com
This vast, high-standard hotel is
near the airport's train terminal.

Proton ₽
*Ulitsa Novozavodskaya 22,
Filevsky Park, 121087*
Tel (495) 797 3300
W protonhotel.ru/index.php/en
Although rather characterless, this
modern hotel has pleasant staff.

Akademicheskaya ₽₽
Ulitsa Donskaya 1, Yakimanka, 119049
Tel (495) 989 6009   **Map** 6 F5
W maanhotels.ru/akademikalabout
A hotel with basic amenities in a
Soviet-era building.

Holiday Inn Vinogradovo ₽₽
*Dmitrovskoe Shosse
Vladenie 171, 127204*
Tel (495) 937 0670
W holidayinn.com
Amenities at this hotel include
mini-golf and tennis.

Ibis Moscow Paveletskaya ₽₽
*Ulitsa Shchipok 22, Str. 1,
Zamoskvorechye, 115093*
Tel (495) 660 7500
W ibis.com
A smart, modern hotel with
spacious, spotless rooms.

Korston ₽₽
15 Kosygina ulitsa, 119334
Tel (800) 100 9989
W korston.ru
Korston offers sweeping city
views from its rooms. It is next
door to a casino.

Volga Apart Hotel ₽₽
*Bolshaya Spasskaya ulitsa 4, Bld. 1,
Krasnoselsky, 107078*
Tel (495) 783 9100   **Map** 3 C2
W hotel-volga.com
In a renovated Soviet-era block,
the rooms here are simply
furnished. There is a play area
for children.

Courtyard by Marriott Moscow
Paveletskaya ₽₽₽
*Ulitsa Kozhevnicheskaya 8, Str. 3,
Zamoskvorechye, 115114*
Tel (495) 287 7722   **Map** 8 D5
W marriott.com
A hotel with a bright, cheerful
interior and polite, efficient staff.

Holiday Inn Lesnaya ₽₽₽
Ulitsa Lesnaya 15, Tverskoy, 125047
Tel (495) 783 6500   **Map** 2 D2
W holidayinn.com
This hotel with excellent business
facilities provides a reliable service.

Katerina City ₽₽₽
*Shluzovaya naberezhnaya 6/1,
Zamoskvorechye, 115114*
Tel (495) 795 2444   **Map** 8 D4
W katerinahotels.com/en
A pleasant hotel with genuinely
helpful staff and cosy rooms,
some with river views.

Sheraton Palace ₽₽₽
*Ulitsa 1-ya Tverskaya-Yamskaya 19,
Tverskoy, 125047*
Tel (495) 931 9700   **Map** 2 E3
W sheratonpalace.ru
This is an immaculate
modern hotel with high
standards and prices to match.
A complimentary fruit basket
is included.

The Olympic-size swimming pool at the Radisson Royal

For more information on types of hotel *see pages 174–5*

WHERE TO EAT AND DRINK

Although eating out was a rare privilege during the Soviet era, and an unaffordable luxury in the years immediately after perestroika (restructuring), Russia has since experienced an astonishing restaurant boom. New places – from student cafés to exclusive sushi restaurants – open and close every week. All the major cuisines are represented, including those from the former Soviet Republics, such as Georgia, Armenia and Uzbekistan. Visitors should have little trouble finding a place that matches their taste and budget. The following pages will help to locate some of the best-quality food and most exciting cuisine on offer in all price categories. A detailed review of selected restaurants is provided on pages 186–9, and ideas for light meals are on pages 190–91.

Where to Eat

Most of Moscow's better-known restaurants are located in the city centre and, therefore, are fairly easy to reach by metro. The area around Tverskaya ulitsa (see p91) has the highest concentration and variety of restaurants, from Russian and Georgian to Italian and Japanese, as well as the now-ubiquitous branches of McDonald's. Krasny Oktyabr, a former chocolate factory across the river from Kropotkinskaya, is now home to the city's most fashionable restaurants and bars, such as Bar Strelka (see p186).

Reading the Menu

Restaurants offering international cuisine often have menus in both Russian and English. Waiting staff will usually know enough English to take orders. In smaller, local eateries, a knowledge of the Cyrillic alphabet will help with deciphering the menu, since many ingredients are phonetic transcriptions of their English equivalents.

Types of Cuisine

There are several excellent Russian restaurants in Moscow, such as Café Pushkin (see p187) and Oblomov (see p188). The best Russian fare is either wholesome dishes and soups from recipes passed down from generation to generation, or cured and salted fish, as well as caviar, for which preparation is more important at its source rather than in the kitchen. Georgian and Armenian cuisines, both of which are delicious and

Stolovaya 57, located within the splendid GUM department store (see p187)

relatively inexpensive, are very good options. Mediterranean and other Western European restaurants, especially Italian ones, are increasingly popular. Chinese and Indian food can sometimes be overpriced and of variable quality. However, there are many excellent Asian restaurants – particularly Japanese, with sushi being a fashionable food trend. Prices are high, since the city is landlocked and fresh fish has to be flown in daily.

What to Drink

Vodka is the alcoholic drink most often associated with Russia. However, beer has become more widely available, and wine often accompanies meals. Most restaurants offer imported and local beer on tap, along with a variety of bottled options. Russian beer is light and generally very good; imported beer is often overpriced. The better European restaurants have commendable wine lists, though good imported wine tends to be quite expensive. It is a shame to visit Moscow without sampling a bottle of Georgian wine (see p185) in one of its many Georgian eateries.

Payment and Tipping

One of the drawbacks of eating out in Moscow is that some restaurants, usually the less touristy ones, only take cash. This situation is changing, but it is still a consideration when deciding where to eat. Generally restaurants that

Smart-casual interior of the popular Ragout (see p189)

serve Western or Asian cuisine will accept credit cards, but it is a good idea to call ahead and check exactly which cards are accepted and whether a surcharge is applied. Prices vary enormously – from around 200 roubles in a cheap cafeteria (*stolovaya*), to closer to 3,500 roubles for exclusive restaurants.

Tipping is not as ingrained in Russia as in other countries. Keeping to international standards of 10–15 per cent if you are satisfied is appropriate, although it is unnecessary to leave more than a few hundred roubles regardless of the total expenditure. In Russian-style restaurants or cafés, it is acceptable to leave small change, or nothing at all. Service is rarely included in the bill.

Bar Strelka, offering picture-postcard views of the Cathedral of Christ the Saviour *(see p186)*

Opening Times

Dinner is the main meal of the day, but many restaurants in Moscow have now adopted the concept of the business lunch. This often takes the form of a fixed-price menu and can be excellent value. Lunch is usually served from noon until 4pm. Most restaurants start serving dinner at around 6pm and stop taking orders at 10:30pm; some family-run Georgian establishments close their kitchens as early as 9pm. Increasingly, restaurants are staying open until the early hours of the morning, and some are even open around the clock.

Making a Reservation

Most international and tourist-oriented restaurants take reservations – indeed, some of the most popular ones require them. Generally, it is best to book ahead whenever possible. However, some of the most popular Georgian and Caucasian restaurants do not take reservations, and these can be busy, especially at weekends.

Etiquette

Casual or semi-formal dress is acceptable in almost every Moscow restaurant. Russians tend to overdress rather than underdress, however, so it is probably safer to err on the formal side. Children are a rare sight at expensive restaurants, and most eateries do not have a special menu for them. Moscow does have a few family-style restaurants, and many of the Western-owned restaurants provide children's menus.

Vegetarians

Much of Russian cuisine consists of meat dishes. Even salads tend to contain meat, so the best option for vegetarians is often a beetroot or tomato platter. Georgian cuisine, featuring numerous excellent bean and aubergine dishes, is usually a better bet for non-meat eaters. Restaurants are increasingly taking into account the demands of vegetarian visitors, and European, Chinese and Japanese eateries usually have some items suitable for vegetarians. There are a few

Stylish dining room of Chicago Prime Steakhouse *(see p187)*

vegetarian restaurants, such as Jagannat *(see p187)* in the city, and the standard of these is rising.

Smoking

There are generally areas for non-smokers in restaurants. However, smoking during meals is considered acceptable in Russia, and smokers sometimes pay scant regard to non-smoking areas.

Disabled Persons

Few restaurants in Moscow have facilities for disabled visitors. Some restaurants are located in basements, making access an issue. It is always best to phone in advance to check if there is full disabled access.

Recommended Restaurants

The restaurants on pages 186–9 have been carefully selected to give a cross-section of the best options in Moscow, from the smartest fine-dining establishments to more low-key budget eateries. Despite the bewildering number of restaurants in the city, a few stand out from the crowd; these have been flagged as a DK Choice. They offer something particularly special, such as exceptional cuisine, a fashionable ambience, family-friendly facilities, a historic background, sumptuous interiors or a combination of these factors.

The Flavours of Moscow

Russia's culinary reputation centres on warming stews, full of wintery vegetables such as cabbage, beetroot and potatoes. Yet Moscow was once the capital of a vast empire stretching from Poland to the Pacific and this is reflected in the variety of food on offer in the city. Aubergines (eggplants) and tomatoes, imported from the Caucasus in the south, bring in the flavours of the Mediterranean, while spices from Central Asia lend an exotic touch. On the stalls of the city's Central Market, crayfish and caviar sit alongside honey from Siberia and melons and peaches from Georgia.

Wild mushrooms

Caviar, the roe of sturgeon from Russia's warm southern waters

Russian Countryside

Many Muscovites have small country houses within easy reach of the city, and spend weekends from spring to early winter lovingly tending their immaculate vegetable gardens, or combing the countryside for wild berries and mushrooms. Much of this bountiful harvest is made into preserves and pickles. There is a refreshing soup, *solianka*, in which pickled cucumbers impart a delicious salty taste. Pickled mushrooms in sour cream make a regular appearance on restaurant menus, as do a variety of fresh berry juices.

In a country where food shortages are a fairly recent memory, very little is wasted. *Kvas*, a popular, mildly alcoholic drink is frequently made at home by fermenting stale bread with sugar and a scattering of fruit. Summer visitors should make a point of trying the delicious cold soup *okroshka*, which is based on *kvas*.

Russia is also a land with hundreds of rivers and lakes, and has a long tradition of fish cookery. Dishes range from simple soups, such as *ukha*, to caviar and sturgeon, and salmon cooked in a bewildering variety of ways.

Blinis · Pickled mushrooms · Spiced feta · Rye bread · Gherkins · Salted fish · Soured cream · Pickled herring

A typical spread of *zakuski* (cold appetizers)

Local Dishes and Specialities

Borscht (beetroot soup) and *blinis* (buttery pancakes) with caviar are perhaps two of the most famous Russian dishes – one a peasant dish which varies with the availability of ingredients and the other a staple for the week leading up to Lent, when rich food would be eaten to fatten up before the fast. Much of Russia's cuisine is designed to make use of what is readily to hand or is warming and filling. A popular main course is *kulebiaka*, a hearty fish pie, larded with eggs, rice, dill and onion and encased in a buttery crust. Another popular dish is beef stroganoff with its creamy mushroom sauce, which was created in 18th-century St Petersburg by the chef of the wealthy Stroganoff family.

Beetroot

Borscht Made with meat or vegetable stock, this beetroot soup is usually served with dill and soured cream.

Major Wi

- Vine-
- Mold
- Ukrai
- Russi

Georgia

Other

Originally
to be ma
ex-Soviet
Armenia
ageing it

Mineral wat

Tea

Russian te
lemon an
glass, calle
(
ja
T
tr
T

A glass of tea, w
(varenye) to swe

Market vegetable stall in central Moscow

The Caucasus

The former Soviet states of the Caucasus – Georgia, Azerbaijan and Armenia – are renowned for their legendary banquets, where the tables are laden with an enormous quantity and variety of food and drink. These regions still supply Russia's cities with a tempting range of fine subtropical produce. Limes, lemons, oranges, walnuts, figs, pomegranates, peaches, beans, salty cheeses and herbs are all shipped in season to Moscow's markets and its many Georgian restaurants. The cuisine of Georgia, with its focus on freshly grilled meats, pulses, vegetables, yogurt, herbs and nut sauces – including the hallmark walnut sauce, *satsivi* – is famously healthy and Georgians are particularly known for their longevity.

Central Asia

From the Central Asian republics of the old Soviet Union, which include Uzbekistan, Turkmenistan and Tajikistan, come a range of culinary traditions based on the nomadic lifestyles of

Freshly picked lingonberries from Russia's bumper autumn harvest

Russia's one-time overlords, the Mongol or Tartar Hordes. The meat of fat-tailed sheep, which thrive in the desert air, is used to make communal piles of *plov* (pilaf) around which guests sit, eating in the traditional manner with their hands. Served in Moscow's Uzbek restaurants, it shares the menu with delicious flat breads, spicy noodle soups, *manti* (tasty dumplings reminiscent of Chinese cuisine) and a variety of melons and grapes, which proliferate in the desert oases, and apricots and nuts, grown in the mountains.

ZAKUSKI

A traditional Russian meal generally begins with *zakuski*, a selection of cold appetizers. These may include pickled mushrooms (*gribi*), gherkins (*ogurtsi*), salted herrings (*seliodka*), an assortment of smoked fish, blinis topped with caviar, various vegetable pâtés (sometimes known as vegetable caviars), stuffed eggs (*yaitsa farshirovanniye*), spiced feta cheese (*brinza*), beetroot salad (*salat iz svyokla*) and small meat pies (*pirozhki*), accompanied by rye bread and washed down with shots of vodka. A bowl of steaming soup often follows, before the main course reaches the table.

Kulebiaka Rich, buttery puff pastry is wrapped around a mix of fish, hard-boiled eggs, rice, onion and chopped dill.

Pelmeni These meat-stuffed dumplings may be served in a clear broth, or with tomato sauce or soured cream.

Kissel A mix of red berries is used to make this soft, fruity jelly, which is served topped with a swirl of fresh cream.

Where to Eat and Drink

Arbatskaya

Baba Marta
Bulgarian   ₽   **Map** 6 E2
Gogolevskiy bulvar 8
Tel (495) 232 9209
Menu favourites at this family-run restaurant include grilled meat dishes with vegetables and cheese. The *banitsa* (sweet and savoury pastries) are particularly recommended.

Chocolate
International   ₽   **Map** 6 F2
Volhonka ulitsa 6
Tel (495) 697 2515
Serving a mixed menu of Russian, Italian and Japanese dishes, this bright restaurant offers excellent service. It has a kids' playroom too.

Obraz Zhizny
International   ₽   **Map** 6 D3
Ulitsa Prechistenka 40/2, Str. 2
Tel (926) 902 3158
With understated decor, low lighting and quirky paintings, this restaurant specializes in traditional Eastern European fare, including Hungarian goulash, Polish *borscht* and Gdansk veal.

Shchisliva
Russian   ₽   **Map** 6 F2
Ulitsa Volkhonka 9, Bld. 1
Tel (499) 393 3961
Brick walls and simple wooden tables create a relaxed setting in which to savour venison *pelmeni* (dumplings) and *schi* soup.

Bar Strelka
International   ₽₽   **Map** 6 F2
Bersenevskaya naberezhnaya 14, Str. 5A
Tel (495) 771 7416
This modern restaurant-bar on an island in the Moskva River offers bistro-style food and great views from the summer rooftop terrace.

Korchma Taras Bulba
Ukrainian   ₽₽   **Map** 6 F1
Ulitsa Mokhovaya 8
Tel (495) 780 7744
Part of a large chain of village-style Ukrainian restaurants in Moscow, this is the place to visit for *pelmeni* (dumplings) and *borscht*.

Twenty-Two
International   ₽₽   **Map** 6 D1
Noviy Arbat 22
Tel (495) 776 8622
A sophisticated clientele comes here for the adventurous Asian–European fusion cuisine, plus the splendid selection of wines.

Vostochnaya Komnata
Indian   ₽₽   **Map** 5 C2
Smolenskaya ploschad 3
Tel (495) 937 8423
Popular with both Russians and ex-pats, this restaurant serves authentic Indian food in the heart of Moscow. Book ahead at weekends.

Zhurfak
International   ₽₽   **Map** 6 E2
Bolshoi Afanasievsky pereulok 3
Tel (985) 212 5050
This popular restaurant with friendly service offers generous portions of Russian and European fare in a laid-back environment.

Zu Café
Asian   ₽₽   **Map** 5 C1
Ulitsa Novyy Arbat 17
Tel (495) 989 6573
Chefs prepare such delights as Thai fish cakes, Asian duck salad and shrimp chips in an open kitchen at this smart restaurant.

Barashka
Azerbaijan   ₽₽₽   **Map** 6 D1
Ulitsa Novy Arbat 21/1
Tel (495) 228 3731
Founded by restaurateur Arkady Novikov, this is a high-class venue serving exquisite meat dishes, as well as some vegetarian options.

Elardzhi
Georgian   ₽₽₽   **Map** 6 E2
Gagarinsky pereulok 15A
Tel (495) 627 7897
The place to see and be seen, Elardzhi serves Georgian staples such as lamb *shashlyk* and *pelamushi* (a dessert made from grape juice and cornmeal).

Industrial-chic interior of the elegant Bar Strelka

DK Choice

White Rabbit
International   ₽₽₽   **Map** 5 C1
Smolenskaya ploschad 3
Tel (495) 663 3999
Enjoy breathtaking views from the comfort of sofas and armchairs beneath a domed glass ceiling at this restaurant perched atop a 16-storey building. White Rabbit is frequented by Moscow's elite, so expect prices to match. Top chef Alexander Mukhin provides a modern take on traditional Russian dishes.

Tverskaya

Bublik
Russian   ₽   **Map** 2 E4
Tverskoy bulvar 24
Tel (495) 629 1342
A deli-style restaurant with an upmarket atmosphere, Bulik serves a range of Russian and international dishes, including lovely savoury and sweet pastries.

Conversation
American   ₽   **Map** 2 E5
Ulitsa Nikitskaya B. 23/14
Tel (985) 443 7344
This New York loft-style café-restaurant serves a great range of cakes and light meals, all prepped in an open kitchen with fresh local ingredients.

Montalto
Italian   ₽   **Map** 2 D4
Sadovaya Kudrinskaya 20
Tel (495) 234 3487
A New York-style pizzeria with exposed brick walls, minimalist decor and a wood-fired pizza oven. Toppings include spicy home-made sausage and wood-roasted mushrooms.

Pizza Peppe
International   ₽   **Map** 2 F5
Gazetnyj pereulok Dom. 9, Str. 2
Tel (495) 629 7945
Simple and unpretentious, this is a great spot for good-value, tasty thin-crust pizzas, salads, pasta dishes and soups.

Retseptor ₽
International **Map** 2 D5
Bolshaya Nikitskaya 22/2
Tel (495) 695 6686
The retro decor here alone makes it worth a visit. The menu includes wholesome dishes such as baked carp and spicy Korean soup.

As Eat Is ₽₽
Russian **Map** 2 E4
Trehprudny pereulok 11/13/2
Tel (495) 699 5313
Traditional Russian dishes with a modern twist here include salad with *omul* fish from Lake Baikal and duck stewed in wine.

Dolkabar ₽₽
International **Map** 2 D3
Ulitsa Krasina 7/1
Tel (499) 254 7908
Established by a Russian travel blogger, Dolkabar is decorated with travel photos and souvenirs.

Hinkalnaya ₽₽
Georgian **Map** 2 E3
Ulitsa Tverskaya 30/2
Tel (903) 728 1874
Tasty specialities such as *pkhali* (chopped vegetables and nuts) and *chikhirtma* (thick chicken soup) are served at this café-style restaurant.

Mari Vanna ₽₽
Russian **Map** 6 D1
Spiridonevskiy pereulok 10A
Tel (495) 650 6500
This restaurant re-creates the look of a cosy pre-Soviet apartment. Home-cooked dishes include baked duck leg with buckwheat. Breakfast is served until noon.

Ulliam's ₽₽
International **Map** 2 D4
Malaya Bronnaya ulitsa 27a
Tel (495) 650 6462
Diners can watch their meal being cooked in the open kitchen at the centre of this small, cosy restaurant. Dishes are mainly French, Italian, American and English.

DK Choice

Café Pushkin ₽₽₽
Russian **Map** 2 E4
Tverskoy bulvar 26A
Tel (495) 739 0033
Oozing with aristocratic charm, this restaurant is one of the best in Russia. It serves beautifully presented traditional dishes – such as thinly sliced frozen wild boar garnished with apple and Russian dumplings – in the magnificent surroundings of an 18th-century mansion.

Pre-Soviet-style decor at the delightfully cosy Mari Vanna

Chicago Prime Steakhouse ₽₽₽
American **Map** 2 F3
Strastnoy bulvar 8A
Tel (495) 988 1717
Diners at this top-rate steakhouse select their raw cuts, which are then cooked to perfection. Great wine list and faultless service.

El Gaucho ₽₽₽
Argentinean **Map** 2 E3
Ulitsa Triumfalnaya 4/10
Tel (495) 699 7974
Cook your own steak on a hot plate at your table at this venue popular with celebrities.

Polo Club ₽₽₽
American **Map** 3 A4
Ulitsa Petrovka 11/20
Tel (495) 937 1024
This plush steakhouse in the Marriott Royal Aurora Hotel also has a good seafood menu, as well as a large selection of desserts and an extensive wine list.

Scandinavia ₽₽₽
International **Map** 2 E4
Bolshoy Palashevskiy pereulok 7
Tel (495) 937 5630
The menu here has quality European cuisine with some Swedish specialities. It is especially popular in summer, when guests enjoy dining under chestnut trees.

Red Square and Kitay Gorod

Jagannat ₽
Vegetarian **Map** 3 A4
Kuznetskiy most 11
Tel (495) 628 3580
This well-established restaurant serves Indian, Mexican, Thai, Chinese and European specialities. There are no alcoholic drinks, so wash your food down with refreshing home-made lemonade and ginger beer.

Ludi Kak Ludi ₽
International **Map** 7 C1
Solyanskiy tupik 1/4
Tel (495) 621 1201
This café with a mosaic floor serves home-baked breads, smoothies and light meals.

Stolovaya 57 ₽
Russian **Map** 7 B1
Krasnaya ploschad 3 (inside GUM department store)
Tel (495) 620 3129
Designed to resemble a Soviet canteen, this is perfect for a quick lunch. The food is excellent, too – far above Soviet standards.

Avocado ₽₽
Vegetarian **Map** 3 C4
Chistoprudny Bulvar 12/2
Tel (495) 621 7719
Healthy and tasty vegetarian dishes here include soups, pasta, *pelmeni* (dumplings) and curries.

Bardak ₽₽
Turkish **Map** 3 B5
Ulitsa Maroseyka 6/8, Str. 1
Tel (495) 624 8878
Well-presented dishes and perfect Turkish coffee are served in a dining room that blends modern and traditional Turkish decor.

Bobby Dazzler ₽₽
International **Map** 3 B3
Kostyansky pereulok 7/13
Tel (495) 608 0383
A popular English pub with a great range of European beers and marvellous dishes, such as salmon sausages. Book ahead.

Liga Pap ₽₽
International **Map** 3 B4
Ulitsa Bolshaya Lubyanka 24
Tel 4956243636
With more than 20 TV screens, this is the ultimate sports bar, with a good varied menu and plenty of chilled beer.

For more information on types of restaurants *see pages 180–81*

DK Choice

Maharaja PP
Indian Map 8 D1
Ulitsa Pokrovka 2/1
Tel (495) 621 9844
Though more expensive than its competitors, Maharaja consistently serves generous portions of delicious Indian cuisine. Tasteful decor and a low-key environment, coupled with attentive service, ensure a thoroughly enjoyable experience. Dishes can be spiced to individual taste.

Petrovich PP
Russian Map 3 B4
Ulitsa Myasnitskaya 24, Bld. 3
Tel (495) 623 0082
This quirky, time-warp basement restaurant celebrates everything Soviet – from the decor to the food and music. It gets very lively at weekends.

Propaganda PP
American Map 6 D2
Bolshoi Zlatoustinskiy pereulok 7
Tel (495) 624 5732
Enjoy great service and large portions at this legendary hang-out that turns into one of Moscow's best clubs at night. Try the home-made pasta dishes.

Tapa de Comida PP
Spanish Map 3 A3
Ulitsa Trubnaya 20/2
Tel (495) 608 2007
Reminiscent of a traditional Iberian café, Tapa de Comida has a wide range of tapas, such as Serrano ham and *croquetas* (croquettes).

U–Me PP
Japanese Map 3 C5
Ulitsa Pokrovka 38A
Tel (495) 621 7840
This restaurant featuring dark wood furniture and paper lanterns has a wonderfully calm ambience, sophisticated service and exquisitely presented dishes.

Volkonsky PP
International Map 3 B5
Ulitsa Maroseyka 4/2
Tel (495) 258 5440
Attached to what is arguably the city's best bakery, this cosy café serves sublime rolls and cakes, plus a good range of mains.

Goodman Steakhouse PPP
American Map 3 A5
Ulitsa Okhotniy Ryad 2
Tel (495) 775 9888
Part of a steakhouse chain, Goodman offers quality steaks and speciality burgers.

Nostalgie PPP
Russian Map 3 C4
Chistoprudny bulvar 12A
Tel (495) 258 5668
A superb wine list accompanies sumptuous haute cuisine in elegant surroundings. Pheasant consommé or warm foie gras are among the menu options.

Schastye PPP
Mediterranean Map 3 C4
Chistoprudniy bulvar 16
Tel (495) 624 6421
Chandeliers, cherubs and whitewashed brick walls create a laid-back vibe at this popular, stylish restaurant, the name of which translates as "Happiness".

Zamoskvoreche

Karavaevi P
Russian Map 7 B3
Bolshaya Ordynka 7/1
Tel (495) 951 6204
Perfect for a quick lunch, this welcoming rustic restaurant has a great selection of sandwiches, pastries, salads and light meals.

Marukame P
Japanese Map 7 B2
Ulitsa Pyatnitskaya 29
Tel (495) 660 5589
Part of a chain with more than 600 restaurants in Japan, Marukame is a self-service noodle bar with consistently high standards and good-value prices.

Aldebaran PP
International Map 7 A3
Bolshoy Tolmachevskiy pereulok 4, Str. 1
Tel (495) 953 6268
In a pleasant location with outside tables, this simple Parisian-style café-restaurant serves a good range of snacks and light meals.

Bottlebar PP
International Map 7 B2
Pyatnitsky pereulok 2, Trade Complex Pyatnitsky, 2nd Floor
Tel (495) 646 4925
The good-value menu at this vibrant restaurant includes steaks, pasta and soups. It doubles as a bar/club with live music, DJs and stand-up comics.

Brix PP
International Map 7 B2
Ulitsa Pyatnickaya 71/5
Tel (495) 925 9594
Renowned for its extensive wine list, Brix is a great place to relax and enjoy imaginative dishes such as black cod with artichokes or lamb ravioli.

The well-stocked bar at friendly, laid-back Delicatessen

Correa's PP
Italian Map 7 B3
Bolshaya Ordynka 40/2
Tel (495) 725 6035
This relaxed, informal restaurant serves imaginative fare such as salmon pizza.

Dorian Gray PP
Italian Map 7 A3
Kadashevskaya naberezhnaya 6/1
Tel (499) 238 6401
Enjoy excellent seafood and pastas, as well as superb service at this elegant riverside restaurant with views of the Kremlin.

Funky Lab PP
International Map 7 A3
Ulitsa Bolshaya Polyanka 7/10, Str. 1
Tel (495) 951 0607
This unpretentious basement restaurant is great value. The tablet menus are a novelty.

Punch and Judy PP
English Map 7 B2
Ulitsa Pyatnitskaya 6
Tel (495) 953 3992
Dishes such as eel salad and beef steak and egg are served at this quirky English pub with a friendly atmosphere and real ale on tap.

DK Choice

Oblomov PPP
Russian Map 7 C4
1yy Monetchikovskiy pereulok 5
Tel (495) 953 6828
Hard to beat for atmosphere alone, this well-established restaurant has long been one of Moscow's best. Ensconced within a historic mansion, it resembles a 16th-century nobleman's palace, while the cuisine is authentic traditional Russian. The wild boar is particularly good. Book ahead.

For key to prices *see page 186*

Further Afield

Casa di Famiglia
Italian   ₽
Ulitsa Metallurgov 7/18
Tel (495) 306 2457
This simple Italian restaurant on the outskirts of Moscow offers a pleasant interior and a good range of home-cooked dishes. Children's entertainment is available at weekends.

Pizzeria Centrale
Italian   **Map** 5 A2   ₽
Kutuzovsky prospekt, Str. 17
Tel (499) 243 5457
Both traditional and unusual combinations can be sampled at this great-value restaurant with a wood-fired pizza oven. The pear, honey and cheese pizza is particularly good.

Tapchan
Uzbek   **Map** 8 F2   ₽
Ulitsa Sergiya Radonezhskogo 2
Tel (495) 228 5050
The delicious selection of dishes at this atmospheric restaurant with friendly staff includes *plov* (rice, meat, vegetables and fruit) and *shurpa* (soup with fatty meat).

U Giuseppe
Italian   **Map** 4 F5   ₽
Ulitsa Samotechnaya 13
Tel (495) 681 1326
At this laid-back Italian *osteria* diners can savour traditional regional specialities and a good selection of home-made pasta dishes. There is a summer terrace for alfresco dining.

Bely Zhuravl
Korean   **Map** 6 D5   ₽₽
Frunzenskaya naberezhnaya 14, Str. 1
Tel (495) 775 0656
Moscow's best Korean restaurant serves gigantic portions of steaming-hot spicy dishes. The menu is very meat-oriented.

DK Choice

Delicatessen
International   **Map** 2 F2   ₽₽
Ulitsa Sadovaya-Karetnaya 20
Tel (495) 699 3962   **Closed** Sun, Mon
Tucked away in a courtyard off the Garden Ring, Delicatessen is a friendly family-run restaurant offering delicious home cooking and a laid-back vibe. The day's menu is scribbled on a blackboard. Sit back and enjoy a great wine list and some of the city's best cocktails.

Druzhba
Chinese   **Map** 2 E1   ₽₽
Ulitsa Novoslobodskaya 4
Tel (499) 973 1212
This hugely popular Chinese restaurant serves enormous portions. The vast selection of dishes includes the usual favourites and many more.

Pane & Olio
Italian   **Map** 6 D3   ₽₽
Ulitsa Timura Frunze 22
Tel (499) 246 2622
Intimate and cosy, this well-established Italian restaurant is reputed to be one of the best in town. Expect attentive service and, perhaps, even a visit from the chef.

Ragout
International   **Map** 1 C4   ₽₽
Bolshaya Gruzinskaya 69
Tel (495) 728 6458
The light and spacious interior of Ragout is reminiscent of a London gastropub combined with a Parisian bistro. The simple menu offers a selection of British and French dishes.

V Temnote?
International   **Map** 2 F1   ₽₽
Oktjabrskaya naberezhnaya 2/4
Tel (495) 688 3396
At this intriguing concept restaurant, diners eat in total darkness and are guided and served by blind waiters. Will you be able to guess what you ate?

Yornik
International   **Map** 1 C2   ₽₽
Ulitsa Gruzinskaya B. 69,
Tel (495) 789 9250
Relax and enjoy the professional and attentive service at this delightful, intimate eatery. Among the inventive dishes created by the British chef are chestnut-crusted veal and salted-caramel ice cream.

Kavkazskaya Plenitsa
Georgian   **Map** 3 B2   ₽₽₽
Prospekt Mira 36
Tel (495) 680 5111
Boasting a terrace and a lovely garden, this brightly decorated restaurant serves a good range of Georgian favourites. Weekends are especially family-friendly, featuring a children's entertainer.

Osteria della Piazza Blanca
Italian   **Map** 2 D2   ₽₽₽
Ulitsa Lesnaya 5A
Tel (495) 508 2517
Book ahead for lunch at this bustling restaurant in a gleaming office complex with efficient service and high-quality Italian cuisine.

Shinok
Ukrainian   **Map** 1 A3   ₽₽₽
Ulitsa 1905 Goda 2
Tel (495) 651 8101
Decorated to resemble a Ukrainian peasant house, this rustic restaurant has a yard with live farm animals. The prices are high, but the food is excellent.

Sixty
International   **Map** 1 B3   ₽₽₽
Presnenskaya naberezhnaya 12, Federatsia Tower, 62nd Floor
Tel (495) 653 8368
Considered the highest restaurant in Europe, Sixty occupies the 62nd floor of a gleaming office tower. Diners come as much for the breathtaking views as for the wide-ranging menu.

Soho Rooms
International   **Map** 5 A4   ₽₽₽
Savvinskaya naberezhnaya 12, Str. 8
Tel (495) 988 7474
This awesome complex of three restaurants, bars and a swimming pool is located in a huge old silk factory that is the night-time playground of Moscow's elite.

Marukame in Zamoskvoreche, part of a Japanese noodle-bar chain

For more information on types of restaurants *see pages 180–81*

Light Meals and Snacks

Moscow has plenty of cafés, bistros, restaurants, bars and fast-food outlets catering for every taste and budget. Russian food, particularly its traditional soups and salads, is perfect for a light meal. A tempting variety of patisserie-style confectionery is also a feature of Russian cuisine, and afternoon tea can be a real occasion, especially in traditional Russian and Central Asian cafés. Pizza, pasta and sushi are in plentiful supply in a wide variety of environments, from bars and cafés to upmarket restaurants. Many restaurants offer a good value "business lunch" or discount on their à la carte menu between noon and 4pm. For a quick bite, snacks such as pancakes and baked potatoes can be obtained from street vendors. The best stalls can be found in Moscow's busiest shopping streets, such as Tverskaya ulitsa and the Novyy Arbat.

Russian

Traditional Russian cafés and bistros are usually rustically decorated, but can be rather smoky. The menu consists of soups such as borscht, and hearty salads including silodka pod shuboi (pickled herring with shredded beetroot). Pirozhki, pastries stuffed with anything from cabbage to liver *(see p183)*, are good fillers. Excellent examples of such offerings can be ordered at **Mari Vanna** and **Café Margarita**, while **Oblomov** and **Art Club Nostalgie** offer both European and Russian food. For a quick meal, the chain restaurants **Moo Moo** and **Russkoe Bistro** serve fast food, Russian style. For Russian food on the move the best option is the blini stalls, which can be found all over the city serving buckwheat pancakes with sweet and savoury fillings.

Ukrainian, Uzbek, Caucasian and Vegetarian

Moscow's ethnic restaurants often have striking Central Asian decor. Guests may well find themselves sitting on cushions at low tables. The food tends to be simple, well-cooked and reasonably priced. Staples from the former Soviet republics of Georgia, Armenia and Uzbekistan, such as *dolmas* (meat and rice wrapped in vine leaves), *shashlyk* (shish kebabs) and *lobio* (a thick spicy bean

soup), are well worth trying. Meals usually involve a soup, grilled meats and a fresh salad. Of the Uzbek restaurants, **Kish Mish** and **Khodzha Nasreddin v Khive** offer good value, tasty food. **Barashka** *(see p186)* serves excellent Azerbaijani food, while **Elardzhi** *(see p186)* has a superb range of Georgian favourites. **Korchma Taras Bulba** is an excellent place to sample Ukrainian cooking.

While vegetarians are better provided for at ethnic restaurants, the options are limited. **Jagannat** is a wholly vegetarian restaurant, serving Indian, Japanese and Chinese meals.

Fast Food, Pizza and Pasta

Restaurant chains tend to predominate for pizza, pasta and fast food. **Akademiya** serves tasty pizzas at a range of locations, while **Pane & Olio** *(see p189)* has pastas, salads and pizzas. For American food, **Starlight Diner** and the **American Bar and Grill** both offer authentic burgers. **Goodman Steakhouse** *(see p188)* is a fashionable restaurant serving high-quality American cuisine, while **Lyudi Kak Lyudi** offers a selection of Russian and international dishes at reasonable prices.

Pastries and Sweets

Russian restaurants and cafés usually have a good range of

pastries and sweets. Western-style cafés such as **Friends Forever**, **Upside Down Cake Co.** and **Cup and Cake** have more international offerings. Russian ice cream is sold in cafés and kiosks and is truly excellent. For picnic supplies, try the delicious cakes and pastries on offer from **Volkonsky Keyser** or **Madame Boulanger**.

Pubs and Bars

Moscow's pubs and bars offer a good range of light meals. So-called art cafés, often featuring live music *(see p202)*, also have excellent menus. In the evening these cafés may be busy, with some form of art-happening taking centre stage, but at lunchtime they usually have a calmer atmosphere. Two good choices are **Kult** and **Kitaiskiy Lyotchik Djao Da**, which both serve good-value, bistro-style food. **Durdin** and **Tinkoff** stock their own microbrewed beers. **Liga Pap** is an upmarket sports bar with a viewing room and plasma TVs screening big sports events. Its drinks and meals are reasonably priced. **Sally O'Brien's** is Moscow's premier Irish bar and provides a range of wholesome pub food. The **Albion Pub** is also a good choice and benefits from a wider menu.

Sushi

Sushi is readily available in Moscow, and can be enjoyed in Japanese restaurants, sushi bars, nightclubs and "art cafés". Despite the capital being landlocked, the sushi on offer is generally fresh and well prepared, though it can sometimes be a little bland.

The **Yakitoria** chain has branches throughout the city. It has traditional Japanese decor and offers good sushi at reasonable prices. **Yapona Mama** is more minimalist in ambience and serves sushi along with a variety of hot dishes, including European ones. Both are reasonably priced. Other good options include **Tanuki** and **Yaposha**, both with branches throughout the city.

DIRECTORY

Russian

Art Club Nostalgie
Арт клуб ностальжи
Chistoprudnyy bulvar 12a.
Map 3 C4.
Tel (495) 258 5668.
w nostalgie.ru

Café Margarita
Кафе Маргарита
Malaya Bronnaya
ulitsa 28.
Map 2 E4.
Tel (495) 699 6534.

Mari Vanna
Мари Ванна
Spiridonevskiy
pereulok 10.
Map 2 E4.
Tel (495) 650 6500.

Moo Moo
Му-му
Ulitsa Arbat 45/24.
Tel (495) 241 1364.
Map 6 D1.

Oblomov
Обломов
1-y Monetchikovsky
pereulok 5.
Map 7 B4.
Tel (495) 953 6828.

Russkoe Bistro
Русское Быстро
Tverskaya ulitsa 16.
Tel (495) 690 9834.
Map 2 F5.

Ukrainian, Uzbek, Caucasian and Vegetarian

Jagannat
Джаганнат
Ulitsa Kuznetskiy most 11.
Map 3 A4.
Tel (495) 628 3580.

Khodzha Nasreddin v Khive
Ходжа Насреддин в Хиве
Ulitsa Pokrovka 10.
Map 3 C5.
Tel (495) 917 0444.

Kish Mish
Кишмиш
Ulitsa Novyy Arbat 28.
Tel (495) 690 0703.
Map 5 C1.

Korchma Taras Bulba
Корчма Тарас Бульба
Pyatnitskaya ulitsa 14.
Map 7 B3.
Tel (495) 953 7153.

Fast Food, Pizza and Pasta

Akademiya
Академия
Kamergerskiy
pereulok 2/1.
Map 2 F5.
Tel (495) 692 9649.

American Bar and Grill
Американ Бар Грилл
Ulitsa Zemlyanoy val 59.
Map 8 E2.
Tel (495) 912 3615.

Correa's
Корреас
Ulitsa Gasheka 7.
Map 2 D3.
Tel (495) 789 9654.

Lyudi Kak Lyudi
Люди Как Люди
Solyankskiy tupik 1/4.
Map 7 C1.
Tel (495) 621 1201.

Starlight Diner
Старлайт дайнер
Bolshaya Sadovaya
ulitsa 16.
Map 2 E3.
Tel (495) 650 0246.

Pastries and Sweets

Cup and Cake
Кап энд Кейк
Ulitsa Nikolskaya 10/2.
Map 3 5A.
Tel (495) 621 2125.

Friends Forever
Френдс Форевер
Bolshoi Kozikhinskiy
pereulok 18.
Map 2 E4.
Tel (495) 699 4302.

Madame Boulanger
Мадам Буланже
Nitiskiy bulvar 12.
Map 2 E5.
Tel (495) 685 9695.

Upside Down Cake Co.
Апсайд Даун Кейк
Bolshaya Gruzinskaya 76.
Map 2 D2.
Tel (495) 926 8397.

Volkonsky Keyser
Волконский Кейзер
Ulitsa Maroseyka 4/2.
Map 3 B5.
Tel (903) 185 3291.

Pubs and Bars

Albion Pub
Альбион
Manezhnaya ploshchad 1
(enter from Alexander
Gardens).
Map 3 A5/7 A1.
Tel (495) 995 9545.

Kult
Культ
Ulitsa Yauzskaya 5.
Map 8 D2.
Tel (495) 917 5706.

Durdin
Дурдинь
Bolshaya Polyanka
ulitsa 56.
Map 7 A3.
Tel (495) 953 5200.

Kitaiskiy Lyotchik Djao Da
Китайский Летчик Джао Да
Lubyansky proezd 25/12.
Map 3 B5.
Tel (495) 624 5611.

Liga Pap
Лига Пап
Bolshaya Lubyanka
ulitsa 24.
Map 3 B4.
Tel (495) 624 3636.

Sally O'Brien's
Bolshaya Polyanka 1/3.
Map 7 A3.
Tel (495) 959 0175.
w sallyobriens.ru

Tinkoff
Тинькофф
Protochnyy pereulok 11.
Map 5 C1.
Tel (495) 780 5888.

Sushi

Tanuki
Тануки
Pyatnitskaya 53.
Map 7 B4.
Tel (495) 951 6973.

Yakitoria
Якитория
Ulitsa Petrovka 16.
Map 3 A4.
Tel (495) 924 0609.

1st Tverskaya-Yamskaya
ulitsa 29/1.
Tel (495) 250 5385.
Map 2 E3.

Yapona Mama
Япона Мама
Smolenskiy bulvar 4.
Map 6 D3.
Tel (499) 246 9967.

Yaposha
Япоша
Tverskaya 20/1.
Map 2 E3.
Tel (495) 650 5918.

SHOPS AND MARKETS

Russia's appetite for Western goods means that Moscow offers most of the shopping facilities of a large, modern Western city. There are supermarkets, department stores stocking imported goods and exclusive boutiques with French and Italian designer clothes and shoes for the new rich. Moscow's most interesting shopping districts are located within the Garden Ring. The main department stores are clustered around the city centre near Red Square, while the best souvenir and antique shops can be found along ulitsa Arbat *(see pp72–3)*, a charming old pedestrian street. For the more adventurous a trip to the weekend flea market at Izmaylovo Park is a must. Here it is possible to buy everything from Russian dolls and Soviet memorabilia to paintings, handmade rugs from Central Asia and antique jewellery.

A display counter in the sumptuously decorated Yeliseyevsky Food Hall *(see p194)*

Opening Hours

Moscow's shops and businesses rarely open before 10am and often not until 11am. Most stay open until around 7pm. A few state-run stores close for an hour at lunchtime, either from 1pm to 2pm, or from 2pm to 3pm. Shops are usually open all day on Saturdays, and most are also open on Sundays, although often for shorter hours. To keep up with increasing consumer demands, a large number of shops and services are now open around the clock, from bookstores to beauty salons.

Markets generally operate from 10am to 4pm but it is necessary to go in the morning to get the best choice of goods.

How to Pay

Nowadays, the *kassa* system of visiting several cashier's desks is pretty rare in Moscow and there are hundreds of Western-type shops of all sizes. Throughout the city there are several chain stores, for example, Sedmoi Kontinent, Kopeika, Perekrestok and Ramstor. The latter offers a huge range of products from food to clothes. There are also a few hypermarkets.

The only legal currency in Russia is the rouble and most shops will not accept other currencies. Vendors at the tourist markets may quote prices in US dollars. However, this will not guarantee a discount and visitors should bear in mind that it is illegal.

Now that the rampant inflation of the early 1990s is under control there should rarely be pressure to pay in hard currency.

Western-style supermarkets and shops, as well as some upmarket Russian boutiques, accept the main credit cards.

Some shops still display prices in US dollars or, very occasionally,

A Western boutique in Moscow's largest department store, GUM

in units that have a fixed rate of exchange with roubles. If so the price will be converted into roubles, at a higher than average exchange rate, before payment is made. Paying by credit card avoids this as credit card slips are nearly always made out in US dollars.

Prices for most goods include 15 per cent VAT. Only staples such as locally produced milk and bread are exempt.

There are a few duty-free shops in the centre of Moscow and at Sheremetevo 2 airport.

Department Stores and Shopping Malls

The most famous department store in Russia is the State Department Store, known by its acronym, **GUM** *(see p109)*. Its beautiful edifice houses three arcades of shops under a glass roof. It was built at the end of the 19th century, just before the Revolution put an end to such luxurious capitalism. During Soviet times GUM stocked the same goods as other department stores in the city and was very dingy and run-down. Following renovation, however, it houses several top Western chains, as well as speciality shops and boutiques. Cosmetics, medicines, cameras and electronic goods are all available along with clothes and household goods.

Moscow's other large department store is **TsUM**, the Central Department Store. Formerly cheaper and a little shabbier than GUM, it has been thoroughly renovated and is too expensive for most ordinary Muscovites.

Replica icons on sale at the Trinity Monastery of St Sergius *(see pp164–7)*

Okhotnyy Ryad is an underground shopping mall, with clothes and electronic goods stores, as well as a food court.

Detskiy Mir (Children's World), the largest children's retailer in Russia, has a large store in the Arbatskaya area. Imported and Russian educational toys, audiotapes, cartoon books and board games can also be found at **Malenkiy Genii** (Little Genius).

Souvenirs on sale at the flea market in Izmaylovo Park

Bazaars and Markets

Many Muscovites buy their cheese, meat, and fresh fruit and vegetables at one of a number of big produce markets dotted around the city. One of the biggest and most picturesque food markets is the **Danilovskiy Market**, which takes its name from the nearby Danilovskiy Monastery *(see pp138–9)*. The market at **Metro Universitet** has a wide variety of fresh produce; there is sometimes a market across the road in which vendors from far-flung Russian regions sell produce and souvenirs. The **Dorogomilovsky Market**, located near Kievsky train station, displays a colourful selection of fresh produce from Russia and the former Soviet Republics. At the upscale **Farmers' Market** on the top floor of the **Tsvetnoy Central Market** customers can purchase ingredients and have them cooked at one of the surrounding restaurants.

Izmaylovo Market is a flea market held every weekend at Izmaylovo Park *(see p143)*. It is a treasure trove of old and new. All the usual souvenirs are on sale, including Soviet memorabilia and painted Russian *matryoshka* dolls *(see p196)*, as well as antique silver, icons, samovars, china, fur hats, amber and some of the best Central Asian rugs in Russia. Many local artists and crafts people have set up their stalls here.

Gorbushka, an indoor market, sells electrical goods, along with DVDs and CDs.

Museum Shops

There is a small, but excellent, souvenir shop at the **Museum of Contemporary History**. Its stock includes old Soviet posters, stamps and badges, amber and lacquer boxes. Both the **Pushkin State Museum of Fine Arts** *(see pp80–83)* and the **Tretyakov Gallery** *(see pp120–23)* sell a good selection of art books with English commentaries.

Bargaining Etiquette

Many market vendors come from long-established trading families and expect buyers to haggle. It may seem a daunting prospect, but bargaining down the price of an item can be extremely satisfying, although visitors are unlikely to get the better of these adept salesmen. Most vendors at souvenir markets speak enough English to bargain. Little, if any, English will be spoken at other markets, so a few Russian words will certainly come in handy.

Occasionally sales people will refuse to drop their price. Try thanking them and turning to leave, to see if they will cut the price further. Their final price, whether bargained down or not, is usually reasonable by Western standards.

A stall selling fresh vegetables and herbs at the Danilovskiy Market

Buying Antiques

It is very difficult to take any items that were made before 1945 out of Russia. All outgoing luggage is x-rayed by customs officials to check for precious metals, works of art, rugs and icons, and complete documentation for all these objects is required before they can be exported. Permission to export antiques and art can only be obtained from the **Ministry of Culture**. This process takes at least 2 weeks and an export tax of 50 per cent of the ministry's assessment of the antiques' value will have to be paid.

It is safest to restrict purchases to items less than 50 years old. However, customs inspectors at the airport may still want to see receipts and documentation that proves the age of the objects.

Samovars and other items for sale in one of the many antiques shops along ulitsa Arbat

Where to Shop in Moscow

The days of Soviet era queues and shortages are long gone. Moscow is a modern city, full of shops, and just about everything that is available in the West can be found here. The Arbat and Tverskaya are the main shopping drags, and are filled with shoppers visiting chic boutiques and other meccas of consumerism. However, high import duties, transportation costs and the relative lack of competition can make some consumer goods more expensive than in the West. The colourful Russian arts and crafts available at many locations throughout the city are popular with visitors as are exotic goods from the ex-Soviet Republics of Central Asia and memorabilia from the Soviet era.

Vodka and Caviar

Russia is the best place in the world to buy vodka and caviar, but buyers must be careful. Caviar should not be bought in the street and it is advisable to buy it in tins rather than jars. Even tins should be kept refrigerated at all times. Caviar is available from most supermarkets but, for a real Russian shopping experience, go to the sumptuous **Yeliseyevsky Food Hall** *(see p91)*. A pre-Revolutionary delicatessen, it was known as Gastronom No. 1 in Soviet times, and boasts chandeliers and stained-glass windows.

There is a great deal of bootleg vodka about, which can be highly poisonous. It is essential to ensure that there is a pink tax label stuck over the top of any bottle of vodka and none should ever be bought on the street. Popular vodkas such as Stolichnaya and Moskovskaya *(see p184)* are available from most supermarkets including **Sedmoi Kontinent**.

Vodka and caviar are also available at the duty-free shops at the airports *(see p216)*, but are much cheaper in town.

Russians never mix vodka, but instead eat snacks or drink juice immediately after a "shot", to cool the aftertaste and increase endurance.

Arts and Crafts

Low labour costs mean that handmade goods are generally cheaper here than in the West and they make exotic and interesting souvenirs to take home. The best places to buy are the markets, such as the **Izmaylovo Market** *(see p193)*, and souvenir shops on ulitsa Arbat *(see pp72–3)*. Lacquer trays and bowls, painted china and *matryoshka* dolls can be bought at **Arbatskaya Lavitsa**. Handmade lace and embroidery are on sale in **Russkaya Vyshivka**, while for Russian jewellery and amber visitors should try **Samotsvety**.

A good range of arts and crafts is also available at shops elsewhere in the city, such as **Roza Azora**, a small art gallery on Nikitsky Bulvar, which sells a curious selection of Soviet bric-a-brac, from lamps to biscuit tins. For more unusual souvenirs, try **Dom Farfora**, which sells hand-painted tea sets and Russian crystal, and the **Salon of the Moscow Cultural Fund**, which has samovars, lamps and whimsical sculptures and mobiles.

Antiques

The new Russian rich are hungry for antiques and dealers know the value of goods, so the bargains of yesteryear are no longer available. It is also worth noting that exporting objects made before 1945 from Russia involves a lot of expense and effort *(see p193)*. However, it is still well worth exploring the many wonderful shops full of treasures.

The area around ulitsa Arbat has many of the city's best antique shops. **Eurasia Gallery**, one of the largest galleries of Eastern antiques in Europe, specializes in Chinese and Japanese art, while **Ivantsarevich** has a variety of interesting Soviet porcelain. For larger pieces and furniture visitors should go to **Rokoko** which sells goods for people for a commission. **The Foreign Book Store**, which is principally a bookshop, also sells furniture, antiques and a lot of china, lamps and bric-a-brac.

Fashion and Accessories

There are many boutiques in the centre of town around **GUM** *(see p109)*, **TsUM** *(see p192)* and **Okhotnyy Ryad**, and along Tverskaya ulitsa *(see p91)*. The centre also has two good arcades. **Petrovskiy Passage** sells clothes and shoes as well as furniture and electrical goods. **Gallery Aktyor**, a modern, three-storey arcade, contains Western and designer stores selling clothes, French perfumes and jewellery from Tiffany and Cartier. Clothes by Russian designers are gradually appearing in Moscow's shops; **Masha Tsigal** sells clothes, handbags and sunglasses.

On the edge of the city centre are the **Evropeiskiy** and **Atrium** shopping centres, which contain a variety of high-street shops, along with cafés, bars and a cinema.

A wide range of authentic Russian fur hats are sold in Petrovskiy Passage and on the second floor of GUM. Alternatively, head to Izmaylovo Market to buy them at much lower prices.

Books and Music

For English-language books, **Dom Inostrannoi Knigi** is probably the best shop to visit. The enormous **Moscow House of Books** sells a good range of English-language books, and also old icons and Soviet propaganda posters. **Biblio Globus** is well worth having a browse in, while the **Moskva Trade House** deals in Russian and foreign books, as well as selling stamps, small antiques and paintings. For vintage and specialist music try **Transylvania**, just off Tverskaya ulitsa.

DIRECTORY

Department Stores and Shopping Malls

Detskiy Mir
Деский мир
10 Vozdvizhenka ulitsa,
Voentorg.
Map 6 D1
Tel 8 (800) 250 00 00
w detmir.ru

GUM
ГУМ
Krasnaya ploshchad 3.
Map 3 A5.
Tel (495) 788 4343.

Malenkiy Genii
Маленький Гении
Bolshoy Kozikhinskiy
pereulok 6.
Map 2 E4.
Tel (495) 691 2147.

Okhotnyy Ryad
Охотный Ряд
Manezhnaya ploshad.
Map 3 A5.
Tel (495) 737 8449.

TsUM
ЦУМ
Ulitsa Petrovka 2.
Map 3 A4.
Tel (495) 933 7300.

Bazaars and Markets

Danilovskiy Market
Даниловский рынок
Mytnaya ulitsa 74.

Dorogomilovsky Market
Дорогомиловский
рынок
Mozhayskiy Val 10.
Map 5 A2.

Gorbushka
Горбушка
Barklaya ulitsa 8.

Izmaylovo Market
Рынок Измайлово
Izmaylovskoe shosse.

Tsvetnoy Central Market
Цветной Централ
Маркет
Tsvetnoy Boulevard 15.
Map 3 A3.

Museum Shops

Museum of Contemporary History
Музей современной
истории
Muzey sovremennoy
istorii
Tverskaya ulitsa 21.
Map 2 E4.
Tel (495) 699 6724.

Pushkin State Museum of Fine Arts
Музей
изобразительных
искусств имени АС
Пушкина
Muzey izobrazitelnykh
iskusstv imeni AS Pushkina
Ulitsa Volkhonka 12.
Map 6 F2.
Tel (495) 609 9520.

Tretyakov Gallery
Третьяковская галерея
Tretyakovskaya galereya
Lavrushinskiy pereulok 12.
Map 7 A3.
Tel (495) 230 7788.

Vodka and Caviar

Sedmoi Kontinent
Седьмой Континент
Bolshaya Gruzinskaya
ulitsa 63.
Map 2 D2.
Tel (495) 721 3874.

Yeliseyevsky Food Hall
Елисеевский гастроном
Yeliseevsky gastronom
Tverskaya ulitsa 14.
Map 2 F4.
Tel (495) 925 2790.

Arts and Crafts

Arbatskaya Lavitsa
Арбатская Лавица
Ulitsa Arbat 27.
Map 6 E1.
Tel (495) 290 5689.

Dom Farfora
Дом фарфора
Leninskiy prospekt 36.
Tel (499) 137 6023.

Roza Azora
Роза Азора
Nkitsky bulvar 14.
Map 2 E5.
Tel (495) 695 8119.

Russkaya Vyshivka
Русская вышивка
Ulitsa Arbat 31.
Map 6 D1.
Tel (499) 241 2841.

Salon of the Moscow Cultural Fund
Салон Московского
фонда культуры
Salon Moskovskovo
fonda kultury
Pyatnitskaya ulitsa 16.
Map 7 B3.
Tel (495) 951 3302.

Samotsvety
Самоцветы
Ulitsa Arbat 35.
Map 6 D1.
Tel (495) 241 0765.

Antiques

Eurasia Gallery
Галерея Евразия
Nikitsky bulvar 12A.
Map 2 E5.
Tel (495) 690 0549.

Ivantsarevich
Иванцаревич
Ulitsa Arbat 4.
Map 6 E1.
Tel (495) 691 7444.

Ministry of Culture
Министерство культуры
Malyy Gnezdnikovskiy
7/6.
Tel (495) 629 2008.

Rokoko
Рококо
Frunzenskaya
naberezhnaya 54.
Tel (499) 242 3664.

Fashion and Accessories

Atrium
Атриум
33 Zemlyanoi Val.
Tel (495) 970 1555.

Evropeiskiy
Европейский
Ploshad Kievskovo
Vokzala 2.
Map 5 B2.
Tel (495) 921 3444.

Gallery Aktyor
Галерея Актер
Tverskaya ulitsa 16/1.
Map 2 F4.
Tel (495) 935 8299.

Masha Tsigal
Маша Цигал
Ulitsa Yazskaya 1/15.
Map 8 D2.
Tel (495) 660 5644.

Petrovskiy Passage
Петровский Пассаж
Ulitsa Petrovka 10.
Map 3 A4.
Tel (495) 625 3132.

Books and Music

Biblio Globus
Библио Глобус
Miasnitskaya ul. 6/3.
Map 3 B5.
Tel (495) 781 1900.

Dom Inostrannoi Knigi
Дом Иностранной
Книги
Ulitsa Kuznetskiy most 18.
Map 3 A4.
Tel (495) 628 2021.

The Foreign Book Store
Иностранная Книга и
Антиквариат
Inostrannaya kniga i
Antikvariat
Malaya Nikitskaya
ulitsa 16/9. **Map** 2 D5.
Tel (495) 690 4082.

Moscow House of Books
Московский Дом книги
Moskovskiy Dom knigi
Ulitsa Novyy Arbat 8.
Map 6 D1.
Tel (495) 789 3591

Moskva Trade House
Торговый дом Книги
Torgovyy dom Knigi
Tverskaya ulitsa 8.
Map 2 F4.
Tel (495) 629 6483.

Transylvania
Трансильвания
Tverskaya ulitsa 6/1, 5.
Map 2 F5.
Tel (495) 629 8786.

What to Buy in Moscow

It is easy to find interesting and beautiful souvenirs in Moscow. Traditional crafts were encouraged by the State in the old Soviet Union, so many age-old skills were kept alive. Artisans today continue to produce items ranging from small, low-cost, enamelled badges through to more expensive hand-painted Palekh boxes, samovars and worked semi-precious stones. Other popular items are lacquered trays and bowls, chess sets, wooden toys and *matryoshka* dolls. Memorabilia from the Soviet era also make good souvenirs and Russia is definitely the best place to buy the national specialities, vodka and caviar.

Samovar

Used to boil water to make tea, samovars *(see p185)* come in many sizes. A permit is needed to export a pre-1945 samovar.

Vodka and Caviar

An enormous variety of both clear and flavoured vodkas (such as lemon and pepper) is available *(see p184)*. They make excellent accompaniments to black caviar *(ikra)* and red caviar *(keta)*, which are often served with blini.

Red caviar

Clear vodka

Black caviar

Flavoured vodka

Malachite egg   Amber ring

Semi-Precious Stones

Malachite, amber, jasper and a variety of marbles from the Ural mountains are used to make a wide range of items – everything from jewellery to chess sets and inlaid table tops.

Wooden Toys

These crudely carved wooden toys often have moving parts. They are known as *bogorodskie* toys and make charming gifts.

Matryoshka Dolls

These dolls fit one inside the other and come in a huge variety of styles. The traditional dolls are the prettiest, but the models painted to represent Soviet political leaders are also very popular.

Chess Sets

Chess is an extremely popular pastime in Russia. Chess sets made from all kinds of materials, including malachite, are available. This beautiful wooden set is painted in the same folkloric style as the traditional *matryoshka* dolls.

Lacquered Artifacts

Painted wooden or papier-mâché artifacts make popular souvenirs and are sold all over the city. The exquisite hand-painted, lacquered Palekh boxes can be very costly, but the eggs decorated with icons and the typical red, black and gold bowls are more affordable.

Palekh Box

The art of miniature painting on papier-mâché items originated in the late 18th century. Artists in the four villages of Palekh, Fedoskino, Mstera and Kholuy still produce these hand-painted marvels. The images are based on Russian fairy-tales and legends.

Bowl with Spoon

The brightly painted bowls and spoons usually known as "Khokhloma" have a lacquer coating, forming a surface which is durable, but not resistant to boiling liquids.

Painted wooden egg

Russian hand-painted tray

Tuners — Strings

Russian Shawl

These brilliantly coloured, traditional woollen shawls are good for keeping out the cold of a Russian winter. Mass-produced polyester versions are also available, mostly in big department stores, but they will not be as warm.

Traditional Musical Instruments

Russian folk music uses a wide range of musical instruments. This *gusli* is similar to the Western psaltery, and is played by plucking the strings with both hands. Also available are the *balalaika* and the *garmon*, which resembles a concertina.

Soviet Memorabilia

A wide array of memorabilia from Soviet times can be bought. Old banknotes, coins, pocket watches and all sorts of Red Army kit, including belt buckles and badges, can be found, together with more recent watches with cartoons of KGB agents on their faces.

Gzhel Vase

Ceramics with a distinctive blue and white pattern are produced in Gzhel, a town near Moscow. Ranging from figurines to household crockery, they are popular with Russians and visitors alike.

Pocket watch

Badge with Soviet symbols

Red Army leather belt

ENTERTAINMENT IN MOSCOW

Moscow offers many forms of entertainment, from great theatre productions, operas and ballets to a wide choice of lively night-life venues. Attending a performance at the Bolshoi Theatre *(see pp92–3)* remains a must for opera and ballet buffs. Other theatres put on an enormous range of productions, including musicals and shows for children. Moscow has several cinemas screening foreign-language films. They usually show the latest releases only a few weeks after they are premiered in the West. The city also has over 300 nightclubs and many late-night bars, some of which have live bands. In addition, there is plenty of free entertainment from street performers, especially on ulitsa Arbat *(see pp72–3)*.

A performance of the opera *Boris Godunov* at the Bolshoi Theatre

Practical Information

Moscow does not have any conventional tourist information offices. However, listings for events such as films, plays, concerts and exhibitions, together with extensive lists of restaurants and nightclubs can be found in the Friday edition of the English-language newspaper *The Moscow Times*. Restaurants and nightclubs are also listed in the English-language *Moscow News*. Both are free and available at large hotels and in most tourist-geared restaurants. Those who can read Russian can make use of the magazine *Afisha*, which has comprehensive listings.

Visitors should note that the safest way to get back from late-night events is in an official taxi booked in advance *(see p221)*.

Booking Tickets

By far the easiest way to book tickets for a concert, a ballet, an opera or the theatre is through one of the main international hotels, even for visitors not staying there. Both Western-style and Russian-run hotels will usually offer this service. However, tickets bought in this way are often more expensive than those available elsewhere. Ticket-booking desks in hotels accept payment by major credit cards, but many will charge a fee for doing so. Visitors who speak Russian will be able to buy cheaper tickets from a theatre ticket kiosk *(teatralnaya kassa)*. These kiosks are scattered all round the city and in metro stations. A particularly useful ticket agency is located on Theatre Square *(see p90)*.

Another alternative is to book tickets at the venues. Although these tickets are usually the cheapest, it can require a lot of patience to obtain them since ticket offices are often open at unpredictable hours. There are ticket touts outside most events, especially those at the Bolshoi Theatre. However, there is a risk that

The Moscow State Circus

Russians have always loved the circus. In the 18th and 19th centuries it was the most popular theatrical entertainment. Troupes travelled round the country performing mostly satirical shows. Today the renowned Moscow State Circus has its permanent home in Moscow. It is famous for its clowns, the breathtaking stunts of its acrobats and trapeze artists and its performing animals. The last often include tigers jumping through burning hoops and bears riding bicycles, and animal-lovers should be aware that they may find some acts distressing. The original venue, now known as the **Old Circus**, was built in 1880 by Albert Salamonskiy for his private troupe. Salamonskiy's Circus became the Moscow State Circus in 1919. The **New Circus** was built in 1973. Both venues are now in use.

The big top of the New Circus, second venue of the Moscow State Circus

their tickets are counterfeit and they will almost certainly be overpriced.

Children's Entertainment

Traditional Russian entertainments for children have always included the puppet theatre, the zoo and the circus. Moscow has two puppet theatres: the **Obraztsov Puppet Theatre** *(see p200)*, which puts on matinee performances for children, and the **Moscow Puppet Theatre**. The **Nataliya Sats Children's Musical Theatre** performs excellent shows, great for children of all ages.

The **Russian Academic Youth Theatre** *(see p90)* puts on a range of performances suitable for children from the age of seven.

Moscow Zoo is a great favourite but, unfortunately, the animals often look underfed and cramped in their cages.

At **Arlecchino Children's Club** children can play with toys and computer games or be entertained by clowns.

The **Durov Animal Theatre**, undoubtedly a much-loved Moscow institution, has attracted a loyal following since its foundation in 1912. Performing animals include cats and dogs, as well as farm animals. The affection and concern for the well-being of the animals is clear to see.

Yuri Kuklachev's unique **Moscow Cats Theatre**, which was established in 1990, has a troupe of more than 100 feline actors of different breeds performing all manner of amazing tricks. Performances include *Olympics Cat Boris* and *Cats of the Universe*, and are both these shows are must-sees for cat lovers.

A scene from the story of Noah's Ark being performed at the Moscow Puppet Theatre

Paddle boats, one of the many attractions on offer in Gorky Park

Spectator Sports

Traditionally, the most popular sports in Russia are football and hockey. Important matches and championships are held at the **Dynamo Central House of Sports**, the **Luzhniki Stadium** and the **Olympic Sports Complex**. On the whole, Moscow's football grounds are safe, although hooliganism is beginning to become a problem. Krylatskoye also has a racecourse and a canal where rowing races take place. The Olympic Sports Complex is Moscow's main venue for tennis tournaments.

DIRECTORY

Children's Entertainment

Arlecchino Children's Club
Детский клуб Арлекино
Verkhnyaya Radishchevskaya ulitsa 19/3, stroenie 1.
Map 8 E3.
Tel (495) 915 1106.

Durov Animal Theatre
Театр Уголок Дедушки Дурова
Ulitsa Durova 4.
Tel (495) 631 3047.
w ugolokdurova.ru

Moscow Cats Theatre
Театр Кошек Куклачева
Kutuzovsky prospekt 25.
Tel (499) 243 4005.
w catstheatre.ru

Moscow Puppet Theatre
Театр Кукол
Spartakovskaya ulitsa 26/30.
Map 4 F2.
Tel (499) 267 4288.

Moscow Zoo
Зоопарк
Bolshaya Gruzinskaya ulitsa 1.
Map 1 C4.
Tel (499) 252 3580.

Nataliya Sats Children's Musical Theatre
Детский музыкальный театр имени Наталии Сац
Vernadskovo prospekt 5.
Near Sparrow Hills *(see p131)*.
Tel (964) 595 2130.

New Circus
Новый цирк
Vernadskovo prospekt 7.
Near Sparrow Hills *(see p131)*. **Tel** (495) 765 0409.

Obraztsov Puppet Theatre
Театр Кукол имени Образцова
Ulitsa Sadovaya-Samotechnaya 3. **Map** 3 A2. **Tel** (495) 699 5373.

Old Circus
Старый цирк
Tsvetnoy bulvar 13. **Map** 3 A3. **Tel** (495) 625 8970.
w circusnikulin.ru

Russian Academic Youth Theatre
Российский академический молодёжный театр
Teatralnaya ploshchad 2.
Map 3 A5.
Tel (495) 692 0069.

Spectator Sports

Dynamo Central House of Sports
Динамо – Центральный дворец спорта
Lavochkina ulitsa 32.
Tel (495) 454 9541.

Luzhniki Stadium
Лужники
Luzhnetskaya naberezhnaya 24.
Tel (495) 780 0808.
w luzhniki.ru

Olympic Sports Complex
Спортивный олимпийский комплекс
Olimpiyskiy prospekt 16.
Map 3 A1.
Tel (495) 786 3333.

The Arts in Moscow

From June until late September most of Moscow's concert halls and theatres close and the city's orchestras, theatre and ballet companies perform elsewhere in Russia and abroad. However, for the rest of the year the city has a rich and varied cultural scene. The Bolshoi Theatre (see pp92–3), Moscow's oldest and most famous opera and ballet house, offers an impressive repertoire. Numerous drama theatres put on a variety of plays in Russian, ranging from the conventional to the avant-garde. For non-Russian speakers there is a wide choice of events, ranging from folk dance and gypsy music to classical concerts by top international musicians. Evening performances at most venues begin at 7pm or 7:30pm, while matinées generally start around noon.

Ballet and Opera

There are numerous venues in Moscow where visitors can see high-quality ballet and opera. Undoubtedly the most famous is the **Bolshoi Theatre**, originally built in 1780. Despite two major fires, the building remains impressive and stands on its original site. Today the Bolshoi is still the best venue in Moscow in which to see opera and ballet. Its magnificent main auditorium has a seating capacity of 1740. World-famous ballets, including *Giselle* by Adolphe Adam and *Swan Lake* and *The Nutcracker* by Pyotr Tchaikovsky, have been danced here by the company. The theatre's operatic repertoire includes a number of works by Russian composers. Among them are *Boris Godunov* by Modest Mussorgsky, *The Queen of Spades* and *Eugene Onegin* by Pyotr Tchaikovsky, and *Sadko* by Nikolai Rimsky-Korsakov.

Another much younger company, the Kremlin Ballet Company, can be seen at the **State Kremlin Palace** (see p58) in the Kremlin. This gigantic steel and glass building, originally constructed in 1961 as a convention hall for the Communist Party, has a 6,000-seat auditorium. It is a prime venue for those wishing to see visiting Western opera singers, as well as for ballet.

Less grandiose, but nevertheless high-quality, operas and ballets are performed at the **Helikon Opera**, the **Novaya**

Opera and the **Stanislavskiy and Nemirovich-Danchenko Musical Theatre**. As its name implies, the **Operetta Theatre** performs operettas, while the **Gnesin Music Academy Opera Studio** stages more experimental productions.

Classical Music

Moscow has a strong tradition of classical music and has long been home to several top international music events. One of Moscow's most famous classical music venues is the **Tchaikovsky Concert Hall**. The main feature of this large circular auditorium is a giant pipe organ, which has 7,800 pipes and weighs approximately 20 tonnes. It was made in Czechoslovakia and was installed in 1959.

The **Moscow Conservatory** (see p96) is both an educational establishment and a venue for concerts of classical music. It was founded in 1866 and Pyotr Tchaikovsky (see p161), then a young composer at the beginning of his brilliant career, taught here for 12 years. Nowadays the conservatory has more than 1,000 music students at any one time.

The Bolshoi Zal (Great Hall) is used for orchestral concerts, both by the conservatory's resident orchestra and visiting orchestras. The Malyy Zal (Small Hall) is used for recitals by smaller ensembles. Over the years many prominent musicians have

performed here and every four years the conservatory plays host to the prestigious Tchaikovsky International Competition (see p35). Moscow's most prestigious classical music gathering is the annual Svyatoslav Richter December Nights Festival (see p37). Held in the Pushkin State Museum of Fine Arts (see pp80–83), the concerts attract a star-studded array of Russian and foreign musicians.

In summer both indoor and outdoor concerts are held outside Moscow at Kuskovo (see pp144–5) on Tuesday and Thursday evenings.

Theatre

Moscow has more than 60 theatres, most of which are repertory. This means that a different production is staged every night. Listings can be found in the Friday edition of *The Moscow Times* (see p215).

The **Moscow Arts Theatre** (see p94) stages a wide repertoire, but it is particularly famous for its productions of Anton Chekhov's plays, such as *The Seagull*. In contrast, the **Lenkom Theatre** produces musicals and plays by contemporary Russian writers. Russia's first drama theatre, the **Malyy Theatre**, across the street from the Bolshoi, played a major role in the development of Russian theatre.

The **Obraztsov Puppet Theatre** (see p199) is as entertaining for adults as it is for children. It was founded in 1931 and is named after its first director, Sergey Obraztsov. The theatre's repertoire is outstanding and most of the plays can be enjoyed without a knowledge of the Russian language. Evening perform-ances may only be open to those over the age of 18.

Performances at the **Gypsy Theatre** consist of traditional gypsy dancing and singing. Performances of Russian folk dancing are held at various venues throughout Moscow.

The **Taganka Theatre**, favourite of Russian president Vladimir Putin, has some excellent productions such as works by Mikhail Bulgakov. The **Mossoviet Theatre** is also among the city's best, showing alternative interpretations of Shakespeare and excellent productions of Russian classics.

Film

The Russian film industry flourished under the Soviet regime and Lenin (see p30) himself recognized the value of films for conveying messages to the people. Specially commissioned films shown throughout Russia on modified trains, for example, informed much of the rural population that there had been a revolution in the capital.

Until the Soviet Union's collapse in 1991, the film industry was run by the state. Films were subsidized and their subject matter closely monitored. Russian film-makers now have artistic freedom, but suffer from a shortage of funding. Cinemas show both Hollywood blockbusters and Russian releases. After a period of stagnation, Russian cinema is enjoying a real boom, and domestically produced films are now more popular than imports.

Many cinemas have out-of-date equipment, muffled sound and uncomfortable seats, but the **Oktyabr Cinema** offers digital sound and good facilities, including an IMAX® screen. The **Illuzion**, located in one of Moscow's Seven Sisters buildings, has preserved the spirit of the era it was built in and screens old Soviet films.

For English-language cinema, there are a few options within the city centre. **Pioneer** caters to foreign tourists well, showing dubbed films as well as some English-language screenings. It also occasionally hosts film festivals. **Eldar** screens mainly blockbusters, while **35mm** specializes in independent foreign films, usually shown in the original language with Russian subtitles. **Rolan** shows art-house movies and festival screenings. The Oktyabr Cinema on Novyy Arbat also puts on English-language films, though the repertoire is more limited.

Some cinemas offer online booking, although at most venues tickets for films can only be bought at the cinemas themselves. At most, payment is in cash.

DIRECTORY

Ballet and Opera

Bolshoi Theatre
Большой театр
Teatralnaya ploshchad 1.
Map 3 A4.
Tel (495) 608 7317.
w bolshoi.ru

Gnesin Music Academy Opera Studio
Театр-студия Оперы Рам Им. Гнесиных
Malyy Rzhevskiy pereulok 1.
Map 2 D5.
Tel (495) 690 2422.

Helikon Opera
Геликон опера
Bolshaya Nikitskaya ulitsa 19. **Map** 2 E5.
Tel (495) 690 0971.
w helikon.ru

Novaya Opera
Новая Опера
Karetny Ryad 3. **Map** 2 F3.
Tel (495) 694 1830.
w novayaopera.ru

Operetta Theatre
Театр оперетты
Ulitsa Bolshaya Dmitrovka 6.
Map 3 A4.
Tel (495) 925 5050.

Stanislavskiy and Nemirovich-Danchenko Musical Theatre
Музыкальный театр имени Станиславского и Немировича-Данченко
Ulitsa Bolshaya Dmitrovka 17.
Map 2 F4.
Tel (495) 723 7325.

State Kremlin Palace
Государственный Кремлевский дворец
Ulitsa Vozdvizhenka 1.
Map 7 A1.
Tel (495) 917 2336.

Classical Music

Moscow Conservatory
Московская консерватория
Bolshaya Nikitskaya ulitsa 13/6.
Map 2 E5.
Tel (495) 629 8183.
w mosconsv.ru

Tchaikovsky Concert Hall
Концертный зал имени ПИ Чайковского
Triumfalnaya ploshchad 4/31. **Map** 2 E3.
Tel (495) 232 5353.

Theatre

Gypsy Theatre
Театр ромэн
Leningradskiy prospekt 32/2.
Map 1 B1.
Tel (495) 614 6058.

Lenkom Theatre
Театр Ленком
Ulitsa Malaya Dmitrovka 6. **Map** 2 F3.
Tel (495) 699 0708.

Malyy Theatre
Малый театр
Teatralnyy proezd 1.
Map 3 A5.
Tel (495) 624 4046.
w maly.ru

Moscow Arts Theatre
МХАТ имени Ап Чехова
Kamergerskiy pereulok 3.
Map 2 F5.
Tel (495) 629 8760.

Mossoviet Theatre
Театр им. Моссовета
Bolshaya Sadovaya 16.
Map 2 D3.
Tel (495) 699 2035.

Taganka Theatre
Театр на Таганке
Zemlyanoy val 76/21.
Map 4 D4.
Tel (495) 915 1217.

Film

35mm
Ulitsa Pokrovka 47/24.
Map 4 D4. **Tel** (495) 780 9142. w kino35mm.ru

Arts Cinema
Художественный кино
Arbatskaya ploshchad 14.
Map 6 E1.
Tel (495) 691 5598.

Eldar
Эльдар
Leninskiy prospect 105.
Map 6 F5.
Tel (495) 735 9944.

Illuzion
Иллюзион
Kotelnicheskaya naberezhnaya 1/15. **Map** 8 D2. **Tel** (495) 915 4339.

Oktyabr
Октябрь
Novyy Arbat 24.
Map 6 D1. **Tel** (495) 545 0505. w karo.ru

Pioneer
Пионер
Kutuzovskiy prospekt 21.
Tel (499) 240 5240.

Rolan
Ролан
Christoprodunyy bulvar 12A. **Map** 3 C4.
Tel (495) 916 9169.

Music and Nightlife

Under the Communist regime, Moscow's nightlife was practically non-existent and those clubs and bars that did exist were for a privileged elite. Today, nightlife in Moscow is booming. Foreign bands, DJs and performers of all types now visit the city regularly, while the quality of the domestic scene has improved markedly. The variety of venues is similarly impressive and ranges from bars where you can see local rock bands to glitzy late-night clubs playing the latest techno music. The Russian take on modern dance music is noteworthy, as Russians like to party hard and long into the night. Venues can be packed and prices high, but it is an experience not to be missed.

Rock Venues

After years of being isolated from major Western pop and rock acts, Muscovites can at last get to see big-name artists in the flesh. Many of the more famous acts from abroad, as well as the best in local talent, play at clubs such as **B2**, which has established itself as one of the capital's best live music venues, hosting a variety of acts from rock to ska.

Among the smaller venues, **PIPL**, **Kitaiskiy Lyotchik Djao Da**, **Gogol** and **Art Garbage** showcase less well known acts. Djao Da is good for acoustic music; Gogol hosts alternative music bands; P!PL plays rock exclusively; and Art Garbage is slightly larger and has a more sophisticated feel.

Major rock concerts usually take place at either **Olympiiskiy Stadium** or **Luzhniki Stadium**.

Jazz, Blues and Latin Venues

Moscow has a vibrant jazz and blues scene, with clubs such as **B2** featuring a live act most evenings. B2 is a one-stop shop for a night out and also has a pool hall, sushi bar and a disco. Other clubs worth checking out are the **Roadhouse Blues Bar** and the **Igor Butman Jazz Club**; both put on good live music, including acts from abroad. **BB King** is a more intimate venue.

Café Ekus, a South American bar and restaurant, is a good bet for Latin American bands and hosts lively merengue and salsa nights, as does **Che**.

Sixteen Tons favours bands playing alternative and independent music.

Nightclubs and Discos

The range of clubs to be found in Moscow is now on a par with other major capital cities and new clubs open every month. As elsewhere, nothing really gets going until around 11pm. Entrance is usually cheaper or free before this time although the queues can be long. Most clubs don't close until 4am; some are open until 6am at weekends.

Domestic preference is still for bass-heavy house music, with trance also becoming popular. Foreign DJs often perform at clubs such as **Propaganda** and **Fabrique**. Propaganda is one of the best known clubs, and plays a variety of styles from the latest electronic sounds to old school disco. Fabrique plays mostly house music. **Cult** offers more urban grooves, including drum & bass and four-to-the-floor techno.

A number of Moscow's leading clubs cater to Moscow's "new-rich", with prices and cover charges to match. **Soho Rooms**, located south of the centre, is worth a visit, if only to spot the partying catwalk models and Russian gangsters. Nearby is **Luch**, an upmarket bar that attracts Moscow's wealthy set and is popular for cocktails.

Krasny Oktyabr, on the site of a former chocolate factory, is home to some of Moscow's most fashionable nightlife venues. They include **Rolling Stones**, which is a popular club with a large summer terrace, and is ideal for those who enjoy more main-stream pop and clubbing tunes. **Gipsy** plays an eclectic mix, from techno to R&B, while **Bar Strelka** attracts large crowds, especially in summer, thanks to its large roof terrace.

The arty **Solyanka** club in the Kitay Gorod district, another of the city's main nightlife areas, attracts a fashionable yet unpretentious crowd and mainly plays house and electro.

Keep in mind that many of Moscow's clubs are marred by the practice of "face control", and the more upmarket venues are likely to look unfavourably on anyone wearing trainers and jeans.

Art Cafés

Some of the city's more unusual clubs are the so-called "art cafés", such as **Art Garbage** or **Drevo**, which promote an eclectic mix of entertainment. One night there might be live music, and the next an alternative fashion show or an avant-garde film. **Krizis Zhanra** has live music and poetry in a cramped but friendly setting. The bohemian **FAQ Café** is a warren of cosy rooms and features concerts on weekends. Many of the art cafés are also good places to visit for a relaxed meal (see p191).

Gay and Lesbian Nightlife

Moscow has a thriving gay community, despite the right-wing stance taken by some political groups. The city has a diverse gay and lesbian club scene. One of the most well-established venues is **Central Station**, a large flamboyant club with nightly stage shows and a karaoke bar. **Sharm** is set on two floors and offers a karaoke room and live shows. Occupying a couple of basement rooms, **12 Volt** is a more laid-back bar that quickly fills up at weekends, while **Propaganda** runs a popular gay night every Sunday.

DIRECTORY

Rock Venues

Art Garbage
Запасник
Starosadskiy
pereulok 5.
Map 3 C5.
Tel (495) 628 8745.
🅦 **art-garbage.ru**

B2
Б2
Bolshaya Sadovaya
ulitsa 8.
Map 2 D3.
Tel (495) 650 9918.
🅦 **b2club.ru**

Gogol
Stoleshnikov
pereulok 11.
Map 3 A4.
Tel (495) 514 0944.
🅦 **gogolclubs.ru**

**Kitaiskiy Lyotchik
Djao Da**
Китайский Летчик
Джао Да
Lubyansky proezd 25.
Map 3 B5.
Tel (495) 624 5611.
🅦 **jao-da.ru**

Luzhniki Stadium
Лужники (Большая
арена)
Luzhnetskaya
nabarezhnaya 24.
Tel (495) 780 0808.

Olympiiskiy Stadium
Олимпийский Стадион
Olympiyskiy prospekt 16.
Map 3 B1.
Tel (495) 786 3333.

P!PL
Пипл
Derbenevskaya 22.
Map 8 E5.
Tel (495) 755 1146.

Jazz, Blues and Latin Venues

BB King
Биби Кинт
Ulitsa Sadovaya
Samotechnaya 4.
Map 2 F2.
Tel (495) 699 8574.

Café Ekus
Кафе Екус
Bolshoi Sukharevsky
pereulok 25/23.
Map 3 B3.
Tel (915) 106 6466.

Che
Че
Nikolskaya ulitsa 10/2.
Map 3 A5.
Tel (495) 621 7477.

**Igor Butman Jazz
Club**
Клуб Игоря Бутмана
Ulanskaya Hotel,
Ulansky pereulok 16.
Map 3 C3.
Tel (495) 632 9264.

Roadhouse Blues Bar
Роудхаус
Starovagonkovsky per. 19,
building 2.
Map 6 F1.
Tel (495) 697 6008.

Sixteen Tons
Шестнадцать тонн
Presnenskiy val 6.
Map 1 B4.
Tel (499) 253 5300.
🅦 **16tons.ru**

Nightclubs and Discos

Bar Strelka
Бар Стрелка
Bolotnaya
naberezhnaya 14.
Map 6 F2.
Tel (495) 771 7416.

Cult
Культ
Ulitsa Yauzskaya 5.
Map 8 D2.
Tel (495) 917 5706.

Fabrique
Фабрик
Kosmodamianskaya
naberezhnaya 2.
Map 7 C2.
Tel (963) 687 8888.

Gipsy
Джипси
Bolotnaya naberezhnaya
3/4, building 2.
Map 6 F3.
Tel (495) 699 8693.

Luch
Лучь
Bolshaya
Pirogovskaya 27/1.
Map 5 B5.
Tel (495) 287 0022.

Propaganda
Пропаганда
Bolshoi Zlatoustinskiy
pereulok 7.
Map 3 B5.
Tel (495) 624 5732.
🅦 **propaganda
moscow.com**

Rolling Stones
Роллинг Стоунз
Bolotnaya
naberezhnaya 3.
Map 6 F3.
Tel (495) 504 0932.

Soho Rooms
Сохо Румс
Sabbinskaya
naberezhnaya 12/8.
Map 5 B3.
Tel (495) 988 7474.

Solyanka
Солянка
Solyanka ulitsa 11/6.
Map 7 C1.
Tel (495) 221 7557.

Art Cafés

Drevo
Древо
Ulitsa Malaya
Nikitskaya 16.
Map 2 D5.
Tel (495) 691 4041.

FAQ Café
Фак Кафе
Ulitsa Bolshaya
Polyanka 65/74.
Map 7 B5.
Tel (495) 951 5227.
🅦 **faqcafe.ru**

Krizis Zhanra
Кризис жанра
Ulitsa Pokrovka
16/16.
Tel (495) 623 2594.

Gay and Lesbian Nightlife

12 Volt
Tverskaya ulitsa 12/2.
Map 2 E4.
Tel (495) 933 2815.
🅦 **12voltclub.ru**

Central Station
Центральная станция
Ulitsa Leninskaya
Sloboda 19/2.
Tel (916) 478 2782.
🅦 **gaycentral.ru**

Sharm
Шарм
Zvenigorodskoye
schosse 11/1.
Tel (966) 027 1460.
🅦 **clubchance.net**

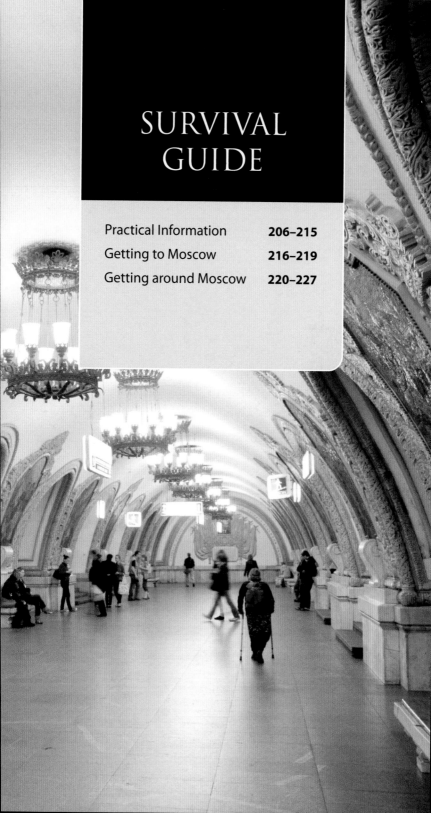

SURVIVAL GUIDE

PRACTICAL INFORMATION

Moscow is not as difficult for visitors to find their way around as it may seem at first. Certainly, the city is vast, street names and signs are in Cyrillic and traffic can be formidably heavy, especially in the centre. On the other hand, public transport is cheap, with an excellent metro system, and locals working in hotels, restaurants and shops will usually help tourists. Nonetheless, it is a good idea for visitors to master a few Russian phrases and familiarize themselves with the Cyrillic alphabet to decipher signs *(see pp260–64)*.

Although Moscow receives more than four million foreign visitors annually, the city's tourist information services are still fairly basic. There is no main Tourist Information Centre, but there is an English-language Tourist Helpline that can offer advice. Visitors requiring information on practicalities and events should look on the Internet or ask their hotel or travel agent. Moscow is one of the most expensive cities in the world to visit compared to Western equivalents, so always enquire about prices before booking something.

St Basil's Cathedral on Moscow's Red Square

When to Go

Visitors should not be daunted by Moscow's long, harsh winters. Between November and late March the temperatures fall to around -8°C, however, the city is well equipped with an army of snow ploughs and street cleaners to deal with the ice and snow. Sturdy footwear, warm layers of clothing and hats are a must. Temperatures in July and August can exceed 30°C, while spring and autumn are usually dry and cool.

Visas and Passports

Citizens from most countries will need a visa to enter Russia. Only those from CIS member states (excluding the Baltic states, Georgia and Turkmenistan) and some Latin-American countries are exempt. Before travelling check the latest

entry requirements with your local Russian embassy. Those arriving by train will also need a transit visa to pass through Belarus. There are three main types of visa: business (for visitors who have been invited by an organization or who want to stay longer than a month), private (for those who have been invited to stay at a private address) and tourist (for those staying at a hotel).

If booking package deals, visas will be arranged by the tour companies. For independent travellers, the easiest way to obtain a visa is to pay a modest fee and get a specialist agent, such as **Andrews Travel House** or **Visa Express**, based in the UK, or **Travisa** in the US, to arrange it on your behalf. Moscow-based **Visa to Russia** can also arrange visas for visitors of any nationality. Alternatively, apply

to the Russian embassy. All visa applications must be accompanied by a letter of invitation, which your hotel, travel agent or host can provide.

Those who are self-employed must provide bank statements with evidence of at least $160 (5,000 roubles) a day in funds for the duration of their trip.

Travellers are required, as a formality, to specify the places they intend to visit and from where they will exit the country. However, visitors are free to change their travel plans once they have arrived in Russia.

Visas normally take around 10 days to process but, if speed is important, all the specialist agents offer an express service for an extra fee. The cost of a visa depends on the length of its validity as well as how soon it is required. UK and US citizens can expect to pay $140 (4,400 roubles) for a single-entry tourist visa valid for a month and issued in advance. EU citizens are charged $50 (1,500 roubles) for the same.

While tourist visas cannot be extended, private and business visa extensions can be made by the organization or individual that issued the invitation. Overstaying your allocated time can lead to a hefty fine.

All foreign nationals must register with the **Federal Migration Service (FMS)**, within 7 working days of arrival. Hotels do this for their guests automatically. If you have a private visa your host must register you at a local police station or FMS office. Non-registration can lead to on-the-spot fines by local police of up to $160 (5,000 roubles) for the host party.

Customs Information

Passports and visas are thoroughly checked at immigration desks. Visitors are given an immigration card by immigration officials on arrival, which must be retained while in the country and presented upon departure. There are no official limits on how much foreign currency may be brought in, but visitors carrying more than $10,000 (320,000 roubles) in cash will be expected to fill in a customs declaration statement. Departure customs are stricter than in other countries, particularly with regard to art and antiques (see p193).

Embassies and Consulates

Every country that has diplomatic relations with Russia has an embassy or consulate in Moscow. Embassy or consular officials can re-issue passports and offer advice and assistance with interpretation in emergencies. Anyone intending to reside in Russia for over 3 months is advised to register with their own country's embassy.

Shop selling traditional souvenirs in central Moscow

Tourist Information

In the absence of any tourist offices in Moscow, travel agents and hotel concierges are often the main source of guidance for visitors. However, an English-language **Tourist Helpline**, a plethora of Moscow city guides on the Internet and **IntoRussia**, a company specializing in Russian travel, provide plenty of easy-to-find and helpful information.

The city's two English-language newspapers, *The Moscow Times* and *The Moscow News (see p215)*, both contain useful listings. The free *Moscow In Your Pocket* guide is another good source of information.

Admission Prices

Moscow can be expensive for visitors as most museums charge higher admission fees for visitors than Russian residents. However there are concession prices for students and seniors.

Opening Hours

In the city centre shops are open 9am–7pm Monday to Saturday and 10am–6pm Sunday. Sights and museums are open from 10am to 6pm, but ticket offices may close an hour earlier. Museums close one day a week and one day a month for cleaning. All museums open on Sundays. Cathedrals and churches are open to visitors, but some are only open during services.

ОТКРЫТО
Sign for open (otkryto)

ЗАКРЫТО
Sign for closed (zakryto)

Language

Cyrillic, the alphabet used in the Russian language, is named after the 9th-century monks Cyril (see p19) and Methodius who invented it. Apparent similarities between Cyrillic and Roman letters can be misleading. Some letters are common to both alpha-bets, others look similar but represent different sounds.

The majority of Russians do not speak English, but those who regularly come into contact with visitors generally do. Knowledge of even one or two words of Russian (see pp260–64) will be seen as a sign of respect.

Igumnov House, built in 1893, now the home of the French Embassy

Visiting Churches

Attending an Orthodox church service is a fascinating experience. The most important services take place on Saturday evenings and Sunday mornings and on religious holidays. In general, services run for several hours. The main Divine Liturgy often goes on for 3 to 6 hours. Russian churches do not have any chairs, and the congregation is expected to stand throughout. While it is acceptable for visitors to drop in on a service for a while, certain dress rules must be observed. Men must remove their hats, while women should not wear low-cut tops and should cover their shoulders and wear a headscarf or hat. Shorts are not suitable for attending a church service.

A woman leaving church after a service dressed in a headscarf

Etiquette and Smoking

Russian manners and attitudes have become more Westernized, but the linguistic distinction between the formal "you" *(vy)* and informal "you" *(ty)* remains strictly in force. On public transport, young men are expected to give up their seats for the elderly or for families with young children.

Smoking and drinking are popular among Russians. Frequent toasts are required to justify the draining of glasses. When invited to someone's home, visitors should offer the toast *za*

Children playing on a cannon at the Armoury in the Kremlin

khozyayku (to the hostess) or *za khozyaina* (to the host).

Many Russians are superstitious. Most prefer not to shake hands across the threshold of a doorway and, if someone accidentally steps on a friend's toes, the injured party pretends to step back on the perpetrator's toes.

Public Toilets

Public toilets are often basic and not pleasant, though most cafés and bars have facilities. It is best to find a toilet in a hotel or department store, where fees may range from 10 to 30 roubles. The attendent who takes the money will also hand out toilet paper rations; it is a good idea to carry your own.

Paying and Tipping

Roubles are the only valid currency in Russia *(see p213)*. Some large shops and hotels display prices in US dollars or euros, but all cash payments must be in roubles only.

Upmarket and mid-range restaurants, hotels and shops accept credit cards, but smaller shops may not, so it is always best to carry cash. Tipping is a matter of choice.

Travellers with Special Needs

Moscow has few facilities for the disabled, but there are signs of gradual improvement. A number of high-end hotels now offer specially equipped rooms, a few central bus routes have introduced wheelchair-accessible vehicles and recently refurbished museums cater for the disabled. Despite these

changes, the city remains a challenge for those with special needs, so it is advisable to use taxis to get around and phone in advance to check if a tourist sight has full disabled access.

Travelling with Children

Russians adore children, and those accompanying visitors to Moscow are likely to attract plenty of compliments.

Children under seven travel free on public transport. Museums are free for under-sevens and offer concession prices to all school children. The city has a wide range of children's attractions including puppet theatres, circuses and parks *(see p199)*.

Gay and Lesbian Travellers

Moscow's gay and lesbian scene continues to thrive *(see p202)* in the face of extreme hostility. In general, however, Russian society is not very tolerant of homosexuality. Gay and lesbian travellers should be aware of this as any public displays of affection will almost always attract unwanted attention.

Travelling on a Budget

Accommodation is expensive in Moscow, so booking a dorm bed in one of the city's many hostels is a good way to save money. Another budget option is **Couchsurfing**,

International Student Identity Card

where you can find places to stay for free.

Bars and restaurants offer a good-value three-course meal on weekdays from noon to 4pm. ISIC card holders are entitled to discounts in museums and on rail and air tickets booked through **STAR Travel**.

Time

As of 2011, Russia has abolished winter clock reversal and Moscow is now 4 hours ahead of Greenwich Mean Time (GMT). This decision is still under discussion.

Electricity

The electrical current in Russia is 220 V and two-pin European-style plugs are used. UK appliances require adaptors and US appliances need a 220 V to 110 V current adaptor.

Responsible Tourism

While Moscow is not renowned as a green city, there are a few (expensive) eco-friendly hotels such as the **Ararat Park Hyatt Moscow** *(see p178)* and **Swissôtel Krasnye Holmy** *(see p178)*, which employ sophisticated energy and conservation systems and recycle much of their waste.

The centrally located **Dorogomilovsky Market** is one of Moscow's largest farmers' markets, selling fresh produce from regional farms, including fresh fruit and vegetables and salted fish.

Moscow recycles just 10 per cent of its waste, but the main municipality has announced plans to introduce a recycling initiative that will provide separate waste collection bins at all metro and train stations, airports, and in residential apartment blocks through-out the city.

Eco-friendly Swissôtel Krasnye Holmy

Conversions

Imperial to Metric
1 inch = 2.54 centimetres
1 foot = 30 centimetres
1 mile = 1.6 kilometres
1 ounce = 28 grams
1 pound = 454 grams
1 pint = 0.6 litres

Metric to Imperial
1 centimetre = 0.4 inches
1 metre = 3 feet, 3 inches
1 kilometre = 0.6 miles
1 gram = 0.04 ounces
1 kilogram = 2.2 pounds
1 litre = 1.8 pints
Russia uses the Metric system.

DIRECTORY

Visas and Passports

Andrews Travel House
23 Pembridge Square,
London W2 4DR.
Tel (020) 7727 2838.
W **andrews-consulting. co.uk**

Federal Migration Service (FMS)
Pokrovka ulitsa 42.
Map 4 D4.
Tel (495) 200 8497.

Travisa
1731 21st St. NW
Washington, DC 20009.
Tel (202) 463 6166.
W **travisa.com**

VisaExpress
Parnell House
25 Wilton Road
London SW1V 1LW.
Tel (020) 7251 4822.
W **visaexpress.co.uk**

Visa to Russia
Leninsky prospekt 29,
Building 8, Moscow.
Map 2 E5.
Tel (495) 956 4422.
W **visatorussia.com**

Embassies and Consulates

Australia
10A Podkolokolny
pereulok 2.
Map 7 D1.
Tel (495) 956 6070.
W **russia.embassy. gov.au**

Canada
Starokonyushenny
pereulok 23.
Map 6 E2.
Tel (495) 925 6000.
W **russia.gc.ca**

Ireland
Grokholskiy pereulok 5.
Map 3 C2.
Tel (495) 937 5911.
W **embassyofireland.ru**

New Zealand
Ulitsa Povarskaya 44.
Map 2 D5.
Tel (495) 956 3579.
W **nzembassy.com/ russia**

South Africa
Granatny pereulok, dom 1.
Map 2 F5.
Tel (495) 540 1177.
W **saembassy.ru**

United Kingdom
Smolenskaya
Naberezhnaya 10.
Map 5 C1.
Tel (495) 956 7200.
W **ukinrussia.fco.gov.uk**

United States
Bolshoy Deviatinsky
pereulok 8. **Map** 2 D5.
Tel (495) 728 5000.
W **moscow.usembassy. gov**

Tourist Information

IntoRussia
18 Norland Road,
London W11 4TR.
Tel 0844 875 4026/
(020) 7603 5045.
W **into-russia.co.uk**

Moscow In Your Pocket
W **inyourpocket.com**

The Moscow News
W **themoscownews. com**

The Moscow Times
W **themoscowtimes. com**

Tourist Helpline
Tel (800) 220 0002.

Travelling on a Budget

Couchsurfing
W **couchsurfing.org**

STAR Travel
Uliysa Novoslobodskaya 3.
Map 2 E1.
Tel (495) 797 9555.
W **startravel.ru**

Responsible Tourism

Ararat Park Hyatt Moscow
Ulitsa Neglinnaya 4.
Map 3 A4.
Tel (495) 783 1234.
W **moscow.park.hyatt. com**

Dorogomilovsky Market
Ulitsa Mozhavskiy val 10.
Map 5 A2.
Tel (499) 249 5553.

Swissôtel Krasnye Holmy
Kosmodamianskaya
naberezhnaya 52,
Building 6. **Map** 7 C2.
Tel (495) 787 9898.
W **swissotel.com/ moscow**

Personal Security and Health

Moscow is a safe city for tourists, despite its reputation. Petty crime should be the visitor's only concern, but can be avoided if sensible precautions are taken. For language reasons it is a good idea to keep a card with the address you are staying at with you at all times for use in taxis and in emergencies. Also keep a copy of your passport and visa. Obtaining medical insurance before you travel is essential, as local healthcare compares poorly with Western standards. Medicines are readily available, but it is best to bring your own.

Police car

Fire engine

Ambulance

A Russian police officer (*militsiya*) patrolling the city streets

Police

Several kinds of police officer operate on Moscow's streets. They change uniform according to the weather, wearing fur hats and big coats in winter. The normal police or *politsiya*, who always carry guns, are more frequently seen. The riot police or OMON, who dress in a camouflage uniform, are rarely seen on the streets.

Totally separate are the traffic police, recognizable by their striped truncheons. Traffic police can stop any vehicle to check the driver's documents and issue on-the-spot fines. Despite government attempts to stamp out corruption, both the *politsiya* and traffic police are known to supplement their incomes by picking people up on minor offences and charging a small "fine" of their own. There have also been instances of bogus policemen approaching tourists for fines, so it's wise

to ask for ID if in doubt. Carry a photocopy of your passport and visa and never hand over your original passport to police.

In an Emergency

The emergency services can be reached by dialling 01 for the fire department, 02 for police and 03 for an ambulance, but the operators are unlikely to speak English so having a Russian speaker to assist you will be essential. If at all possible, seek help first from your embassy or consulate.

What to be Aware of

The greatest danger for visitors comes from thieves who might become violent if they encounter resistance. As in any country, it is advisable to hand over belongings if they are demanded with menace. Travellers are advised to remain vigilant against pickpockets, particularly at popular tourist attractions where large crowds of people are gathered. Women on their own may be approached by kerb-crawlers, who are best ignored, or may be propositioned if alone in bars and restaurants. Both male and female travellers should exercise caution if invited to drink with strangers as instances of drinks being spiked are not uncommon. At night it is safer to use taxis booked in advance rather than those hailed on the street. Travellers, especially women, should avoid walking alone in the city late at night.

Lost and Stolen Property

Visitors should be vigilant of pickpockets when travelling on public transport and in crowded areas. Being a victim of pickpockets can be avoided by steering clear of overcrowded public transport and not carrying money in open pockets or displaying large sums of money in public. Bags should be kept closed and roubles kept apart from foreign currency and credit cards. It is advisable to carry only a small sum of money for purchases and keep the rest separately or in the safe at your hotel.

It is best not to stop for gypsies who sometimes frequent Tverskaya ulitsa and the central metro stations, apparently begging. Hold tight to valuables and walk resolutely on without aggression. It is absolutely essential to report thefts to the police in order to obtain certificates for insurance claims. Report first to the hotel security staff who can deal with the whole matter. Embassies will help with serious situations.

Hospitals and Pharmacies

Most upmarket hotels have their own doctor and this should be the first port of call for anyone who falls ill. There are several companies, notably the **European Medical Centre** and the **American Medical Center**, that specialize in healthcare for visitors. They can provide everything that travellers are likely to need, from basic treatment to dental care, X-rays, ultrasound scans and even medical evacuation home. Their charges are very high, but they are all used to dealing with foreign insurance policies. The UK and Russia have a reciprocal healthcare agreement, so basic treatment for UK citizens in state hospitals should be free of charge. **US Dental Care** provides a full range of dental treatment. For those in need of urgent attention,

Pharmacy, identified by the word *apteka*

without the time to contact any of the above, the casualty department of the **Botkin Hospital** is well equipped and used to dealing with foreign nationals.

Pharmacies in Russia are all signed by the word *apteka* and usually have an illuminated green cross hanging outside. They sell many imported medications, some with the instructions still in the original language. Prescriptions are not necessary for any purchase, so antibiotics and other strong medications can be bought over the counter. All the assistants are trained pharmacists and can suggest a Russian alternative to visitors who name the drug they are seeking. However, visitors with specific requirements, particularly insulin, should bring enough with them for their whole stay. Moscow has a number of all-night pharmacies (*see Directory*).

Health Precautions

Visitors should not drink the tap water in Moscow and should avoid fruit and raw vegetables that may have been washed in tap water, sticking to drinking bottled water. Food in a foreign country often unsettles the

stomach and eating the meat and sausage pies (*pirozhki*) sold on the streets is sure to cause an upset tummy.

Mosquitoes (*komari*) are rife in the summer months of June to late September. Plug-in chemical mosquito coils are available in pharmacies. Alternatives are sprays, or citronella oil repellents used in vaporizers or burned in candles. Ticks are common in rural areas.

Travel and Health Insurance

A comprehensive travel insurance policy is recommended for all visitors. While travel health insurance can be purchased separately, most travel insurance policies cover medical treatment as well. Hospital bills can be very expensive so it's best to choose a provider that will reimburse the hospitals directly while on your trip.

Vaccinations

Diphtheria has increased among the local population, and there is also a low risk of rabies, polio and hepatitis A and B. It is advisable to be inoculated against these before travelling to Russia.

DIRECTORY

Emergency Services

Ambulance (skoraya pomoshch)
Tel 03.

Fire (pozhar)
Tel 01.

Police (politsiya)
Tel 02.

Hospitals

American Medical Center
Американский медицинский центр
Amerikanskiy meditsinskiy tsentr

Prospekt Mira 26, Building 6.
Map 3 B2.
Tel (495) 933 7700.
w amcenter.ru

Botkin Hospital
Боткинская больница
Botkinskaya bolnitsa
2-oy Botkinskiy proezd 5.
Map 1 A1.
Tel (495) 945 0045.

European Medical Centre
Европейский медицинский центр
Yevropeyskiy meditsinskiy tsentr

Spiridonievsky pereulok 5, Building 1.
Map 2 D4.
Tel (495) 933 6655.
w emcmos.ru

US Dental Care
Американский стоматологический центр
Amerikanskiy stomatologicheskiy tsentr
Bolshaya Dmitrovka 7/5, Building 2.
Map 2 F4.
Tel (495) 933 8686.
w usdentalcare.com

Pharmacies

Apteka 36.6
Аптека 36,6
Ulitsa Tverskaya 25/9.
Map 2 E3.

Ulitsa Valovaya 2–4/44.
Map 7 B5.

Leninskiy prospect 16.
Map 1 B1.
Tel (495) 797 6366.
w **366.ru**
(Open 24 hours)

Banking and Currency

All major credit and debit cards can be used in Moscow to pay in hotels, upmarket and mid-range restaurants and shops. Everywhere else, however, cash is the norm, so carry some at all times. Roubles are the only legal currency, although prices are also quoted in US dollars and euros. There are numerous ATMs and bureaux de change located throughout the city and visitors can exchange currency or get roubles with a debit or credit card. Bureau de change offices usually offer the best exchange rates, although rates of commission may vary.

SBERBANK

Sberbank logo

Banks and Bureaux de Change

Roubles can be obtained outside Russia, but the rates of exchange are usually better at the bureaux de change found around Moscow, including at the airports. Some offices are open 24 hours a day. A passport usually has to be shown when changing money. Any defect on foreign bank notes, especially vertical tears or ink or water stains, makes them invalid and they will be refused.

There are only a few foreign banks in Russia and they generally do not offer over-the-counter services. Most Russian banks, however, do have on-the-spot exchange services. They will exchange a variety of currencies as well as offering

cash advances against credit and debit cards. **Alfa-Bank** and **Sberbank** offer the best rates. For anyone wishing to have money sent to a bank in Russia, these are also the most reliable banks. **Master Bank** and **Bank Moskvy** also offer money transfer and accept American Express travellers' cheques, and prepaid currency cards can be used to withdraw cash at many ATMs. **Western Union** will transfer money to and from Russia through a large number of banks and post offices in Moscow; check the website for details of agent locations and transfer rates.

Most independent bureaux de change offices in Moscow will also accept all worldwide currencies to convert, although be aware that some exchange offices may only convert US dollars and euros.

A sign for a currency exchange office
(obmen valyuty)

DIRECTORY

Banks

Alfa-Bank
Альфа-Банк
Kuznetskiy Most 9/10, Building 2.
Map 3 A4.
Tel 495 (620) 9191.
🆆 alfabank.ru

Bank Moskvy
Банк Москвы
Ul. Novy Arbat 36/9.
Map 5 C1.
Tel (495) 925 8000.
🆆 bm.ru

Master Bank
Мастер Банк
Runovskiy pereulok 12.
Map 7 C3. **Tel** (495) 232 2324.
🆆 masterbank.ru

Sberbank
Сбербанк
Gazetny pereulok 17, Building 2.
Map 6 D2.
Tel (495) 692 3869.
🆆 sbrf.ru

Western Union
🆆 westernunion.co.uk

Lost or Stolen Cards

American Express
Tel (495) 933 8400.

Visa
Tel (866) 654 0164.

ATMs

ATMs can be found all over Moscow and sometimes in the most unlikely of places. The usual precautions apply – avoid using machines that are not attached to a reputable bank if at all possible.

Credit and Debit Cards

Credit and debit cards are readily accepted in mid-range and upmarket hotels, restaurants and shops. Cards can be used to withdraw roubles, euros, and US dollars from ATMs. The most commonly accepted card is **Visa**, with Diners, MasterCard, Eurocard and **American Express** less widely used. Lost or stolen credit cards should be reported immediately to your credit card company.

ATMs at a branch of Alfa-Bank

Currency

The Russian currency is the rouble (or ruble), written **рубль** or abbreviated to ₽ or **руб**. The higher denominations of roubles are available in banknotes, which all bear images of well-known Russian cities, the lower denominations in coins. The kopek, of which there are 100 to a rouble, is issued in coins.

Banknotes

There are five denominations of banknote, with face values of 10, 50, 100, 500, 1,000 and 5,000 roubles, and they have the same designs as their pre-revaluation equivalents. When changing money check that the notes correspond to those shown here.

10 roubles

50 roubles

100 roubles

500 roubles

1,000 roubles

5,000 roubles

Coins

The revaluation of the Russian rouble in 1998 led to the revival of the long-redundant but much-loved kopek. Traditionally, the rouble had always consisted of 100 kopeks. In addition to coins for 1, 2 and 5 roubles, there are now coins valued at 1, 5, 10 and 50 kopeks. Any coins issued before 1997, prior to revaluation, are essentially valueless. Visitors should therefore always examine change they receive and refuse to accept any of these old coins.

1 rouble

2 roubles

5 roubles

1 kopek

5 kopeks

10 kopeks

50 kopeks

Communications and Media

Moscow has an excellent city-wide and international telephone service. There still remain some telephone boxes on the streets, although card-operated phones are more widespread than coin-operated ones and most Russians use mobile phones. There has also been an increase in Internet usage and the proliferation of magazines, newspapers and television channels. Russia's postal system has also improved, but remains considerably slower than its Western counterparts.

Using mobile phones for calls and Wi-Fi in public spaces

International and Local Telephone Calls

While payphones can still be found around the city, they are becoming ever rarer. The few available payphones that accept coins are less reliable than those that accept credit or debit cards or phone cards.

Directions on how to use a payphone appear in English when the receiver is lifted. If using a credit or debit card, insert the card and wait 15 seconds for card verification before dialling.

Phone cards come in 25, 50, 100, 120, 200, 400 and 1,000 units and are available from kiosks and post offices. To make an international call at least 100 units are needed. International and inter-city calls are cheaper from 10pm to 8am in the week and all weekend.

The **Central Telegraph Office** has phones available to make international and local calls, paid for at the counter. A cheap way to call abroad is to buy an international calling card from a kiosk or post office, which can be used with all payphones and landlines.

Mobile Phones

If roaming is activated on your mobile phone it can be used in Russia, but the charges are likely to be exorbitant. Calls made to Russian numbers from your mobile should start with the country code (+7) followed by the city code and number.

Prepaid Russian SIM cards are a much cheaper option if your phone is unlocked. Your passport is required for registration when buying a SIM. These are available contract-free from the main mobile network operators – **MTS**, **Megafon** and **Beeline** – and can be topped up at phone shops, ATMs and top-up points in underpasses.

Internet

The easiest way to access the Internet, if you have a laptop or smartphone, is to use the free Wi-Fi provided by most cafés, restaurants, bars, hotels and public spaces. Wi-Fi has also been introduced on the Ring Line of Moscow metro. There are many Internet cafés in the city centre. **Café Max,** is one of the largest and opens 24 hours a day.

Internet café with computer access

Addresses

Russian addresses are given in the following order: post code, city, street name, house (dom) number and, finally, apartment (kvartira) number. If a flat is part of a complex, a korpus (k) number will also be given to indicate which block it is in. When visiting a flat, it is useful to know which entrance (podezd) to the block to use and when sending letters to a Russian address it is crucial to include the correct six digit postcode.

Useful Dialling Codes

- Local directory enquiries (Moscow only): dial 09.
- Local calls: dial 8 (wait for the tone if using an analogue phone) then the city code if necessary (Moscow has two codes: 499 and 495) then the number.
- International calling cards: Dial the local access number followed by the card number and the PIN, then dial the number starting with the country code and omitting 00.
- Direct international dialling: Dial the country code followed by the number:
  UK: 044 followed by the area code (omitting the first 0) and number.
  USA: 001 then the area code (omitting the first 0) and number.
  Australia: 0061, then the area code (omitting the first 0) and number.
  New Zealand: 0064, then the area code (omitting the first 0) and number.
  Irish Republic: 00353, then the area code (omitting the first 0) and number.
  Italy: 0039, then the area code (including the first 0) and number

Romanesque-inspired façade of Moscow's grand Main Post Office

Postal Services

The **Main Post Office** and the Central Telegraph Office are Moscow's most central post offices. Smaller post offices are marked **почта** (*pochta*), and can be found all over the city. They generally have blue post boxes outside. Russian postboxes are also marked **почта** and are plentiful in the city centre.

Tourists should use the small pale blue post boxes. The yellow ones are used for special delivery local services only. Post offices sell regular and commemorative Russian stamps, postcards, envelopes and phonecards.

International post is usually reliable, but often quite slow and is probably best avoided except for postcards. For important documents use a courier service, such as **DHL FedEx, Pony Express** and **TNT Express Worldwide**. Keep in mind that anything other than paper will be checked by customs which may delay dispatch by an extra day or so.

Newspapers and Magazines

Moscow has one major English-language daily newspaper, *The Moscow Times*, which covers both domestic and foreign news. *The Moscow News*, the city's oldest English-language newspaper, is published twice a week and has similar content. Both papers are distributed free in cafés, bars and hotels and have excellent websites.

In Your Pocket Moscow is a useful free guide published in English every two months. There is also a Russian-language version of the UK magazine *Time Out*, which has extensive listings as well as articles. It can be bought at most newsstands.

To keep up with world events, however, you are better off visiting international news websites or tuning into foreign television.

Television and Radio

Hotels have long offered Eurosport, CNN, BBC and NBC channels. Russian-language television is dominated by imported soap operas, which are generally dubbed into Russian rather than subtitled. The best national news in Russian is on NTV, and the best local news on TV-Tsentr.

The BBC World Service no longer transmits in Russia except via satellite, but you can tune in with a special receiver or listen online, and other English-language radio stations are also accessible online.

Ekho Moskvy (91.2 FM) provides a news service in Russian. Popular stations include Radio Maximum (103.7 FM) and Love Radio (106.6 FM), both of which play Western music, and Russkoe Radio (105.7 FM), which plays Russian music.

Newspaper and magazine kiosk near Arbatskaya metro station

DIRECTORY

Telephone Services

Central Telegraph Office
Центральный телеграф
Tverskaya ulitsa 7.
Map 2 F5.
Tel (495) 504 4444.
Ⓦ moscow.cnt.ru

Mobile Phones

Beeline
Ⓦ beeline.ru

Megafon
Ⓦ megafon.ru

MTC
Ⓦ mts.ru

Postal Services

DHL
1st Tverskaya-Yamskaya ulitsa 11.
Map 2 D3.
Tel (495) 956 1000.
Ⓦ dhl.ru

FedEx
Sokolnicheskiy Val 1L.
Tel (495) 737 5223.
Ⓦ fedex.com/ru

Main Post Office
Главный почтамт
Ulitsa Myasnitskaya 26.
Map 3 C4.
Tel (495) 624 0250.
Ⓦ moscowpost.ru

Pony Express
Ulitsa Pyatnitskaya 74.
Map 7 B2.
Tel (495) 981 1956.
Ⓦ ponyexpress.ru

TNT Express Worldwide
UlitsaBolshaya Nikitskaya 22/2.

Map 2 D5.
Tel (495) 690 5568.
Ⓦ tnt.ru

Internet

Café Max
Ulitsa Pyatnitskaya.
Map 7 B2.
Ⓦ cafemax.ru

Centre Internet Club
Kuznetskiy most 12.
Map 3 A4
Tel (495) 625 9288.
Ⓦ gpntb.ru

GETTING TO MOSCOW

The quickest and most comfortable way to get to Moscow is by plane. Travelling overland, especially by road, can be difficult and often involves crossing numerous borders and negotiating roadworks and pot-holed roads. However, if cost is the priority, arriving by train or coach are cheaper alternatives, especially for visitors travelling from St Petersburg or from neighbouring countries, such as the Ukraine or Belarus. Whichever route is chosen, it is worth shopping around to find the best deal as flight prices fluctuate greatly throughout the year. Many companies also offer package deals.

Arriving by Air

There is a good choice of flights to Moscow from the UK. **British Airways**, **BMI**, **Aeroflot** and **Transaero** operate direct flights, while several other airlines, including **SAS**, **KLM** and **Austrian Airlines** run a variety of flights via a number of destinations. Transaero, which flies direct from London, is the only reliable Russian alternative to Aeroflot. **Delta** has direct flights from the US along with Transaero and Aeroflot, which also operate long-haul flights from Australia and Canada. Despite popular belief that Aeroflot's flights and in-flight service is of an inferior quality, its international fleet is maintained to a high standard and the service is usually of a high standard.

Tickets and Fares

Cheap trips are advertised online and in the travel sections of many newspapers and magazines. Websites such as www.lastminute.com and www.skyscanner.net can find the cheapest tickets and there are several agencies in London and New York that book trips to Russia. Some only sell flights while others, such as **Russian National Group**, also book hotel accommodation or offer inclusive package deals. These deals can be cheaper than booking flights and accommodation separately.

Some agencies also arrange visas for travellers (see p206). **Andrew's Travel House** can offer visas and provide detailed travel itineraries for your stay in Moscow. They can even

Passenger Terminal at Domodedovo airport

make restaurant and theatre reservations on your behalf before your arrival.

Airports

Moscow has three main airports, each servicing both domestic and international flights. The largest is **Domodedovo**, to the south of the city, which is closely followed by **Sheremetyevo**, which has six terminals. **Vnukovo**, which is the smallest of the three, has three terminals and has been undergoing a programme of expansion.

Domodedovo lies 42 km (26 miles) southeast of Moscow and, like all three airports, is easily accessible by the **Aeroexpress** rail link. Sheremetyevo is situated about 29 km (18 miles) northwest of the city centre and has a reputation for lengthy queues at check-in. Vnukovo is closest to the centre (28 km/17 miles). Information desks, exchange offices, ATMs, duty free stores, cafés and the like can be found at all three airports.

All of Moscow's main airport terminals have free Wi-Fi Internet access and are served by 24-hour information desks manned by helpful, multilingual staff who can provide airport and flight information and advice to travellers about transport to Moscow and other cities. Although they are unable to make hotel bookings, they can assist with locating pre-booked hotels and will also contact hotels on behalf of travellers if necessary.

Lost luggage desks are located next to the baggage carousels in the various terminals of the airports.

On Arrival

Travellers flying into Moscow will need an immigration card. At Domodedovo a printed-out card will be given to travellers by immigration officials, and this should also be the case at Sheremetyevo. Passengers flying in to smaller airports such as Vnukov will be given a card by flight attendants shortly before landing, which should be completed with personal details including address, visa number and departure date. The card has two parts – one for entry and the other for exit. The entry half will be retained and you must keep the exit slip and present it to passport control on departure. There is no need to fill out a currency declaration statement unless you are carrying over 320,000 roubles ($10,000) cash.

Зал прилёта
Arrivals

Розыск багажа
Lost and found

Хранение багажа
Left luggage

Airport signs in Cyrillic and English found in all Moscow's airports

Transport from the Airport to the City

The easiest way to get to and from all three airports is the **Aeroexpress** rail link – a dedicated train service that links the airports with train and metro stations on the Circle line. One-way tickets cost 320 roubles ($11) and trains depart every 30 minutes from 6am to midnight. The journey from Domodedovo takes 45 minutes and terminates at Paveletsky station; the Sheremetyevo train takes 35 minutes and terminates at Belorussky station;

and the Vnukovo train takes 35 to 40 minutes and terminates at Kievsky station.

Frequent bus services also connect the airports with the city centre. Buses leave between 6am and midnight but traffic congestion often causes delays. Bright blue buses departing every 15 minutes connect Domodedovo with Domodedovskaya metro station; bus 851 takes around 40 minutes to connect Sheremetyevo with Rechnoy Vokzal metro station; and bus 611 from Vnukovo to YugoZapadnaya metro station takes 25 minutes.

It is recommended that passengers arriving after midnight use a taxi to reach the city centre, however, it is also possible to wait at the airport for the next available train or bus link to the city.

Official airport taxis can be pre-booked by your hotel or from desks within the terminal. Unofficial drivers also ply their trade inside and outside the airports. They are generally safe, but it is much better to use the official taxis. The taxi meters, installed in most taxis, are rarely used so it is vital to negotiate a price for the trip beforehand – the cost should be around

Official taxis, which provide easy access to the city centre

1,600 roubles ($54) to the city centre. This price is for a standard "economy class" car. Most drivers increase their fares when they have higher-quality "business class" vehicles. No tips are necessary. The journey takes about 40 minutes, depending on traffic.

Internal Flights

All of Moscow's airports handle domestic flights. Passengers usually need to show their passports on departure despite the fact that they will not be leaving the country.

The majority of Aeroflot's domestic flights use Sheremetyevo Airport's Terminal D, while the popular low-cost airlines **S7** and Transaero fly to and from most major Russian cities from Teminal B at Domodedovo airport.

All domestic flights from Vnukovo Airport fly to and from Terminal A, from where the low-cost airline **UTair Aviation** has flights to destinations around Russia.

On Departure

The maximum baggage allowance per passenger is 23 kg of hold luggage and 10 kg of hand luggage. Departure customs are stricter than in other countries, particularly with regard to art and antiques *(see p193)*.

If you have lost the exit half of your immigration card, you will need to visit the Immigration Service offices in the airport terminal to request a replacement card.

Aeroexpress rail link, which connects to the Circle line metro in the city centre

Belorusskiy railway station

Arriving by Train

Moscow can be reached easily by train from Paris, Brussels, Berlin and several other European capitals, but the trip will take at least 24 hours and you will need a transit visa for Belarus. Be prepared for a lengthy wait at the Russian border as all of the train's wheels will be changed to fit the wider Russian tracks before proceeding.

Interior of an overnight sleeper compartment

Three of Moscow's main railway stations are situated on Komsomolskaya ploshchad *(see p146)*, also known as ploshchad Trekh Vokzalov (Square of the Three Railway Stations). **Yaroslavskiy** and **Kazanskiy** serve domestic routes only. **Leningradskiy** is the terminus for trains from St Petersburg and Finland. Of the other stations, **Rizhskiy** serves the Baltic and **Kievskiy** serves Eastern Europe, while at **Belorusskiy** trains arrive from Western Europe, Kaliningrad and Poland. **Paveletskiy** and **Kurskiy** stations handle arrivals from southern Russia and parts of the Ukraine. All eight railway stations are easy to access as they are located close to main metro stations.

All tickets must be booked in advance. Due to the long distances, the majority of trains to Russia are overnight sleepers, but some standard trains operate on the shorter routes. Trains can be express *(ekspressy)* trains, direct between Moscow and St Petersburg only; fast *(skorye)* trains, which operate on long journeys and stop at only a few stations; passenger *(passazhirskie)* trains, which also operate on longer routes, but stop at most or all stations; and suburban *(prigorodnye)* trains *(see p227)*.

Arriving by Coach

Arriving by coach is only worth it if travelling from a neighbouring country or on a tight budget. Routes to Moscow leave Germany, the Czech Republic, Slovakia, Poland, Hungary, Latvia and Estonia. Some run via the Ukraine, while others enter via Belarus, for which a visa will be required. From Ukraine or Belarus takes 12–16 hours.

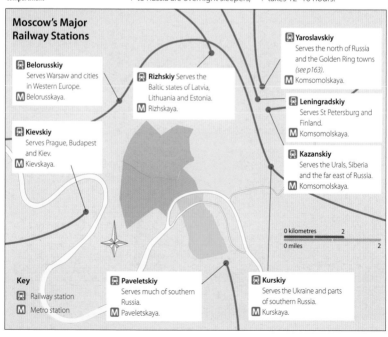

Moscow's Major Railway Stations

Belorusskiy
Serves Warsaw and cities in Western Europe.
Ⓜ Belorusskaya.

Rizhskiy Serves the Baltic states of Latvia, Lithuania and Estonia.
Ⓜ Rizhskaya.

Kievskiy
Serves Prague, Budapest and Kiev.
Ⓜ Kievskaya.

Yaroslavskiy
Serves the north of Russia and the Golden Ring towns *(see p163)*.
Ⓜ Komsomolskaya.

Leningradskiy
Serves St Petersburg and Finland.
Ⓜ Komsomolskaya.

Kazanskiy
Serves the Urals, Siberia and the far east of Russia.
Ⓜ Komsomolskaya.

0 kilometres   2
0 miles   2

Key
Ⓡ Railway station
Ⓜ Metro station

Paveletskiy
Serves much of southern Russia.
Ⓜ Paveletskaya.

Kurskiy
Serves the Ukraine and parts of southern Russia.
Ⓜ Kurskaya.

Travelling to Moscow from St Petersburg

The easiest way of getting to Moscow from St Petersburg is by train. Express trains run from Moskovskiy station in St Petersburg to Leningradskiy station in Moscow. Tickets can be bought through a hotel or from a travel agent.

Red Arrow train to Moscow from St Petersburg

The most atmospheric trains are the night-time *Red Arrows* that were once used by the Communist elite. Nos. 1 and 3 travel from St Petersburg to Moscow, and Nos. 2 and 4 from Moscow to St Petersburg. The *Grand Express* No. 54 is considered the most luxurious as it offers Grand Delux cabins with a toilet, DVD player and complimentary slippers. All these services leave at midnight and arrive at 8am the next morning. Travellers should be wary of thieves on the overnight trains. Most

compartments have locks, which should be used, especially at night.

From Moscow to St Petersburg the high speed *Sapsan* trains run daily and cover the distance in under 4 hours at speeds of up to 150 mph (250 km/h). Ticket prices vary depending on class and the services included. There is a choice between *sidyashchyy* (sitting) tickets and more expensive sleeper options. Food may be available, but visitors are advised to bring their own. Bed linen costs extra.

Alternatively a flight takes 50 minutes, but allow plenty of time to get to and from the airport *(see p216)*.

DIRECTORY

Airlines

Aeroflot
Аэрофлот
Tel (495) 223 5555.
w aeroflot.ru

Austrian Airlines
Tel (495) 995 0995.
w austrian.com

BMI
Tel (0844) 848 4880.
w flybmi.com

British Airways
Tel (495) 363 2525.
w britishairways.com

Delta
Tel (404) 773 0305.
w delta.com

KLM
Tel (495) 937 3839.
w klm.com

S7
Tel (3832) 599 011.
w s7.ru

SAS
Tel (495) 961 3060.
w flysas.com

Transaero
Трансаэро
Tel (495) 788 6150.
w transaero.ru

Utair Aviation
Tel (495) 228 0380.
w utair.ru

Tickets and Fares

Andrews Travel House
23 Pembridge Square, London, W2 4DR.
Tel 020 7727 2838.
w andrews-consulting. co.uk

Russian National Group
224 West 30th St, Suite 701, NY 10001.
Tel (877) 221 7120.
w russia-travel.com

Airports

Aeroexpress Airport Rail Link
Tel (800) 700 3377.
w aeroexpress.ru

Domodedovo
Домодедово
Tel (495) 933 6666.
w domodedovo.ru

Sheremetyevo
Шереметьево
Tel (495) 578 6565.
w svo.aero

Vnukovo
Внуково
Tel (495) 937 5555.
w vnukovo.ru

Arriving by Train

Belorusskiy
Белорусский
Tverskoy Zastavy ploshchad 7. **Map** 1 C2.
Tel (499) 623 8557.
w belorussky.dzvr.ru

Kazanskiy
Казанский
Komsomolskaya ploshchad 2.
Map 4 D2.
Tel (499) 266 1994.
w kazansky.dzvr.ru

Kievskiy
Киевский
Ploshchad Kievskovo vokzala.
Map 5 B2.
Tel (499) 240 7339.
w kievsky.dzvr.ru

Kurskiy
Курский
Ulitsa Zemlyanoy val 29.
Map 4 E5.
Tel (800) 775 0000.
w kursky.dzvr.ru

Leningradskiy
Ленинградский
Komsomolskaya ploshchad 3.
Map 4 D2.
Tel (495) 663 1398.
w leningradsky.dzvr.ru

Paveletskiy
Павелецкий
Paveletskaya ploshchad 1.
Map 7 C5.
Tel (800) 775 0000.

Rizhskiy
Рижский
Ploshchad Rizhskovo vokzala.
Tel (495) 266 8512.
w rizhsky.dzvr.ru

Yaroslavskiy
Ярославский
Komsomolskaya ploshchad 5.
Map 4 D2.
Tel (499) 266 9320.
w yaroslavsky.dzvr.ru

Arriving by Coach

General Enquiries
Tel (499) 748 8029.
Ticket Bookings
Tel (499) 748 8718.
w busmow.ru

Moscow Central Bus Station
Московский автовокзал
Moskovskiy avtovokzal
Nr Shchelkovskaya metro, Uralskaya ulitsa 2.
Tel (495) 468-0400, or 468-4370.

GETTING AROUND MOSCOW

Moscow's vast metro network has stops close to all the major sights and is the most reliable way of travelling around the city. However, it can get extremely crowded. Moscow is also served by buses, trolleybuses and trams and services are relatively frequent. Knowledge of the Cyrillic alphabet will help with reading signs on these services, although there are some English signs. Suburban buses are useful for travelling to Moscow's outlying districts and bus routes start at all major metro stations. Trams run as far as the outskirts of the city and trolleybuses cover the popular routes in the city centre. Taxis are the most flexible, but also the most expensive, way of getting around.

Cycling along the Moskva river

Green Travel

As green initiatives are limited in Moscow, an easy way to reduce your carbon footprint is by choosing a centrally located hotel for ease of access to the main sights. The centre can be covered on foot and guided walking tours are run throughout the year. There are no city-run cycle initiatives in Moscow, but cycle hire is possible and is a great way to get around the city. In the winter months it is best to use public transport, an eco-friendly alternative to taxis or cars. Some Muscovites even cross-country ski to get around the suburbs.

Guided Tours and Excursions

Hotels can book places on group guided tours and day trips. Alternatively, agencies such as IntouristUK offer a wide range of themed tours, including city trips and special trips to areas out of town. **Patriarshy Dom Tours** organize tours in English, including trips around the KGB Museum, the Kremlin and State Armoury, as well as hiking expeditions. Tours should generally be booked at least 48 hours in advance.

Anyone interested in a unique visitor experience away from the tourist sights should try **Moscow Greeter**, who offer a free walking tour with a local resident.

Walking

Moscow covers a vast area so is not easily negotiable on foot. However, the central area within the Boulevard Ring, where many sights are located,

Walking through the cultural district of Old Arbat

offers good opportunities for walking. At the heart of the city are Red Square (see p108) and the Kremlin (see pp55–69), which are only accessible on foot. Visitors should allow 3 hours to cover this area, including all the cathedrals in the Kremlin.

Across the river from here, beautiful Zamoskvoreche (see pp116–27) is another district to be enjoyed on foot.

Muscovites themselves are not great walkers but, in the evenings or at weekends, they can often be seen taking a stroll around the Old Arbat (see pp72–3), a district of the city frequented by artists, musicians and street performers. Other places to enjoy a walk are Tverskoy Bulvar, numerous parks – in particular Gorky Park (see p131), Izmaylovo Park (see p143) – and by the Moskva river.

When walking around the city, wear sturdy shoes, and preferably old ones as Moscow can be dirty. Traffic is heavy and major roads can often be crossed via subways. Alternatively use a zebra crossing if a green light shows: drivers in Moscow do not stop at zebra crossings without lights.

It is not advisable to walk around the city alone at night.

Cycling

Although there are no cycle routes in Moscow, there are some lovely parks to discover and the roads next to the Moskva river are wide enough for cyclists and pedestrians, making it a great way to explore the centre. Cycle rental outlet

Double-decker river boat, a good way to view the sights along the river

Kruti-Pedali offers bikes and equipment by the day costing around 700 roubles ($21). To hire a bike leave a passport or a cash deposit of 3,000 roubles ($95). Bikes can be rented between 10am and 10pm. Cycle guides can be arranged.

Taxis

For safety reasons it is best to travel only by official taxis, which come in a range of guises but should at least have a taxi light on the roof and some kind of chequered markings. Restaurant or hotel staff can be asked to book one by phone or you can try **Taxi956**, which employs some English-speaking operators. A minimum fare for journeys up to 40 minutes costs around 500 roubles ($15), while other taxis have meters starting from 200 to 300 roubles ($6–9). Journeys within the city should not cost more than 500 roubles ($15). It is always best to agree on a fare before the start of the journey. It is possible to flag down a taxi on the street. Some switch on a green light, either on their window or on their roof, to indicate they are free.

Taxis to the airport should be booked in advance and cost around 1,600 roubles ($54). Some hotels have their own taxi ranks, but these can be very expensive.

River Cruises

River cruises are popular in summer, as it is a great way to see the sights lining the river. **Capital Shipping Company** run cruises from May to October along the Moskva river. The main pick-up point for these cruises is opposite Kievskiy station. Stops are located along the river so you can hop on and off using either a single or a day ticket.

DIRECTORY

Guided Tours

Moscow Greeter
W moscowgreeter.ru

Patriarshy Dom Tours
Vspolniy pereoluk 6.
Map 2 D4. **Tel** (495) 795 0927.
W toursinrussia.com

Cycling

Kruti-Pedali
Universitetskiy prospekt 6/1.
Map 2 E4. **Tel** (495) 6421942.
W kruti-pedali.ru

Taxi

Taxi956
Tel (495) 956 8956.
W taxi956.ru

River Cruises

Capital Shipping Company
Tel (495) 225 6070.
W cck-ship.ru

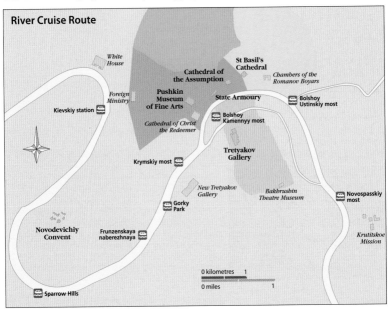

River Cruise Route

White House

Cathedral of the Assumption

St Basil's Cathedral

Chambers of the Romanov Boyars

Foreign Ministry

Pushkin Museum of Fine Arts

State Armoury

Bolshoy Ustinskiy most

Kievskiy station

Cathedral of Christ the Redeemer

Bolshoy Kamennyy most

Tretyakov Gallery

Krymskiy most

New Tretyakov Gallery

Bakhrushin Theatre Museum

Novospasskiy most

Gorky Park

Krutitskoe Mission

Novodevichiy Convent

Frunzenskaya naberezhnaya

0 kilometres   1
0 miles   1

Sparrow Hills

The Metro

Moscow is a sprawling, hectic city. One of its great assets, however, is its excellent metro network, which extends from the centre right out to many of its suburbs. During the rush hour, in particular, heavy traffic means that it is often faster to travel by metro than by car or any other form of public transport. For years all transport in the Soviet Union was extremely cheap and metro fares are still very good value. Passengers pay the same fare regardless of the length of their journey. The metro system is reliable with trains running frequently throughout the day. Constructed as part of Stalin's grand plan for rebuilding Moscow, the metro stations are also a popular tourist attraction *(see pp40–43)*.

Metro train ready to depart from Mayakovskaya metro

The ornate, cavernous interior of Arbatskaya metro

The Network

The Moscow metro network is well planned and extensive consisting of 12 lines that cover the whole city except its outermost suburbs. One feature worth noting is the Circle line connecting all the mainline railway stations *(see p218)*. Changing between the metro and a mainline station is generally easy as both have the same name, but with a slightly different ending. Belorusskiy railway station, for

The imposing marble arch entrance of the Kropotkinskaya metro station

instance, links to Belorusskaya metro and Kievskiy railway station to Kievskaya metro. However, Komsomolskaya, also on the circle line, is the exception. It links to three mainline railway stations – Leningradskiy, Kazanskiy and Yaroslavskiy.

The metro lines are colour-coded and numbered 1 to 11 and M1. Metro station signs are in English and Cyrillic, but a basic grasp of the Cyrillic stop names will be useful. Trains arrive every 1–2 minutes on weekdays, while services are slightly less frequent at weekends. During the rush hour the waiting time for trains is usually under a minute. Stops are announced on board the train and the exits are marked выход (vykhod).

The Moscow metro is on the whole safe and reliable. All the stations are staffed, although metro attendants are unlikely to speak languages other than Russian. Metro stations are buried deep underground and escalators lead down to the platforms. Several stations are equipped with lifts for disabled access; check http://engl.mosmetro.ru for more information.

Travellers who have a large bag or a suitcase will be asked to pay an added charge.

Changing Lines

For those unused to the complexity of Moscow's metro system, journeys can be made even more confusing by the fact that stations where it is possible to change between metro lines often have two or more separate names, one for each line involved. On the metro map *(see p224)* these interchange stations are bracketed together. For instance, near the centre of the city there is an interchange between four lines – 1, 3, 4 and 9 – each of which is served by a different station. Correspondingly, four station names are given on the map: Biblioteka imeni Lenina, Arbatskaya, Aleksandrovskiy Sad and Borovitskaya.

When changing lines at an interchange station it is therefore important to know the name of the station on the other line. It is then easy to reach the right platform by following the *(perekhod)* – or "interchange" – signs indicating this name.

Tickets and Travel Cards

There are no 1-day travel cards in Moscow. Instead passengers should buy a smart card, which can be credited with 1, 2, 5, 10, 20 or 60 journeys, or with a travel pass that allows unlimited travel for 3 months up to a year.

A single journey has a flat rate of 40 roubles ($1), whether your journey is a couple of stops or the length of the network. This also means that it is possible to change as many times as necessary if exploring the metro's architectural highlights *(see pp40–43)*. Buy enough rides for your stay at one time to avoid waiting at the ticket machine or **касса** *(kassa)* – counter, where queues can be long during rush hour.

At the automatic barrier simply swipe your smart card across the yellow detector that reads the information. Any number of people can travel on the same card since they all pay exactly the same fee for their journey. When the card is swiped at the barrier, the passenger is allowed through if the card is valid and the number of journeys left will be reduced by one. The number of remaining journeys will then flash up on the barrier display.

There are no child tickets on the metro, but children under seven travel free. Metro ticket counters also sell phone cards and tickets for buses, trolley-buses and trams *(see p225)*.

Magnetic smart card being held over a detector at a metro barrier

Making a Journey by Metro

1 Study the metro map *(see p224)* and plan your journey in advance as the station names on each platform are not visible from inside the train. It is well worth learning the pronunciation of the station names as announcements will indicate which station you are approaching. It is also a good idea to count the number of stops.

2 Purchase a smart card from the **касса** *(kassa)*, the counter situated just inside the metro station. Swipe the card over the yellow detector at the automatic barrier to gain access to the train platforms.

3 To find the right platform follow signs headed **к поездам до станции** *(k poezdam do stantsiy)*, which show the stops in each direction from the station you are at. These signs are sometimes colour coded.

Stops in one direction

4 On the platform, consult the signs showing all the stops of the line you are using. Trains always stop at each one. Look at the vertical lists beneath each interchange station. These show which subsequent stations you reach by changing at that point.

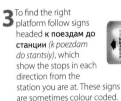

Colour of intersecting line   Stops on other lines   Line

5 Look at the digital board showing the time that has elapsed since a train last left the station. On weekdays another one will usually arrive within 1 or 2 minutes.

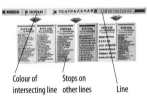

Current time   Minutes and seconds since last train

6 If you change to a different line during your journey, follow the signs marked with either **переход** *(perekhod)* or **на станцию** *(na stantsiyu)* and the appropriate station name. Once at your destination follow signs for **выход** *(vykhod)* to locate the exit.

Interchange sign

Exit and interchange sign

The Moscow Metro

Key

- line 1
- line 2
- line 3
- line 4
- line 5 (Circle)
- line 6
- line 7
- line 8
- line 9
- line 10
- line 11
- line M1 (monorail)
- ═○═ under construction

Travelling by Tram, Trolleybus and Bus

Moscow has extensive bus, trolleybus and tram routes and some of the most useful ones are identified on the transport map on the inside back cover of this book. Some routes link to the metro network *(see pp222–4)*, often starting at one metro station and terminating at another. Main avenues are generally served by both buses and trolleybuses. Trams are less useful, but as a sedate form of transport they are great for sightseeing. Busy routes can get extremely crowded during the morning and evening rush hours and traffic is often slow-moving at these times. Moscow's more remote suburbs are well served by these forms of transport. Bus stops are clearly signed and are at frequent intervals. Tram stops are occasionally further apart.

A tram passing through Moscow on route to suburban areas

Trams

Trams remain Moscow's most traditional means of transport. They provide an interesting way to see the city and the ride itself is an experience. Although services have been cut back over the years, trams are gradually being re-introduced as a historical form of transport along the more popular routes in the centre.

The remaining tram services run frequently, especially those operating in the suburbs, providing good links to metro stations and apartment blocks. Tram stops are marked by a sign labelled "Tp" in Cyrillic with a tram symbol on a white background and usually have a semi-circular shelter with a bench. Trams have one or two carriages, each with three doors. Enter via the front door.

Tram route A, which starts at Chistye Prudy metro is one of the city's oldest and, along with 39 and 3, it is the most useful route for visitors to the city as it passes close to the many major sights located in the centre of Moscow.

Trolleybuses

Trolleybuses are an environmentally friendly way of travelling around the city centre. Even though local residents prefer travelling by bus, most of the routes are still busy during rush hours. Trolleybus stops are often shared with bus stops and marked by a sign with a bus symbol on a white background and the Cyrillic letter "T". Trolleybus 3 travels around the Garden Ring and is good for getting to the major sights,

while trolleybus 2 follows ulitsa Novy Arbat to the centre where it passes around Red Square and the Kremlin *(see p108)*.

Buses

Buses are useful for travelling to Moscow's outlying suburbs where distances between metro lines are much greater than in the city centre. Bus stops are often shared with trolleybus stops and marked by a white and yellow sign showing the Cyrillic letter "A". Buses are yellow, red, or red and white. Bus services within the city centre are limited and there are none running along Tverskaya ulitsa. There are, however, several bus routes that run up Kutuzovskiy prospekt past the Borodino Panorama Museum, the Triumphal Arch and Victory Park.

Tickets and Travel Cards

One-day travel cards are not available in Moscow, but you can buy tickets valid for 1, 2, 5, 10, 20 or 60 journeys. The same tickets can be used on buses, trolleybuses and trams and are valid for a single journey without changes. Buy tickets from kiosks located next to bus stops or from the driver paying in cash. If the bus or trolleybus has a turnstile at the front, you'll need to insert your ticket before entering. If there's no turnstile, get on the bus and validate your ticket by inserting it into one of the yellow ticket readers, which will stamp the time and date on the ticket.

Passengers boarding a bus

Driving in Moscow

Driving in Moscow can be quite gruelling and it is not advisable for the uninitiated. The city suffers from chronic traffic congestion and most driving regulations that would be considered common sense elsewhere are ignored. For instance, although the majority of drivers will stop at red lights, some carry on regardless. Cars travel in disorderly lanes and veer dangerously to avoid pot holes. Drivers tend to be aggressive and inconsiderate about giving way to one another. Road signs mostly follow international conventions but are rarely bilingual, so it is well worth drivers familiarizing themselves with Cyrillic place names in advance.

Driving

Driving regulations in Moscow are complex. Russia's traffic police *(see p210)* have the right to stop drivers at any time and ask for documents. They can issue fines on the spot for infringements such as not having a fire extinguisher or first-aid kit and not wearing seat belts. It is compulsory for both drivers and front-seat passengers to wear seat belts, although many people do not. Drivers are not allowed to drink any alcohol at all and fines for drink-driving can be very high. It is illegal to make U-turns on many of Moscow's main streets.

Priority is always given to traffic approaching from the right unless a yellow, diamond-shaped sign indicates otherwise. The buying of driving licences, rather than obtaining them through legitimate means is common in Russia so visitors should not necessarily assume that all road users are qualified and responsible.

In winter, drivers must use studded tyres as roads are icy and covered with snow. Driving in these conditions is dangerous and not advisable.

Parking

On-street parking is free in central Moscow, but drivers should park carefully because fines for parking in restricted areas (marked with international signs) are high and illegally parked cars are frequently towed away. Car parks are identified by a white letter "P" on a blue back-ground. Car parks are open 24 hours. Many of the larger hotels have parking facilities.

Car Hire

Several well-known companies operate in Moscow. **Hertz** and **Avis** have offices at all three airports, while **Europcar** has offices at Sheremetyevo and Domodedovo airports as well as

Multiple lanes of traffic in central Moscow

in the city centre. Visitors hiring a car must show a driving licence, passport and credit card on collection. Some of the larger hotels can arrange car hire on your behalf.

Driving Outside Moscow

The roads leading out of Moscow are in reasonable condition, but Kutuzovskiy prospekt is particularly well-maintained because it is used by government officials and the New Russians who own *dachas* (second homes) in this area. It is vital to have a good map because side roads to small villages can easily be missed. Road signs outside of Moscow will be in Cyrillic.

Excursions from Moscow

Arrangements to visit sights outside Moscow *(see pp128–69)* can be made through either a hotel or a travel agency, or the trip can be made independently by train, bus or car. Most of the places mentioned below are not far from Moscow and can be visited on a day trip. A few, such as Suzdal and Vladimir, take two days. Patriarshy Dom Tours *(see p220)* offers a wide range of excursions to the major sights around Moscow. It is advisable to enquire in good time as reservations with them have to be made 48 hours before departure.

Train arriving at Sergiev Posad for the Trinity Monastery of St Sergius

Using Trains and Buses

Suburban trains *(prigorodnye poezda)* to the nearer sights can be caught at the appropriate mainline station *(see p218)*. They offer good value for money as foreign nationals pay the same fare as Russians. The more distant sights are served by passenger trains *(passazhirskie poezda)*.

Suburban buses *(prigorodnye marshruty)* to closer sights leave from Moscow Central Bus Station outside Shchelkovskaya metro station in the northeast of the city. Towns outside Moscow are served by inter-city buses *(mezhdugorodnye avtobusy)*.

One-Day Trips

Novodevichiy Convent *(see pp132–3)* and Kolomenskoe *(see pp140–41)* are both south of the city centre, the former close to Sportivnaya metro, the latter to Kolomenskaya metro. Kuskovo *(see pp144–5)*, in eastern Moscow, is reached by metro, to Ryazanskiy Prospekt or Vykhino. The estate is a short bus ride away.

Arkhangelskoe *(see p160)*, 20 km (12 miles) to the west of the city centre, is served by Tushinskaya metro and then a bus. By car it is on a straight route out along Volokolamskoe shosse or Rublevskoe shosse.

It takes around 2 hours to travel to the village and battlefield of Borodino *(see p160)* by train from Belorusskiy station. It can also be reached by bus from Moscow Central Bus Station or by car leaving the city on Mozhayskoe shosse. The Tchaikovsky House-Museum *(see p161)* is 2 hours northwest of the city by car on Leningradskoe shosse. Trains leave from Leningradskiy station and buses from Moscow Central Bus Station.

Abramtsevo Estate-Museum *(see p162)* is situated to the northeast of Moscow just off Yaroslavskoe shosse. Trains leave from Yaroslavskiy station and buses depart from Moscow Central Bus Station. The journey takes on average an hour.

The Trinity Monastery of St Sergius *(see pp164–7)* is also to the northeast along Yaroslavskoe shosse and the journey takes just over an hour. It is possible to get there by train or by bus from Yaroslavskiy station, and by bus from Moscow Central Bus Station.

Pereslavl-Zalesskiy *(see p162)* can be reached by car along Yaroslavskoe shosse, by train from Yaroslavskiy station, or by bus from Moscow Central Bus Station. The trip along all routes takes approximately 2 hours.

Two-Day Trips

Suzdal *(see p168)*, 200 km (124 miles) northeast of Moscow, is reached by leaving the city on Gorkovskoe shosse. Buses to Suzdal leave from Moscow Central Bus Station and take about 4 hours.

Vladimir *(see pp168–9)* is also situated northeast of the city along Gorkovskoe shosse. The 170-km (106-mile) trip can be made by bus from Moscow Central Bus Station or by train or car in 3 hours.

Yasnaya Polyana *(see p169)* is 180 km (112 miles) south of Moscow on the Simferopolskoe shosse. Buses from Moscow leave from Domodedovskaya, Prazhskaya, ulitsa Akademika and Yangelya metro stations to Tula, where you change for Yasnaya Polyana.

It is also worth considering combining a trip to Vladimir and Suzdal, as there are frequent buses that run daily from Shchyolkovsky station between the two and the journey takes 4 hours. Patriarshiy Dom Tours offer overnight packages to both towns and guided day trips to Yasnaya Polyana.

Day-trip buses awaiting passengers outside Kievskiy station

MOSCOW STREET FINDER

The key map below shows the areas of Moscow covered by the *Street Finder*. The map references given throughout the guide for sights, restaurants, hotels, shops or entertainment venues refer to the maps in this section. All the major sights have been marked so they are easy to locate. The key below shows other features marked on the maps, such as post offices, metro stations and churches. The *Street Finder* index lists street names in transliteration, followed by Cyrillics (on maps, Cyrillics are only given for major roads). This guide uses the reinstated old Russian street names, not the Soviet versions. Places of interest are listed by their English names.

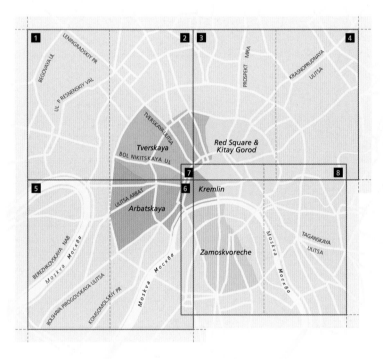

0 kilometres 1

0 miles 1

Key to Street Finder

Major sight		Hospital	
Place of interest		Police station	
Other building		Orthodox church	
Train station		Non-Orthodox church	
Metro station		Synagogue	
Main tram stop		Mosque	
Main trolleybus stop		Pedestrian street	
Main bus stop		Railway line	
River boat pier		41» House number (main street)	

Scale of Map Pages

0 metres 300

0 yards 300

Street Finder Index

Abbreviations & Useful Words

ul.	ulitsa	street
pl.	ploshchad	square
pr.	prospekt	avenue
per.	pereulok	small street/passage/lane
	most	bridge
	podezd	entrance
	proezd	small street/passage/lane
	sad	garden
	shosse	road
	stroenie	building
	tupik	cul-de-sac

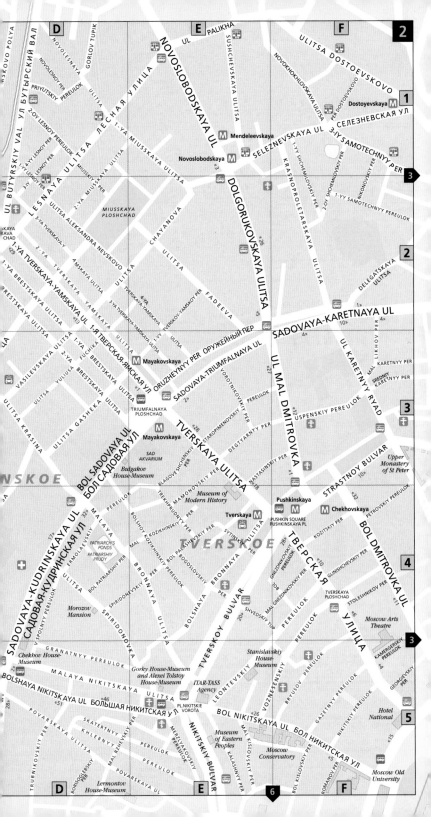

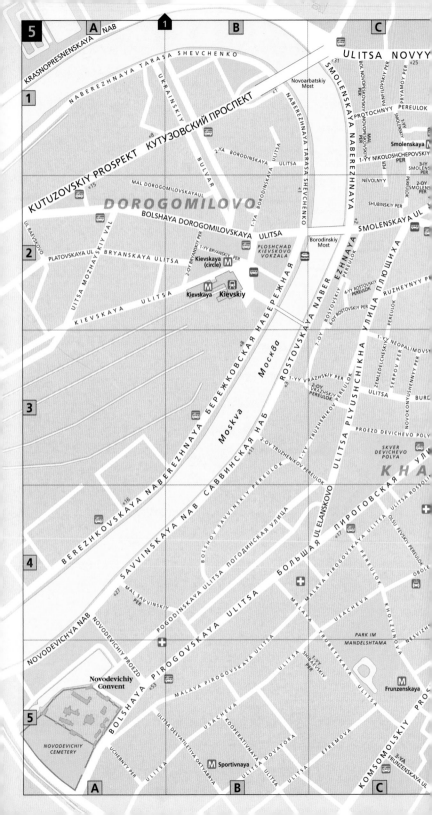

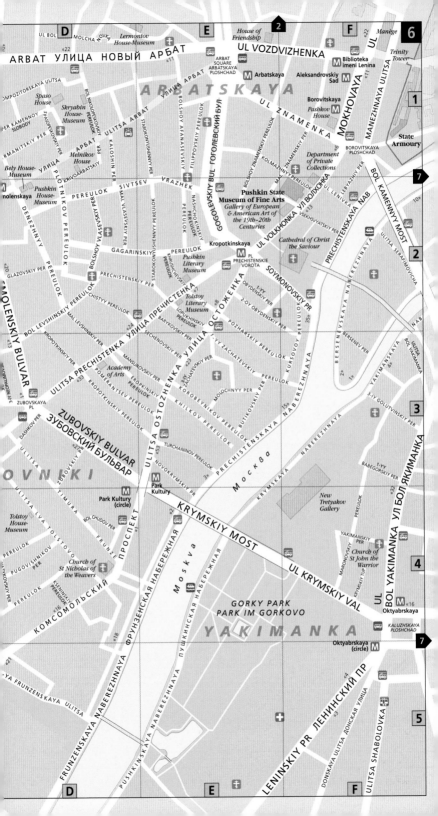

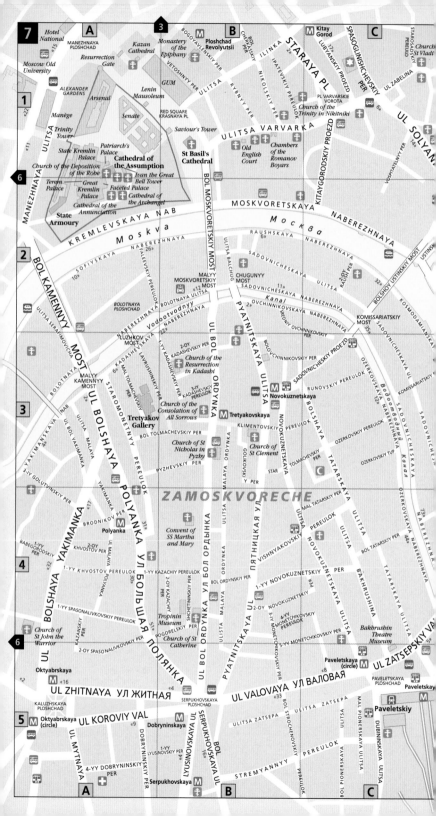

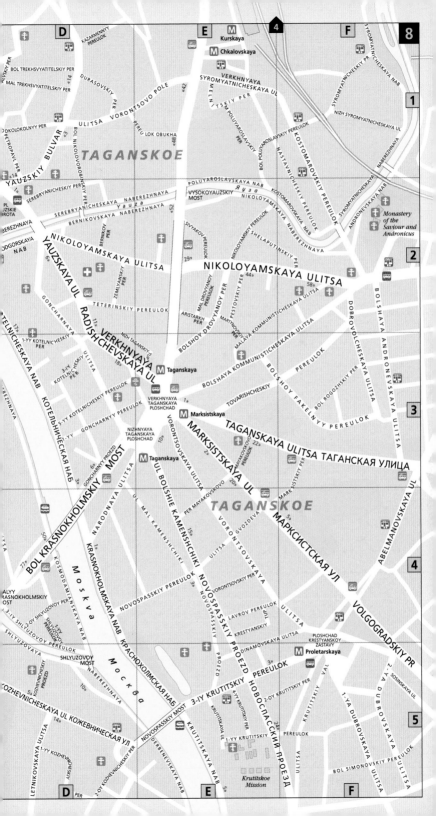

General Index

Acknowledgments

Dorling Kindersley would like to thank the following people whose contributions and assistance have made the preparation of this book possible.

Main Contributor
Chistopher Rice holds a PhD in Russian history from the University of Birmingham. He and his wife Melanie, also a writer, first visited Russia in 1978 and have been returning regularly ever since. They have written numerous travel guides to the city, and to a variety of other destinations including Prague, Berlin, and Istanbul, as well as the *Eyewitness Travel Guide to St. Petersburg.*

Additional Contributors
Rose Baring studied Russian from the age of 12. She has an MA in Modern History and divided her time between London, Moscow and St. Petersburg for much of the early 1990s. She has written guides to St. Petersburg, Moscow, and other destinations, including the *Eyewitness Travel Guide to Istanbul.*

Marina Boughton has a BA in Film Studies from the University of Central London. She also studied in Russia and has worked there for a number of years. She is now a correspondent for BBC Radio in Moscow.

Sergey Konstantinovich Romaniuk is a graduate of the Moscow State University. Specializing in Economic Geography and the history and cultural life of Moscow, he has written around 200 articles and books about the city.

Senior Editor Anna Streiffert
Managing Editors Fay Franklin, Georgina Matthews
Managing Art Editor Annette Jacobs
Senior Managing Editor Vivien Crump
Deputy Art Director Gillian Allan

Special Assistance
Dorling Kindersley would like to thank Ian Wizniewski (food and drink author), Frank Althaus (hotels), Radhika Jones (restaurants), Natasha Linkova (researcher in Moscow), Maria Fetisova (photo permissions), Elena Mirskaya (DK Moscow), Oleksiy Nesnov (language consultant), Victoria Rachevskaya (language consultant), and Sylvain Borsi of Nikita's restaurant, London (food preparation for *What to Eat in Moscow*).

Proofreader
Judith Bamber, Stewart J Wild.

Production
Jo Blackmore, David Proffit.

Revisions Team
Namrata Adhwaryu, Brigitte Arora, Liz Atherton, Claire Baranowski, Marc Bennetts, Marta Bescós, Sonal Bhatt, Hilary Bird, Andrei Bogdanov, Laurence Broers, Louise Cleghorn, Dawn Davies-Cooke, Kiki Deere, Claire Folkard, Rhiannon Furbear, Lydia Halliday, Freddy Hamilton, Leanne Hogbin, Rupanki Kaushnik, Nicola Malone, Sarah Martin, Sam Merrell, Adam Moore, Casper Morris, Pure Content, Susie Peachey, Rada Radojicic, Ellen Root, Rough Guides/ Jonathan Smith, Luke Rozkowski, Sands Publishing Solutions, Pamela Shiels, Jaynan Spengler, Priyanka Thakur, Ingrid Vienings, Dora Whitaker, Matt Willis, Veronica Wood.

Additional Illustrations
Paul Weston, Joy Fitzsimmonds.

Additional Photography
Andy Crawford, Erich Crichton, Neil Fletcher, Steve Gorton, Ian O'Leary, Gary Ombler, Clive Streeter.

Photography Permissions
Dorling Kindersley would like to thank all those who gave permission to photograph at the various cathedrals, churches, museums, restaurants, hotels, shops, galleries and transport services and other sights too numerous to thank individually.

Picture Credits
a-above; b-below/bottom; c-centre; f-far; l-left; r-right; t-top.

Works of art have been reproduced with the permission of the following copyright holders:

Young Acrobat on a Ball, Pablo Picasso © Succession Picasso/DACS 2011 50cl.

The publisher would like to thank the following individuals, companies and picture libraries for their kind permission to reproduce their photographs:

123RF.com: Boris Breytman 112bl

Academic.RU: en.academic.ru 213clb; **Adrimi Apartments:** 176bc; **Aeroexpress:** 217bl; **AISA, Barcelona:** 23br, 24clb, 48tr, 61tc, 61cra, 63cr, 66bl; **AKG, London:** 20cb, 29cl, 30br, 30–31c, 31ca, 57br, 109b, 120br, 122cra, 123bc, 163cra/bl; Erich Lessing 28tr, 30bl, 163cl; **Alamy Images:** Bart Pro 207tr; Cullinganphoto 149cr; Eastland Photo 94tl; Bernie Epstein 152cla; ITAR-TASS Photo Agency 214crb; Jon Arnold Images 11tl; Buddy Mays 225br; Anatoliy Minkov 214cla; P E Forsberg 210cra; RIA Novosti 215crb; Robert Harding Picture Library Ltd/Sylvain Grandadam 182cla, 183tl; Alex Segre 204-5; Sunpix Travel 210tr; Peter Titmuss 227br; **Alfa-Bank:** 212bl; **Ararat Park Hyatt:** 173br; **Arkhnadzor:** 118cl, 124bl; **Artephot, Paris:** 18, 120bl; **AWL Images:** Walter Bibikow 134-5; Paul Harris 2-3; **Axiom Photographic Agency:** Luis Castaneda/ Tips 78-9.

Baltika Breweries: 185c; **Kathleen Berton Murrell:** 44clb, 64bl; **Bolshoi Theatre:** 92tr/bl, 93tl/cra; **The Bridgeman Art Library, London/New York:** The Hermitage, St. Petersburg 27tl; Kremlin Museums 66cl; Mark Gallery 167tr; Novosti 23crb, 27crb; Private Collection 25crb, 31tr; Pushkin Museum, Moscow 81tl, 83tr; Tretyakov Gallery 24tr, 49bl, 120cla, 121tl, 122br, 123tl.

Demetrio Carrasco: 119cra; Jean-Loup Charmet: 20tr; Catherine Cooke; 73bc; Chicago Prime Steakhouse: Alexey Dovgan 181bc; Corbis UK: Dean Conger 5tr, 36cra, 198cl; Rob Howard 183c; Library of Congress 30cla.

David King Collection: 29tr, 31tl, 32tl, 42cla, 77br, 113br; Delicatessen, Moscow: 188tr; Dreamstime.com: Alenmax 220cla; Andrey Bayda 70, 170-1; Boris Breytman 69tc; Dance60 154-5; Ignor Dolgov 54; Ekaterina Fribus 100; Vladislav Galenko 13bl; Afonskaya Irina 34cla; Julia161 84tl; Kuzma 110cla; Vladimir Melnik 183br; Pavel Parmenov 146tl; Pingvin121674 13tr; Sailorr 38, 128; Scaliger 52-3; Salazkin Vladimir 156; Natalia Volkova 118cla.

Efremova M: 125tl; Et Archive: 26–7c.

Fotolia: pressmaster 185bl, Frank Spooner Pictures: Georges Merillon/Gamma 33tl; John Freeman: 39cla, 56cl, 57bc, 60cla, 62bl, 64t, 65tc/br, 98cr.

Getty Images: Panoramic Images 10b; Jonathan Smith 217tr; Giraudon: 26bl; Bildarchiv Preussischer Kulturbesitz 27br; Bridgeman 121cra; Lauros 63t; Golden Apple Boutique Hotel: 173tl, 177tr.

Robert Harding Picture Library: 65cla; Franz Marc Frei 86; Igor Sinitsyn 148; Hilton Leningradskaya: 174bc, 178tr; Michael Holford: 19cra, 22br, 24c; Hulton-Getty: 184tr.

Ibis Moscow Paveletskaya: Francois Kotler 172br; Intouristuk: 206cla.

James Davis Travel Photography: 59tr, 62tr; Jon Arnold Images: Demetrio Carrasco 11br.

Kadashevskaya, Moscow: 174tl; Kea Publishing Services: Francesco Venturi 49tl.

Mari Vanna: 187tr; Marukame, Moscow: Dmitry Metkin 189br; Mary Evans Picture Library: 23tc, 24bc, 26br, 31crb, 136tr; John Massey Stewart: 21crb, 59clb; Moscow Domodedovo Airport: 216cra; Moscow Metro: 222bl, 223tr, 223cra, 223bl; Moscow Suites Apartments: 175br.

Network Photographers: A Reiser/Bilderberg 74crb; Nikolai Ignatiev 33crb; Novosti (London): 21ca, 22cla, 28clb, 32clb, 34cr/bl, 36bl, 37crb, 58c/bl, 63cla, 95tc, 114c, 126bl.

Oronoz, Madrid: 25ca. Plodimex Aussenhandels Gmbh, Hamburg: 184cr/bl.

Raymond Mander & Joe Mitchenson Theatre Collection: 93bl; Rex Features: Image Broker 12tc; SIPA 32cr; Radisson Royal Hotel, Moscow: 172cla, 179br; Ragout Moscow: 181bc; Ellen Rooney: 35bl, 37bl, 58tl, 150bl; Russian Railways: 218t, 218cl, 219cla.

Sberbank: 212cla; Photo Scala, Florence: Pushkin Museum Bacchanal Peter Paul Rubens (1577–1640) 81crb. Gregor M Schmid: 61cr, 67cb/cr; Seasons Hostel: 175tl; Vladimir Sidoropolev (www.photographers direct.com): 10cra, 149bl, 152tr; Siny Most: N Alexeiev 22clb, 39cl, 50bc, 57cra, 67tl; V Tetebenine 26cla; Jon Smith: 150cla, 151tl, 151cr, 151bc, 152br, 153tr, 153ccb; Society for Cooperation in Russian and Soviet Studies: 20br, 66tr; Novosti 199c; STA Travel: 208br; Stolovaya 57, GUM Department Store Moscow: 180ca; Bar Strelka, Moscow: 181tr; Superstock: age fotostock 199tr; Fine Art Images 116; LOOK-foto/LOOK-foto 91tr; Swissôtel Hotels & Resorts: 209tr.

TRIP: N & J Wiseman 162br.

Visual Arts Library: 27cra, 63ca, 75tc, 83cb, 122cla.

Zefa: Stockmarket 59br.

Front Endpapers - Dreamstime.com: Andrey Bayda Lclb; Igor Dolgov Rcr; Ekaterina Fribus Rtr; Sailorr Lbc; Salazkin Vladimir Lbr; Robert Harding Picture Library: Franz Marc Frei Ltl; Superstock: Fine Art Images Rbr.

Jacket Front and spine– Alamy Images: Ivan Vdovin. Map Cover - Alamy Images: Ivan Vdovin.

All other images © Dorling Kindersley.
For further information see: www.dkimages.com

Phrase Book

In this guide the Russian language has been transliterated into Roman script following a consistent system used by the US Board on Geographic Names. All street and place names, and the names of most people, are transliterated according to this system. For some names, where a well-known English form exists, this has been used – hence, Leo (not Lev) Tolstoy. In particular, the names of Russian rulers, such as Peter the Great, are given in their anglicized forms. Throughout the book, transliterated names can be taken as an accurate guide to pronunciation. The Phrase Book also gives a phonetic guide to the pronunciation of words and phrases used in everyday situations, such as when eating out or shopping.

Guidelines for Pronunciation

The Cyrillic alphabet has 33 letters, of which only five (a, к, м, o, т) correspond exactly to their counterparts in English. Russian has two pronunciations (hard and soft) of each of its vowels, and several consonants without an equivalent.

The right-hand column of the alphabet, below, demonstrates how Cyrillic letters are pronounced by comparing them to sounds in English words. However, some letters vary in how they are pronounced according to their position in a word. Important exceptions are also noted below.

On the following pages, the English is given in the left-hand column, the Russian and its transliteration in the middle column. The right-hand column provides a literal system of pronunciation and indicates the stressed syllable in bold. The exception is in the Menu Decoder section, where the Russian is given in the left-hand column and the English translation in the right-hand column, for ease of use. Because of the existence of genders in Russian, in a few cases both masculine and feminine forms of a phrase are given.

The Cyrillic Alphabet

А а	a	**a**limony
Б б	b	**b**ed
В в	v	**v**et
Г г	g	**g**et (see note 1)
Д д	d	**d**ebt
Е е	e	**ye**t (see note 2)
Ё ё	e	**yo**nder
Ж ж	zh	lei**s**ure (but a little harder)
З з	z	**z**ither
И и	i	**s**ee
Й й	y	bo**y** (see note 3)
К к	k	**k**ing
Л л	l	**l**oot
М м	m	**m**atch
Н н	n	**n**ever
О о	o	r**o**b (see note 4)
П п	p	**p**ea
Р р	r	**r**at (rolling, as in Italian)
С с	s	**s**top
Т т	t	**t**offee
У у	u	b**oo**t
Ф ф	f	**f**ellow
Х х	kh	**kh** (like loch)
Ц ц	ts	le**ts**
Ч ч	ch	**ch**air
Ш ш	sh	**sh**ove
Щ щ	shch	fre**sh sh**eet (as above but with a slight roll)
ъ		hard sign (no sound, but see note 5)
Ы ы	y	l**i**d
ь		soft sign (no sound, but see note 5)
Э э	e	**e**gg
Ю ю	yu	**you**th
Я я	ya	**ya**k

Notes

1) Г Pronounced as v in endings -oro and -ero.
2) Е Always pronounced ye at the beginning of a word, but in the middle of a word sometimes less distinctly (more like e).
3) Й This letter has no distinct sound of its own. It usually lengthens the preceeding vowel.
4) О When not stressed it is pronounced like a in across.
5) ъ, ь The hard sign (ъ) is rare and indicates a very briefpause before the next letter. The soft sign (ь, marked in the pronunciation guide as ') softens the preceeding consonant and adds a slight y sound: for instance, n' would sound like ny in 'ca**ny**on'.

In an Emergency

Help!	Помогите! *Pomogite!*	pama**gee**tye!
Stop!	Стоп! *Stop!*	Stop!
Leave me alone!	Оставьте меня в покое! *Ostavte menya v pokoe!*	ast**a**vt'ye my**e**nya v pak**o**ye!
Call a doctor!	Позовите врача! *Pozovite vracha!*	pazav**ee**tye vrach**a**!
Call an ambulance!	Вызовите скорую помощь! *Vyzovite skoruyu pomoshch!*	vizav**ee**tye sk**o**ru-yu p**o**mash'!
Fire!	Пожар! *Pozhar!*	pazh**a**r!
Call the fire brigade!	Вызовите пожарных! *Vyzovite pozharnykh!*	vizav**ee**tye pazh**a**rnikh!
Police!	Милиция! *Militsiya!*	mee**lee**tseeya!
Where is the nearest...	Где ближайший... *Gde blizhayshiy...*	gdye bleezh**a**ysheey...
...telephone?	...телефон? *...telefon?*	...tyel**yefo**n?
...hospital?	...больница? *...bolnitsa?*	...bal'**nee**tsa?
...police station?	...отделение милиции? *...otdelenie militsii?*	...atdyel**ye**nye meel**ee**tsee-ee?

Communication Essentials

Yes	Да *Da*	da
No	Нет *Net*	nyet
Please	Пожалуйста *Pozhaluysta*	pazh**a**lsta
Thank you	Спасибо *Spasibo*	spas**ee**ba
You are welcome	Пожалуйста *Pozhaluysta*	pazh**a**lsta
Excuse me	Извините *Izvinite*	eezveen**ee**t-ye
Hello	Здравствуйте *Zdravstvuyte*	zdr**a**stvooyt-ye
Goodbye	До свидания *Do svidaniya*	da sveed**a**nya
Good morning	Доброе утро *Dobroe utro*	d**o**bra-ye **oo**tra
Good afternoon/day	Добрый день *Dobryy den*	d**o**bree dyen'
Good evening	Добрый вечер *Dobryy vecher*	d**o**bree v**ye**chyer
Good night	Спокойной ночи *Spokoynoy nochi*	spak**o**ynay n**o**chee
Morning	утро *utro*	**oo**tra
Afternoon	день *den*	dyen'
Evening	вечер *vecher*	v**ye**chyer
Yesterday	вчера *vchera*	fchy**era**
Today	сегодня *sevodnya*	syev**o**dnya
Tomorrow	завтра *zavtra*	z**a**ftra
Here	здесь *zdes*	zdyes'
There	там *tam*	tam
What?	Что? *Chto?*	shto?

Where?	Где? *Gde?*	*gdye?*
Why?	Почему? *Pochemu?*	*pachyemoo?*
When?	Когда? *Kogda?*	*kagda?*
Now	сейчас *seychas*	*seychas*
Later	позже *pozzhe*	*pozhe*
Can I...?	можно? *mozhno?*	*mozhna...?*
It is possible/allowed	можно *mozhno*	*mozhna*
It is not possible/allowed	нельзя *nelzya*	*nyelzya*

Useful Phrases

How are you?	Как дела? *Kak dela?*	*kak dyela?*
Very well, thank you	Хорошо, спасибо *Khorosho, spasibo*	*kharasho, spaseeba*
Pleased to meet you	Очень приятно *Ochen priyatno*	*ochen' pree-yatna*
How do I get to...?	Как добраться до...? *Kak dobratsya do...?*	*kak dabrat'sya da...?*
Would you tell me when we get to...?	Скажите, пожалуйста, коеда мы приедем в...? *Skazhite, pozhaluysta, kogda my priedem v...?*	*skazheet-ye, pazhalsta, kagda mi pree-yedyem v...?*
Is it very far?	Это далеко? *Eto daleko?*	*eta dalyeko?*
Do you speak English?	Вы говорите по-английски? *Vy govorite po-angliyski?*	*vi gavareet-ye po-angleeskee?*
I don't understand	Я не понимаю *Ya ne ponimayu*	*ya nye paneema-yoo*
Could you speak more slowly?	Говорите медленнее *Govorite medlennee*	*gavareet-ye myedlyenye-ye*
Could you say it again please?	Повторите, пожалуйста *Povtorite, pozhaluysta*	*paftareet-ye, pazhalsta*
I am lost	Я заблудился (заблудилась) *Ya zabludilsya (zabludilas)*	*ya zabloodeelsya (zablaodeelas')*
How do you say... in Russian?	Как по-русски...? 	*kak pa-rooskee...?*

Useful Words

big	большой *bolshoy*	*bal'shoy*
small	маленький *malenkiy*	*malyen'kee*
hot (water, food)	горячий *goryachiy*	*garyachee*
hot (weather)	жарко *zharko*	*zharka*
cold	холодный *kholodnyy*	*khalodnee*
good	хорошо *khorosho*	*kharasho*
bad	плохо *plokho*	*plokha*
okay/fine	нормально *normalno*	*narmal'na*
near	близко *blizko*	*bleezka*
far	далеко *daleko*	*dalyeko*
up	наверху *naverkhu*	*navyerkhoo*
down	внизу *vnizu*	*fneezoo*
early	рано *rano*	*rana*
late	поздно *pozdno*	*pozdna*
vacant (unoccupied)	свободно *svobodno*	*svabodna*
free (no charge)	бесплатно *besplatno*	*byesplatna*
cashier/ticket office	касса *kassa*	*kasa*

avenue	проспект *prospekt*	*praspyekt*
bridge	мост *most*	*most*
embankment	набережная *naberezhnaya*	*nabyeryezhnaya*
highway/motorway	шоссе *shosse*	*shasse*
lane/passage	переулок *pereulok*	*pyereyoolak*
square	площадь *ploshchad*	*ploshat'*
street	улица *ulitsa*	*ooleetsa*
flat/apartment	квартира *kvartira*	*kvarteera*
floor	этаж *etazh*	*etash*
house/block	дом *dom*	*dom*
entrance	вход *vkhod*	*fkhot*
exit	выход *vykhod*	*vikhot*
river	река *reka*	*ryeka*
summer country house	дача *dacha*	*dacha*
swimming pool	бассейн *basseyn*	*basyeyn*
town	город *gorod*	*gorat*
toilet	туалет *tualet*	*tooalyet*

Making a Telephone Call

Can I call abroad from here?	Можно отсюда позвонить за границу? *Mozhno ostyuda pozvonit za granitsu?*	*mozhna atsyooda pazvaneet' za graneetsoo?*
I would like to speak to...	Позвоните, пожалуйста... *Pozvonite, pozhaluysta*	*pazaveet-ye, pazhalsta...*
Could you leave him/her a message?	Вы можете передать ему/ей? *By mozhete peredat emu/ey?*	*vi mozhet-ye pyeryedat' yemoo/yay?*
My number is...	Мой номер... *Moy nomer...*	*moy nomyer...*
I'll ring back later	Я позвоню позже *Ya pozvonyu pozzhe*	*ya pazvanyoo pozhe*

Sightseeing

castle	замок *zamok*	*zamak*
cathedral	собор *sobor*	*sabor*
church	церковь *tserkov*	*tserkaf'*
circus	цирк *tsirk*	*tseerk*
closed for cleaning "cleaning day"	санитарный день *sanitarnyy den*	*saneetarnee dyen'*
undergoing restoration	ремонт *remont*	*remont*
exhibition	выставка *vystavka*	*vistafka*
fortress	крепость *krepost*	*kryepost'*
gallery	галерея *galereya*	*galeryeya*
garden	сад *sad*	*sad*
island	остров *ostrov*	*ostraf*
kremlin/fortified stronghold	Кремль *kreml*	*kryeml'*
library	библиотека *biblioteka*	*beeblee-atyeka*
monument	памятник *pamyatnik*	*pamyatneek*
mosque	мечеть *mechet*	*myechyet'*
museum	музей *muzey*	*moozyey*
palace	дворец *dvorets*	*dvaryets*
park	парк *park*	*park*

parliament	дума *duma*	*dooma*
synagogue	синагога *sinagoga*	*seenagoga*
tourist information	пункт информации для туристов *punkt informatsii dlya turistov*	*poonkt eenfarmatsee-ee dlya tooreestaf*
zoo	зоопарк *zoopark*	*zapark*

Shopping

open	открыто *otkryto*	*atkrita*
closed	закрыто *zakryto*	*zakrita*
How much does this cost?	Сколько зто стоит? *Skolko eto stoit?*	*skol'ka eta stoeet?*
I would like to buy…	Я хотел (хотела) бы купить… *Ya khotel (khotela) by kupit…*	*ya khatyel (khatyela) bi koopeet'…*
Do you have…?	У вас есть…? *U vas yest…?*	*oo vas yest'…?*
Do you take credit cards?	Кредитные карточки вы принимаете? *Kreditnye kartochki vy prinimaete?*	*kryedeetnye kartachkee vy preeneemayete?*
What time do you open/close?	Во сколько вы открываетесь/ закрываетесь? *Vo skolko vy otkryvaetes/ zakryvaetes?*	*Va skol'ka vy atkrivayetyes'/ zakrivayetyes'?*
This one	этот *etot*	*etat*
expensive	дорого *dorogo*	*doraga*
cheap	дёшево *deshevo*	*dyoshyeva*
size	размер *razmer*	*razmyer*
white	белый *belyy*	*byelee*
black	чёрный *chernyy*	*chyornee*
red	красный *krasnyy*	*krasnee*
yellow	жёлтый *zheltyy*	*zholtee*
green	зелёный *zelenyy*	*zyelyonee*
dark blue	синий *siniy*	*seenee*
light blue	голубой *goluboy*	*galooboy*
brown	коричневый *korichnevyy*	*kareechnyevee*

Types of Shop

bank	банк *bank*	*bank*
bakery	булочная *bulochnaya*	*boolachna-ya*
bookshop	книжный магазин *knizhnyy magazin*	*kneezhnee magazeen*
butcher	мясной магазин *myasnoy magazin*	*myasnoy magazeen*
camera shop	фото-товары *foto-tovary*	*foto-tavari*
chemist	аптека *apteka*	*aptyeka*
delicatessen	гастроном *gastronom*	*gastranom*
department store	универмаг *univermag*	*ooneevyermag*
florist	цветы *tsvety*	*tsvyeti*
grocer	бакалея *bakaleya*	*bakalye-ya*
hairdresser	парикмахерская *parikmakherskaya*	*pareekmakhyerskaya*
market	рынок *rynok*	*rinak*
newspaper stand	газетный киоск *gazetniy kiosk*	*gazyetnee kee-osk*
post office	почта *pochta*	*pochta*
record shop	грампластинки *gramplastinki*	*gramplasteenkee*
shoe shop	обувь *obuv*	*oboof'*

travel agent	бюро путешествий *byuro puteshestviy*	*byooro pootyeshestvee*

Staying in a Hotel

Do you have a vacant room?	У вас есть свободный номер? *U vas yest svobodnyy nomer?*	*oo vas yest' svabodnee nomyer?*
double room with double bed	номер с двуспальной кроватью *nomer s dvuspalnoy krovatyu*	*nomyer s dvoospal'noy kravat'-yoo*
twin room	двухместный номер *dvukhmestnyy nomer*	*dvookhmyestnee nomyer*
single room	одноместный номер *odnomestnyy nomer*	*adnamyestnee nomyer*
bath	ванная *vannaya*	*vana-ya*
shower	душ *dush*	*doosh*
porter	носильщнк *nosilshchik*	*naseel'sheek*
key	ключ	*klyooch*

Eating Out

A table for two, please	Стол на двоих, пожалуйста *stol na dvoikh, pazhalsta*	*stol na dva-eekh, pazhalsta*
I would like to book a table	Я хочу заказать стол *Ya khochu zakazat stol*	*ya khachoo zakazat' stol*
The bill, please	Счёт, пожалуйста *Schet, pozhaluysta*	*shyot, pazhalsta*
I am a vegetarian	Я вегетерианец (вегетерианка) *Ya vegeterianets (vegeterianka)*	*ya vyegyetareeanyets (vyegyetareeanka)*
breakfast	завтрак *zavtrak*	*zaftrak*
lunch	обед *obed*	*abyet*
dinner	ужин *uzhin*	*oozheen*
waiter!	официант! *ofitsiant!*	*afeetsee-ant!*
waitress!	официантка! *ofitsiantka!*	*afeetsee-antka!*
dish of the day	фирменное блюдо *firmennoe blyudo*	*feermenoye blyooda*
appetizers/starters	закуски *zakuski*	*zakooskee*
main course	второе блюдо *vtoroe blyudo*	*ftaroye blyooda*
meat and poultry dishes	мясные блюда *myasnye blyuda*	*myasniye blyooda*
fish and seafood dishes	рыбные блюда *rybnye blyuda*	*ribniye blyooda*
vegetable dishes	овощные блюда *ovoshchnye blyuda*	*avashshniye blyooda*
dessert	десерт *desert*	*dyesyert*
drinks	напитки *napitki*	*napeetkee*
vegetables	овощи *ovoshchi*	*ovashshee*
bread	хлеб *khleb*	*khlyeb*
wine list	карта вин *karta vin*	*karta veen*
rare (steak)	недожаренный *nedozharennyy*	*nyedazharenee*
well done (steak)	прожаренный *prozharennyy*	*prozharenee*
glass	стакан *stakan*	*stakan*
bottle	бутылка *butylka*	*bootIlka*
knife	нож *nozh*	*nosh*
fork	вилка *vilka*	*veelka*
spoon	ложка *lozhka*	*loshka*
plate	тарелка	*taryelka*

napkin	*tarelka* салфетка	salfyetka
salt	*salfetka* соль	sol
pepper	*sol* переЦ	pyeryets
butter/oil	*perets* масло	masla
sugar	*maslo* сахар	sakhar

Menu Decoder

Russian	Pronunciation	English
абрикос *abrikos*	abreekos	apricot
апельсин *apelsin*	apyel'seen	orange
апельсиновый сок *apelsinovyy sok*	apyel'seenavee sok	orange juice
арбуз *arbuz*	arbooz	water melon
белое вино *beloe vino*	byelaye veeno	white wine
бифштекс *bifshteks*	beefshtyeks	steak
блины *bliny*	bleeni	pancakes
борщ *borshch*	borshsh	borsch (beetroot soup)
варенье *varene*	varyen'ye	Russian syrup-jam
варёный *varenyy*	varyonee	boiled
ветчина *vetchina*	vyetcheena	ham
вола *voda*	vada	water
говядина *govyadina*	gavyadeena	beef
грибы *griby*	greebi	mushrooms
груша *grusha*	groosha	pear
гусь *gus*	goos	goose
джем *dzhem*	dzhem	jam
жареный *zharenyy*	zharyenee	roasted/grilled/fried
икра *ikra*	eekra	black caviar
икра красная/кета *ikra krasna-ya/keta*	eekra krasna-ya/kyeta	red caviar
капуста *kapusta*	kapoosta	cabbage
картофель *kartofel*	kartofyel'	potato
квас *kvas*	kvas	kvas (sweet, mildly alcoholic drink)
клубника *klubnika*	kloobneeka	strawberries
колбаса *kolbasa*	kalbasa	salami sausage
кофе *kofe*	kofye	coffee
красное вино *krasnoe vino*	krasnoye veeno	red wine
креветки *krevetki*	kryevyetkee	prawns
курица *kuritsa*	kooreetsa	chicken
лук *luk*	look	onion
малина *malina*	maleena	raspberries
минеральная вода *mineralnaya voda*	mineral'naya vada	mineral water
мороженое *morozhenoe*	marozhena-ye	ice-cream
мясо *myaso*	myasa	meat
оглец *ogurets*	agooryets	cucumber
осетрина *osetrina*	asyetreena	sturgeon
нельмени *pelmeni*	pyel'myenee	meat or fish dumplings
персик *persik*	pyerseek	peach
печенье *pechene*	pyechyen'ye	biscuit
печёйка *pechenka*	pyechyonka	liver
печёный *pechenyy*	pyechyonee	baked
пиво *pivo*	peeva	beer
пирог *pirog*	peerok	pie
пирожки *pirozhki*	peerashkee	small parcels with savoury fillings
помидор *pomidor*	pameedor	tomato
продукты моря *produkty morya*	pradookti morya	seafood
рыба *ryba*	riba	fish
салат *salat*	salat	salad
свинина *svinina*	sveeneena	pork
сельдь *seld*	sye'ld'	herring
сосиски *sosiski*	saseeskee	sausages
сыр *syr*	sir	cheese
сырой *syroy*	siroy	raw
утка *utka*	ootka	duck
фасоль *fasol*	fasol'	beans
форель *forel*	faryel'	trout
чай *chay*	chai	tea
чеснок *chesnok*	chyesnok	garlic
шашлык *shashlyk*	shashlik	kebab
яйцо *yaytso*	yaytso	egg
слива *sliva*	sleeva	plum
фрукты *frukty*	frookti	fruit
яблоко *yabloko*	yablaka	apple

Transport

English	Russian	Pronunciation
north	север *sever*	syever
south	юг *yug*	yook
east	восток *vostok*	vastok
west	запад *zapad*	zapat
airport	аэропорт *aeroport*	aeraport
aeroplane	самолёт *samolet*	samalyot
traffic police	ГАИ *GAI*	Ga-ee
bus	автобус *avtobus*	aftoboos
bus station	автобусная станция *avtobusnaya stantsiya*	aftoboosna-ya stantsee-ya
bus stop	остановка автобса *ostanovka avtobusa*	astanofka aftoboosa
car	мащина *mashina*	masheena
flight	рейс *reys*	ryeys
metro (station)	(станция) метро *(stantsiya) metro*	(stantsee-ya) myetro
no entry	нет входа *net vkhoda*	nyet fkhoda
no exit	нет выхода *net vykhoda*	nyet vikhada
parking	автостоянка *avtostoyanka*	aftostoyanka
petrol	бензин *benzin*	byenzeen
railway	железная дорога *zheleznaya doroga*	zhelyezna-ya daroga
railway station	вокзал *vokzal*	vagzal
return ticket	обратный билет *obratniy bilet*	obratnee beelyet
seat	место *mesto*	myesta

suburban train	пригородный поезд *preegaradnee* prigorodniy poezd *po-yezd*
straight on	прямо *pryama* pryamo
taxi	такси *taksee* taksi
ticket	билет *beelyet* bilet
token (for a single metro journey)	жетон *zheton* zheton
to the left	налево *nalyeva* nalevo
to the right	направо *naprava* napravo
train	поезд *po-yezd* poezd
tram	трамвай *tramvay* tramvay
trolleybus	троллейбус *tralyeyboos* trolleybus

Numbers

1	один/одна/одно *adeen/adna/adno* odin/odna/odno
2	два/две *dva/dvye* dva/dve
3	три *tree* tri
4	четыре *chyetir-ye* chetyre
5	пять *pyat'* pyat
6	шесть *shest'* shest
7	семь *syem'* sem
8	восемь *vosyem'* vosem
9	девять *dyevyat'* devyat
10	десять *dyesyat'* desyat
11	одиннадцать *adeenatsat'* odinnadtsat
12	двенадцать *dvyenatsat'* dvenadtsat
13	тринадцать *treenatsat'* trinadtsat
14	четырнадцать *chyetirnatsat'* chetyrnadtsat
15	пятнадцать *pyatnatsat'* pyatnadtsat
16	щестнадцать *shestnatsat'* shestnadtsat
17	семнадцать *syemnatsat'* semnadtsat
18	восемнадцать *vasyemnatsat'* vosemnadtsat
19	девятнадцать *dyevyatnatsat'* devyatnadtsat
20	двадцать *dvatsat'* dvadtsat
21	двадцать один *dvatsat' adeen* dvadtsat odin
22	двадцать два *dvatsat' dva* dvadtsat dva

23	двадцать три *dvatsat' tree* dvadtsat tri
24	двадцать четыре *dvatsat' chyetir-ye* dvadtsat chetyre
25	двадцать пять *dvatsat' pyat'* dvadtsat pyat
30	тридцать *treetsat'* tridtsat
40	сорок *sorak* sorok
50	пятьдесят *pyadyesyat'* pyatdesyat
60	шестьдесят *shes'dyesyat* shestdesyat
70	семьдесят *syem'dyesyat* semdesyat
80	восемьдесять *vosyem'dyesyat* vosemdesyat
90	девяносто *dyevyanosta* devyanosto
100	сто *sto* sto
200	двести *dvyestee* dvesti
300	триста *treesta* trista
400	четыреста *chyetiryesta* chetyresta
500	пятьсот *pyat'sot* pyatsot
1,000	тысяча *tisyacha* tysyacha
2,000	две тысяч *dvye tisyach* dve tysyach
5,000	пять тысяч *pyat' tisyach* pyat tysyach
1,000,000	миллион *meelee-on* million

Time, Days and Dates

one minute	одна минута *adna meenoota* odna minuta
one hour	час *chas* chas
half an hour	полчаса *polchasa* polchasa
day	день *dyen* den
week	неделя *nyedyel-ya* nedelya
Monday	понедельник *panyedyel'neek* ponedelnik
Tuesday	вторник *ftorneek* vtornik
Wednesday	среда *sryeda* sreda
Thursday	четверг *chyetvyerk* chetverg
Friday	пятница *pyatneetsa* pyatnitsa
Saturday	суббота *soobota* subbota
Sunday	воскресенье *vaskryesyen'ye* voskresene

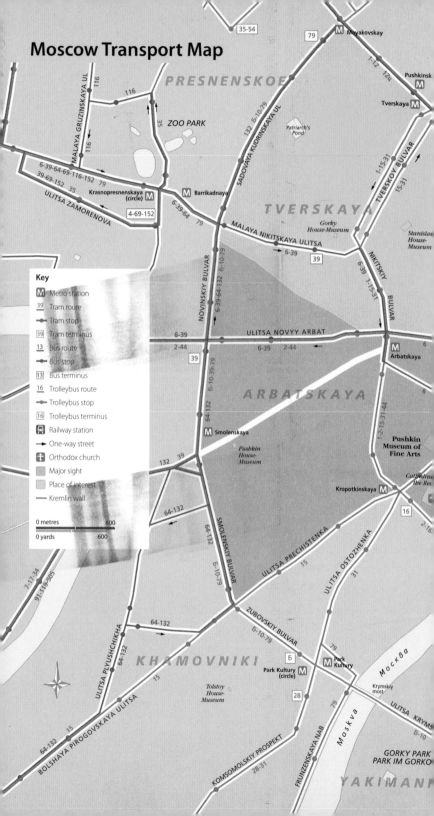